BEYOND THE MASK
THE RISING SIGN

BEYOND THE MASK
THE RISING SIGN

CREATIVITY AND SPIRITUALITY IN THE SECOND HALF OF LIFE

PART I: ARIES - VIRGO
&
PART II: LIBRA - PISCES

KATHLEEN BURT

Beyond the Mask: The Rising Sign
Creativity and Spirituality in the Second Half of Life
Volume I: Aries-Virgo & Volume II: Libra-Pisces
Copyright © 2010 by Kathleen Burt

ISBN 978-1-926975-08-5 Paperback

Published simultaneously in Canada, the United Kingdom, and the United States of America. For information on obtaining permission for use of material from this work, please submit a written request to:
books@genoahouse.com

Every effort has been made to trace all copyright holders; however, if any have been overlooked, the author will be pleased to make the necessary arrangements at the first opportunity.

Genoa House
www.genoahouse.com
books@genoahouse.com

Cover Photo *Tuscany: Aurora Consurgens*, Pari, Italy,
Copyright © 2012 by Mel Mathews

Contents

Preface

Almost twenty years ago I wrote a book on Sun Sign astrology called *Archetypes of the Zodiac*.[1] The same year that Archetypes appeared in bookstores several of us, students, clients, friends and I, participated in a Mask-making workshop offered by Friends of Jung, San Diego. When we discussed the experience later, we were all curious about how the astrological Mask, the Rising Sign, differed from the Sun Sign archetype. Was there a distinct pattern for the Rising Signs? Synchronistically, a few months later I was asked to contribute a chapter to Joan McEvers' anthology, *Spiritual, Metaphysical, & New Trends in Modern Astrology*.[2] The perfect opportunity to have a look at the Rising Signs through their spiritual (esoteric) rulers! When my chapter was finished, I knew I wanted to explore the topic more fully. But first I'd need enough accurate horoscopes to establish a pattern.

Years passed before I discovered Lois Rodden's wonderful celebrity database, which includes famous writers. What a delight to spend time with the horoscopes of my favorite authors, both fiction and non-fiction; writers whose books have meant so much to me over the years! As I collected and read their memoirs, autobiographies, and biographies, twelve distinct Rising Sign patterns emerged.

However, there was now too much data, too many good stories for one book! I needed only a few examples for each Sign. Thinking about that mass of material, I felt like a village housewife in India sitting with her winnowing fan, sorting the best kernels of rice and removing the pebbles. Overwhelmed by my attempt at winnowing in isolation, my next step was to design a series of yoga/astrology retreats: weekend workshops featuring the Rising Sign, including myth, folk tales, poetry, the authors' Rising Signs, and breaks for hatha yoga stretches. The students' reactions to the storytelling—folk tales and stories from the authors' lives—helped in choosing the best examples, those that sparked enthusiasm and discussion.

Meanwhile we all grew older; friends, clients, workshop participants, myself. We discussed how, as our Solar ambitions and interest in our past accomplishments waned, time and space opened to us. There was room in our lives for new beginnings. After my husband Michael and I moved to Florida, the Rising Sign workshops assumed a different shape: the Mask and the Second Half of Life. The stories in this book are Elder Tales.

1 Kathleen Burt, *Archetypes of the Zodiac*, (St. Paul: Llewellyn Publications,) 1988
2 Burt, "The Spiritual Rulers, Their Practical Role in the Transformation," Llewellyn: 1988, 76-101.

The Mask after Fifty

In youth, the Mask protects our Solar dreams and goals until we're prepared to go public with them. As children, we may have hidden behind a moody or introverted Mask or a chatty extraverted Mask. Perhaps we had a grumpy relative or teacher who, if he knew about those dreams, would discourage us. As adults, our Mask shielded us from the boss or project director who felt threatened. But now, we're free!

One of the most interesting observations from my client work was the number of people who came for readings just as the progressed Ascendant was about to change Signs. They sensed that something was changing or, if they were not as self-aware, others close to them noticed that they were behaving differently—either way, they wondered what was happening and scheduled a reading as the Mask changed. Some called it "my first reading ever." Though they'd been "curious about astrology for a long time," now they actually came for a reading.

Watching the change in slow motion, from the time the Ascendant enters the new Sign until it makes its first major contact (aspect) to a natal planet is a lot like watching a butterfly emerge from its chrysalis. At first we feel vulnerable, unsteady and uncertain; then we grow a bit braver, and several years later when the Ascendant contacts a natal planet, we know we can fly. We're ready to catch a breeze and soar.

Though our progressed Ascendant has already changed Signs once by midlife, this second change is more interesting, because the second progressed Ascendant has more in common with the Natal Mask by Element and Mode. So, it's easier to work with than the first Progressed Rising Sign. It also opens new possibilities, new ways of being. Two constellations are coming into contact. Constellations are vast and expansive.

We all feel vulnerable at first. Our old cocoon feels desiccated; the energy behind our old Mask wanes; we're not yet aware of who it is that we're becoming. We need to be patient with ourselves.

When my second Mask, Cancer waned, the energy for one-on-one client consultations dropped away. I had less and less "nurturing" patience available to me every year. Client work that used to be energizing was now enervating! I retired, read biographies and wondered how to support myself! I enrolled in a teacher's training in hatha yoga. I'd loved yoga for twenty years and wanted to learn more about it. I told myself at the time. "I'd never actually teach yoga, of course! I have no sensate function!" Five years later, the progressed Ascendant contacted a Natal planet in five degrees, a planet in my career house: I was a fledgling yoga teacher.

When you're a changeling, it's good to ask yourself, "what would I like to do?" No expectations, no pressure, just "what would I enjoy?" The answer to this question is a direction, a starting point but not a destination. And it's important to avoid people who resemble that grumpy relative or negative teacher from younger days.

Mine would have said, "are you insane? You admit you'd never teach yoga! Why invest in a two-year training? At your age, you should hang on to your retirement money!" As time passes, the progressed Ascendant degree will eventually contact a natal planet whose nature: earnest or playful, active or reflective, creative or inspired, helps set the tone for our new thirty-year cycle.

The Second Half of Life can be a playful time. We experience the constellations differently. As our Mask changes, we gain a new understanding of the Natal Rising Sign through the perspective of the new Progressed Ascendant. Transits cycles of the outer planets add to the mix. We experience Jupiter Returns at age 48, 60, 72 and 84.

We create new rituals, we travel, we find new wellsprings of joy. On the Second Saturn Return, age 58-59, we simplify life, clean out our closets and leave behind old support structures. A chapter closes. Saturn is Chronus, Father Time. Uranus' cycle brings insight and freedom. Neptune's cycle offers inner peace (the River Lethe Experience: forgiving and forgetting) and creative inspiration. We release those Masks associated with our old responsibilities. The Second Half of Life is a time for imagination, for creativity and passion, for seeking and sharing inspiration. It's an exciting time!

"Is life no more than a series of Masks?"
W.B. Yeats, from his astrology journal[1]
Vacillations, IV

"my fiftieth year had come and gone,
I sat, a solitary man
In a crowded London shop,
An open book and empty cup
On the marble table-top.

While on the shop and street I gazed
My body of a sudden blazed;
And twenty minutes more or less
It seemed so great my happiness
That I was blessed and could bless."[2]

---

1 W.B. Yeats, *Memoir*, Journal. Denis Donoghue, ed, (NY: Macmillan), 1972. There are many entries about his progressions, his natal Mars/Moon opposition and his efforts to be more patient with others.

2 Yeats, "Vacillations, IV," *The Collected Poems of W.B.Yeats*. Richard L Finneran, ed., (NY: Scribner), 2001, p. 251. Richard Ellmann learned from Yeats' wife that the experience affected him deeply, "he attached great importance to it." This poem was originally entitled, "Wisdom." Ellmann, *Yeats: The Man and the Masks*, (NY: Norton & Co), 1979, xviii; 276 (Wisdom.)

INTRODUCTION

The Rising Sign and the First House
Frequently Asked Questions

What is the Rising Sign?

It's the astrological *persona* or Mask. Technically, it's the constellation coming up over the horizon at the *time* of birth, in the *location,* the city or town where we were born. Because it's rising overhead, this constellation is also called the Ascendant.

Located on the Cusp of the First House, (Identity) the degree of the Rising Sign is our personal, symbolic place in time and space. An accurate time of birth is very important.

How does my Rising Sign differ symbolically from my Sun Sign?

Here are some technical differences to ponder:

The Sun is a star around which planets revolve. The Rising Sign is an entire constellation. The Ascendant Sign changed every two hours the day we were born, while the Sun Sign was shared with a greater number of people born within several weeks of us. The Twelve Rising constellations have different types of charisma and magnetism.

The Rising Sign is associated with dawn and new beginnings. We experience this when transits of the faster-moving planets—Mercury, Mars, Venus or the Luminaries (the Sun and Moon) cross the Ascendant and move through our First House. With transiting Mars on the Ascendant, we may decide to sign up at the gym or take karate. With Mercury transiting, our new endeavor may be a craft class or a letter to the editor. We can follow the motion of planets across our Ascendant in the ephemeris. Slower-moving planets may influence the Ascendant for several years. We adjust, then get used to them being around and they no longer feel new.

What does the Sun symbolize in the horoscope?

You may recall from *Archetypes of the Zodiac* that for every planet there are two levels of symbolism, esoteric (spiritual) and mundane (instinctual.)

At one level, the Sun symbolizes the Ego. Symbolically, the planets in the horoscope are to the Ego as the physical Sun is to the Solar System: the Sun is the source of light and heat and the planets play a subordinate role. They represent qualities or attributes of the Sun. (Mercury symbolizes the Ego's curiosity, its ability to learn and communicate knowledge; Mars, the Ego's flight-or-fight response; assertiveness, competitive spirit, agility, coordination, passion. Venus represents the Feeling Function and the way that the Ego relates to others (preferably harmoniously, non-competitively) as well as aesthetics and the individual'sl taste.

But for those interested in spiritual symbolism, the Sun is a symbol of the Self. Its alchemical metal is gold. Poets and storytellers through the ages have made use of the metals associated with the planets to let us know that a poem or story has a deeper message. "The Golden Fleece" alluded to in the Aries Rising chapter is such a tale, a Search for the precious treasure, the Self. William Butler Yeats, who studied astrology with the Golden Dawn Society, ended his poem, "The Song of Wandering Aengus" with the lines "…and pluck till time and times are done/the Silver Apples of the Moon/the Golden Apples of the Sun." There's a sense of eternity: "till time and times are done." Golden Apples are delicious, but actual silver ones are hard to find!

Modern seekers after "the Grail" or the "Golden Fleece" learn a great deal about themselves by hindsight after transits to the Sun by outer planets, (Saturn and beyond.) Others pass through the same transit cycles and only want to know "when will this finally end?" There are two distinct levels.

Are there different levels to the Rising Sign constellations too? Or is the Mask just a superficial face we present to the world? Just "putting our best face on things?"

Absolutely, there's a deeper level. An astrological Mask represents an entire constellation *of possibilities.* It's like owning a shelf of actor's Masks. Or we may wear a series of Masks over the years. Let's consider a constellation with a wide range of possibilities: Gemini Rising. We all know chatty, gossipy Gemini Rising people. We see Hermes-the-Trickster or Prankster in them. We've met Peter Pan and Tinkerbelle, Gemini Rising people who don't want to grow up! Jung's puer and puella. But there are also brilliant Gemini Rising people with a wry sense of humor, like Henry Kissinger; talented teachers like Marcel Marceau who opened his school of mime to preserve the Harlequin tradition. There are talented Gemini Rising craftspeople. There are Gemini Rising lecturers who seem to ramble but then surprise us by summing everything up beautifully with a power point presentation, bringing all the pieces together at the end.

Gemini Rising people can be highly intuitive, like Jeanne Dixon and Mira Alfassar

Richard, The Mother of the Aurobindo Ashram in Pondicherry, India. We see this when Gemini Rising attunes not only to Hermes/Mercury but also to its esoteric ruler.

Venus rules aesthetics and values. *So many Masks* are possible for Gemini: journalist, talk show host, Advisor to the King (Kissinger) Court Jester (juggler or mime), author, teacher, psychic and more. The more spiritual Geminis seem able to reconcile the pillars of Hercules (the glyph for the Twins) in a harmonious manner. They're attuned to Venus, the principal of harmony.

Is it true that the Rising Sign, not the Sun Sign is what people usually come up with at parties when they try to guess your Sign? They see the Mask?

Yes, that happens fairly often. Most of us prepare our party-going-Mask carefully; we put thought and attention into it. Still, the Mask will reflect the planet close to the Rising Sign if we have one there. Uranus near the Ascendant, or contracting it, usually means a zany choice of apparel, Saturn near the Ascendant tends towards a businesslike, serious Mask. The look is "classic"—often black or the latest "new black." The briefcase is left home but the wallet or purse contains business cards in case they're needed. Mars near the Ascendant: elegant sportswear to show off a buff body. Venus near the Ascendant: style; a sense of color that accentuates the hair, the eyes, the complexion or hides flaws. Moon near the Ascendant may discuss an "ex" or a close family member they're concerned about, their pet, or, worst case-scenario, their dreadful "ex" at the party. Whether or not the person is a nurturer, they appear to be.

Here's where the confusion occurs: a person might guess "Libra Rising" when Venus is on the Ascendant in some other Rising Sign. Or guess "Cancer Rising" when the Moon is on the Ascendant, regardless of Rising Sign. The businesslike person would seem like Capricorn Rising because Saturn's on the Ascendant. If any of these planets were in the middle of the First House, they'd still affect the magnetism but to a lesser degree.

Are First House Planets part of the Mask, or just the Rising Sign Degree and the planet closest to it?

The entire First House is part of the Mask, including all its planets. Twelfth House planets within five degrees of the Rising Sign influence the Mask, too.

Each planet in the First House contributes something of its own nature to our magnetism. With Saturn-in-the-First House, others probably see you as a responsible, well-organized person, disciplined, and focused. This will draw you a lot of work! By the age of 30, you'd most likely be hard on yourself as a result of your perceptions about *others* unfulfilled expectations of you. (Perhaps parents and mentors never really expected that of you! It's *your* First House Saturn, after all, not theirs!) At work, you've come to believe, "the buck stops here" on your desk. Or, with Mars in your First, you see yourself as an active person, (you were probably athletic in youth) but by now, at 55, your may feel frustrated because you no longer have the physical stamina or agility you had at 35. Or you may forget this on occasion, overexert yourself and pull a muscle or develop a hernia.

So, the Mask not only symbolizes how others see us; it *also colors how we perceive ourselves.* It's possible to over-identify with First House planets after Midlife. Our First House Saturn keeps overachieving but we may no longer enjoy our jobs. Or, our First House Moon still wears an outdated Supermom Mask. Wearing a Mask that no longer serves often interferes with drawing new friends or participating in activities that we would now enjoy. Our days are filled with people who wear old Masks, like ours.

The Venus-in-the-First House sorority girl or Adonis-the-handsome-salesman particularly feel a sense of loss as beauty fades after Midlife. For Mercury-in the-First House, multi-tasking becomes more difficult. (With aging they're more forgetful.) The Masks that worked for us in youth become difficult to maintain; we invest more and more energy in keeping their veneer fresh and shiny as the decades pass.

How can I find my Rising Sign? And how can I find out if I have any First House planets?

The information you need for calculating your horoscope, including the Rising Sign and the houses is on your birth certificate. If you don't have a copy, it's available from the Department of Vital Statistics in the capitol of the state where you were born.

A word of caution, though. Some states have two-page certificates with the time of birth on the second page. So, it's a good idea to ask, "is there is a second page?" when you call to order it. If so, do request both pages. Otherwise, they may send only the first page. If the time of birth is missing, you'll have only half the information. (If you know your latitude and longitude, you'll know your symbolic place in space but not in time.) Once you have the information, you can proceed to an internet site and fill in the data or see an astrologer for a private session. If you have a serious interest in calculating many horoscopes, software is available for purchase through Solar Fire, Matrix or Astrolabe.

What if I don't have any First House Planets?

Don't worry about it. Not everyone has a planet sitting right on his Ascendant or in the First House. Planets in other houses will likely make contacts (aspects) to the Ascendant degree. Novelist Simone de Beauvoir and psychologist Sigmund Freud didn't have any.

First look for the planet or planets that rule your Rising Sign. Simone de Beauvoir had

Scorpio Rising. Scorpio has two ruling planets. One of them, Mars, trined the Ascendant from the Fifth House; she was passionate about Life.

The other ruler of Scorpio, Pluto was in her Seventh, long-term relationships, in an unstable aspect (inconjunct) to the Ascendant.

John Paul Sartre, the love of her life for fifty years, put her through a great deal with his many love affairs, about which he wrote her in great detail (in spite of her objections that she didn't care to be in the bedroom as a voyeur.) Also painful were his doubts about Existentialism, the philosophy of personal freedom by which they'd both lived their lives, in his later years. But his adopting a young woman as his "literary heir" and advisor, a position that she'd previously held herself, was probably the greatest shock.

The major theme of the Mask and the obstacles it faces; the adjustments that must be made are described.

Next, look for *any* planet that contacts *the Ascendant degree* to learn about your Mask. Beauvoir's Moon and Saturn in Pisces were conjunct her Fifth House Mars. They were in a nice free-flowing trine to the Ascendant; she was Sartre's anchor (when he tired of a lover or the woman became too demanding, Simone got rid of her for him, because she said "we had spoiled Sartre; he didn't like unpleasantness and I was tough." As editor, she helped structure his work Structuring is a Saturn function. Her Pisces Moon was very sacrificial around the "creative genius." If she wanted to go to New York and Sartre was invited to Yugoslavia, she went with him instead.

As the years pass, transiting and progressed planets will cross the Ascendant and move through your Identify House. *It isn't really empty.* By the time Simone was at the Sorbonne, her progressed Ascendant had entered Sagittarius. When it reached (conjuncted) Sartre's Natal Sagittarian Ascendant degree, he invited her to join his group of friends (she had excelled on the exam that Sartre had failed.) He nicknamed her "Castro" (Beaver) because she studied so hard. After she joined the group, he studied and passed the exam the next time with high marks.

If *no* planets contact the Ascendant degree, it's also possible that your mother remembered your birth time incorrectly (especially when you're part of a large family.) If you haven't a copy of your birth certificate, it's a good idea to obtain one and check the time. If you cannot easily obtain yours (adopted children sometimes have difficulty) it's also a good idea to look for an astrologer who does rectification.

What else influences the astrological Mask besides First House Planets and the spiritual and instinctual planets that rule the Ascendant?

The Elements and the Modes. Let's visualize meeting someone for the first time. A person who might become important to you. Let's say you're at Starbucks to meet an Internet e-mail pal in person; someone from your forum. How do you seem to them? Grounded/Earthy? Imaginative/Watery? Enthusiastic/excited /Firey? Or Aloof, objective/ Airy. Air is usually reserved at the first meeting, Though the Airy Mask is friendly, Air is wondering whether they *really* want to get involved. Air is thinking, "He or she might be okay at a distance, I enjoy those e-mails, but do I really want this person any closer than my inbox?"

The Modes (also called Qualities) are influential too: **Cardinality (Aries, Cancer, Libra, Capricorn)** seems authoritative; "together," well organized. The Mask projects: "I have the entire project under control. Let me run through it for you from beginning to end." You'd feel very comfortable having your child or grandchild in his classroom or carpool. Cardinal Masks work well for us when it comes to competition for promotion.

Fixity (Taurus, Leo, Scorpio, Aquarius) has real *presence* but is quite stubborn. Fixity knows who she is; she's sure of herself and quite comfortable in her body. Fixity has the courage of his convictions. He won't be easily persuaded to change his opinions; in fact, he might try to convert you to his religion, philosophy, cause (Aquarius) or political affiliation. (Any Mask, of course, may hide a fragile ego.)

Mutability (Gemini, Virgo, Sagittarius, Pisces) is impressionable, reasonable and maybe even too accommodating (can seem wishy-washy.) They're nice, helpful, impressionable, and suggestible. Like young Professor Mutable. On the first day of class a student wanted to do a term paper on an obscure hobby-topic. The student was very excited about it and Professor Mutable's Mask absorbed the enthusiasm. But the small college library lacked books on the subject, so Professor Mutable brought the student a stack of books he had checked out from a large university library. When the books went missing from the student's locker, Professor Mutable was left with an enormous bill.

It helps if Mutables are in touch with a boundary-setting planet (usually Saturn or Pluto) elsewhere in the chart. Mutable Rising Signs absorb others' energy more than the other Modes, with the exception of Cardinal Water. (Cancer is the psychic-sponge.)

Someone said I have an Intercept. What is that ? How do I work with it?

An entire workshop could be devoted to intercepts! They come up when we use the Tropical Placidus or Tropical Koch formula to calculate horoscopes. By definition, an intercepted Sign is wholly contained within a House but does not appear on a Cusp. People born in the Northern Latitudes are more likely to have them than others.

I don't know whether or not you have planets in your intercept. Intercepted planets usually develop in a solitary way, taking longer to express themselves. There's an excellent book by Joanne Wicklenburg: *Your Hidden Powers, Retrograde Planets and Intercepted Signs.* (American Federation of Astrologers, 1992.) Some people who have intercepted planets are original thinkers; quite imaginative. They seem to have a different perspective on the intercepted House than the rest of us.

As I understand it, I have my Natal Rising Sign for life, though I can also absorb the positive attributes of the Progressed Ascendant as well?

You're right. We came to earth at a certain time and place. That doesn't change as we progress through the next two or three signs. Let's take an example: Scorpio is a very stubborn (Fixed) Rising Sign. As a child, Scorpio Rising Simone de Beauvoir threw tantrums, or held her breath until she fainted in order to get her own way. It worked for her; her father was absent, her mother at a loss about how to discipline Simone.

As a teenager, she came up against a situation that she couldn't control, even with the Pluto-Ascendant aspect. She wanted to marry her cousin Jacques, who visited often and seemed interested. When she learned that his marriage was already arranged to a wealthy young woman, Simone, who had no dowry, was devastated. She decided never to marry.

Once she progressed into Sagittarius, she found it easier to compromise. With her Fixed Scorpio discipline, she threw herself into her studies at the Sorbonne. She saw philosophy as the key to a "passionate life," the only kind worth living. Influenced by Jean Paul Sartre, whose mind she fell in love with, she renounced the bourgeois values of her upper middle class, conservative Catholic parents for Existentialism and free love. But the mental stimulation was not enough. Her Scorpio libido wanted more.

During the Capricorn progression Beuvoir wrote two novels and her most famous book, *The Second Sex,* without any input from Sartre. Capricorn is the zenith of fame, (symbolically, the Tenth House, the apex house) and she soon had as many fans as Sartre. She was sought as a feminist speaker across America. (The Progressed Ascendant sextiled her Natal Sun and Mercury during this cycle.)

By the time she progressed into Aquarius, Simone lived the "authentic life" she'd longed for as a child. With Chicago author Nelson Algren, she satisfied her Scorpio physical passion and experienced far more than a "marriage of minds!" Though Algren tried to convince her to move to Chicago, she knew Paris was where she belonged. And Algren couldn't accept her relationship with Sartre, with whom she travelled and spent several hours a day.

Her unusual relationship with Sartre included an adult child they had each legally adopted. The two young adopted women sometimes travelled with them; they were an unusual joint family! On Ascendant- square-Ascendant Sartre died; she had a falling-out with his "literary heir."

According to Carl Jung, the *persona* is like an actor's Mask, *but the Mask adapts over time*. In astrology, the progressed 30-year-cycles describe the adaptation.

PART I: ARIES - VIRGO

CHAPTER ONE

Aries Rising - Inspiration

Rev. Billy Graham, "I've read the last page of the *Bible*. It's all going to turn out all right."

Rev. Terry Cole-Whittaker, *What you Think of Me is None of My Business,* a title which resonated with so many Aries Rising clients. The book came out in the 1980s.

John Lennon, "I have always had to lead."

Henry Miller, "Every man has his own destiny: the only imperative is to follow it; accept it, no matter where it leads him." *The Wisdom of the Heart.*

—— "Sex is one of the nine reasons for reincarnation. The other eight are unimportant." *Sexus,* Chapter 21, 1949.

Marcel Proust, "Every reader finds himself. The writer's work is merely a kind of optical instrument that makes it possible for the reader to discern what, without this book, he would perhaps never have seen in himself."

—— "If a little dreaming is dangerous, the cure for it is not to dream less but to dream more, to dream all the time." *In Search of Lost Times,* Vol. II. 1918.

Reverend Aimee Semple MacPherson, "Will I marry a third time? He would have to be very handsome, have a radio show, and maybe play the trombone. Angeles Temple could use a trombone player. But I doubt I would marry again. Jesus is my bridegroom now."

Annie Besant, "I'm married to Theosophy." *An Autobiography,* 1893.

The Aries Rising Mask in Youth - The Mask of Bravado

The Hero or Heroine has the gift of persuasion. Decisive, direct and impulsive, assertive and sometimes aggressive; Aries rushes in to save the day, share wisdom and inspire others, to rally others to their cause or raise funds to promote their organization.

How to Recognize the Aries Mask

In my astrology practice I have encountered mainly thin, wiry Aries Rising bodies. Many people with this Ascendant keep trim by practicing their favorite sports or martial arts from their twenties through their seventies. Others seem to avoid exercise altogether yet appear to have a metabolic rate that the rest of us would envy! Mars, the mundane ruler is associated with heroic impulses, sports competitions (Mars was invoked before events in the Roman stadium) and the martial arts, as well as reflexes and co-ordination.

However, First House planets have an impact on the physique too. Some Aries Rising athletes have stocky figures like basketball center Shaquille O'Neal with Venus conjunct his Ascendant. If Venus or Jupiter conjuncts or otherwise contacts the Ascendant degree, or is located in the First House, the person usually requires an exercise regimen to keep off excess weight. The same is true for the Moon in the First. The Moon rules the tides and is associated with fluid retention.

There's another way to recognize Aries Rising: *Aries is usually in motion.* They'll be rushing off to an appointment or telling you what they're going to do next. When Aries sits down to write his memoirs, he's likely to be eighty years old, like Reverend Billy Graham.[1]

Though most Aries Rising people are too busy enjoying life to write about their experiences. Theosophist Annie Besant is an exception to the rule. At 57, during her Second Saturn Return, she took time out to write about "moving through the storms" of the First Half of Life "to inner peace."[2]

Max and Augusta Heindel are correct in *Message to the Stars:* Aries Rising does tend to have a high forehead and a pointed chin.[3] I've also found the Heindels accurate about the Aries tendency to run very high fevers, yet survive. But my Aries clients don't just survive, they carry right on with their agenda when the rest of us would be popping aspirin on our way to the doctor's office. Aries' stoicism is somewhat similar to that of the two Saturn-ruled Signs, Capricorn and Aquarius.

The Mode and the Element

---

1 Reverend Graham's autobiography, *Just As I Am,* though full of interesting accounts of places he visited and famous people he met, doesn't discuss his inner struggles, unlike Yeats' *Memoir* (above) or Annie Besant's *An Autobiography.*

2 *Annie Besant: An Autobiography* (1893) with her 1908 preface, (n.c: Kessinger publications,) 2007.

3 Max Heindel and Augusta Foss Heindel, *The Message of the Stars,* (Oceanside: Rosicrucian Fellowship,) 1980, 92-3.

The most independent of the Rising Signs, this Cardinal Sign presents to the world a confident, authoritative Mask: the Mask of leadership. "I'm a master at my work: the competition pales in comparison" comes through their aura in the office, lab or studio. John Lennon, who gave us the inspiring song, "Imagine," put this well during his famous *Playboy* interview, "I've always had to lead." At the astrology session, these words are usually followed by, "I'm going to leave my company soon, I cannot put up with one more bad executive decision." Or, "I've made plenty of suggestions on how to streamline the process; I have my own approach, but nothing ever changes." None of the Cardinal Sign Masks suffers fools gladly, but Aries will move on sooner than the others.

Aries' Element is Fire, bringing the *persona* warmth and magnetism. But this Solar Rising Sign (the Sun is exalted in Aries) generates not only heat, but light too.

Fire is an energetic, active, inspiring Element. If you've read through the quotations from famous Aries Rising people (above) you'll have noticed a number of ministers, ranging from Evangelicals to Pentecostals, from Theosophy to the Church of Religious Science.[4] Others look to Aries Rising for inspiration.

Reverend Billy Graham, who tells us that the Bible has a happy ending (above) is probably the most famous of the ministers. Now in his 80's, Graham's charisma, personal warmth and enthusiasm still attract large crowds. And he exhibits another attribute of Cardinal Fire: he doesn't micromanage. Evangelical Web site testimonials refer to his leadership style, based upon the Parable of Talents. Those drawn to his Christian ministry are free to apply their talents wherever they see an opening.

Volunteers are drawn by his passion for his beliefs. Like most Aries Rising people, Graham is neither petty nor narrow-minded. He respects Catholicism and the Mormon church; he believes heaven is open to sincere pagans who are unfamiliar with the *Bible*.

The Planetary Rulers - Instinctual and Spiritual

The mundane (instinctual) ruler is Mars, symbolizing the *persona's* tremendous passion, vitality, drive, assertiveness, decisiveness and enthusiasm. But it also symbolizes the Mars' inclination to anger, arrogance (if aspected to Jupiter or Pluto) restlessness, impulsiveness, and impatience.

---

4 Astrologers will be interested to know that A.S. McPherson, A. Besant, O. Roberts and Shaquille O'Neal all had Mars in Fall or in Detriment. Nobody in this chapter had Mars in Rulership or in Exaltation.

All the Cardinal Signs are competitive but Mars bestows a competitive edge on Aries: As athletes put it, Aries is a "contender."

The spiritual (esoteric) rulers are Mercury and the Goddess Athena, the Wise Counselors. Both are associated with an incisive mind, skillful communication, and the ability to see through complicated problems and find solutions rapidly. When Mars and Mercury work well together in the horoscope Aries communicates clearly and directly. When they don't, Aries may not communicate as well, but still expects others to come to the point quickly. The two rulers of Aries Rising also describe a person's reflexes and mind-body co-ordination.

In classical times, two Wise Counselors, Mercury and Athena offered guidance to young, temporarily discouraged heroes in the epics of Homer and Virgil.

Sometimes they brought the message in person, as Athena did to Telemachus in the *Odyssey*, "be patient just a little while longer and your father will return." And sometimes they came in dreams, as Mercury to Virgil's protagonist in the *Aeneid*, "stop wasting time! Get on with it! Break out of prison, go to Athens, become a squire and win the fair maiden!"[5] Sometimes Mars' impulse to fight (or argue) is appropriate, sometimes it's best to sublimate; Aries retreats and fights another day.

We still look to Wise Counselors for inspiration in our dreams and in person. People are drawn to the positive Aries Mask. They respond with, "whatever that speaker has, *I want!*"

Annie Besant spoke in person to large, enthusiastic crowds on behalf of both Theosophy and Home Rule for India, but we live in a fast-paced media-world. Aries Rising inspirational speakers have all adjusted to it well. In the early Twentieth Century, Aimee Semple McPherson, who arrived in Los Angeles from Western Canada with only her tent, a tambourine and a ten dollar bill, soon had a large Pentecostal Temple. People came from across the city to her Sunday service. A client who experienced it as a child described Aimee's dramatic entrance: "she marched up the aisle to the front the Temple in

---

5 and Krishna to Arjuna on the battlefield of the Dharma in the Mahabharata, "enough sitting and reflecting, it's time to fight." Though there was an actual war, this is usual interpreted as fighting our inner battles with negative emotions and addictive habits.

her flowing white dress; everyone was awestruck and excited! I can still picture it now, in my late seventies."[6] Aimee soon had a radio program.

Oral Roberts also began in the "revival tent era." He left the tent behind to found a university and healing center. He let God and others know exactly how much money he needed at every stage of the process! And of course, Billy Graham still fills stadiums in his 80's.

Terry Cole-Whittaker drew great crowds every Sunday in La Jolla, Ca. She had a television show. In the 1980s she broke from the Church of Religious Science to establish her own church. On Easter Sunday, 1985 feeling burnt-out, Terry left California, to organize a foundation in Hawaii. She took time off to visit spiritual pilgrimage centers. Still in demand as a motivational speaker, her positive message is similar to Oral Roberts': God wants us to be healthy and prosperous. The Aries Mask of Inspiration is a powerful magnet.

The Mask of Rebel or Social Critic - Henry Miller and Pearl Buck

Pearl Buck, daughter of missionaries to China and wife of another, included in her novel, *The Good Earth* numerous injustices she observed in the orient, particularly toward women. She had Jupiter conjunct her Ascendant and Mars square the Moon's nodes. She thought of herself as a writer from childhood, as did Henry Miller.

Miller assumed the author *persona* in Paris, where he lived for two decades. He fought against a taboo of his era, the prohibition against explicit sex in novels. His first novel, *Tropic of Cancer,* was published at 49. Both this and his next one, *Tropic of Capricorn,* were banned in America. Miller's interest in sexuality—Mars, is his passionate mundane ruler—also comes through the quote (above) on why people reincarnate. In biology, Mars is the glyph for the masculine sex.

Miller had Mars conjunct rebellious Uranus and his Moon in his Seventh House. (Scorpio.) Though he seemed to wear the mask of the industrious self-made man, he had

---

6 Virginia Lingren, La Mesa, California. For Aimee's story see Lately Thomas, (pseud.) *The Vanishing Evangelist: The Aimee Semple McPherson Kidnapping Event,* (New York: Viking,) 1959. After facing the grand jury, "she returned to Foursquare Temple and was cheered as no football hero was ever cheered. She radiated confidence, courage and defiance and stood before the congregation like a triumphal Empress." Thomas is quoting the *Los Angeles Examiner* on her return from court; the paper had been critical of her, p. 112 and p. 362.

no planets in his First House; he succeeded with a lot of help from his friends, including five wives and his mistress of many years Anais Nin (see Libra Rising.)

The Atypical Aries Rising
Marcel Proust Neptune on the Ascendant

If by chance you know someone with Aries Rising who does *not* wear the Mask described: an Aries Rising person who is a dreamer, not a doer: introverted, highly introspective, indecisive, at times even lethargic, you may want to stop at this point and re-read the two quotes from Marcel Proust about dreaming and about the writer's work as an "optical instrument." Proust was born with Neptune on his Ascendant and is most famous for *In Search of Lost Times,* a seven-volume opus considered to be one of the Twentieth Century's major novels. The Aries Rising person you know may have Neptune in the Seventh House, opposite the Ascendant. Many Aries Rising Baby Boomers have Neptune there; it sends and receives mixed signals. Proust is very different from the typical Aries Rising person, where what you scc is what you get.

Proust's metaphor about a writer's work as an "optical instrument that helps the reader see things about himself he's never noticed" is apt.

Proust himself had that talent. Neptune Rising at birth does function like an opaque lens; It's like having a unique window on life. Many readers enjoy his novels because they're fascinated with his era as seen through his mind's eye.

A *visionary* planet, Neptune favors the world of the creative imagination over the mundane world. Proust was fascinated with dreams and fantasy, with the sudden awakening of lost memories by sounds, smells or taste. If we scan through the list of quotations above, we see that his writing style was very different from that of the other Aries Rising authors.

Neptune on the Ascendant, regardless of Rising Sign is a permeable Mask. Others project qualities on the Neptunean Mask that a person may not have, or may have had *for awhile,* but not for long.

Some critics read the "Sodom and Gomorrah" book in *Temps Perdu* (Lost Times) and were certain Proust was a latent or a closet homosexual. That may or may not have been true. With Neptune it's hard to discern truth from appearances, especially given the author's metaphorical (Neptunean) writing style. Still, Neptune on the Ascendant is a wonderful placement for a poet or an interpreter of dreams.[7]

The Macho Mask and Creativity
The Second Half of Life

At thirty, John Lennon told the *Playboy* Interviewer that he was tired of the "Macho" Mask and tired of fighting. He'd put a lot of energy into his Leadership Mask. When he met Yoko Ono, he decided to remove it and leave the Beatles. Though he had many reasons for leaving, the strongest was his creative impulse; he felt he was entering a new cycle of creativity about the time he wrote "Imagine." His "best songs" lay ahead. Unfortunately, he was assassinated within a year of the interview.[8]

Many Aries are still seeking the Golden Fleece in the community, or as Jung called it, the Collective. What brings Aries Rising contentment and inner satisfaction after fifty? For many Aries Rising people, there's still a great deal of joy to be found in inspiring or motivating others. They're still energized by the role of Wise Counselor. And by then they speak from experience.

Aries Rising memoirs like Besant's, direct, open, and honest about her inner struggles while wearing the Mask of Leadership, are valuable. She told her readers that even at 57,

---

7 *In Search of Lost Times* is now the preferred translation of *a La Recherche du Temps Perdus*. Formerly, *Remembrance of Times Past*. Since Proust later wrote about "Found Times," (*Temps Trouves*) he apparently meant lost and (later) recovered memories. Proust's Neptunean style is in sharp contrast to Walt Whitman's terse lines in *Leaves of Grass*; Walt Whitman had Aries Rising too, but had Saturn on the Ascendant. Whitman's work was very structured.

8 *The Playboy Interviews with John Lennon and Yoko Ono*, David Sheff, (NY: Playboy Press,) 1981, 245, "I was lying fallow creatively." Saturn opposed his Mercury as it returned to its natal position at 28. It was a depressing time. The band's manager, Brian Epstein insisted upon the famous "Beatles sound," which "worked for them." The others were still happy with the Group Mask: the haircut and dress style that characterized the band. But John wanted to write songs on the Vietnam War, "commercials for peace." Epstein saw the war as "an American problem; not the business of a British group," pp. 32-33. John met Yoko and moved on. She was ready to manage the business; he was ready to "be a peaceful house husband, stay home with Sean and write songs. I was a hitter, a man of violence, but now I'm a man of peace." p. 154.

she still stood backstage trembling and full of anxiety.[9] But once on stage, she connected immediately with her audience. She, and each of them, were all one soul.

She'd come a long way from the young bride of the country minister who fetched things herself rather than ask the servants. (The daughter of Mrs. Wood, Anglo-Irish widow and impoverished tutor to the aristocracy, Annie had been afraid of servants!) She was the first woman to stand up before a judge in England and fight for her children (sadly, she lost them to the minister husband.) Friend to socialist Member of Parliament Charles Bradlaugh she helped organize the girls' strike at a London matchbook factory, she became the leader of the Indian Theosophists and of the All India Congress Party in India in 1917.

Annie had little time to meditate but always "knew" when to move on and what course to take. Like Terry Cole-Whittaker, "what others thought of her was none of her business!" A risk-taker, the Mars-ruled *persona* enjoys new challenges to the very end of life.

Jason and the Dragon's Teeth Warriors
An Episode in his Quest for the Golden Fleece

This is a good story for those of us who enjoy symbolism. It's a solar story (the Sun is Exalted in Aries) that's not about Ego aggrandizement. There's a clue to alert us that this story is really about the Self: Jason seeks a rare object, the Golden Fleece. Gold is the Sun's metal. So, this is a treasure well worth the struggle (a challenge worthy of Aries Rising.) Like the golden chalice (the Holy Grail) in the Medieval story, the Golden Fleece is a priceless object sought for its own sake. It has an intrinsic value to the Seeker but no resale value whatsoever.

When our story begins, Jason, the Seeker, has been at sea for quite some time. He has courageously faced many challenges; his confident masculine side has already been tested many times. However, we sense a little battle-fatigue. Many of us can identify with that after living five or more decades ourselves. We've begun to wonder if we'll ever reach our destination or find the elusive treasure?

Jason and his crew, the Argonauts arrive in the kingdom of Colchis. Once again, a local

---

9 The success of a speech was "proportional to her nervousness ahead of time." The more anxiety she felt, the better she would be. *Autobiography,* cited above, pp. 161-2. One major regret about communication was the time lost in defending herself and in arguing. She wished she had it back.

ruler asks their help in return for his aid in finding the Golden Fleece. Jason and the crew are used to this by now.

Though Jason wears the Mask of the Hero, at this point in life he no longer considers himself invincible or indestructible. He asks for and accepts help when needed.

The king of Colchis sets the task, The challenge is to cross the plains of Ares and secure the wild, fire-breathing bulls. "I want those sacred bulls," he says, "yoke them for me!"

But how to accomplish this? Jason seeks advice from the sorceress Medea: "sow the furrows with Drakon's teeth, just as a farmer would sow corn," she says, "And the teeth will sprout as fully-grown, battle-ready warriors. They'll be armed with spears and shields. No matter how strong the enemy appears, *you must attack.*

Jason misreads the situation but he quickly agrees to the plan. He expects to accomplish this task quickly: the teeth will spout immediately and the warriors will become instant allies. He brings the dragon teeth, a gift of Goddess Athena to a King in a previous episode, and sows them on both sides of the field wherein the bulls are snorting fire. "That went pretty well, he thought," then he waited.

And finally, as the poet Ovid tells us in *Metamorphoses*:

> when within the dark and pregnant earth the forms of men were finished, up they rose from the whole teeming field, and each came forth clashing—most wonderful sight—the arms of war... As the Earthborn men shot upon the field, the deadly War-god's sacred plot bristled with stout shields, double-pointed spears, and glittering helmets.

Jason was astonished and shaken to see what he'd done. Suddenly hundreds of invincible warriors stood between him and the sacred bulls!

But clearly they were not his allies, they were there to guard the bulls from him! He and his crew were astonished.

Ovid tells us that even Medea, "the foreign witch" was shaken by the sight:

> ...when the Greeks beheld the multitude with sharp spears poised to hurl at Jason's head, their brave hearts failed; fear was on every face; she too who had made him safe was filled with dread, and when she saw him there alone, attacked by foes so many, sudden terror drained her blood away, and cold and faint she sat. Lest her herbs should fail she reinforced them with her spells and summoned secret charms.
>
> Then she invoked Hecate, the Goddess of the Night.

Nor did Jason forget the counsel from Medea of the many wiles: "attack, no matter how strong they seem!" He picked up an enormous round boulder, "one that Ares himself might have thrown, but four strong men together could not have budged from its place."

Rushing forward, he "hurled it far away among the Earthborn men." Then he crouched behind his shield, "unseen and full of confidence," confusing them.

> They turned their onslaught from himself upon each other; then by mutual wounds in civil strife the Earthborn brethren died.
>
> The Greeks acclaimed the victor and embraced their glorious prince with eager arms; and she, the foreign witch, longed to embrace him too, but modesty—and her fair name—forbade. With silent secret joy her heart was full of gratitude to her triumphant spells and to the gods who gave their magic power.
>
> The splendor of it flashed through the air above and struck Olympus. Indeed, this army springing from the earth shone out like the full congregation of the stars piercing the darkness of a Murky night, when snow lies deep and the winds have chased the wintry clouds away.
>
> The Colchians gave a mighty shout like the roar of the sea beating on jagged rocks; and the king himself was astounded as he saw the great boulder hurtle through the air. But the Earthborn men, like nimble hounds, leapt on one another and with loud yells began to slay. Beneath each other's spears they fell on Mother Earth, As pines or oaks are blown down by a gale.
>
> And now, like a bright meteor that leaps from heaven and leaves a fiery trail behind it, portentious to all those who see it flash across the night, Jason hurled himself on them with his sword unsheathed and slaughtered them, striking as he could, for many of them had but half emerged and showed their flanks and bellies only, some had their shoulders clear, some had just stood up, And others were afoot already and rushing into battle.
>
> Thus Jason cut his crop of Earthborn Men. Blood filled the furrows as water fills the conduits of a spring. And still they fell, some on their faces biting the rough clods, some on their backs, and others on their hands and sides, looking like monsters from the sea.
>
> Many were struck before they could lift up their feet, and rested there with the death-dew on their brows, each trailing on the earth so much of him as had come up into the light of day. They lay like saplings in an orchard bowed to the ground after Zeus has sent torrential rain and snapped them at the root.[10]

Jason yoked the bulls of Ares for Colchis, received directions from the grateful King and set out on the next stage of his journey, his final destination not yet on visible on the horizon.

This story is replete with Ares/Mars symbolism: A hero ready to do battle, seemingly

---

10 Ovid, *Metamorphoses*, VII, G.P. Goold, ed, F.J. Miller, trans., *Loeb Classical Library* #42, (NY: 1984,) pp. 347-51 on Jason's vow to Medea; Medea's help and invocation of Hecate. For Athena's gift, see Apollonius Rhodius, *Argonautica* 3. 1179 ff See also Seneca's play, *Medea*.

invincible warriors and a battlefield called the "plains of Ares." And most important, the dragon's teeth, the sharp teeth of Drakon, "serpent-guardian of Ares' sacred spring." Originally a gift of Goddess Athena (Wise Counselor) to King Cadmos, Jason received them in return for his help earlier in his voyage.

There's even a symbol of the coming Taurus progression, the bulls he yoked represent Taurus, though they "belong to Ares." And a hint of the second progressed Ascendant Sign, Gemini: Castor and Pollux shine down upon him as he yoked them.

Because the Golden Fleece is a symbol of the Self, we know that Jason is a conscious hero, not a man driven entirely by his instincts, in contrast to the Dragon-Teeth-Warriors who acted from battle lust and limited awareness.

But key to Jason's success (and to balanced living after fifty) is following the wise counsel of the feminine, intuition. This is a challenge in youth, when pausing on life's battlefield to get in touch with intuition can be very dangerous. When we haven't much experience, it's often more appropriate to go with our gut instincts. And nobody lives in-the-moment more than Aries![11]

In youth, it's hard to hold back impulsive Mars; difficult to wait for Gaia's womb—the womb of "the dark and pregnant earth"—to grow the seeds to maturity. The creative process takes time.

But unless the seeds spring up immediately, Aries is tempted to plough them over and move on to a different project.

But as soon as Jason followed his intuition, the scene quickly changed! The boulder landed; the warriors became confused, thinking one of their own had thrown it. They forgot all about Jason and turned on each other. Soon it was all over for them.

Where would Jason have been without Athena's Dragon Teeth to distract the bulls, Medea's herbs and prayers, or Hecate to darken the skies?[12] Or perhaps most important, his faith that, as Reverend Graham said of the Bible, the story will have a happy ending.

Even though the destination and the treasure—the Golden Fleece—are not yet visible on the horizon, the journey continues.

---

11 In the first half of life most of my Aries Rising clients seem to agree with John Lennon's philosophy that "life should be a fast run." Ray Coleman, *John Winston Lennon,* (London: Sedgwick & Jackson,) 1984, 245. Unfortunately, accidents do occur while gong at full throttle. Aries Rising Isadora Duncan caught her long scarf in the car door and strangled herself. Better to check your surroundings before stepping on the accelerator! Several Aries Rising clients have been in motorcycle accidents.

12 Another Goddess is present, too, by implication: Gaia, the Earth Mother. The dragon-teeth-warriors are her Earthborn sons, (the *terragenae*.)

Creativity After Fifty - Taurus and Gemini Progressions

During the Taurus-ruled progression, Aries' client base stabilizes and gradually expands or there are step raises and promotions: Aries Rising usually has a Capricorn Midheaven, which Taurus trines.

With the exception of extreme risk-takers, many of whom have a void or very few planets in Earth or Water, or have a high percentage of planets in Air and Fire, or have Mars or Uranus in houses 1, 4, 7 and 10. (Remember Henry Miller's Mars-Uranus in the Seventh!)—except for them, this is an enjoyable cycle. For the risk-takers, the Taurus progression can seem dull; they long for the challenge of new quests, new fair maidens or new handsome lovers.

"What's the purpose of this long, humdrum Taurus cycle?" Aries asks.

"It develops such underrated virtues as patience and humility. It brings balance to the personality. Others will see you as reliable rather than restless," the astrologer says.

"It doesn't matter how others' see me. It sounds as if this cycle will benefit my family and my business associates more than me," says Aries Rising. "Do you mean that I'm going to be easier *on other people?*"

There *is* truth in that!

On the other hand, the slower thirty-year-cycle resonates for clients with many Earth and Water planets. Clients with Taurus planets in their First House, particularly Moon-in-Exaltation there, enjoy the cycle. When the Ascendant degree contacts Taurus Moon, Aries Rising often discovers a latent interest in the visual arts, poetry, or sculpture. Occasionally music, but usually the arts. Some develop an interest in meditation, chanting, or spontaneously see auras when the Exalted Moon is contacted.

One Aries Rising client embarked upon his "path to recovery" and began the Twelve Step program when the progressed Ascendant degree contacted his First House Moon. He'd thought about it before, but now he was ready: "I'm serious this time about the Higher Power," he said, "I see the benefits of the serenity prayer." Years later, he seems happier and more balanced.

With Venus-in-Taurus in the First House, Aries' romantic magnetism increases now. He makes time for romance. (Venus is already magnetic in Rulership in the First House, but this enhances her charms.)

Pisces (Water) planets in the Twelfth House really come alive during the sextile from Taurus: intuition, artistic interests, dream work, metaphysical studies are featured. With

Cancer planets in the Fourth, Aries at least considers more land, a bigger house, pets and/or children are featured during the Taurus progression.[13]

The Gemini Progression - Creativity and Communication
A Modern Aries Rising Tale

In my experience, this story describes the Aries Rising persona from cradle to grave. For most of us, a task that we eagerly undertook at 25 and set aside at 35 can seem overwhelming if we return to it at 50, 60 or 70. But it doesn't seem as daunting to the Aries Rising Mask. Or to people with Mars in the First House.

An Aries Rising woman friend, a former teacher who hadn't taught in decades, recently went on a job interview. Her family's business was going through its Saturn Return. So, during the recession, so she sought a teaching position at 59: "I need to be an employee for awhile. I know that a lot of people are competing for jobs, but I can still get back in the game!" And she was right.

The five prospective teachers interviewed ahead of her seemed very unhappy on their way out. One of them looked almost ill. When it was her turn, she learned why. She was asked about her "familiarity" with a certain software program for writing lesson plans. I'd seen it on a shelf in Office Depot, so, yes, it did sound familiar. And it seemed important to the interviewer so, I said, 'sure, I know that program!' And he looked really pleased. Relieved, even, because the school district requires it now. So, I got the job! I'm off to buy the software and teach myself to use it. After all, I've taught myself business software. *"Should be a piece of cake."*

I thought about the other five women interviewed who weren't "familiar with the program," some of whom had probably seen it in the store too, and I thought of Jason's fearful crew.

Later, my friend was surprised when the classroom situation proved more of a challenge

---

13 My Aries Rising clients don't ordinarily have a lot of children; one or two is the norm. None thus far has expressed an interest in adopting seven children as Pearl Buck (Moon and Venus in Cancer in the Fourth) did after her second marriage, or had five like Reverend Billy Graham (exalted Jupiter in Cancer in the Fourth.) Independent Aries Rising women I have known seem to follow the pattern of Annie Besant, Aimee Semple McPherson (see above list of quotes) and Terry Cole-Whittaker. After Midlife, their passion and energy are still focused on "the Work" as spiritual leaders, ministers, or as persuasive salesmen and fund-raisers. My Aries Rising male clients are more inclined to serial monogamy, like Henry Miller.

than expected, but like Jason, it didn't take her long to get her "snorting bulls" under control.

A strong *persona*, the Aries Mask covers and hides the less courageous side of their personality.

Obstacles seldom slow Aries down. The adrenalin rush Jason experienced when he lifted and hurled his boulder is often accessible to Mars' optimistic children.

Aries Rising usually presents a businesslike masculine side and wears a Mask of bravado. Aries also releases expectations quickly,—"what! Those warriors are not my friends? I'd expected them to help me!" But then Aries shrugs and completes the task.

At the end of the long progression through Earth (Taurus) Aries Rising has (at least theoretically) become grounded. Perhaps he's assimilated such Taurus attributes as perseverance, stamina, endurance, patience and more rarely, calm in times of crisis.

While Jason was yoking the sacred bulls for the king, "Castor and Pollux shone down on him" in the Roman story. The twin stars symbolize Gemini, the next stage of his journey. Natal Aries and Gemini are both logical Signs. Mercury connects the progression to the Natal Ascendant: it's the mundane ruler of Gemini *and* the esoteric ruler of Aries. So, as they progress through Gemini, Aries Rising people may develop a detached perspective and/or objectivity.

The Air Element has more in common with Natal Aries than the Earthy Taurus cycle did. My friend from the earlier anecdote returned to teaching three years after progressing to Gemini Rising.

However, had her astrologer predicted a few years ago, while she was still wearing the Taurus Businesswoman Mask, that she'd teach again, she would have laughed! Why leave the family business? She had a comfortable (Taurus) routine. She set her own schedule. She could take off for the gym on slow days. She thought she had a perfect, if dull, job situation.

So, I asked the Gemini cycle question. Have you anything left *to learn* in the family business? She doubted that she did.[14]

She joked that maybe she'd purchase screenplay software in a few years, "they say that's required in Southern California, that if we don't write a screenplay we'll eventually be told to leave!" But it turned out to be lesson-plan software instead, for now at least. For most Aries Rising people the new Mask is a new, unexpected change, drawing on the talents of

---

14 She did say (with her new *persona* in zero Gemini,) "it feels like something is shifting; like tectonic plates are sliding around inside me. Oh, and *my husband* thinks I'm restless." Others often pick up the changing Mask before we do. Our body language gives us away.

the Natal Mask. Others, like Henry Miller, come into their own in this phase. Miller, who'd always wanted to be accepted as an author, was published during the Gemini cycle.

In the Cancer progression, a nurturing phase which brought out her Fourth House Cancer planets, Annie Besant's children, Digby and Mabel came from England to see her, in spite of their minister-father's negative remarks about her work. Both had studied Theosophy. She was delighted. She was very happy, too with the progress of her protégé, Jeddu Krishmurthi, then living in Ojai California.

Her most lasting contribution is probably Hindu College, Varanasi, India, which she nurtured in several ways: she worked on the curricula; she raised fund and served on the board.

She also raised money for Jeddu and his brother Nityananda to study in England.[15]

Leo Rising - The Trine to the Ascendant

I haven't had the opportunity of knowing many Aries Rising people in late old age. Those I do know discussed golf and restoring classic cars (the men) or having free time, at last, to play with their grand or even great-grandchildren (the women.)

For all of us, play time is very important in old age, whether creativity means cooking, quilt-making, gardening, or playing video games with grandchildren. Leo, more than any other Sign, is creative about play, the fifth Sign and the Fifth House have an affinity for it.

---

15 She'd hoped Nityananda would heal in the dry climate but he succumbed to tuberculosis. Like many others with Aries Rising, Annie excelled at fund-raising. When she lived in England, she had raised money to create a home for the match book factory girls, who had little to eat and slept on rags. She saved what she earned from her articles for them. In India, she convinced Sri Prakasa's father to give up his career as a magistrate and volunteer full time at the college. Sri Prakasa was 18 when they went riding together. He paced himself slowly for the 67-year-old, but Annie raced her horse around him, shouting, "hurry up!" See Sri Prakasa, *Annie Besant as Woman and as Leader,* (Bombay: Bharatiya Vidya Bhavan), Bhavan's B.R. University Series, Vol. 24, 1962, 126.

Aries Rising Bibliography

Besant, Annie Wood, *Annie Besant: An Autobiography,* *(1893)* incl. 1908 preface, (Kessinger's Publishing, www.kessinger.net) no city; no date.

Buck, Pearl S., *The Good Earth* (NY: John Day Co.,) 1945.

—— *The Goddess Abides,* (NY: John Day Co.,) 1972.

Cole-Whittaker, Terry, *What You Think of Me is None of My Business,* (La Jolla: Oak Tree Publications,) 1979.

Colman, Ray, *John Winston Lennon,* (London: Sedgwick & Jackson,) 1984.

Duncan, Isadora, *My Life,* (NY: Liveright,) 1995.

Graham, Billy (Rev.), *Just as I Am: The Autobiography of Billy Graham,* (San Francisco: Harper,) 1997.

Heindel, Max and Augusta Foss Heindel, *The Message of the Stars,* (Oceanside: Rosicrucian Publications,) 1980.

Thomas, Lately, (pseudo.) *The Vanishing Evangelist, The Aimee Semple McPherson Kidnapping Event,* (NY: Viking,) 1959.

Lennon, John, *The Playboy Interviews with John Lennon and Yoko Ono,* David Sheff, interviewer, G. Barry Golson, ed., (NY: Playboy Press,)1981.

—— "Imagine," from the CD, *Imagine,* 2000.

Miller, Henry, *Tropic of Cancer,* preface by Anais Nin, (NY: Grove Weidenfeld,) 1961.

Ovid, (Publius Ovidus Naso) *The Metamorphoses, VII: Jason & the Dragon's Teeth Warriors,* G.P. Goold & T.J. Miller, eds., Loeb Classical Library #42 (no city or press) 1984.

Prakasa, Sri, *Annie Besant as Woman and as Leader,* (Bombay: Bharatiya Vidya Bhavan,) B.R. University Series, vol. 24, 1962.

Proust, Marcel, *In Search of Lost Times, (Remembrance of Times Past,)* Christopher Prendergast, ed, (London: Allen Lane,) 2002.

Roberts, Oral (Rev.), *The Call: An Autobiography,* (NY: Doubleday,) 1972.

Taylor, Anne, *Annie Besant, A Biography,* (NY: Oxford University Press,) 1992.

CHAPTER TWO

Taurus Rising - Resourcefulness

Anna Freud to her biographer, Robert Coles. "What would I do if I wanted to introduce psychology in Brazil? I'd do it exactly the same way as (I did it) in Vienna and in London. Of course, I'd have to find someone to teach me the local language. Then I'd open a facility, perhaps a school. Children would come and through them I'd meet their parents."

Taurus Rising C.P.A., "More changes in the tax code this year! I see no need to re-invent the wheel."

Herman Melville to D.H. Lawrence, "What do you mean, why am I working here in the custom's office? Why aren't I traveling; collecting experiences for books? I already have enough material for the rest of my life!"

Taurus Rising yoga center owner, "If it's not broken, why fix it?"

Werner Erhard, founder, EST transformation seminars, "Mastering life is the process of moving from where you are to where you want to be."

Irish-American grandfather, "I know the Church demoted St. Christopher, but mine own opinion is mine opinion still." (About the statue on his dashboard.)

Queen Latifah, "I wish every woman would love herself and embrace what she was given naturally." *Woman's World*, June 7, 2005.

William Randolph Hearst, "Keep your mind on the objective, not the obstacle."

—— "Whatever begins as something tranquil is gobbled up by something not tranquil."

—— "When in doubt, money is always a good gift."

Bonnie Raitt, "I would rather feel things in extreme than not at all."

—— "Religion is for people who are scared to go to hell. Spirituality is for people who have already been there."

—— "There's nothing like living a long time to create a depth and soulfulness in your music."

Taurus Rising in Youth
The Mask of Stability, Practicality, Groundedness, Common Sense

I am loyal, dependable and determined. I am warm, sociable, sensual, charming and sometimes industrious. I love to beautiful things. Just don't invade my comfort zone, for I am stubborn as a bull. I do **not** like change and I'm adamant about that.

How to Recognize Taurus Rising

Taurus Rising has *presence*. However, that warm, magnetic Aphrodite smile masks a shrewd, businesslike approach to life. Astrologers traditionally recognize this Ascendant by the stocky body and the strong bull-like neck, which tends to thicken as they age. *Message to the Stars* mentions a sullenness in their eyes when challenged (in contrast to the firey glare of the previous Rising Sign) heavy jaws, a thick, stubby nose and firm calves. I agree with the Heindels[1] on all but the nose. I find that noses and hair color vary greatly within the twelve Rising Signs. Most of my Taurus Rising clients are short in stature. They seem to retain their physical stamina into late old age. They're appropriately dressed to make a good impression: the artistic Taurians are colorfully dressed while the professional and business Taurians are usually attired in tailored suits. Vernon Jordan, an attorney who serves on several corporate boards has the quintessential successful Taurus Rising Mask. Even on the golf course he could be photographed for the cover of *Gentleman's Quarterly*.

Unless there are many planets in the Air Element, especially Gemini, Taurus Rising is *not* known for its sense of humor or quick grasp of new information. However, they love practical knowledge. And they learn their craft very thoroughly.

The Mode and the Element

Fixed Earth is as solid as a rock. Once established, Taurus is unlikely to change careers, move away or take long vacations. If you need to refer a friend or client with a serious problem, a Taurus Rising therapist or social worker might be your best solution. This also works in choosing an instructor for your new endeavor: a Taurus Rising bead shop owner, yoga studio owner or a personal trainer will usually be there as long as you have an interest.

The most stubborn of the Fixed Signs, (Taurus, Leo, Scorpio, and Aquarius) Taurus will

---

1 Max Heindel and August Foss Heindel, *Messages*, cited above, 93-4.

persevere on a project long after the rest of us have given up. They'll continue in the same direction longer than anyone else. And they also hate to throw anything out. Relatives of Taurus Rising, or Taurus Moon-in-the-First House often see this as hoarding; they wish Taurus would sell their collections on e-Bay and give their old clothes to Good Will. So, this must be said in defense of Taurus: hanging on to that unfinished short story from high school can prove extremely useful!

Toni Morrison, known for *Beloved*, her most famous novel, did exactly that. Unaware of why she saved it, Toni set aside an unfinished story about a young African-American girl who wished she had blue eyes. The girl had lovely brown eyes that suited her, when blue eyes would not have, but she had a strong desire for blue eyes. Decades later, Toni returned from Europe as a divorced single mom with two small children. She retrieved and completely rewrote the story as a novel.[2]

This story launched a successful writing career, but even after *Beloved* became a movie, after she'd won major literary prizes and could support herself as an author, she still saw herself primarily as a teacher. She enjoyed teaching, but she also felt secure with the salary.[3]

The Earth Element

Morrison is not alone in her appreciation of a stable, salaried position. In contrast to the previous Sign, a Fire Sign that lives in the moment,[4] Taurus Rising is an Earth Sign. Taurians are very concerned about saving for the future. They plan well for a comfortable old age. Though they take pride in their homes and possessions, they also see them as long-term investments, sources of revenue for the uncertain future ahead. Not for them, the Mask of Bag Lady or Dumpster Diver!

---

2 *The Bluest Eye* was published in 1970 when she was 39. Morrison attended Howard and Cornell Universities, taught at Princeton and became a Random House editor. She retired from Princeton in 2006.

3 *Beloved*, like most of Toni's novels, explores the theme of loss and adjusting to change. She reduced her teaching hours when she became an editor. She told interviewer Kathy Neustadt that she began thinking of herself as an author at 42 after *Sula* was published. See Danielle Taylor-Guthrie, ed., *Conversations with Toni Morrison*, (Jackson: University of Mississippi Press,) 1994, 88.

4 Aries Rising John Lennon put this well in the *Playboy* interview. When David Sheff asked him if he wrote the song, "Yesterday," John replied, "No, Paul (McCartney) wrote that. I do *not* believe in yesterday. Yesterday is gone forever." Cited above, 71-2. Seldom nostalgic, Aries is focused on today and tomorrow.

Nor does Taurus want to be uncomfortable *in the present.* The other two Earth Signs might starve in a garret for the sake of art or science[5] but it's a rare Taurian who'll give up his comfort.[6] A good, steady income; a job with benefits and a pension plan appeals to Taurus Rising, unless there is a high percentage of Air and Fire in the horoscope, or risk-taking Mars is in a strong House (1.4.7,10.)

Taurus Rising often has a gift for business creativity, especially with a high percentage of planets in Earth. Newspaper magnate William Randolph Hearst (see below) had fifty percent of his planets there; Vernon Jordan, attorney and corporate executive, has two imaginative planets in Virgo, including Venus trine his Ascendant. Toni Morrison worked for Random House.[7] Most Taurians I know have solid business instincts. Most of my clients are professionals: psychologists, social workers, teachers, and CPAs. Psychologists Joyce Brothers and Anton Janov have had long, interesting careers. Dr. Janov is still training primal therapists, and Dr. Brothers, now eighty three, was until recently a talk show guest and syndicated advice columnist. Taurians in the graphic arts and music also seem to have good business instincts.

The Mundane and Spiritual Rulers

A few years ago, a young friend was outraged to read that her Rising Sign, Taurus, is "the most materialistic." She didn't see herself as a hoarder or as extravagant. She "lived in sweat suits and casual clothes." She *did* love beautiful jewelry, which she called, "my only vice." That, and, of course, her seven types of sports shoes — she needed those— her Club Med vacations; her spacious house with its gorgeous view. She pointed out that she was a kind, loyal friend, and seldom missed a class reunion, "people are more to me important

---

5 See below, Virgo Rising and Capricorn Rising, on how the Mercury and Saturn-ruled Earth Signs differ from Aphrodite-ruled Taurus. Anna Freud seems unique among Taurus Rising women in sublimating her libido completely into her work. (On Anna's libido, see Elisabeth Young-Bruehl, *Anna Freud, A Biography,* (London: Summit Books,) 1988, 288.

6 During those periods when Taurus is not as industrious as the other two Earth Signs, they're not always resting on their laurels, "lazy" or "complacent." It's more likely that the Taurian has gone to the spa or the golf course between creative or business projects.

7 Her Random House career dovetailed well with teaching. She didn't see her job as motivating students, "as teaching passion or vision" but as helping students improve: learn to write seamlessly and to fix their mistakes and "remove the cataracts." She brought in manuscripts purchased by her publisher and asked the students to fix them. A practical Taurus Rising approach. See Conversations with Toni Morrison, cited above, 86-7.

than money." A modern Aphrodite, dressed in organic cotton at home and business suits at work! Like Queen Latifah[8] (see above quote) she "embraced her natural good looks" and as a result, she has a certain *presence*.

As mundane ruler, Venus-Aphrodite symbolically contributes charm, sociability, friendliness, and often a melodious voice. Surrounded by the Graces and the Muses, she won the beauty contest and was awarded the apple as a prize. Aphrodite is vain and she can be lazy. But is she materialistic?

We don't know whether or not she shared that apple. That would seem key to answering the question. Does Taurus hoard? or does Taurus share with those in need?

In the (above) list of Taurus Rising quotes, William Randolph Hearst, the wealthy newspaper publisher, suggested, "when in doubt, money is a good gift." He valued it; he shared it with others. And probably found them appreciative!

Werner Erhard, a modern media success, was a controversial figure because of his problems with the Internal Revenue Service. A multimillionaire, he replaced his famous EST transformational seminars with a different model, called the Forum. He does conflict-resolution.

Vernon Jordan began his career as a civil rights attorney in the days of segregation. He later became famous as Bill Clinton's friend. He now serves on several corporate boards. Associated with liberal causes in his youth, later in life he became a great deal more conservative.

Publishing tycoon William Randolph Harrison fits that same pattern, as do many of my Taurus Rising clients.[9] But when it comes to the environment—the Earth my Taurian friends and clients seem to have retained their youthful values.

---

8 Queen Latifah has a cosmetics brand named for her. The cosmetics industry is ruled by Venus. She's not merely a spokesperson; she attends corporate meetings and plays an active role to assure that only quality products carry her name. "The Queen" is an atypical Taurus Rising in that her Venus-Ruled Ascendant has *Mars* conjunct it. We associate Mars with the martial arts, and she did learn karate. Her Mask is much more assertive and overtly competitive than the usual Taurus-Rising Mask. The ruler of the Seventh House cusp conjunct the Ascendant is called a Detriment position. (Mars rules Scorpio on the Seventh, so it is in Detriment in the Sign Taurus.)

9 William Randolph Hearst, whose newspaper editorials promoted the Spanish American War, (1898) was twice elected to the House of Representatives as a Democrat. In 1932, he broke with Franklin D. Roosevelt to become a Republican. He went to work in the family publishing business at age 23. He hired talented writers, Mark Twain Jack London, Stephen Crane. The movie *Citizen Kane* is based on his life.

The Esoteric Ruler - Vulcan
Alchemy and Inner Resources

The esoteric ruler of Taurus is Vulcan-Haephestus. A gifted artist, he created Achilles' shield on which he etched the daily life, heroic battles, and cultural accomplishments of the Greeks. An equally talented blacksmith, he made Achilles' shield durable: a well-wrought instrument for a noble warrior.

We know that Haephestus faced many obstacles, starting with his angry mother, Hera, who tossed him off the top of Mt. Olympus. The fall left the Immortal with a limp. His marriage to Aphrodite was arranged. Zeus and Hera decided that the restless Goddess of Love must be wed: it was not a love match. As a couple, they resembled Beauty and the Beast. Then handsome Ares appeared on the scene to seduce the bride and cuckold Haephestes. He was betrayed.

So, we have the mundane interpretation: the love triangle involving the Old Man, the young Trophy Wife and her Handsome Lover. But the story doesn't always turn out badly. Some trophy wives, like Anna Nicole Smith, contend that they're very happy with the wealthy older man. There are still cultures where these arranged marriages are practiced between lovely young women and wealthy older men.

In esoteric symbolism, Haephestus-Vulcan is a *Wise* Old Man who's been through the fires of life experience.[10] The symbolism includes the alchemical forge, the "wounded" (lame) smith or artist, the metal or *prima materia* to be transformed (in this case, Taurus Rising,) obstacles to the creative flow, and finally the process of refining out the dross and fashioning a beautiful object. Liberating Psyche is a creative process.

The mature soul, after facing and transcending the Ego's fears is one *knows who he is*. Of course not everyone emerges from the firey forge like Haephestus able to create beautiful objects, songs or novels. However, those who emerge and are not jaded are often able to create new lives for themselves in ways they never before imagined.

When Taurus Rising individuals find themselves suddenly standing near Vulcan's forge, "life heats up."[11] Aphrodite's children can no longer be complacent; they cannot sit and wait for the situation to go away! The Fixed Mode resists change, as does patient Earth. But Vulcan lights a fire under Taurus Rising.

William Randolph Hearst had a piece of practical advice for when life heats up: "Keep

---

10 In Handel's Messiah there's a simile, "for He is like a Refiner's Fire." Vulcan, the Roman Haephestus, is a cognate of the word *volcano*. The heating-up process for Taurus Rising is similar to a volcano erupting in that it usually happens suddenly and often comes as a complete surprise.

11 "Life heating up" is known as *tapas* in Patanjali's Yoga Sutras.

your eye on the objective, not on the obstacle." After living through the Great Depression, watching his newspaper empire die, whether Hearst liked it or not, he had to accept that change is constant. As he put it, "everything that seems tranquil is gobbled up by something not so tranquil." After a court-ordered bankruptcy, his antiques went on the auction block. He began anew.[12]

Resourcefulness
Taurus Rising and the Second Half of Life

Two Taurus Rising women emerged from Vulcan's forge. Both were changed. They were stronger. They were able to draw on their talents and experiences in new, creative ways. The first is Viennese child psychologist Anna Freud—possibly the most underrated psychologist of the last century. The second is American songwriter and performer, Bonnie Raitt, whose fans agree with her that, "there's never been any music quite like what we came up with." [13]

Anna Freud was the youngest child of Austrian psychiatrist, Sigmund Freud (Scorpio Rising.) Between the ages of 15 and 18 she told her dreams to her father, who analyzed them and published several. She absorbed psychoanalytical theory at home. However, she was mainly interested in the welfare and education of children; she became a teacher. In her early twenties, she published on child psychology and child welfare. After reading her books, her father's friend Sandor Ferenczi wrote him to comment on Anna's "sagacity, intelligence, humanity and maturity."[14] Very proud of her, Sigmund Freud responded to others' praise of Anna by replying that she was also a great help to him.

By her late twenties,[15] Anna was a child psychoanalyst in private practice and had begun teaching at the Vienna Psycholoanalytical Training Institute. At forty she was a Director

---

12 His Natal First House Gemini planets indicated resilience; he was back in the newspaper game quickly after the Great Depression. He went towards tabloid journalism.

13 The Raitt quotations are from brainyquote.com. Whenever I hear "Nick of Time," I'm reminded of events in my life like the disastrous hailstorm that threatened an ashram vegetable garden just as 150 people were arriving for a weeklong retreat. It was a vegetarian group, so we depended entirely on the garden. The hailstorm suddenly stopped while we were harvesting and the weather remained sunny all week; we could hold activities outside as planned. Bonnie's song brings back that and other dramatic memories.

14 The quotes are from the Carter-Jenkins Center homepage, www.cjc.org.

15 Her Saturn Return was in 1923-4. Born in 29 Taurus, she had progressed to the Cancer Mask.

of the International Psychological Association, and the next year, 1936, she published her famous book on the ego's defenses against anxiety.[16] Life seemed to be going smoothly for Anna. Then, suddenly, Hitler came to power and everything changed. There were knocks on doors at night; people disappeared. She worked with traumatized children.

On March 22, 1938, nine days after the German army arrived in Austria, she was arrested and kept overnight by the Gestapo.[17] Anna was "terse" with her biographer about what happened that night, saying only that "much worse had happened to others during those years than happened to me." Anna was told that world opinion wouldn't protect her father much longer. They were give a few days to pack and leave the country, otherwise they would be arrested. Born in his family home, her father wanted to die in it. When she packed her suitcase he was finally convinced to leave.[18] As they boarded the train, she thought of the children left behind. Her life changed dramatically.

Soon she had English children. She helped found a facility in the countryside where she taught orphans and lonely, frightened children whose parents had sent them out of London during the Blitzkrieg.

After the war, she helped found and worked in an orphanage for surviving refugees. As her circumstances changed, her understanding of psychology changed. She wrote on the importance of the children's peers as listeners; sometimes peers are of greater help than adult analysts.

Anna visited the United States during her mid-seventies. Medical doctors and university theorists sat spellbound by the quiet, calm, older woman whose only credential came from a *lycee*.[19] When someone remarked, "but that's only common sense," she quickly replied that there's nothing *common* about common sense! With no planets in Earth, Anna was still an extremely grounded, resourceful woman. With forty percent of her planets in Air, she was, surprisingly, a good listener.

Like Toni Morrison and Anna Freud, Bonnie was raised by parents who encouraged her talents and goals.[20] A client with Taurus Rising told me that in early childhood, "the Venus Rulership felt like being born under a lucky star." She had the right parents; she

---

16 *The Ego's Mechanisms of Defense* (1936.) She presented it to her father on his 80th birthday. Her *Introduction to the Technique of Child Analysis* was published at the age of 31 (1926.)

17 Sigmund Freud's diary noted simply, "Anna bei Gestapo." Robert Coles, *Anna Freud: The Dream of Psychotherapy*, (NY: Addison-Wellesley Radcliff Series,) 1992, p.186.

18 He was dying of jaw cancer. They left in 1938, he died in England in September of 1939.

19 a public secondary school.

20 Education was an important value for Toni's parents, Bonnie's were in the music and the entertainment industry.

had the emotional and financial support for her particular set of talents. Still, the volcano erupted.[21]

Both Bonnie's parents John Raitt and Marjorie Haydock performed. She was surrounded by blues singers, country and Western, rock and roll and by her father's Broadway friends. She learned the acoustic guitar and sang in cafes.[22] Soon she had a record contract with Warners. She seemed on track to success.

A few years later, however, she was protesting the Vietnam War, dropping out of college and caught up in the drug scene. She lost her contract and her relationship. Because a happy marriage was really important to her, she fought her way back to recovery. By the late 1980's she was happily married, had a contact with Capitol Records and recorded her Grammy-winning album, "Nick of Time."

Taurus wears the Mask of Resourcefulness which, like all Masks, requires energy and effort to maintain.

Novelist Herman Melville, known to us as the author of *Moby Dick* was born into a prominent family that traced its origins to the colonial period in New York.[23] He'd expected to attend an Ivy League college like his contemporaries, Nathaniel Hawthorne and R.W. Emerson. But his father died when he was thirteen, then his prominent grandfather died a year later. When the wealthy grandfather's will was read, Melville's branch of the family discovered they were bankrupt.[24]

So at the age of twenty, Melville signed on and went to sea as a lowly cabin boy. He said at the time that he shipped out because he wanted to send money home to his sisters. Unfortunately, he was never able to help them. As he told the story, he barely survived. Life on shipboard was a long series of misadventures involving mad, power hungry captains who ran out of food, disease-infested islands, and mutinous crews. He filled his notebooks with all the details.

Between voyages, he wrote two short novels which Hawthorne helped him to get

---

21 It can happen in many different ways. The loss or long hospitalization of a parent, or an illness of their own. (Anna Freud suffered periods of depression.)

22 With a close Venus trine to the Rising Sign (magnetism and presence) and apex Jupiter, Bonnie had luck as well as talent. Apex Jupiter is associated with performing abroad.

23 His Mother was Maria Gansevoort of Albany, N.Y, descendant of Dutch patroons, one of whom fought in the Revolutionary War. Major Melville, his paternal grandfather, participated in the Boston tea party. Elizabeth Hardwick, *Herman Melville,* (NY:Viking-Penguin,) 2000, pp. 10-18.

24 Herman's grandfather subtracted his father's debts from the inheritance, the family had nothing. It was very embarrassing. The property went into receivership; the furniture was carried out.

published,[25] and years later, his opus *Moby Dick*, the tale of Captain Ahab, obsessed with revenge against the whale who took his leg. The opus was a moderate financial success but won him a literary reputation. At the end of his life, Melville told D.H. Lawrence that he was *not* hen-pecked and he liked his quiet life working in the Custom's House. He had no interest in voyaging and enough material to last him the rest of his life. And like Anna Freud, he lived a long time.

Family resources, even parents who are recognized in their field and who have important contacts, will not guarantee success or a smooth life. Friends like Nathaniel Hawthorne do help somewhat. In modern times, Oprah Winfrey's Book Club is helpful to Toni Morrison. But *inner resources* are more important than those in the outer world.

In summary, symbolically, Vulcan-Haephestus shocks Taurus out of his settled life and pulls him into the forge. The dross is burned away, the Mask is re-fashioned and Taurus eventually emerges anew, like Freud, Morrison and Melville. Afterwards, the Taurians seem less willful, more creative and more insightful. We see it in their songs and novels, and in their work with others.

There's usually a happy ending, but as my dear friend, Jungian analyst Monika Wikman says, "*Individuation always comes with a price.*" A Vulcan initiation affects us at the very core of our being. Understanding the experience takes time, sometime decades.

And shortcuts seldom work. There's a Russian tale about that called *The Magic Beans*.[26] An impoverished couple lived in a hut on the edge of a forest. One day, they returned home from gathering firewood and found a small bunch of beans on their wooden table.

"Humph," the wife grunted, "not enough beans for a soup." She flung them to the dirt floor in disgust. Time passed; they forgot about the beans. Then, one day they came home to find a tall beanstalk had sprung up through a hole in the table and pushed itself through their roof. They went outside for a closer look at it but they could not see to the top.

The woman remembered those peculiar beans that required no watering. "Aha! Those were *magic beans*. It's a *magic* beanstalk. Our problems are solved! We'll climb to heaven; God will reward our efforts with treasure! We'll be rich!" she said.

They made several attempts at the climb, but every time they doubted they could reach

---

25 *Typoo and Omoo*, circa 1849. *Moby Dick*, his fifth novel, was published in 1851. He was 32, married with a second son on the way. Walt Whitman, another literary contemporary, gave him positive reviews.

26 I heard this story at the 1992 International Urania Conference in Moscow. It's similar to another Russian story, "The String Bean That Went Through the Roof of the World," in Ann G. Thomas, *The Women we Become, Myths, Folktales and Stories About Growing Older*, (Rocklin: Prima) 1997, 76-85.

the top or complained about having to make such a strenuous effort at *their age,* they slid back down.

And then one day they reached the top, passed through the clouds and arrived at their destination. They paused to catch their breath and heard a voice say: "An old couple just climbed the beanstalk."

"Oh?" said, second Voice, "ask them the question. If they answer correctly, let them stay."

The man and wife turned to each other, puzzled. They hadn't intended *to stay,* it was much too soon! Surely they had years left on earth. Their plan was to return home with the treasure.

Then the second Voice said, *"I see you're not ready."* And they found themselves falling back down the beanstalk to their kitchen.

The old couple preferred their familiar cottage with its dirt floor and their difficult life on earth to heaven. They had a narrow, literal view—a totally materialist view—of heaven's treasures. They weren't even curious about whether they knew the answer to the question.

The Gemini Progression

In the *Magic Beans* story, the old couple at first failed to identify their resource: they didn't trust in the power of creativity, symbolized by the beanstalk. This often happens. We're unaware of the value of our life experience (a treasure trove) or that of the creative process, which like the beanstalk, requires very little attention. We're too focused on the destination, the goal, and our illusions about it.

The couple's expectations didn't pan out. When that happens, flexibility and resilience, two attributes of Mutable Gemini are required.

Natal Taurus Rising is a serious Mask, not known for its ability to laugh at itself or its miscalculations. But Gemini is optimistic, curious, and able to laugh all the way back to earth when "heavenly" hopes are not fulfilled. After dropping back to earth, (reality) Gemini will shrug off the disappointment and approach life with a sense of wonder; expecting something positive, or even miraculous, welcoming new opportunities even in old age. These are some tasks for Taurus' progression.

Born with 29 Taurus, the last degree, Rising and three planets in Gemini in her First House, Anna Freud's Mask began to absorb Gemini qualities when she was a year old. Her father remarked to his friends that she was a mischievous child. (We're reminded of Hermes the Prankster.) Sigmund Freud's guests conversed in several European languages and Hebrew. Precocious Anna began to pick up their vocabulary, as well as the psychological terms, from the conversations. She learned a great deal about dream analysis when her father worked with hers between the ages of 15 and 18. She attended a *lycee* in Italy for awhile, and spent a holiday in England at nineteen; Anna had opportunities to expand her horizons and practice foreign languages.

Bonnie Raitt has worn her eclectic Gemini progressed Mask for twenty years, but this year the progressed degree conjuncts her Natal Moon: a good time to reach an audience through her Natal lunar versatility. (The Moon symbolizes the media.) She has ten years left of the Gemini cycle, a good one for sending out her messages in lyrics.

Progressed Cancer - Imagination and Nurturing

Around the time of her Saturn Return, (age 28-29) Anna Freud's progressed Mask moved from Gemini to Cancer, a nurturing Sign that has more in common with Natal Taurus. She'd already worked with children for decades, but under the Cardinal influence of Cancer, her peers began to respect her contributions to child psychology, an area where few psychoanalysts had yet to venture. Though she had no children of her own, and no Natal Cancer or Fourth House planets, the new Mask was a good fit professionally.

Born at the end of Taurus Rising, Toni Morrison progressed into Gemini when she was around six years old. She demonstrated her versatility in several Mercury areas: teaching, editing and writing. In 1965, she progressed into Cancer in 1965. She had two sons during the 1960's, and wrote while they slept. In this period, Toni lived in her imagination, creating stories that helped bring the African American experience to mainstream literature. She identified with the creative Mask of author after seven years in the Cancer cycle.

Queen Latifah will progress into Cancer in 2011-12. The first Natal planet the progressed Ascendant will touch upon is Neptune, the next is Jupiter. She may portray a Wise Woman in a film in the years ahead or make an impression as a cultural emissary abroad. Lunar Imagination will bring out Natal planets in the early degrees of Taurus and Leo. With Mars there, she might do an action movie.

Cancer is usually more conservative than Gemini. W.R. Hearst, decided it was his patriotic duty to editorialize against American involvement in World War I "it's not America's fight." He and Vernon Jordan, a former Civil Rights attorney, both became more conservative during progressed Cancer.

Progressed Leo - Name and Fame

Around the time of her Second Saturn Return (58) thirty years later, Anna Freud's progressed Ascendant entered Leo, symbolically, the Sign of Fame. She already enjoyed a reputation in Britain, America and the German-speaking world. Now, however, she was no longer viewed primarily as the Great Man's daughter but as an elder, an authority in her own right and as a creative contributor to her field. She also took on new challenges. Psychology, she believed, should no longer limit itself to the needs of middle-class children but should also address the needs of poor children.

William R. Hearst gained notoriety in old age. His newspapers acquired a reputation for sensationalism. Vernon Jordan took on a leadership role in the corporate world and became a presidential advisor.

Toni Morrison, winner of many prestigious literary awards, novelist, playwright, editor, professor and critic progressed into Leo in 2005 and retired from teaching in 2006. Once she's adjusted to the power and authority of the Fixed Fire Mask, she may become an influential spokeswoman for a cause that's close to her heart. The progressed Ascendant degree contacts her natal Mercury in 2009-10.

Virgo Rising - The Trine

Like Werner Erhard, Joyce Brothers and Anna Freud, my Taurian clients enjoy being productive in extreme old age: Work is play.

Taurus Rising Bibliography

Bartley, William Warren III, *Werner Erhart, The Transformation of a Man, the Founding of EST* (NY: Clarkson Potter,) 1988.

Brothers, Joyce, *How To Get Whatever You Want Out of Life,* (NY: Ballantine,) 1987.

—— *Widowed,* (NY: Ballantine,) 1992.

Coles, Robert, *Anna Freud and the Dream of Psychoanalysis,* (Cambridge, Mass: Radcliffe Biography Series,) 1993.

Freud, Anna, *The Ego and the Mechanisms of Defense,* (London: Karnac,) 1993.

Hardwick, Elizabeth, *Herman Melville,* (NY: Viking,) 2000.

Heindel, Max and Augusta Foss Heindel, *The Message of the Stars,* (Oceanside: Rosicrucian Publications,) 1980.

Janov, Arthur, *Primal Healing: Access the Incredible Power of Feelings to Improve Your Health,* (n.c: New Page Books,) 2006.

Latifah, Queen, (Dana Owens) *Ladies First: Revelations of a Strong Woman,* (NY: HarperCollins-Quill,) 2000.

Morrison, Toni, *Beloved,* (NY: Vintage,) 2004.

—— *The Bluest Eye,* (NY: Vintage International,) 2007.

Relph, Monika, *Pregnant Darkness: Alchemy and the Rebirth of Consciousness,* (Berwick: Nicholas Hays,) 2004.

Raitt, Bonnie, songs, "Nick of Time," from the CD, *Nick of Time.* 1990.

Taylor-Guthrie, Danielle, ed., *Conversations with Toni Morrison,* (Jackson: University of Mississippi Press,) 1992.

Thomas, Ann G., *The Women We Become: Myths, Folktales, and Stories about Growing Older,* (Rocklin: Prima Publishing,) 1997.

Young-Bruehl, *Anna Freud, a Biography,* (NY: Summit Books,) 1988.

CHAPTER THREE

Gemini Rising - Insightfulness

Erica Jong, "Ambivalence is a wonderful tune to dance to. It has a rhythm all its own."

—— "I write lustily and humorously. It isn't calculated; it's the way I think. I've invented a writing style that expresses who I am."

George Bernard Shaw, "I dread success. To have succeeded is to have finished one's business on earth…I like a state of continual becoming, with a goal in front and not behind."

—— "Life isn't about finding yourself. Life is about creating yourself."

—— "Am I an atheist? Certainly not. I worship the Creative Evolutionary Life Force. Feel free to criticize my deity if you wish."

—— "Some look at things that are, and ask why. I dream of things that never were and ask, why not?"

Luigi Pirandello, "A fact is like a sack - it won't stand up if it's empty. To make it stand up… you have to put in it all the reasons and feelings that caused it."

—— "Whoever has the luck to be born a character can laugh even at death. Because a character will never die! A man will die: a writer, the instrument of creation: but what he has created will never die!"

—— (to Benedetto Croce,) "There will always be some anguish about not being able to reconcile the opposites. But how much better to live with honest anguish than to opt out and be reconciled with dishonesty."

Henry Kissinger, "I am being frank about myself in this book. I tell of my first mistake on page 850."

—— "Corrupt politicians make the other 10% look bad."

—— "Even a paranoid man can have enemies."

Marianne Williamson: "If I choose to bless another person, I will always end up feeling more blessed."

Mira Alfassa (The Mother) "I belong to no nation, no civilization, no society, no race, but to the Divine. I obey no master, no rules, no law, no social convention but the Divine. To Him I have surrendered all, will, life and self; for Him I am ready to give all my blood, drop by drop, if such is His will, with complete joy, and nothing in His service can be sacrifice, for all is perfect delight."

The Gemini Mask

I usually appear as the Mask of Comedy or Court Jester but I'm a shape shifter; I can don almost any Mask. If required, I can even wear the Mask of Tragedy for a short time. I'm loquacious. At social events I shine brightly like the twin stars, Castor and Pollux. I am of two minds on most subjects. I'm tolerant: "live and let live" is my philosophy. Objective, detached and curious, I have a childlike sense of wonder. I love new facts. Though I learn quickly, I'm restless and easily bored. I'm famous for my sense of humor, which is usually lighthearted, though I can be sardonic or sarcastic with the influence of Saturn, Pluto, or Scorpio planets. In a crisis, I'd rather laugh than cry. The most versatile of Signs, I work best with the Air and risk-taking Fire planets in the horoscope. I'll eagerly enroll in anything the Ego chooses to study, though I prefer a short program.

How to Recognize Gemini Rising

My Gemini Rising friends and clients, unlike the Heindels'[1] have not been particularly tall or slender. Only a few of them are close to six feet; most fall between five-foot-two and five-foot-six. It's true that older Gemini Rising relatives have shown me pictures of themselves as very thin school children. However, as the years went by and the progressed Ascendant shifted to Cancer; the Gemini Rising faces and figures in the family album became rounder. The one exception was the smoker, who remained thin. (His health suffered, however.) Gemini is associated with the lungs in astrology.

Message to the Stars notes Gemini's short attention span. It's true that when bored, their eyes glaze over. A teacher once told me that she could actually observe Gemini switching mental channels to a more stimulating topic than hers! When she saw the change in Gemini's eyes, she quickly injected humor into her presentation. As soon he heard others laughing, Gemini's attention returned to the classroom. Keeping Gemini engaged helps prevent their inner Court Jester (see above, The Mask) from emerging as Class Clown.[2]

The Heindels found Gemini Rising to have longer limbs than other Signs. I haven't noticed that, but I and many other astrologers *have* noticed that Gemini Rising speakers

---

1 Max and Augusta Foss Heindel, *Message,* cited above, pp. 95-6 (Gemini Rising's appearance.)
2 The Class Clown reaction is a form of "acting out" that sometimes occurs after a divorce, death or other sad event at home. Precocious Gemini responds with humor; he gains the attention of his peers and of adults in the school system. He does not want to dwell on/discuss the sad event at home.

can be recognized by their (sometimes wild) gestures. While other speakers will rotate their hands up or down from the wrists, Geminis, excited by the concepts, will get their entire arm and shoulder involved in the gesture.

Astrologers are aware that cuts and bruises to the limbs indicate that Gemini Rising is moving through the day too rapidly; the mind is moving faster than the body. Like Aries Rising, Gemini has many tasks to accomplish—the day is too short—but Gemini's energy is mental, rather than physical. Many operate on frenetic nervous energy; this accelerates when they ingest too much caffeine, and, preoccupied, bump into, or cut themselves on, objects around them.[3] As the body ages, it becomes even more important to pay attention when chopping vegetables and carrying heavy objects through doorways. A nervous laugh may also be an indicator that Gemini needs to slow down. Gemini's taste in apparel changes with their Mask.

The Mode

The Mutability Mode does well with change; Gemini is very different from the previous, Fixed Rising Sign, Taurus. As chameleons, Geminis instinctively try to fit in by adapting to the circumstances around them. If born into a family that encouraged them to think for themselves, they're likely to become independent thinkers, otherwise the Heindels are right, they'll tend to parrot others' ideas.[4]

When Gemini changes environments for the first time—if the family moves to a different region or leave for college— they usually discover that new people around them do not share the opinions of their parents and teachers back home. This comes as a shock to the chameleon. Some feel that their parents let them down by not explaining "how the world really is." They may reject earlier teachings; change their Mask to blend in, or assume the ideas of a lover, a college organization or a charismatic faculty member.

However, if they have a high percentage of Fixed planets or a "heavy" First House planet like Uranus, they'll emerge from the experience as independent thinkers. (Many of the Baby Boomers have Uranus-in-Gemini in the First House.) If Saturn is there, they usually

---

3 Yoga stretches for relaxation, limiting the amounts of coffee and soda ingested are recommended. If there are many Fire planets in the horoscope, Gemini will get enough exercise, balancing physical and mental energy and releasing tension from the nervous system. Gemini may need to ask his doctor if he needs B-complex vitamins.

4 *Message to the Stars,* cited above, 95. Most are well-read; they'll quote the book they just finished.

have the discipline to finish their credential. With either "heavy" planet, they'll want to be in control of their lives. They'll form their own opinions. The nature of the First House planets, if they have some, will describe their interests and direction. Otherwise, look for planets aspecting the Ascendant degree and the Mundane and Esoteric Ruler.

Like Fixity, Saturn helps to slow restlessness, discover and persevere in a career choice (rather than change majors four times, spending six years in college) and conclude their studies with a conventional Mask to put on the shelf, a teaching or nursing credential as a fallback position. The Heindels found Gemini Rising good at science (a Uranus and Saturn area) but Gemini can do almost anything when they apply themselves.

The Element

Gemini's Element is Air, Gemini is impersonal, objective, detached, and witty. George Bernard Shaw, Erica Jong, and Henry Kissinger exemplify different types of Gemini humor, (see above quotations.) Gemini is usually friendly, especially when they meet someone mentally stimulating.

If this adage is true: "high intelligence is the ability to hold two contradictory ideas in your mind simultaneously," then many people with the Sign of the Twins Rising qualify as highly intelligent! Still, one person who meets Gemini Rising may think, "frivolous," while another person who meets the same individual may conclude, "genius."

Air usually prefers theory to practice. The percentage of Earth and Fire in the horoscope will describe Gemini's practicality and actions. Gemini usually benefits from a hands-on internship before committing to a graduate program. Earth-Sign-Rising professionals, like Anna Freud in the previous chapter, judge others "by their deeds rather than their idealistic words;"[5] an internship or volunteer work on the resume demonstrates that Air Rising "did something" beyond reading.

Mercury (Hermes) - The Mundane Ruler

Hermes' myths reveal him to be a Prankster or Magician a Trickster and a Precocious Child. He learns quickly. He evaluates his environment sets out to accomplish his desires. As a child, he outsmarted the older God, Apollo when he stole his cattle. Hermes was not malicious, just precocious. He seemingly did this to show the other gods *he could*. When

---

5 She discussed this with her biographer, Robert Coles, *Anna Freud*, cited above, p. 147.

he returned the cattle, Apollo laughed, the way most of us do at Gemini's jokes. Original and inventive, young Hermes made the first lyre from a tortoise shell. He's associated with music and crafts.

Mercury moves on winged feet, and has a cap—or sometimes a wand—that renders him invisible at will. As Messenger God, he travels the Three Worlds: Mount Olympus, (the world of the Gods) the World of Mankind (waking state awareness) and the Underworld, (the World of the Dead or the world of Dreams, where he appeared as Psychopomp) bringing messages to heroes and Gods. Today, his Gemini children often bring others the precise information they need in a timely manner.

Several clients have dreamt of Hermes standing at a fork in the road, sometimes leaning on his Herm (stone marker.) They were usually considering a major decision, a new direction at the time.

In astrology, Mercury is the Sun's (Ego's) intellect, its ability to process information from the five senses and pass it on to the other planets in the horoscope. If it's in Earth, Mercury filters the facts in a literal, practical way (adding up the pros and cons,) if it's in Air, a glib or theoretical way, if in Fire a quick, (seemingly-effortless) instinctual way and, if in Water, a sensitive, caring way: (whose feelings could get hurt if I did this? Mine? Someone I care about?)

If you have Gemini Rising, you might want to find your Mercury, and review the House position, Element, Mode and aspects. If Mercury is bored or restless at this stage of your life; if symbolically, you stand at the crossroads, you might want to look at your progressions for a new Hermes' interest or a new direction.

The Esoteric Ruler - Venus, and Her Daughter, Harmonia
Luigi Pirandello, G.B.S., and Mira Alfassa Richard

The glyph for Gemini, the Sign of the Twins, resembles Roman Numeral Two and is said to symbolize Hercules' pillars. These pillars were said to stand on the edge of the inhabited world.[6] To pass through the pillars was to leave behind everything familiar, all that people knew and understood. Symbolically, both pillars *together* were the gate to a new dimension, beyond time, space and the logical (mercurial) mind.

This was frightening to Homer's readers. Only a hero like Hercules would attempt to pass through. It's still true today. We experience the tension of the opposites when we

6 The known world was called the *oecumene*, Hans Biederman, *Dictionary of Symbolism: Cultural Icons and the Meanings Behind Them*, James Hulbert, ed.,(NY: *Facts On File*,) 1992, p. 267.

attempt to bring two different areas of life into balance. Consciously or not, we're always trying to bring House Four, (home life and family,) into balance with House Ten opposite it, (our career.) There's plenty of "creative tension" right here in the dimension *we inhabit*. Moving into the Unknown, symbolically, the Edge of the Earth, seems more dangerous still.[7] Yet that's what the artist in his studio, the inventor in his lab, and the mystic all do, they courageously passes through Hercules' gates into the Unknown.

The inventor is alone in unfamiliar territory, trying to get it right. There are no prototypes for what he's attempting to do. As Playwright Luigi Pirandello put it so well in the (above) quote, "there will always be a certain anguish in reconciling the opposites. Yet, how much better to live with honest anguish than to opt out and reconcile them dishonestly."

Pirandello received a Nobel prize for his play, "Six Characters in Search of an Author," in which he described so well how the Gemini Rising mind—the Hermes' mind—works when operating without any help from its esoteric ruler.

In "Six Characters," four actors played various members of the same family, the others were "Director" and "Playwright." Tension built as the characters fought with the director. Two insisted that the story must be told from their point of view. One character refused to go on stage with another, a family member to whom she was not speaking! She demanded the scene be re-written; her conflict aired and resolved. She had a point. It would have been a fine drama, just not in *that* play.

In the last act, the director gave up. He fired the actors and told the characters they portrayed: "go find yourselves another author." Plays have their limits, he explained, there are only a certain number of acts in which to resolve the theme. Nor can a playwright have too many themes in the same play. He makes an important point for Gemini Rising. It's valid not only in art but also in life.

The esoteric ruler, Venus Aphrodite, rules Art, Beauty, Aesthetics and Value Judgments made by the Feeling Function ("I like *this*; I don't like *that*." "I know what I like," "I have *good taste*")[8] and perhaps most important, she's brings along her daughter, Harmonia.

---

7 Fortunately after fifty, this usually gets easier. Empty Nesters find both career and home life less demanding. The children move out; the hours at work are cut back, or they're downsized. They then focus on balancing the Community's Needs (House Eleven) with the House of Creativity (House Five: personal projects.)A new pair of opposites comes into play.

8 C.G. Jung, *Aion*, CW, IX(Princeton: P.U. Press) 1975, 28-32. We prioritize based on our feeling perceptions: we say things like *this* is the most important part of my dream! Or, "*This* is the best thing I've ever written." We're no longer dependent upon our peer group's taste: "I like Hip Hop (or Jazz)" because others do. With a strong Feeling Function, we rely on our own judgment. We're confident in our own response to music, art poetry. A prominent Venus is similar.

Harmony is the Venusian principle that unites the opposites and resolves those conflicts so central to dramatic writing. (It's almost impossible to design a plot that works without conflict.) But even Harmonia can' resolve every conflict. Sometimes, like Pirandello's director, Gemini must do the honest thing: walk away. "False attempts at reconciling the opposites" don't work.

Feeling is vitally important for Gemini. Without it Hermes retreats into his head, where every line of his well-written play looks equally good and equally necessary. Without Venus, Hermes has difficulty evaluating and prioritizing. Integrating Aphrodite and Hermes, Feeling and Thinking, is a challenging task that leads to Wholeness.

With feeling comes subjectivity; attachment. Pirandello felt the characters' pain but knew they couldn't work together. Editing can be a painful process for Gemini.

Esoteric Geminis move past knowledge to wisdom and love. As astrologer Alan Oken once said in an evening lecture, "those who have moved past knowledge to love are sought out; they're magnetic. Others feel good around them."

That night, I thought of Pirandello's line (above, list of quotes) that facts without feeling are empty sacks that easily fall over. This is true with glib Hermes-the-Trickster. But Esoteric Gemini's facts are not empty, they have feeling and purpose behind them. They stand up alone.

With Venus on his Ascendant at birth, Pirandello was attuned to Aphrodite. He was known as the "Values Playwright" for his sense of honesty (artistic integrity) and his sense of beauty (aesthetic values.)

He also said, "dilettantism and narcissism after forty lead to pessimism and exhaustion." This is true of the perennial student, the Peter Pan who never grows up. He avoids adult responsibilities and may also develop nervous system problems. When there's too much heat in the brain and not enough heartfelt passion about life or relationships with others, Harmonia's balance is missing.

George Bernard Shaw, known for his famous "Shavian wit," had Gemini Rising. His esoteric ruler conjuncted his Sun, but didn't aspect Mercury or the Ascendant. Imaginative Neptune made the closest aspect to his Ascendant, a square from Pisces at the apex of his horoscope. Neptune comes through Shaw's later plays (after 1921) though he continued teasing William Butler Yeats about mysticism and fairies.

Born into an Anglo-Irish aristocratic family like Oscar Wilde, Annie Besant and William B. Yeats, Shaw is considered an Irish playwright even though he lived in London.[9]

Attuned to Venus early in life, Shaw lived in a home where art was valued. "He was passionate about drawing" he "prowled Dublin's National Gallery looking at paintings by the old masters."[10]

Shaw usually enjoyed St. Stephen's Green, Dublin's large central park, with his nanny. Sometimes, though, she took him along to a tenement on the other side of the city on visits to her family.

The boy was unfazed by the poverty or the dirt. What disturbed him was the lack of art on the walls; the lack of beauty of any type in her part of town. He wondered how children could be allowed to grow up like that. Later, as an adult, Shaw said his interest in middle class (Fabian) socialism took root long ago, in his Dublin childhood.

His mother and his sister both sang and performed, he heard arias practiced in the living and went to the theater. By osmosis, Shaw picked up enough knowledge about music from their tutor—his mother's lover—to become a music and theater critic for a London newspaper.

It's a type of Hermes magic! This chameleon Rising Sign seems to absorb information by osmosis. They'll listen and watch as others work, then, later, in a new environment, they'll hang out their shingles as psychotherapists, astrologers, healers, or consultants. The Rising Sign draws clients and patrons who appreciate Gemini's techniques and talents. Credentialed professionals can appear dull by comparison.

Though art and music surrounded him, Shaw really wanted to write. His progressed ascendant moved into Cancer at the age of ten. He began submitting essays to contests. However, at fourteen, his father apprenticed him with a banker friend as a cashier. The job was Gemini's worst nightmare: Shaw was told not to discuss his personal views with the customers, particularly topics like vegetarianism and the evils of alcohol. Gemini Rising was not allowed to express himself!

When he was sixteen, Shaw's mother announced that she was leaving his alcoholic

---

9 Shaw and Annie shared an interest in socialism; they dated for several years. Anne Taylor wrote that Besant liked having a handsome man on her arm at events: M.P. Charles Bradlaugh, Shaw, and Theosophist Colonel Olcott later. Shaw joked that Annie's hair turned white right after the break-up. He said she had no sense of humor. "I could sometimes make her laugh, but never at herself." Anne Taylor, *Annie Besant, A Biography,* (Oxford; Oxford University Press,) 1992, 184.
10 He wanted to be a great artist who drew the human figure like Michelangelo. He also wrote dramas as a child. Michael Holroyd, *Bernard Shaw, The Search for Love.* (NY: Random House,) Vol. I, 1998, 37.

father.[11] She and his sisters were moving to London with the music teacher. Four years later, his younger sister Agnes died. He resigned from the bank and left for her funeral. He was free! In London, he became a music, art and theater critic; a "street orator" in Hyde Park, (lecturing on equality for both sexes and all classes,) and contributed articles to Annie Besant's magazine, *Our Corner*.[12]

Literature, however, was the most important of his eclectic interests. He wrote five novels replete with theories and idealistic philosophy. When they didn't sell, Annie Besant printed one in serial form in her magazine. She gave him the study in her apartment to write when he tired of hearing music students practicing at home.[13]

After his fifth try, Shaw realized he wasn't a novelist. Most of us would have quit sooner, but Shaw had Saturn-in-the-First-House. And it was in Cancer, a hard-working Detriment position.[14] His Saturn placement exemplifies the adage, "when at first you don't succeed try, try, again." And again and again. Meanwhile he sang at parties; edited Sydney Webbs' *Fabian Essays*, and wrote features for the Saturday *Review* on Ibsen's plays and Wagner's operas. He studied Danish and German for a deeper understanding of his favorites.

At thirty-two, the progressed Ascendant conjuncted his Mercury in Cancer. He seemed to be taking a long time to "create himself."[15] It bothered Shaw that Oscar Wilde's mother held a London salon where famous and well-connected people met and conversed. Oscar attended, made important contacts and was very successful with the critics. Shaw was unable to participate for lack of a proper salon-going wardrobe.

Looking back in old age he commented on feeling the need as a young man to construct a *persona* that would fit into the world of "dashing men," actors, orators, theater owners,

---

11 Though Neptune in the Tenth House may indicate that the person himself drinks to excess, in Shaw's case it referred to his father. (In youth, Houses Four and Ten are associated with one's parents.) Shaw's reaction to his father's drinking was to reject liquor himself. He abstained from meat and alcohol his entire life.

12 See Aries Rising for Annie Besant. Shaw didn't visit Ireland again until after midlife marriage, when his wife, Charlotte Payne-Townsend, insisted he accompany her.

13 He wanted to help Annie, too. He introduced her to Fabian socialist Sydney Webb but it didn't work out. She preferred organizing strikes to "the Fabian discussion group." Sidney told her that she wouldn't fit in: they already had "too many chiefs and not enough followers;" she'd be "a Fifth Wheel," which Webb knew would *not* work for a leader like her.

14 In 1888, at 32, he decided novels were a clumsy art form. Holroyd, *Shaw*, cited above, 121. A planet in Detriment is in the Sign 180 degrees away from the Sign it rules, this is considered an uncomfortable position, but a position which leads to success over time. There is more on Detriments in my CD set, "The Rising Sign and Writers: a Workshop for the Second Half of Life."

15 See above, from the list of Shaw quotes.

politicians, journalists. He'd "always lived in the world of the imagination." Their world was alien to him.[16] In the first decade of the Twentieth Century he progressed into Leo Rising, his Leo Ascendant conjuncted his Sun/Venus, and he felt more at home among the dashing. His confidence grew; his plays improved. His message came across powerfully.

The Winower's House, an early play about slumlords, was as he admitted, "unpleasant." Only in his forties did he his plays become lighter, the audience no longer felt harangued, and success followed quickly. Shaw's sense of humor was his greatest asset: theatergoers loved to laugh at his irony, satire, paradoxes and witticisms. There were no more depressing slumlords.

He wrote several plays after World War I about The New Woman (he had Moon conjunct Uranus) who would be the equal of any man: independent and self-supporting. Shaw's play *Major Barbara,* about the Salvation Army major was a great success, followed by *Pygmalion* and *St. Joan.* His *Arms and the Man* and many others are still performed today.

Like many people with Gemini Rising, Shaw's was a complicated personality. A social reformer and crusader for justice, he was also a mystic with Neptune square the Ascendant. He once told his theater manager that he refused to cut out a long monologue because the Creative Evolutionary Life Force had dictated it. He couldn't say 'no' to God, so the monologue had to stay. But the actress didn't understand it and refused to recite it. The theater owner agreed: he doubted the audience would understand it, either.

Gemini Rising decided to compromise. Wearing his critic's hat, he lauded the man's current play (a flop) and reported that it would be held over a few more weeks. Reading this, people flocked to the theater to see why the reviewer liked it, giving Shaw time to shorten his monologue.

His most famous collaboration with the Creative Evolutionary Life Force was five plays in a prophetic series called "Back to Methusaleh." While writing them, he knew they were unlikely ever to be performed, but still he kept at it, channeling the message. When finished, he put them in a drawer and left their future up to the Life Force.

Years later, a man from a distant town knocked on his door. "I want to do a play nobody has ever seen. I was told you might have one."

"Well, I have these," said Shaw, handing him *Methusaleh,* "but I hope you aren't expecting a great success."

"No," said the man, "some people own thoroughbred horses, my expensive habit is my

---

16 An optimist, Shaw disliked tragedies, yet said Shakespeare's *Hamlet* was more real to him than contemporary politicians. Holroyd, *Bernard Shaw,* Vol. I, cited above, 41.

theater." After the first play was performed, Shaw joked that it made five pounds' profit. It was later tried in London and lost money.

Still, George Bernard Shaw had faith in the Life Force and in his own talents. He finished his last play at ninety-one. Mahatma Gandhi, who had met Shaw in a vegetarian restaurant and enjoyed his company, called him "Puck, the Arch Jester of Europe." He also said that everything of Shaw's he had ever read had a religious center to it.

Mira Alfassa Richard, known as the Mother at the Aurobindo Ashram (Pondicherry, India) was a prophet ahead of her time. She and G.B.S. had many traits in common: they were optimists; they were drawn to the esoteric ruler even before developing the mundane ruler. Attracted to Beauty, they both loved to draw when very young. Both saw life on earth as God's experiment, and both expected progress: the experiment would have a positive outcome, in spite of a few glitches along the way. Both had an Airy, scientific outlook. And both wanted to do whatever they could to serve the Divine in the evolutionary process.[17]

The Mother expressed Impersonal Divine Love and Wisdom beyond learning. The closest aspect to her Ascendant in early Gemini was the square from Sun/Venus in Pisces at the apex of the chart. She had several spontaneous visions in her childhood; they were Her greatest joy. She was married to a journalist, Paul Richard, and had a son when she visited Pondicherry and met Sri Aurobindo. They left when World War II intervened, but she returned later to stay. She was drawn to His work as much as she was to Aurobindo Ghose.

After the Sun Venus conjunction, Pluto was the planet closest to Her Ascendant, conjuncting it from the Twelfth House. She was not at all saccharine! I was surprised to discover later, when I saw Her horoscope, that Pluto made a *loose* conjunction because " Her Force," as the Pondicherry disciples called her magnetism,[18] was so intense.

This intensity was first quality people felt as they stood in the long reception line for *darshan* —they felt pulled towards her, as if hypnotically, though the line was long and

---

17 Shaw knew that some of the Life Force's experiments, like his *Methusaleh* plays, were doomed to failure. The Mother was never surprised when certain people left Pondicherry, often after writing her long letters on how to improve the ashram. When I was at the guest house in 1970, someone wrote to ask her if Pondicherry would become more spiritually advanced than Auroville because the celibates in 'Pondi' are more spiritual than the householders in Auroville. She said joyfully, "who knows what will happen? It's all an Experiment of the Divine." (The earnest disciple sought to choose the *right* place to live, 'Pondi' or Auroville, "the place with the higher vibration.")
18 perhaps they still do. I'm speaking of 1970.

moved slowly.[19] Only upon reaching the front, standing a few feet from Her did the joy and gentleness of the Pisces conjunction come through.

She spoke prophetically about a time to come when people would live on vitamins and oxygen alone; cooking and shared meals would be a social custom entirely. We could then all put our efforts into other, more interesting activities. Nationalities would preserve their cultures but get along harmoniously together: no more World Wars. People would live forever—the cells in their bodies would change; resist aging and decay. She experimented on the cells in her own body, to bring down the Divine to the molecular level.

At the same time, She was very practical and had a unique sense of humor. According to local tradition, the breakfast cook once complained that Her instructions about serving eggs as protein[20] were rejected by the most conservative local Brahmans. They refused to eat his hard boiled eggs. In their philosophy, an egg was a potential chicken; a life-form not to be destroyed!

Then one day The Mother appeared at breakfast with a large basket of hard boiled eggs. She stood in the doorway and handed them out as *prasad*—a gift of the Guru—to everyone who entered the dining room, including the conservative Brahmans. She stood there, waited, watched and smiled until they finally grimaced, cracked and ate their eggs.

The Mask in Youth - Peter Pan and Tinkerbelle
Eclectic and Versatile - Magician and Jester

To summarize, from the example of G.B.S. in youth, Geminis love to talk. It's difficult for Gemini if adults ask them to keep quiet about their latest interest, even though the subject may seem over-the-top, eccentric, or strange, as vegetarianism and abstinence from liquor seemed to the Irish banker to whom Shaw was apprenticed. Silencing quells their natural exuberance; they'll soon seek an escape route, as Shaw did.

On the other hand, their curiosity and extraverted nature is welcomed at social events.

---

19 A skeptical Italian journalist there for a story commented after passing through the line, "that is *a very strong soul* in a very old body. I somehow forgot to tell the camera man when to take the pictures. I've never done that before."

20 A European, born in Paris of Egyptian and Turkish parents, She knew that Western guests would feel deprived in Pondichery without protein. The manager of the guest house where I stayed was a former Jain who had previously worn a mask to avoid inhaling insects. He was told he must purchase chickens for the Westerners and serve in the house. He did so saying, "come, dinner is served, one chicken has been sacrificed to your Western stomachs!"

Well-versed in most subjects, Gemini Rising if seated next to the most morose guest, entertains him and soon has him laughing at an anecdote. If the guest was sullen over the stock market, Gemini will remember that. He'll network: the next day his new acquaintance will receive a call from Gemini's stockbroker friend who "will do a better job for you than your current broker."

It's seems almost impossible for young Gemini Rising not to cut in and interrupt. Actress Florence Farr dated both Irish playwrights, G.B.S. and William Butler Yeats at different times while starring in their plays. She commented that G.B.S. talked and she listened but Yeats listened and she talked. To her, that was the major difference.[21] She added, though, that "Shaw was a terrible gossip." When she mentioned it to him, he claimed it was an Irish trait. He added that the Irish were not malicious; "we mean no harm by it. We think well of the people we gossip about." Maybe so, but it's also a Gemini Rising tendency.

As they get older many Gemini Rising people learn the art of listening, particularly during the Cancer progression, when relationships become more important. Gemini tends to become interested in houses, pets, relationships and sometimes children. Their relieved relatives mention that they have "settled down."

Most Geminis are natural mimics. Marcel Marceau, who had Gemini Rising "felt like a modern Ulysses, always getting on and off airplanes." Dedicated to preserving the Harlequin Tradition of Mime, he established a school and also performed around the world to keep it alive. He drew rapt audiences who lost all sense of time, became caught up in his skits and were touched by his characters.

Gemini Rising is usually very restless in youth, especially those who, Hermes-like, feel a need to bring their message to others. They'll travel to conferences around the world to share their ideas.[22]

I've encountered people several with this Ascendant who had the type of dedication that Shaw and Marceau exhibited, but I've met a many more who spent three or four decades trying on various masks in an attempt to find one that fit. Gemini Rising chameleons seem to need a longer adolescence than other Ascendants.

During graduate school I met many perennial students with Gemini Rising. They

---

21 Holyroid, cited above, p. W.B. Yeats is discussed in Capricorn Rising.

22 We also see this message-sharing in the progressed Gemini cycle of the preceding two Rising Signs. Annie Besant's story is remarkable. Anna Freud taught students from nursery school age to older psychoanalysts; wrote, had a private practice, and helped her father with his books. She brought his message to England and America. Toni Morrison was very eclectic in her Gemini cycle. She juggled her numerous interests successfully.

enjoyed reading but found they didn't enjoy the activity for which the program prepared them. They soon found themselves back on campus starting over in a different field.

The Gemini Mask in the Second Half of Life
Insightfulness - Wit and Wisdom

Several of my Gemini Rising clients married in their late forties or early fifties for the first and only time. Like G.B.S, they used their insights into human nature in choosing a partner for the Second Half of Life. To the best of my knowledge, the majority of them chose well and are happy. Shaw's first and only marriage at age forty-two lasted until his nineties; Catherine Payne-Townsend predeceased him by a year or two. He made a wise choice.

Gemini Rising "eternal children" will list a variety of reasons for marrying, as if convincing themselves to take the risk. Shaw, the Great Conversationalist, met a woman with whom he had a true meeting-of-the-minds. Unlike his earlier love interests, Catherine did not pressure Shaw to be monogamous. She said their views were similar; that though she favored anarchism to socialism, *they were both opposed to marriage.* He felt safe. Her cook learned vegetarian recipes. She typed and edited his work.

Then, as soon as he began to feel comfortable, Catherine announced she was leaving for six weeks in Italy. He missed the bicycle rides and the conversation; he worried that she'd meet a new man. Six weeks was a long time.

Like my clients, Shaw was lonely at midlife. Charlotte had excellent timing. After his friends Sidney and Beatrice Webb married, the tone of the Fabian Society changed. There were more couples and fewer single people. His lover Florence Farr, who had divorced her husband for him, left the London theater to become headmistress of a Hindu girl's school in Ceylon. Annie Besant had moved to India. Just as he'd predicted, the "New Women"[23] upon whom so many of his plays were based had made "independent decisions in favor of their work." But his letters reveal that he missed them.

When Catherine returned, she proposed marriage. He asked his friends to convince him not to do it. He was weakening! But they failed. True, she was unattractive and not

---

23 His mother and his sister Lucy were also strong, independent women. It's likely that they, too, influenced his New Woman concept.

very passionate but they shared cultural interests. She was wealthy and had social status. Hers was a more important Anglo-Irish family than Shaw's.[24]

In the end, he accepted her proposal and they both compromised. She didn't want to change her name to Shaw but she acceded. He found a new typist; Catherine felt free to travel whenever she liked. The unusual marriage fit Shaw's Moon/Uranus. One good thing about the Mutable Signs, they adapt to change, even later in life.

Because Geminis don't want to grow old, they're likely to consider plastic surgery years earlier than other Rising Signs. But the thing they miss most, *after* their firm, youthful, wrinkle-free body, is the ability to multi-task. Most were quite proud of the mind-body co-ordination that allowed them to do several things simultaneously like a good juggler keeping all his plates in the air. This ability diminishes with age. Around fifty-five, Geminis tell me in a shocked tone, "You know, I can only do one or two things at a time now without *losing it*."

"Good Advice"

There's an Italian folk tale which seems appropriate for Airy Gemini. It involves curiosity; Hermes' cunning, gossip and rumor.

Once upon a time there was a peasant who had a wife and six sons. He and his hungry family lived on land owned by the Church. His landlord, a local priest, charged so much rent that they had very little left for food. So the peasant complained to the North Wind, "my family is often hungry." The Trickster Wind gave him a box with two instructions: "open it when you're hungry and tell no one about this box."

The peasant took it home. That night and every night thereafter the hungry family ate well. But one day his wife couldn't stand it any longer. How could she keep the magic box a secret? What a silly rule! She told a neighbor, who told someone, who told someone else. Finally the gossip reached the ears of the landlord-priest. He demanded the box for himself. If they refused to give it to him, they would be evicted.

The cunning peasant knew, though, that the priest did not really want them to leave.

---

24 For a Socialist, he was at times a snob. He commented on Wilde's family having a big house in Merriam Square, Dublin. He liked Charlotte's family connections. He may have hesitated to return to Ireland because his father, no longer able to afford the family home, lived in furnished lodgings. Annie Besant, whose mother had been a tutor to the Anglo-Irish aristocracy's children, lacked both the money and social position of Catherine Payne-Townsend.

So, he said, "all right, I'll take my box, my family and go. But then, who is going to work this land for you? Or perhaps you have something to trade me for the box? In that case, we'll stay."

But the priest was cunning, too. He gave the peasant a box of dried grass and took away the magic box.

The peasant went back to the North Wind and humbly explained everything that had transpired. The North Wind gave him a second, even heavier box with the same instructions, "open only when hungry. *And this time, tell no one.*"

This time, the man was curious. Half way to his cottage, he opened it. A thug jumped out and beat him up. After much exertion, he finally pushed the thug back into the box and dragged it home. He was exhausted. The next morning, he told his wife the story.

She didn't believe him. "How could a big thug fit into that small box?" she asked. As he dressed to go to the fields, she opened it. Six big thugs jumped out and beat the woman, her husband and their sons.

After the family had finally gotten the thugs back into the box, they discussed ways to get rid of it. The couple decided to start a rumor designed to reach the priest. The peasant woman told her neighbor: "we now have a newer, bigger and better magic box."

And sure enough, a week before the bishop was due to visit the landlord, the priest sent his messenger to the cottage. "Your new box is required in time to prepare a banquet for the bishop," he solemnly said.

The cunning husband was very quiet, as if thinking it over. Next he hemmed and hawed, refusing to give up his new treasure. The messenger insisted. Finally, the peasant said, "perhaps we could trade again." He allowed the priest's emissary to convince him to exchange the bigger magic box for the smaller box which the priest had taken.

On the eve of the bishop's visit, the landlord returned the first box and left with the new, larger one.

The rest is left to our imagination. It's doubtful, though, that the bishop enjoyed his visit.

Hermes is both clever and inventive. The peasant thought about his unpleasant situation—his box of thugs and his obnoxious landlord—and intuited a way to combine the two to his advantage. This type of practical wisdom, based on an understanding of human nature, works well in the Second Half of Life. As the "Twins," Geminis are likely to have two simultaneous problems at any stage of life. However, when they're older and more experienced, their ingenuity is likely to solve them in a unique way.

The story also seems to say, "as we age, it's important not to lose our Trickster cunning because we need it now more than ever."[25]

The Progressed Mask

As the progressed Mask changes, Gemini Rising[26] is still a networker, though their rolodex or computer phone list seems to shrink as they grow older. Still curious about others' lives, they draw quieter guests out at parties. And they still can't resist a good story; even esoteric Geminis will gossip. Most Geminis retain their childlike sense of wonder. Some, like Shaw, continue to use humor or nervous chatter as a shield to deflect personal questions. Most have learned to become better listeners.

In Cancer, they're at their most imaginative. If they've written articles during their youth, they may do longer or in-depth pieces now. They may know artists or other creative people. With Water planets or Earth planets in the chart they'll enjoy longer relationships, most will marry and have families. Some become consultants. They enjoy nurturing others' projects when they haven't one of their own. Some become interested in psychology, but Gemini prefers short-term client work and *no pathology please,* nothing really depressing unless there are several Scorpio or Eighth House planets. Gemini's positive attitude comes out during the Leo cycle.

On of the best examples of Gemini insightfulness over fifty is Erica Jong. Mars and Jupiter are conjunct her natal Ascendant, indicating restlessness in youth; difficulty settling anywhere for long. Married four times, her modern journey is similar to that of many women clients in California, as Shaw's is similar to those of many Gemini Rising men.

Jong's poetry and novels written during her Cancer progression reflect the lifestyle of the 1960's and 70's. Her readers remember *Fear of Flying* (1973) for being sexually explicit. In a sense, her protagonist is the modern equivalent of Shaw's New Woman. *Flying* seemed as shocking in 1973 as Henry Miller's *Tropic of Cancer* in the 1950's. (Women already knew how their bodies reacted when panicky of course, but had never before seen it in print.) After *Flying,* women writers felt they could more be explicit themselves. Her fans enjoy her bawdy humor.

---

25 Italo Calvino, *Italian Folklore*, trans, George Martin, "Good Advice," (NY: Harcourt-Harvest,) 1992.

26 You might also want to review the Gemini progressions at the end of the FAQs (Introduction) as Gemini was the example used for the progressed cycle.

The occupations of two husbands married during her Cancer cycle are intriguing: a psychiatrist (Alan Jong) and a novelist-social worker. They're in healing and imaginative careers.

Later in life she made a wiser choice; her longest and happiest marriage is to attorney Ken Burrows. Jong is a trendsetter; when she and her husband burned their pre-nuptial contract because "they no longer needed it," some of her fans did as well.

Her title choice for *Fear of Fifty* was published the year her progressed Ascendant changed from Cancer to Leo. Natal Gemini Rising abhors the aging process. As a progressed Leo, she spoke powerfully to many of her generation who identified with the emotion behind the title.

Jong's 2007 book, *Seducing the Demon, Writing for My Life* may interest creative writers and memoirists , especially those who were unhappy in their relationships prior to fifty. Erica's progressed Ascendant degree conjuncted Chiron when she wrote it, symbolizing the healing of old wounds through the writing process. The dramatic Leo Mask works well with Gemini (a symbolic Sextile.)

Unfortunately, some Geminis become cynical on the Virgo square to the Natal Ascendant. As they age, like Aries, Gemini enjoys spending time with grandchildren or step-grandchildren. Most were so busy when their children were young that they missed out on play time (though they enjoyed increasing their children's vocabularies during quality time.)

During the Virgo progression Gemini may finally tire of learning new skills. They're more likely to exchange talents they've already developed for others' knowledge: "I'll set up your website if you'll upholster my chairs; I don't really want or need to learn upholstery."

Gemini Rising might write "how-to-do-it" books or articles during this double-Mercury cycle, drawing upon a wealth of practical knowledge and experience from one of their earlier careers.

In the Virgo progression, Geminis may become more selective about their interests. As the dilettante energy winds down, there are definite compensations. It becomes easier to focus. This can be a great blessing for Jong and other Natal Geminis with Jupiter-in-Detriment on the Ascendant. Natal Jupiter accentuates the restlessness; Geminis may view themselves as citizens of the world and want to see as much of it as possible.

In youth, Jupiter's influence may overextend Natal Gemini Rising. Gemini may attempt to become "supermom," "super wife" and "super author" simultaneously. Later in life,

Virgo's narrower range of interests may help to offset Jupiter, particularly when supported by practical Earth planets.

I haven't known many Gemini Rising people who've reached the Libra cycle, the symbolic Air trine to the Natal Ascendant. As this is a Venus-ruled progression, we might expect it to be tranquil and enjoyable, especially for those Geminis in loving relationships.

Gemini Rising Bibliography

Calvino, Italo, *Italian Folklore*, "Good Advice," George Martin, trans, (NY: Harcourt-Harvest,) 1992.

Chinen, Allan B., *Saga Vol. I: Best New Writings on Mythology*, "Adult Liberation and the Mature Trickster," ed., Jonathan Young, (Ashland: White Cloud Press,) 1996.

Henderson, Archibald, *George Bernard Shaw*, (NY: Hesperides Press,) 2006.

Holroyd, Michael, *Bernard Shaw*, vols. I-IV, (NY: Random-Vintage,) 1991-1993.

Jong, Erica, *Fear of Flying*, (NY: Penguin,) 1995.

—— *Fear of Fifty, A Midlife Memoir*, (NY: HarperCollins/Perennial,) 1997.

—— *Love Comes First: Poems*, (NY: Tarcher-Penguin,) 2009.

—— *Seducing the Demon: Writing for Your Life*. (NY: Tarcher,) 2007.

Jung, C.G. *Aion: Researches into the Phenomenon of the Self*, R.F.C. Hull, trans., Bollingen Series XX, (New Haven: Princeton University Press,) pp. 28-31.

Pirandello, Luigi, *Six Characters in Search of an Author*, trans. John Livstrum, (London, Methuen,) 2004.

Richard, Mira Alfassa, *Collected Works, Questions and Answers, Vols. 5-10*, "The Mother," Centenary Edition, (Pondicherry: Aurobindo Ashram Press,) 1973.

Shaw, George Bernard, "Major Barbara," "Back to Methusaleh," "Arms and the Man," "Man and Superman," "Mrs. Warren's Profession."

Williamson, Marianne, *A Return to Love, Reflections on A Course in Miracles*, (NY: Harper Paperbacks,) 1996.

CHAPTER FOUR

Cancer Rising - Active Imagination

James M. Barrie, "God gave us our memories so that we might have roses in December." *Peter Pan.*

—— "The reason birds can fly and we can't is simply that they have perfect faith, for to have faith is to have wings."

Joan Didion, "We tell ourselves stories in order to live."

—— "Was it only by dreaming or writing that I could find out what I thought?"

—— "Was there ever in anyone's life span a point free in time, devoid of memory, a night when choice was any more than the sum of all the choices gone before?"

Christopher Isherwood, "I am a camera with its shutter open, quite passive, recording, not thinking."

—— "Life is not so bad if you have plenty of luck, a good physique, and not too much imagination."

William Blake, "I must create a system or be enslaved by another man's. I will not reason and compare: my business is to create."

—— "To see a world in a Grain of Sand/ and a Heaven in a Wild Flower/ Hold Infinity in the Palm of Your Hand/ and Eternity in an Hour."

—— "The man who never in his mind and thoughts travel'd to heaven is no artist."

Lord Byron, "…in solitude, where we are least alone."

—— "I know that two and two make four-and should be glad to prove it too if I could, though … if by any sort of process I could convert 2 and 2 into five it would give me much greater pleasure."

—— "Love will find a way through paths where wolves fear to prey."

—— "Sometimes we are less unhappy in being deceived by those we love, than in being undeceived by them."

Joni Mitchell, "You could write a song about an emotional problem you are having, but it would not be a good song, in my eyes, until it went through a period of sensitivity to a moment of clarity. Without that moment of clarity to contribute to the song, it's just complaining."

—— "There are things to confess that enrich the world, and things that need not be said."

Jerry Lewis, "A woman doing comedy doesn't offend me, but sets me back a bit. I, as a viewer, have trouble with it. I think of her as a producing machine that brings babies into the world."

The Cancer Mask

I seem caring, sympathetic, and concerned about you, but you'd better not say anything negative about my mother! I am moody; sometimes crabby. I have an innate ability to find and push others' emotional buttons to further my agenda. Cautious as a crab, I walk sideways around problems, circling them before choosing an option. Decisions once made and directions once taken are difficult to reverse.[1]

My crab-shell is tough. Self-protective and sensitive to slights, I'm quick to take things personally. I have an excellent memory and a powerful imagination which tends to exaggerate my grievances. Home and family are more important to me than my ambitions.[2] If I have no children, I'll fight to protect those in need. Tenacious as a crab, I'm the ideal ombudsman for my spouse or lover, surrogate child, client, elderly relative, and defenseless animals. I'm responsible. I plan to live a long time and enjoy a financially secure old age.

How to Recognize Cancer Rising

Most of my Cancer Rising clients are short, though a few are as tall as the model, Cheryl Tiegs. The upper body is usually larger than the lower body. The men tend towards barrel chests and the women towards full-figured torsos, especially after midlife. As Moonchildren, (the Moon is the mundane ruler) Cancers are said to have round (Moon-shaped) faces and paler skin than the other Signs. They need gardening hats and sunscreen in summertime. When Cancer Rising gains a few pounds, the neck and face fill out right away. You may remember former Vice President Al Gore's wife Tipper on the campaign trail: the grueling combination of eating-on-the-run, poor sleep and little exercise takes

---

1 See Joan Didion, above, "was there ever…a point in time… devoid of memory when choice was any more than the sum of all the choices gone before?"

2 The Sun or a high percentage of planets in Fire increases ambition, as does Mars-in-Capricorn (Exalted) opposite the Rising Sign: Jerry Lewis and Elizabeth Claire Prophet (Sun in Aries) have the Mars placement. Stephen Spielberg has Mars-in-Capricorn in his Sixth House. Capricorn and Cancer are the two most conservative Signs.

its toll. She began the campaign quite toned, but her face filled out quickly.[3] Cancers need to watch their calories after midlife, or the abdomen, too, will be round.

Cancer Rising may tell you their worries about a child, a close relative, or their own health. Joan McEvers put this well in *12 Times 12: 144 Sun/Ascendant Combinations,* Cancer Rising "practically invented ulcers."[4] Astrologers see a symbolic connection between the ability to digest or assimilate one's life experience and the ability to digest one's food. Emotions interfere with digestion. A former apartment mate of mine with Cancer Rising used to fast all day before a job interview, even when it took place in the late afternoon. "Why put up with an upset stomach if I don't need to?" she asked. She had a point.

But Pisces Rising will tell you their worries, too. An even stronger indicator that you are sitting across the desk from Cancer Rising is this: they'll unconsciously pick up your mood and mirror it back to you.

Cancer Rising usually arrives in your office in the same mood as the last person they encountered. It might have been a sad grocery clerk, a bored co-worker, or their angry spouse. But if you greet Cancer warmly and you're in a cheerful mood, they'll soon pick that up and mirror it back to you. Astrologers consider Cancer Rising to be a psychic sponge: they absorb others' moods and emotions.

It's as important for psychic sponges to associate with happy people as it is for the highly suggestible Mutable Rising Signs. Cancers who spend too much of their time with a bitter or cynical relative need cheerful, optimistic friends. Otherwise, the protective crab shell hardens over time and Cancer Rising risks becoming like the Maiden visited by her angel in the dream:

> I dried my tears and arm'd my fears,
>
> With ten thousand shields and spears.
>
> Soon my Angel came again;
>
> I was arm'd; he came in vain.

---

3 Tipper is also very kind to the needy. Her daughters, interviewed on T.V. spoke of her bringing homeless people to lunch at Blair House, the Vice President's official home, while a magazine photographer was attempting to take pictures of the festive Christmas decorations. Mrs. Gore has Venus-in-Cancer in the First House.

4 She added that some Cancer Rising people even walk around with a hand on their stomach. McEvers, (San Diego: 1983,) 71-2. I find, as McEvers did, that many with this Ascendant have green eyes. I've also met many with blue eyes, or hazel eyes that change color with the color of their clothing.

> For the time of youth was fled
>
> And grey hairs were on my head.[5]

William Blake, the Cancer Rising poet who wrote these lines, dreamed of himself as a "Maiden Queen" twice visited by her angel, once in youth and once in old age. He urged his readers to open themselves to new experiences; to remove their armor; to let go of old grievances. Blake had a deep understanding of the Cancer Rising journey.

Cancer Rising men tend to think of women as Earth Mothers or housewives who've mysteriously turned up in the business world by mistake because, of course, they'd really prefer to be home! These men are easily recognizable from remarks like that of Jerry Lewis, (the great friend to disabled children,) about a woman comedian, "I think of her as a producing machine that brings babies into the world" and "I'm troubled" to see her on stage. (The full quote is on the list, above.)

They are chivalrous; they often open doors for women, and pull out chairs for them in restaurants. They're attentive to their mothers. They like to entertain at home, they're house-proud. They're also very thrifty. If you go out to dinner in a group, the Cancer Rising man will read the bill carefully to be sure he pays only his family's share. He looks forward to a financially secure old age; he'll probably achieve his goal.

The Mode

Cardinality is an authoritative or executive Mode. Cardinal Signs are very well-organized. Many of my Cancer Rising clients own small businesses; others schedule their own time in home health care or child care. Several are realtors who love matching the right family with the right home, or teachers, who have the ability to manage a classroom of restless students while making their subject interesting.

Cancer Rising may not appear to be a leader at first. They seem soft-spoken and quiet (unless Mars or Uranus aspects the Ascendant, or the Sun Sign or Moon Sign is extraverted.) On the surface Cancer is less dramatic than Aries and less ambitious than Capricorn.

But many corporate power plays occur beneath the surface, where Cancer's talents lie. You'll discover that their friends and proteges are promoted quickly; Cancer Rising knows

---

5 William Blake, *The Angel, Songs of Experience*, Plate 41, in *William Blake, The Complete Illuminated Works*, (NY: Thames and Hudson,) 2002, 83.

how to build an empire unobtrusively, usually without offending others. And at meetings, they'll speak up forcefully in defense of their department's budget. While other Cardinal Signs *manage* departments, Cancers prefer to *create* them, from selecting high-level staff to choosing the plants on the windowsills.

Their employees are considered family. Cancer Rising Ross Perot, for instance, conducted his own foreign policy during the Iranian Hostage Crisis, much to the chagrin of the American President. Jimmy Carter had declared, "we do *not* negotiate with terrorists," but Ross Perot, CEO of Electronic Data Systems did it anyhow. He made his deal and brought his two employees—his "family"—home before word leaked to the press. The Texas billionaire ran twice for the presidency for the Reform Party. When Republican candidate Robert Dole asked Perot to quit the race, he said that he was "in it till the bitter end. " A triple Cancer, with his Sun and Moon in the Sign as well, Perot refused to quit in spite of the expense and the odds against him.[6]

Pluto, the "power planet," is conjunct his First House Moon. The Moon symbolizes the media and the general public; Perot drew his share of media attention.

Pluto enhances Perot's Cardinality from the middle of the First House. But many other Cancers born around the time of the Great Depression had it conjunct their Ascendant degree, an even stronger position. We recognize some of them as soon as we hear their voices, like Jerry Lewis and Eva Gabor. With a close conjunction of Pluto to his Ascendant, columnist Jack Anderson influenced readers' opinions for decades.

Film director Steven Spielberg, a member of the Baby Boomer generation, has Cancer Rising with Pluto in the First House *in Leo*. He continues to make an impression on popular culture.

Perhaps the most famous corporate leader of our times with Cancer Rising is Bill Gates, the founder of Microsoft. Gates has Uranus in his First House. Though his parents worried when he dropped out of Harvard, he succeeded beyond their expectations. Retired now, Gates and his wife manage the family's charitable foundation. Uranus in the First House often coincides with liberal politics. Gates was a Clinton supporter.

Salvatore Ferragamo, the successful Italian shoe designer has Cancer Rising as well. Though he has no First House planets, his Moon makes a 150-degree contact to the Ascendant. Women love his shoes!

Cancer Rising builds personal relationships at work. They make certain that employee

---

6 The late Anne Richards, former Democratic governor of Texas, claimed that Perot held a grudge against George H.W. Bush, and that the grudge was his real reason for running against Bush Senior, even though he knew he couldn't win. Perot later supported "W," so Richards may have been right.

birthday cards are purchased and signed by everyone, sometimes they even bring the cake themselves. When an employee's spouse or child is sick they'll say a kind word or if the schedule permits, give him time off. They invest time and energy in training a protégé. They're sad when he leaves; if he goes to the competition, they often feel betrayed. Like a good parent, a Cancer boss is supportive. Like Cancer Rising's children, their employees may feel sorry, even guilty when the time comes to leave "home."

The Water Element

Many of us associate the Water Element with the Creative Unconscious. We may dream of being in, on, or near water when life is about to flow in a new, often creative direction. Such dreams catch our attention; we remember them when we wake up.

The fertile water of the imagination is important. Unless we're first able to *imagine* a new direction, then visualize ourselves moving towards it, we'll most likely remain stuck in our ruts; ten years from now we'll still be sitting here worrying about the same old problems.

Though Cancers may complain about their present situation, they're also attached to the security and continuity it represents. Cancer will say, "I can't imagine life without so-and-so," the very person who "drives them crazy," the same person who supports their lifestyle.

Imagination is probably the greatest gift of the Water Element, whether Water Rising applies it in business (like the CEOs, above) healing, psychology (like Assagioli's guided imagery) or the arts. Cancer Rising author H. Rider Haggard imagined and created Ayesha, the White Queen in *She,* and Allan Quartermain, the treasure-hunter in *King Soloman's Mines.* Ayesha and Allan have long outlived their creator. In addition to millions of readers, large audiences know these characters from the movie theater. At least nine movies have been made about the novel *She,* from silent films[7] through black and white to color, including the most recent version with Ursala Andress. In Ayesha, Haggard created a powerful Goddess, his imagination touched upon an archetype.

When C.G. Jung read *She,* he saw Ayesha as a guide, or *anima* figure for men. And she did expound on her philosophy to Leo. Haggard's protagonist, Ayesha, a.k.a. "She-Who-Must-Be-Obeyed," is a 2,000-year-old queen who became immortal by leaping into a pillar of fire on the edge of a volcano. She spoke of love *and power;* she killed her enemies. She wanted Leo to jump into the fire with her and become immortal. As a guide, she seems

7 Haggard collaborated on the first version of *She. King Soloman's Mines* is also a movie.

more like the Hindu Goddess Kali or the Hawaiian volcano Goddess Pele than Dante's gentle Beatrice. If I were a man, I think I'd prefer a tamer Guide.

Haggard had a powerful imagination. He also had a Grand Trine in Air, including Venus-in-Gemini, its Sign of Esoteric Rulership.[8] A versatile and prolific author, Haggard wrote over eighty books: romances, adventure stories, a psychological novel, historical novels, fantasy, even a ghost story. In one year, 1887, he wrote three novels, including *She* and a sequel to *Soloman's Mines.* He set several novels in places he'd never seen, like Mexico and the South Seas.

His body of work includes several non-fiction books about the regions of Africa where he lived and traveled, Natal and Transvaal; the *Poor and the Land,* about contemporary Britain, and his research on colonial migration. Haggard ran unsuccessfully for Parliament as a Conservative, but was knighted for his service to the Government. When he died, he left behind four completed, unpublished novels.

Playwright and children's author James M. Barrie also created a character who lives on, *Peter Pan.* Peter and the lost boys are close to Carl Jung's archetype: the *puer* or *puella aeternus.* Barrie had Venus-in-Cancer on the Ascendant.

In his novel *Berlin Diaries,* Christopher Isherwood created a nightclub singer character, Sally Bowles. Sally lived on in many different media, most recently in the musical *Cabaret* and the movie version with Liza Minelli. Neptune was conjunct Isherwood's Ascendant.

Another noteworthy character who lives on is Franksenstein, created by Mary Wollstoncraft Shelley, wife of the famous poet. Stephen King has Cancer Rising, too. Whether or not we appreciate the horror genre, most of us will admit Mrs. Shelley wrote well and King is an exceptional storyteller.[9] King has Mars conjunct his Ascendant from his Twelfth House. Mary Shelly had Saturn in her First House.

Water is very different from logical, objective, impersonal Air. (See Chapter III, Gemini Rising for the contrast.) Emotional, subjective and personal, Water is seldom convinced by logical arguments. Cancer's decisions are supported by strong emotions.[10]

When Ross Perot decided to send supplies on his own to soldiers in Vietnam, the fact that they probably wouldn't get through didn't faze him; he had to try anyway. Later,

---

8 Also in the Grand Trine: Moon-in-Aquarius and Mars-in-Detriment (Libra.) He has a Sun-Saturn conjunction in the Twelfth House.

9 Movies have been made of 26 of King's novels.

10 As Gemini Rising Luigi Pirandello said (see Chapter III) a fact is an empty sack. It only stands up by itself when there's an emotion inside; the emotion is its reason for being. For instance, pollster's cold statistics will not provide a "full sack" of emotions or persuade people with the opposing view.

during the hostage crisis, Perot wanted his two employees back immediately. When President Jimmy Carter asked him not to interfere with the larger negotiation, he was unfazed. He *felt* his decision to be the right one and acted accordingly. "To thine own self be true" means, for Water, the response to any situation must "feel right." Sometimes Cancer Rising's decision works and sometimes it doesn't. Perot lost the supplies, but he brought the hostages home.

Subjectivity works very well in art, music, drama, sculpture, novels, and poetry. The artist's, musician's or songwriter's unique perspective often finds an appreciative audience.

But when Cancer applies its personal perspective—what's best for *my* family, *my* company's investors and directors, *my* employees—the outer world may respond negatively. Other power players who find Cancer's viewpoint too narrow will challenge them. Under Bill Gates, Microsoft's intransigence about allowing other browsers to compete led to a costly lawsuit in Europe. So, before the crab commits to "holding on until the bitter end," he might want to seek an outside, *objective* opinion and seriously consider it.

Water takes things personally and Cancer has a long memory. Personal grudges consume time, mental energy and financial resources that Cancer could employ in other ways.

Though attached to their perspective, Cancer is usually kind, unless the Moon is afflicted and fears or jealousy blind them.[11] Many with this Cardinal Ascendant are active on behalf of a cause close to their hearts, like Jerry Lewis, ("Jerry's kids,") Ross Perot (the Vietnam soldiers and his employees) and the Gates Foundation. Two of my Cancer Rising clients rescue stray animals.

The Mundane Ruler - The Moon

"My Empire is Thy Imagination"
Queen Ayesha to Leo Vincey

The Moon is the Mother of Form in Plato, the archetype from which we create. Many Cancer Rising people honor Her by acting on their intuition and doing what "feels right." As a result, their lunar intuition increases. Whether they like it or not, Cancers may

---

11 Cancer Rising William Blake has a poem in *Songs of Experience,* cited above, called, *The Poison Tree.* Negative thoughts watered it; One beautiful poisoned apple grew, which his enemy stole and ate. The poisoner awoke one morning to see his enemy lying dead under the tree. Joan Didion has also written about jealousy. Cancer Rising often writes about emotions.

develop reputations as psychics. Some are very private people, with their planets mainly in the bottom hemisphere of the horoscope. Or perhaps they have a high percentage of Earth and Water planets.

Others with Cancer Rising enjoy media publicity; they have Sun or Moon and a high percentage of planets in Fire and Air. Whether or not Cancers resist the limelight or try to ignore their psychic side, others will often feel their lunar gift. They may see the Moonchild as a mind-reader, or come to Cancer Rising for advice about their problems.

Because Cancer's feelings are close to the surface of the *persona*, they're often visible to others. Most prefer to "cry today," rather than set their emotions aside and "cry tomorrow," like Scarlett O'Hara. Aquarius and Capricorn Rising may wear a convincing poker face, but not Cancer.

Moonchildren are comfortable writing about their feelings. Openness about their personal lives draws empathetic readers. Joan Didion's *Year of Magical Thinking* takes us through the shock of her husband's death and the grieving process as if we were there. The same is true of Isherwood's *Mr. Norris Takes the Train.* We know the character and we feel for him. William Blake revealed a great deal about himself in his poems, *The Angel* and *The Poison Tree.* In the latter poem, we have a sense of his jealousy and frustration that "lesser poets" were admitted to the Royal Academy: poets who didn't marry a servant, a lowly woman who might not know how to behave at tea with genuine ladies![12]

Cancer Rising authors are so different from Airy George Bernard Shaw, whose plays were moved along by dialogue; by the characters' witty banter on Shaw's favorite topics. (As he put it, "I don't see the point of a play *without a point.*")

Isherwood once said that if a student read his novels in chronological order they'd have read his autobiography.[13] Joan Didion's works are similar, If we began with her book about Northern California where she grew up and kept reading, we'd know who she is. Cancers' personal experience is their material. And they're not afraid to share it.

Like Jungian Individuation, creativity has its price: solitude. We have more time for that in the Second Half of Life. Solitude is required to develop *any* lunar gift, poetry, novels, any art form, from reading Tarot cards, meditation to enhanced intuition. Neptune, the esoteric ruler, enjoys solitude. (See below.)

Cancer Rising horoscopes with most of the planets in the upper hemisphere, or horoscopes that are strong in the extraverted Elements, Air and Fire know they're gifted.

---

12 Nor did they write polemics in favor of the French Revolution, which the government feared might spread to England.

13 "my work is all part of an autobiography." In James J Berg, ed., *Conversations with Christopher Isherwood,* (Jackson: University of Mississippi Press,) 10.

However, they're also very active; often quite social. They'll say "I know I can write better novels than the ones in the airport bookshops." (And it's true; the talent is there.) Then they'll quickly add, "but of course, I'm *too busy living my life.*"

Many famous writers have—or had—the Moon in the angular houses: 1, 4, 7, and 10.[14] There's an inner tension, a psychic pressure for the Moon in these houses to develop their gifts. The Moon seeks approval from the outside world.

The Moon is Mother. Symbolically, she's the first Goddess we encounter in life; our first example of the feminine. We may criticize her ourselves—she's human—but we usually protect her, too. We don't like others criticizing her. If Cancer has a nurturing mother, wonderful. If not, most imaginative Cancers will re-fashion her in their memories, removing her flaws until she's perfect.[15]

The author of *Peter Pan* is a double Cancer: Cancer Moon conjunct Cancer Rising. A double Cancer, he wore his heart on his sleeve. James M. Barrie grew up with a mother who stopped responding to him coherently after the death of his older brother. In a dreamlike state, she would open her eyes and reply to James, "my David is dead." Adrift on the seas of his imagination, the hypersensitive six-year-old retreated into the fantasies that sustained him. Barrie's mother lived on, ghost-like in his adult mind. In *Mary Rose,* his last play, the character Henry returned home from his life at sea to connect with his mother's ghost. He tried to put the relationship to rest.[16] At the end, the ghost was free to move on and Henry "felt his prayers were answered." The play was not a great success. Sometimes we write for ourselves, and it can be cathartic.

Generations of children have enjoyed *Peter Pan,* but few of us would want to trade places with James Barrie!

Christopher Isherwood, whose line "I am a camera" expresses so well Cancer's nearly photographic memory (another symbolic meaning of the Moon is memory)[17] had an angular Moon, too. His was in the Tenth House in the Water Sign, Pisces. He said that his mother Kathleen was both his strongest critic and his biggest fan. Though he lived thou-

---

14 The Moon in House Seven (partnership) will often succeed with the help of one or more supportive women but the person, too, has a need for recognition. See Henry Miller, Aries Rising.

15 I have yet to meet a Cancer Rising person who could see dad's side of the divorce. They're definitely Moonchildren.

16 *Mary Rose* was written 15 years after *Peter Pan,* when Barrie was sixty. See John Lahr, "Trapped in Time: The Ghost Worlds of J.M. Barrie and Tom Stoppard," *The New Yorker,* March 5, 2007.

17 Joan Didion, author of *The Year of Magical Thinking* goes into such detailed description of the night her husband died that it's as if her memory stored everything photographically, to be replayed later in slow motion as she wrote.

sands of miles from her—he lived in Berkeley, California; she lived in England—he called to read her parts of his novels. He really missed her after she died.

Yet, he found it hard to forgive her for sending him away to school at eleven, the year his father was killed in action. The other boys saw his black arm band, punched him in the shoulder and said, "tough luck old lad." Some of the others had lost fathers too, but they were expected to go away to school, they accepted it. However *they* didn't have Cancer Rising or a Tenth House Pisces Moon.

As an adult, Isherwood requested his parents' wartime correspondence for a book he planned to write about them, called *Frank and Kathleen.* As he read his mother's letters to his father, Isherwood came to understand those years from her perspective.

The crab shell can harden like a suit of armor; tenacious crabs may find it difficult to open their claws and let go. Sometimes a writing project can be a catalyst to healing.

H. Rider-Haggard, who gave us Queen Ayesha was the eighth child in his family. His mother, a published poet, must have been extremely busy, yet she encouraged him to write. He gave some of his characters different versions of her name.

His Air Sign Moon was in the Eighth House in a Grand Trine, he seems to have had a happy marriage to an older, wealthy woman with a spirit of adventure.[18] Neptune, another imaginative planet, squared his Ascendant from the Tenth House.

Barrie loved to write. He left his career as a barrister to become a full-time author. His novels read as if he enjoyed writing them.

Psychic, artistic, and literary inspiration are not the only examples of lunar creativity. During the First Half of life, biological creativity—children— is the main focus of many Moonchildren. This is discussed in "The Mask in Youth."

In summary: for Cancer Rising the Moon Sign is at least as important as the Sun Sign. The House placement is important, too. To better understand family members, it helps to know their Moon Signs.

New and Full Moons are periods of greater emotional sensitivity. It helps if we can be patient with ourselves and others during these times.

Neptune - The Esoteric Ruler
Creativity and Spirituality

Trident-wielding Neptune (a.k.a. Poseidon) ruled the seas in classical times. The seas, of

---

18 She went to Transvaal to live on his ostrich farm until the Dutch asked them to leave.

course, symbolize the Creative Unconscious. As they left port, Greek sailors would drop an offering into the sea as a sacrifice to Poseidon. Neptune is associated with sacrifice. In astrology Neptune rules Pisces, the Sign whose faith is strongest.

The Greeks also had several important rivers, among them Lethe, the River of Forgetfulness. Memory is a lunar function. Moonchildren are gifted with the best memories in the Zodiac. However, not all memories are positive. Cancer is also known for remembering slights, grievances, and painful situations: Bad Things that should never happen to Good People.

William Blake, a double Cancer, was fascinated with the *Book of Job*. He engraved a series of pictures to illustrate his poems about it; he spent a long time on a search for answers similar to Job's.

Why did his brother have to die? Why did untalented artists who were willing to compromise their standards receive commissions and not him? Why was he still designing pottery catalogues for Josiah Wedgwood? Why did that soldier he slapped take him to court, causing all those sleepless nights?[19]

By the end of his life, Blake had turned away from *The Poison Tree* and its bitter apple. In a vision, Blake saw a host of angels and heard voices singing, "Holy, Holy, Holy." Afterwards, he painted the famous watercolor, "The River of Life," with the souls of the departed swimming to the Face of God. He later did a series of engravings called, "All Religions are One." At the end of his life Blake was often in ecstasy—-his wife Catherine told visitors he "spent so much time in Paradise" that she scarcely saw him. He departed from the earth in great joy.[20]

Neptune (a.k.a. Dionysus, the God of ecstasy) was in Leo (Exalted) in his First House, opposite Saturn in his Eighth. It wasn't easy for him to find the River of Forgetfulness, let go of his grievances, forgive and forget. It can take a long time to seek out the Lethe.

It's often difficult for Cardinal Signs to surrender. That's a Yin process and they're Yang people: *doers.*[21] Christopher Isherwood asked many questions the day he met Swami Prabhavananda and decided to move to California. Isherwood might walked away had the Swami given a different answer to his question on homosexuality. But when

---

19 He was nearly arrested for printing seditious pamphlets against the King of France but an important patron came to his defense.

20 Some thought him a madman, but the poet Wordsworth said he would rather spend time with the madman Blake than many so-called sane people.

21 Annie Besant, Cardinal Fire Rising, wrote in her autobiography that the day she met her teacher, Helena P. Blavatsky, did not intend to become a disciple. Blavatsky told her she was as proud as Lucifer.

Prabhavananda said, "it's a form of attachment, like everything else, " he felt comfortable. The Swami added, "However, if you want to live in the ashram you must be celibate." A difficult sacrifice but Isherwood made it and stayed for awhile.[22]

Christopher had Neptune conjunct the Ascendant in Cancer. Many seekers have been grateful for the time he spent in the ashram helping the Swami translate Indian scriptures into coherent English. Their book on Patanjali's Yoga Sutras: *How to Know God,*[23] is still available.

H. Rider Haggard's character Leo Vincey went to Africa on a quest for his identify, his "legacy." Vincey was also a seeker of sorts, a follower of Queen Ayesha, who thought of him as her reincarnated lover, Kalikrates. Haggard's Tenth House Neptune is in close square to his Ascendant degree. At the esoteric level, Neptune seems to symbolize mystics, potential seekers, and those who write about them. There are other avenues to Dionysian ecstasy than drugs and alcohol!

The Shining Fish

An elderly couple lived in a cottage at the edge of the sea, where the water met the land and crashed against the rocks during stormy weather. Grieving the loss of their three sons, the old couple were fearful. There was no one left to help them now.

One day, the old man went out as usual to gather wood, but this time a surprise awaited him. He met a stranger on what was usually his solitary walk. He greeted the man without fear or suspicion. The stranger gave him a few gold coins and went away.

The old man was happy at first. But then his mood changed and his dark side emerged. When he looked at the coins again, he suddenly decided to keep them for himself. He went home and hid the coins under a manure pile. "She'll never find them there," he thought.

His wife wondered why he returned early without any wood for the fire. And no wood to sell in the market. There would be no food! Then she thought of the manure pile. She could sell it for fertilizer.

---

22 "meeting Prabhavananda had a lot to do with rooting me here (Ca.)…It still seems an important reason for staying." *Conversations with Christopher Isherwood, James J. Berg,* ed, cited above, 66. See also, *Where Joy Resides: A Christopher Isherwood Reader,* intro by Gore Vidal, Don Bachardy, ed., (NY: Noonday Press,) 1989, pp. 269-96.

23 *The Yoga Aphorisms of Patanjali: How to Know God,* Isherwood and Prabhavananda, (n.c: Vedanta Press,) 2007. He also worked on the translation of the *Upanisads* and the *Bhagvat Gita.* Eventually, he collaborated with the Swami in writing the biography of Ramakrishna.

So, the next day while the old man was in the forest, the old woman prepared the manure to take to market, and discovered the gold coins.

The old man was furious to find them gone. "That woman is so wasteful," he muttered.

He hoped to see the rich stranger again, and sure enough, the next day, there he was. This time he was given a sack of gold, which he hid under the ashes in the hearth.

And the old woman, of course, decided to sweep up the ashes and found the sack immediately. "Why, there's enough gold here to keep us for a long, long time," she said to herself.

Again her husband was furious to find his sack of gold missing. On the third day he eagerly looked around for the stranger, hoping for an even larger sack. But it was dusk before he saw him and this time the stranger was less generous. He was also vague. (Neptune is vague, it's a cognate of nebulous.) Instead of gold, the stranger gave him a large bag of frogs.

"You're clearly not destined to be rich, but this will help a little," said the stranger. Sell the frogs and buy a fish. But not just any fish! You must buy the biggest fish you can find."

"All right," said the wood gatherer. He took the sack of frogs. Of course he'd sell them, "but why buy *a fish* when there are so many wonderful things at the market?" he wondered. "After all, we'd eat the fish and then it's gone. That's not very practical."

And he had faith in the stranger, after all, the man had come through for him twice before. He would do as he was told.

So, faith overcame fear and greed. The old man sold the frogs; sought out the fish vendor and spent everything on the biggest fish he could find. And he somehow felt good about it. When he reached his cottage it was too late to clean the fish, so he hung it from a rafter near the window overnight.

A few hours later, a tremendous storm came up and rattled the cottage. Then came a loud knock at the door. He opened it to find a group of young fishermen, laughing and singing.

"Thank you for saving our lives," they shouted over the rain crashing against the rocks. We were lost at sea in the storm and didn't know how to set our course till you put that light in your window."

"Light? What light?" asked the old man. And the sailor pointed to the window. The old man turned to see his large fish shining so brightly that it could be seen for miles.

And every stormy night thereafter the couple hung out the fish. In return, the fishermen

73

shared their catch with the old couple. And they lived in comfort and dignity the rest of their lives.[24]

The Neptune sacrifice, "sell everything for the fish," represents trusting in Life. For Cancer Rising, it also means, "trust your intuition." The old man trusted the stranger who provided the resources. With Neptune as esoteric ruler there are usually sacrifices along the way —"lessons in non-attachment"— as Isherwood's Swami would say. But the esoteric lifetime usually ends in contentment. Sometimes, as for William Blake, it ends blissfully.[25]

We can waste time and energy complaining about the sacrifice or n we can move on from "woe is me" to acceptance. When we do, there's often a boon. William Blake painted a happy ending for Odysseus, the sailor who had forgotten Neptune's sacrifice when he set off for the Trojan War. As a result Odysseus was lost at sea for fifteen years.

In Blake's painting, Athena, Goddess of Wisdom, tossed Odysseus her girdle and looked on as he, in turn, tossed it into the sea. Then the wanderer set sail, for he knew the way home.

William Blake, who had his vision while painting, valued the imagination so highly that he spoke of it as the Son of God, the Second Person of the Christian Trinity.[26] He believed that we are closest to the Creator God though our imagination, when we're engaged in the creative process. Christopher Isherwood said that art rightly practiced is a form of religion.

More authors claim William Blake as an influence on their work than any other English language writer. Blake's poetry and his Vision have been pondered by writers as diverse as William Butler Yeats, Alan Ginsberg and Joyce Carol Oates. All three had their own sudden experiences of cosmic consciousness.

The Mask in Youth - The Nurturer

With very few exceptions, family is extremely important to my Cancer Rising clients. In youth, most were eager to marry and have children. Cancer Rising women often acquired

---

24 Allan B. Chinen, "The Shining Fish, the Elder Cycle Completed," *In The Ever After: Fairy Tales and the Second Half of Life,* (Wilmette: Chiron,) 1989, 139-49.

25 as opposed to the "mundane Neptune story" which involves addiction to drugs or alcohol.

26 Kathleen Raine thinks Blake follows Jacob Boehme on the subject, *Golgonooza, City of the Imagination: Last Studies in William Blake,* (NY: Lindisfarne,) 6, that the Image of God within us is actually our imagination.

a skill that enabled them to work part time; a flexible schedule was more important than salary. Nurturing professions like nursing appealed.[27] Several were substitute teachers; others were involved with Sunday school. Some enjoyed their role as soccer moms or scout den mothers. Whenever possible, they volunteered to help handicapped children.

Several young women with a predominance of planets in Earth and Water told me that they'd prefer to be stay-at-home moms but economic pressures intervened; it took two salaries to keep afloat.

With a predominance of Air and Fire, Cancer Rising often experiences cabin fever. Working outside the home, having a schedule to juggle leaves mother less crabby for "quality time" in the evenings.

I didn't know as many young men with Cancer Rising. The ones I knew gravitated toward family law, medicine, and accounting (CPAs) Two excelled at cooking and could have been professional chefs. There were many talents in their horoscope but unfortunately they had little time to develop them.

When several Cancer Rising women told me they'd like four or more children but couldn't afford them, I consulted the database for the Ascendant to see if this desire for large families extended beyond my own clientele. It did. Cancer Rising people in the celebrity database could afford large families; many had or adopted four or more children.[28]

Columnist Jack Anderson (a Mormon) had nine; Ross Perot had five, biographer and mystery novelist Lady Antonia Fraser had six, as did Salvatore Ferragamo. Jerry Lewis had six children from his first marriage and adopted one after his second. Steven Spielberg had seven after his second marriage (a combined family) with plans to adopt more.

There would no doubt be more examples had my search extended beyond creative writers, directors, performers and CEOs. (I didn't check the data base for the other Rising Signs' children, only the Cancer archetype: home and hearth/the Fourth House.)

---

27 Psychology or social work interested a few in college, but their psychic sponge *persona* absorbed too much sadness. They appreciated the knowledge but changed majors. Only one woman client continued with psychology in graduate school.

28 Mary Wollstonecroft Shelley had three children in four years. Had her husband, Percy Bysshe Shelley not drowned, they may have had more. Natal Saturn (in Detriment) on her Ascendant enhanced her organizing skills, she edited his manuscripts and quickly got them published to support herself and her young children.

The Imaginative Mask - Cancer Rising After Midlife
The Wise Matriarch/Patriarch

Not surprisingly, children and grandchildren are a great source of joy after midlife. Unless the Moon is badly afflicted, Cancer Rising has given their children all the attention, love, and support possible. They usually come "home" to celebrate all the milestones: retirement, holidays, and those birthdays and anniversaries that end in a zero.

Children and grandchildren usually value Cancer's advice. An intuitive, Cancer may wear the Mask of Prophet, coming up with creative alternatives and imaginative solutions no one else sees. William Blake, known for his own prophetic writing, said that prophecy and poetry are gifts of the Holy Spirit. They don't belong to the ego. Cancer Rising's intuition is not always 100% accurate, but when Cancers are "on," they're "on."[29]

Most Cancer Rising parents are very proud of their adult children. If I'd come across psychiatrist George E. Vaillant's excellent study on aging earlier and asked my clients his question for men over fifty, "what have you learned from your adult children?" I'm quite sure that many Cancers would respond with Ross Perot, "I'm 100% satisfied with five out of five," and only a few would change the subject to complain about the child who disappointed them "after all we've done for him."[30]

Cancer Rising parents sometimes wonder why it seems to take their married children so long to have children of their own. Partly, it's the economy; it takes longer now to get established. But their children also might also be in awe of Cancer's parenting skills. A Cancer Rising parent can be a hard act to follow. This is especially true of horoscopes low in the Water Element.

If Cancer Rising has an Air or Fire Moon in his horoscope, it's likely their children were raised to be independent, which will give the Cancer Rising grandparent more free time. The Air or Fire Moon is probably ready for adventure: travel, a new hobby subject or sport.

With a high percentage of Earth and Water, the adult children may be more dependent. They may move in with Cancer between jobs or decide to live nearby so that Cancer can babysit. With the Moon in Earth or Water, Cancer might not mind though; playing with grandchildren can be relaxing. Several with Earth and Water Moons told me that they looked back on the time when their children were young as the happiest period of their

---

29 As example would be Elizabeth Clare Prophet who has Cancer Rising and many followers. When she's "on" she's very accurate but few psychics are "on" all the time.
30 *Aging Well: Surprising Guideposts to a Happier Life*, (NY: Little, Brown and Co,) 2002.

lives. They looked forward to re-living it again with grandchildren, this time without the pressures of earning a living.

The Leo Progression

William Blake was born with the last degree of Cancer Rising and progressed into Leo Rising when he was a year old. His Cancer Mask began to assimilate a bit more of Leo's *presence*, confidence, will power and stubbornness every year until he entered Virgo Rising close to age twenty-nine.

As the progressed Ascendant degree moved a degree deeper into Leo each year, it connected with and brought out the attributes of Blake's North Node and five Natal planets in Fire. At the age of five, for instance, it conjuncted his North Node in the First House, his sense of destiny. Before the age of ten, his progressed Ascendant had trined his Natal Sun and Jupiter in Fire in the creative Fifth House. With Jupiter in Sagittarius (Rulership) young William wanted to travel and study the Great Masters' art. However, his family couldn't afford it; he was limited to the illustrations in books. Still, he had a sense of himself as an artist at a very young age. At ten, the Ascendant degree conjuncted his first house Neptune, the planet of dreams, fantasies and Visions.

At fifteen his father apprenticed him to an engraver (the anvil and the hammer in his poem, *Tyger, Tyger* were objects present in his daily life, though they can also be read as symbols of the inner, alchemical transformation.) The apprenticeship was to last seven years.

Impatient and frustrated at twenty, when the progressed Ascendant reached the degree of his Mars-in-Leo (Second House) and trined Pluto in his Fifth[31] he wanted out of the apprenticeship early. The engraver didn't consider him ready. We associate Mars, especially in Leo, with a hot temper. They argued. He apparently left a year before the contract specified but on good terms with his employer.

Blake hung out his shingle at twenty-one and began taking commissions as an engraver and illustrator of books and catalogues. Never a commercial success, Blake did attract patrons and agents who liked his work. At twenty-two he enrolled at the Royal Academy of Art school for the six year program but disagreed with its president, Sir Joshua Reynolds, who was in Blake's view "too general and abstract." "To generalize is to be an idiot," said

---

31 Both planets were in 20 degrees. Pluto existed then of course, though it had not been officially discovered; his astrologer/landscape painter friend who did readings wouldn't have known of it.

Blake. Mars-in-Leo does not suffer fools gladly. But later Sir Joshua's opinion mattered when candidates for the Royal Academy were chosen and Blake was not.

He met and married Catherine at the age of twenty-five. They were known as a happy couple. He and his brother Robert opened a print shop together the next year. One of their first commissions was an illustrated book for Mary Wollstonecraft, Mary Shelley's mother, who belonged to the Swedenborg Church Blake attended at the time.

Within his family, he was closest to his brother Robert, nine years younger, to whom he taught most of his art and engraving techniques. His brother's death affected Natal Cancer Rising deeply; he sat alone for hours in Westminster Abbey sketching in his brother's notebook. He carried it for years, jotting down his insights and sketches. Robert appeared to him in dreams with messages about his work.

His anger at God over his brother's death brought him to the *Book of Job*. He spent a long time thinking about Job's relationship with God and working on the poems and illustrations for his own book, *Job*.

By the end of the Leo cycle, many people with First House Leo planets are like Blake, certain they're destined for fame.

The Virgo Progression

In his thirties Blake invented a new process called relief etching, to replace the earlier intaglio process. His wife taught him to color the illustrations in his books.

The progressed Ascendant aspected, over the years, five planets in Earth and Water: Cancer Moon, Uranus (known to his astrologer as Hershel, from the astronomer who discovered it) Venus and, at the last few years of the Virgo cycle, Mercury and the Natal Ascendant degree, 29 Cancer.

The Virgo progression involved squares to his Natal Sagittarian planets: Jupiter, Sun, Pluto. During this time, Blake worked on developing and illustrating his unique religious philosophy, so he wouldn't have to live by someone else's. (See the quote at beginning of the chapter.) Today his admirers consider him the greatest artist ever produced. But sadly, his peers were not as impressed.

The couple lived in very small quarters which they could barely afford. Though patrons opened their large country homes to him so he could finish their projects in comfort, Blake resisted being beholden to them. The artist who dreaded setting aside *his* projects in favor of *theirs* was always happy to return to his cramped London quarters, his wife, and his visions.

Virgo is very detail-oriented. Blake's complex personal philosophy and prophecies would be even harder to grasp without his intricately-designed illustrations. Other "detail-people" (especially Virgos) will appreciate his many long hours spent etching those lines on copper plates, hoping to share his message with the world.

But in spite of all his talent and efforts, "lesser artists" had greater recognition and commercial success. During the Virgo cycle, humility, (a virtue Blake had called "hypocrisy" during his Leo cycle,) is often developed.[32]

Around the age of sixty, as the Ascendant sextiled Natal Cancer Rising, he seems to have mellowed. Though still sensitive to criticism, he transcended his jealousies.[33] Blake met a young engraver, John Linnell, who appreciated his work and found him large, interesting projects to illustrate. They remained friends to the end.

The Libra Progression

The last ten years of Blake's life corresponded to the Libra progressed cycle. Friendship became more important to Blake as he entered the more sociable Libra period. His engraver friend Linnell and his astrologer-landscape painter friend John Varley[34] visited frequently,

He last project was Dante's Divine Comedy.

Libra is an artistic cycle. It's interesting that by the end of his life, Blake was known more as an artist than as a poet.

With his devoted wife and his friend John Linnell beside him, with angels surrounding his bedside, Blake sang joyfully during his last few hours on earth.

---

32 He was speaking of Sir Joshua's humility, which he thought pretentious at the time.

33 See James King, *William Blake, His Life*, (NY: St. Martin's Press,) 2002 on mellowing close to sixty, Blake's friendship with Linnell, and his deriving comfort from the childhood visions.

34 An unknown artist sketched John Varley, his astrologer/landscape painter friend, doing a reading for Blake. Varley told Blake that the newly-discovered planet Hershel trined Blake's Cancer Moon and indicated artistic genius. (It likely also contributed to his radicalism, so lamented by the government of his time.) Varley seemed influenced by Blake's theories in his book *Zodiacal Physiognomy* (1828.)

Cancer Rising Bibliography

Bachardy, Don and James P. White, eds., *Where Joy Resides, A Christopher Isherwood Reader,* "Goodbye to Berlin," "Kathleen and Frank," "My Guru and His Disciple" "A Single Man," (NY: Noonday Press,) 1989. Introduction by Gore Vidal.

Berg, James J. and Chris Freeman, eds., *Conversations with Christopher Isherwood,* (Jackson: University of Mississippi Press,) 2001.

Blake, William, *The Complete Illuminated Books,* (NY: Thames and Hudson,) 2005. "Tyger, Tyger," "The Angel," "The Poison Tree."

—— *Jerusalem, The Emanation of the Giant Albion.* (n.c: Kessinger,) 2004.

Chinen, Allan B., *In The Ever After, Fairy Tales and the Second Half of Life.* "The Shining Fish," (Wilmette: Chiron Publ,) 1989.

Didion, Joan, *The Year of Magical Thinking,* (NY: Vintage,) 2007.

—— *Where I Was From,* (NY: Vintage,) 2004.

Frye, Northrup, *Fearful Symmetry, A Study of William Blake,* (Princeton: Princeton University Press,) 1990. (Chapter Nine: The Refiner's Fire: Blake's Stages of Life.)

Haggard, H. Rider, *She,* (NY: Oxford University Press,) 2008.

King, James, *William Blake, His Life.* (NY: St. Martins Press,) 2002.

McEvers, Joan, *12 Times 12: 144 Sun/Ascendant Combinations,* (San Diego: ACS,) 1983.

Paley, Morton D., *Energy and the Imagination, A Study of the Development of Blake's Thoughts,* (London: Oxford University Press,) 1970.

Raine, Kathleen, *Blake and Antiquity,* (Washington D.C: National Gallery of Art,) 1977.

—— *Golgonooza, City of Imagination, Last Studies in William Blake,* (NY: Lindisfarne,) 1991.

—— *William Blake,* (NY: Thames and Hudson,) 1970.

—— *William Blake,* The World of Art Series, (NY: Thames and Hudson,) 1982.

Shelley, Mary, *Mary Shelley's Frankenstein,* (NY: W.W. Norton & Co,) 1995.

Vaillant, George E, *Aging Well: Surprising Guideposts to a Happier Life,* (NY: Little, Brown and Company,) 2003.

CHAPTER FIVE

Leo Rising - The Playful Dance of Life

Pablo Picasso, "My mother said to me, 'If you are a soldier, you will become a general. If you are a monk, you will become the Pope.' Instead, I was a painter, and became Picasso."

—— "God is really only another artist. He invented the giraffe, the elephant and the cat. He has no real style, He just goes on trying other things."

Alexander Dumas Senior, "Nothing Succeeds like Success."

Sting, "You can scratch the surface of my songs pretty lightly and you'll find someone who wanted to be James Taylor at the age of 14. He's also a brilliant and ridiculously under-rated guitar player and blessed with a voice that could melt ice caps."

—— "I want to get old gracefully. I want to have good posture, I want to be healthy and be an example to my children." (Among his reasons for yoga practice.)

Frida Kahlo, "I paint my own reality. The only thing I know is that I paint because I need to, and I paint whatever passes through my head without any other consideration."

Henri Matisse, "I do not literally paint that table, but the emotion it produces upon me."

Edouard Manet, "I need to work to feel well."

—— "It is not enough to know your craft—you have to have feeling. Science is all very well, but for us (artists) imagination is worth far more."

Edgar Cayce, "You grow to heaven. You don't go to heaven."

—— "The conquering of self is truly greater than were one to conquer many worlds."

Paramahansa Yogananda, "The happiness of one's own heart alone cannot satisfy the soul; one must try to include, as necessary to one's own happiness, the happiness of others."

—— "The season of failure is the best time for sowing the seeds of success."

The Leo Mask

I'm the Mask of royalty. When I make my dramatic entrance, heads turn and faces light up! The king or queen has arrived; let the festivities (or rehearsal or staff meeting) begin! But as soon as things become boring, I'll make my excuses and leave.

I'm the Mask for performing and visual artists. Like Edouard Manet, (above quote) my health is better when at work on a project. Like Sting, I wonder what people who lack creative outlets *do* with their intense emotions; their failures and their pain. Clinging to negative feelings is unhealthy. Actually, the stronger the emotion—be it joyful or painful—the greater the energy available for my art or my performance.

I'm also the actor's, director's and producer's Mask. (Think Aaron Spelling, Garry Marshall, and Vicki Gloor.) My desire for fame rarely diminishes with age. Even an old lion doesn't really mean it when he says, "it was such an honor to be nominated. I'm so happy for the deserving winner." Not if he's wearing *my* Mask! Proud as a lion, he knows perfectly well that *his* was the best performance !

When I cannot wear my sunny smile because of a blue mood, I prefer to stay home. A dejected lion or lioness is not a pretty sight, and besides, I dislike feeling eclipsed.

I'll call you later with my usual high energy when there's upbeat news to report. I'm generous;[1] I'll take you to lunch. You can catch me up on anything I missed by leaving the meeting early.

A loyal friend, if you help me I'll be forever grateful. I'll soon find an opportunity to return the favor. I'd love to be part of that event you're planning, but I'll need creative control over my contribution, from beginning to end. I hope your dance card isn't full and, like Zelda Fitzgerald, I hope you'll save the last dance for me.

How to recognize Leo Rising

Leo Rising is recognizable from several yards away by their regal posture and graceful gait. In the *Yoga Journal* interview with Ganga White, Sting mentioned that among his reasons for practicing yoga was to maintain his good posture with age.[2] Leo Rising Maya Angelou has a regal bearing.

Those of us familiar with William Butler Yeats' Leo Rising muse, the lovely actress Maud Gonne, may recall these lines Yeats wrote about her, looking back on her youthful

---

1 Unless Saturn is in negative aspect to the Sun or in the First House. Then Leo isn't as instinctively generous and may expect favors in return.

2 December, 1995, still posted on www.Sting.com/news/interview as of October 10, 2009. He mentioned being more energetic and flexible. Running had resulted in tight hips and hamstrings.

beauty: "Maud Gonne at Howth station waiting a train/Pallas Athena in that straight back and arrogant head/All the Olympians, a thing never known again."[3]

She often treated "Willie Yeats," as she called him, with leonine arrogance; he proposed marriage and she refused him. First she preferred a French Member of Parliament and later, the dashing hero of the Boer War and the Irish Independence movement, John MacBride.[4]

Leo Rising is recognizable by their flashing eyes, usually full of fun, but sometimes flashing in anger like Zelda Fitzgerald's when she accused her husband, Scott, of plagiarism. (She had a point, their conversations, taken from her diary, did appear in some of his novels though Scott's words were part of the conversation, too.)

Many astrologers would list the "lion's mane"—Leo's thick and well-styled hair—ahead of their flashing eyes as the dominant Leo characteristic. It's true that even if Leo shaves his heads or tattoos it, the large head is still a Leo Rising characteristic.

Yet, so much of the personality shines through the eyes: Leo's intelligence, humor and warmth. The eyes reveal whether or not Leo Rising is able to laugh at his own foibles. It's a good sign when he can. Fun-loving Zelda Fitzgerald was not a great beauty according to the couples' friend Gerald Murphy, "her beauty was all in her eyes."[5]

Lady Augusta Gregory, Yeats' patroness, found Maud Gonne arrogant. She knew that if Maud married Yeats, the beautiful actress would challenge Lady Augusta's influence over the young poet.[6] Maud Gonne spoke from her heart. She was direct and persuasive.

The heart is the organ associated with Leo. It's not only important for Leo to get things off their chests as Maud Gonne did by speaking directly, but as Leo Rising ages, it's also important to exercise regularly and watch their cholesterol.

In addition, whenever it feels as if life is getting out of balance in ways that Leo Rising is powerless to control, Leo needs an outlet. I see this so often with artistic clients. A dear

---

3 "Beautiful Lofty Things," is in Finnerman's *The Collected Works of W.B. Yeats*, cited above. He included his patroness Lady Gregory and his father, addressing a crowd from the stage of the Abbey theater in the same poem. There are photographs of Maud on the Web. She was quite beautiful.

4 MacBride was killed after the Easter Rebellion in Dublin in 1916. He told the firing squad to skip the blindfold; he was used to looking down gun barrels. His death left Maud free again.

5 Nancy Mitford, *Zelda: A Biography*, (NY: Harper and Row,) 1970, 124.

6 Lady Gregory told others that Maud was a traitor to her class, (the Anglo-Irish aristocracy) a rabble-rouser who harangued the masses with radical speeches. Lady G. was pleased when Yeats later proposed to Maud's daughter Iseult; she preferred young, malleable Iseult to Maud as a prospective bride. (Isolde refused him too; he eventually married Georgia Hyde-Lee.) Ellmann, cited above, *Yeats, The Man and the Masks*, introduction, vii-xii.

friend, an outstanding watercolorist and abstract painter, develops physical symptoms if she goes too long without a gallery show. (She has the Sun in her Sixth House.)

An extraverted Ascendant, Leo needs not only to create, but to perform or exhibit as well; to share what they've done with others.

A double Leo, (Leo Sun and Leo Rising) with nothing in the Earth Element, Zelda Fitzgerald tried desperately to find a creative direction. As much as she loved her husband, and her marriage was vitally important to her, it was not enough; she needed something for herself.[7] Their friend Gerald Murphy said that Scott neglected her.

The Queen of Jazz toured with a professional dance troop in southern France. She painted, published several short stories, wrote a play, "The Vegetables," and eventually her novel, *Save Me the Waltz.* But her husband, F. Scott Fitzgerald (Aquarius Rising) was not supportive of her creative efforts.[8] After the couple had spent years in therapy, their therapist, Dr. Meyer, noted that most of their arguments were about "the material;" they both wanted to write about the marriage.[9]

In her manic phases Zelda wrote very quickly, especially when in a facility that offered her a structured routine, like the mental institutions where she was at times confined. Her husband took seven years to finish *Tender is the Night.* He was angry that Zelda's short stories, published earlier and without his permission, had used the same anecdotes and plot as his novel-in-progress.[10]

Some astrologers associate Leo Rising with lower back pain. I've found that to occur when Leo Rising is combined with several Libran planets.[11] Most astrologers agree, I think, that Leo Rising usually has a somewhat square body shape. When asked about

---

7 Mitford, cited above, p. 160.

8 Not only Gerald Murphy but Rebecca West and Hemingway's first wife Hadley remarked about it. Hadley said, "he treated her as if her life were raw material for one of his novels." Mitford, cited above, 114.

9 Mitford, *Zelda,* cited above, pp. 1-55. The Doctor also mentioned Scott's refusal to give up drinking. 170. Scott's solution to resolving their marital difficulties was a second child to keep Zelda busy. She refused. He used her letters to him when they were young in *This Side of Paradise,* and The *Debutante:* "dull men are afraid of her intelligence and intellectual men are afraid of her beauty." When Zelda had an outbreak of eczema, a character in *Tender of the Night* developed it, 168.

10 *Ibid.,* Mitford, 218, When she published *Save Me the Waltz,* which was "hers alone," Scribners applied half the royalties to Scott's debts. Mitford, 225.

11 Saturn is exalted in Libra and rules the sacral/tailbone area. Libra is the sign of the Scales—symptoms sometimes occur in that area when life is unbalanced in one direction or another.

height, though, there was a lack of consensus: one astrologer would have short Leo Rising clients while another's would be mostly over 5'4."

The majority of mine have been 5'4" or taller with shorter Leos the exception. However, with height, as well as eye and hair color, the influence of genetics seems greater influence than that of astrology.

The Fixed Mode - Will Power and Stubbornness

Leo Rising is a Fixed Sign, and like the other Fixed Signs (Taurus, Scorpio and Aquarius) has *presence*. In Leo's case, it's star power. Leo is not ruled by a planet, but by a star called the Sun (see below, mundane ruler.) This "star power" distinguishes Leo's Mask from the other Fixed Signs, each of which has its own charisma. Unless the mundane ruler is badly afflicted, the Leo Mask exudes a type of confidence that others might envy.

Fixity is willful and stubborn. When two Fixed Signs have a confrontation, as often happens, the referee who jumps in might instinctively decide Leo Rising is right because Leo is so sure of himself. Or, the referee might conclude that Leo Rising is bullying the other person. In either case, if he asks Leo to back off and think it over, Leo usually does so quietly, unless his dignity has been threatened. He or she has been in such situations before and knows the best response is magnanimity: the King or Queen is gracious. And it works. Leo's generosity will be remembered; he will be treated generously in return.

We associate Fixity with physical stamina. Zelda's perseverance at ballet, which she began studying late, (she was twenty-seven,) revealed not only her strong will but a physical strength and stamina that surprised both her husband and her doctor.

Like the other Fixed Ascendants, Leo Rising is determined, persevering, steadfast and usually loyal to their spouse. In the opinion of her friend Gerald Murphy, Zelda Fitzgerald's extramarital love affair was designed to draw her husband's attention back to her, away from his writing and his drinking. But it might have been, at least in part, retaliation for his conduct with other women.

The Element - Fire

Leo is symbolically associated with the heart. Leo Rising goes at life passionately and wholeheartedly, unless the Sun is afflicted. Fire is courageous, sometimes even reckless. Both

Maud Gonne the Anglo-Irish radical and Zelda Fitzgerald were fearless. Scott Fitzgerald said he "fell in love with Zelda's courage, her sincerity, her flaming self-respect."[12]

Maya Angelou took a risk when she married an African. A strong-willed American woman with Leo Rising, Maya took a job as a journalist in Africa. Her husband told her that "nice women don't work" in Egypt. "I Know Why the Caged Bird Sings," resulted from her experiences.

Leo brings drama to other' lives, as Maud did for Yeats and Zelda did for Scott Fitzgerald. Michael Moore brings drama to his audiences when he takes on the Powers That Be in ironic films like "Sicko," about the American Health Care System and "Capitalism: A Love Story," about the recession and the Wall Street bailout. Singer Willie Nelson battled with the Internal Revenue Service and did a series of concerts to help farmers save their land from tax auctions.

Sting was fearless when he left *The Police* at the peak of the trio's success. He believes that God looks after creative people who take the risks necessary to their art. Both Michael Moore and Sting have Pluto in the First House, the former conjunct his Ascendant and the latter in the middle. Willie has a Mars/Neptune conjunction in Virgo at the bottom of his First House and Saturn (government organizations) opposite the Ascendant.

Many of my Leo Rising clients have Pluto-in-the-First like Sting and Michael Moore. (Pluto was in Leo for nearly thirty years.) Power is associated with Pluto. Personal power comes through Leo Rising's stance, their eyes, and their voices at job interviews or in confrontations with authority figures. The Mask conveys, "What you see is what you get. If you don't want me, I'll leave." Even when they really need the job, Leo Rising never seems desperate.

In romance, Leo Rising is spontaneous. Most, like Angelou, will risk everything for love. Leo Rising loves wholeheartedly *unless* their opposite-sex-parent cheated on the same-sex-parent. If that happens, Leo seems to have a difficult time in his first marriage. My clients have said that when "trust issues" arise, it's not so much that they don't trust their spouse as that they're not sure *marriage* works. Therapy around the relationship with the opposite sex parent sometimes helps to understand and forgive the parent, trust life and move on.

Leo Rising actor and musician Sting candidly discussed his own childhood experiences,

---

12 Mitford, cited above, 66-69. In her autobiography, Maud tells of "Willie Yeats attempting to lock her in a room for her own protection. She got away and dashed into the melee on the street below. Furious, she told him she it was cowardice to hide. Maud Gonne, *Autobiography: In Service of the Queen,* (Chicago: Univeristy of Chicago Press,) 1995, 217-18.

the "détente" between his parents and his feelings about it in his autobiography, *Sting: Broken Music.*[13]

Fire is a passionate element. Though the other two Fire Signs are passionate as well, Fixity seems to strengthen the candle wick, allowing the flame to burn without flickering for a long time.

Solar and Lunar Creativity

There's a workshop exercise my students seem to enjoy, intended to clarify the difference between the lunar creativity of Cancer Rising and Leo Rising's solar creativity. You might want to try it: close your eyes for a moment and visualize the night sky with a Crescent Moon overhead. Then change your image to a Full Moon. Now add a lake or a snowy landscape beneath. Notice the pale, silvery light the Moon casts upon the scene below.

Now release the lunar image and visualize the Sun overhead in the noonday sky. It's a hot summer day; you can feel the heat. Bring up some clouds in front of the Sun. That should be cooler. Next, slowly watch the Sun sink towards the West. Now it's shining through the clouds. There's a beautiful rainbow sunset of yellow, orange and coral hues, then the Sun makes its dramatic exit; the day comes to an end.

In this exercise, we have a visual contrast of the Moon as ruler of the night sky and the Sun as ruler of the day sky. The Moon's silvery light is more subtle, less bright than that ball of fire, the Sun, overhead in summer time.

The Moon, on the other hand moves through many phases. Poetically, we say its twenty-eight day cycle has many moods.

In this visualization we have a sense of the Sun as the source of heat and light. Practically speaking, we also know that when there's too much heat, our air conditioning bills rise and when there's too little, our heating bills climb. Even in the digital world of the Twenty-First Century, the Sun's power is vital to our lives. We depend upon it; we wouldn't survive without it.

The Sun rules the day sky as a *strong and constant light*. It looks the same to us every day. Unlike the Moon, it has no phases.

The Sun represents, symbolically, our Waking State Awareness. We associate it with

---

13 Sting, *Broken Music: A Memoir*, (NY: Dial Press,) 2003, pp. 299-300. His mother was "the archetype of the fallen woman conflated with the artistic muse;" he "vacillated between anger and devotion to her," 177.

stamina, vitality and dynamic energy, three qualities we appreciate more and more as we grow older.

In the horoscope, the Sun is analogous to the Ego. It's the central character in the cast. Just as the planets revolve around the Sun in the Solar System, in our horoscopes, they're symbolically said to revolve around the Sun Sign, the Ego, with its desires and its aversions, its ambitions and its procrastination tendencies. (Venus is the Sun's capacity to love, Mercury, it's capacity for logical thinking and communication: getting the message out, and so forth.)

The Moon rules the night sky, symbolically, our night time awareness. Unless we work the night shift, we're free from the daytime pressures of earning a living. The metabolism slows; it's time to meditate, write, study, engage in artistic projects, read or relax in front of the TV.

Then, finally we fall asleep. Our inner film producer takes over, searching through the archives of our life experience, past and present, for images and scenarios to catch the Sleeping Ego's attention. Our nocturnal producer hopes Ego will awaken retaining something —maybe just a strong feeling—from his movies (or the short trailers if he has a dream series planned.) If Ego pays attention and honors the producer's works; perhaps begins to write the dreams down, more will come.

Cancer Rising's creativity, lunar creativity, is similar to the work of the nocturnal dream producer. The Creative *Un*conscious contributes through subtle feelings, intuitions, inklings, perceptions about life and art that the Ego, moving routinely through his day with his lists and his goals may have missed.

Leo Rising's creativity is different. Solar will power is *consciously applied* as Leo Rising proceeds towards his goal.

Leo Rising's Mundane Ruler - The Sun

"Creating a Life" or "Living Life on Your Own Terms"

There's a quote attributed to Pablo Picasso, "my mother said to me, if you become a soldier, you will be a general. If you become a monk, you will be Pope. I was a painter and I became Picasso." Whether the quote is accurate or not, it suits him. Artists like Picasso, Manet and Matisse go beyond creating works of art, they invent themselves as well.[14]

---

14 Frida Kahlo and Andy Warhol also have Leo Rising.

Leo Rising may be a Mask, but a great deal of energy and effort goes into creating it, with the aid of the Sun Sign. If unafflicted, the Natal Sun delights in its public *persona* however "unapologetic, arrogant and cocksure," as Sting called the collective Mask of his group, *The Police*.[15] It's fascinating to watch Leo Rising friends and clients invent and re-invent themselves over time, sometimes by changing regions of the country or even citizenship.

Leo Rising often leaves home by their mid-twenties for the big city and the bright lights in search of fame. Sting (Gordon Sumner) is another example. Unlike Zelda, though, Sting came from a working class family. Born in Wallsend, between Newcastle and the North Sea, he set out for London at twenty-six with his wife Frances and his infant son. By then, he'd had a variety of experiences, a wealth of material for songs. A credentialed teacher, Sting had taught nine-year-old children, taught jazz, and had done myriad gigs. He'd played a cruise ship.

En route to London, his family asleep in the back seat of the car, he realized that the other members of his band weren't going to join him. They wouldn't risk uprooting themselves from their day jobs, or live in squalid housing in pursuit of their dream.[16] Like Zelda with Scott Fitzgerald, he was happy that he had Frances. Re-inventing yourself can be a lonely process. In his late twenties, though, fame arrived with *The Police*, a trio with Sting as lead songwriter, lead singer and bassist. Frances found acting work in two BBC dramas. Sting's song, "So Lonely," was updated with new chords.

Over the course of the next decade, Sting would move from jazz to punk, then to pop music with reggae overtones, and finally to rock. His progressed Mask would incorporate dynamic Mars-in-Leo and by the mid 1980's, Venus-in-Virgo in his Second House. As a songwriter, his royalties increased; his adaptability and resilience were rewarded.[17]

In the 1980's he left the group to record his first solo album featuring Branford Marsallas, *The Dream of the Blue Turtles*.[18] He also continued with acting in *Dune*, *Plenty* (with Tracey Ulllman) and *Stormy Monday* (with Melanie Griffith.) His song, "Here Comes the Sun," is a good fit for the Leo Rising Mask.

Sting been elected to both the Songwriters' and the Rock and Roll Hall of Fame and has won many music awards, including a Golden Globe for his song, *Demolition Man*.

But Sting is not simply out-for-fame, or satisfied with creating a successful life for himself

---

15 *Broken Music*, cited above, 301.

16 Sting, *Broken Music*, 225.

17 Eventually Gerry, one member of his original band did move to London but Sting was with *The Police* then, and the trio didn't need a keyboard player. *Broken Music*, 268.

18 The group got together again in 2007 for a world tour.

and living it on his own terms. Sting has done many benefits for Amnesty International and environmental groups. In addition to his creative and altruistic interests, Sting has a spiritual practice, yoga, which he hopes to continue the rest of his life.

The Esoteric Ruler - The Sun as the Higher Self

In esoteric astrology the Sun rules Leo Rising at two different levels. At the mundane level (see above) the Sun represents the Ego. During the First Half of Life, while the Ego acquires the credentials and/or skills it needs to earn a living and support a family, Leo Rising is ruled by the Sun at the mundane level.

At the same time, the Ego also builds a public *persona* as a shield, to deflect criticism and pain while focusing on creating a life. Leo's Mask adapts in response to transits to the First House; to the Sun Sign, and the rest of the horoscope. New people come into our lives, old friends move on; the culture changes around us. Leo Rising, becomes more flexible.

Many people continue at the mundane level their entire lives; they're only interested in collecting more material possessions and greater worldly success. Their Mask sometimes hardens into a suit of mail. They go on in the same direction, incensed that a new generation with new ideas has begun to replace them.

But there are others with Leo Rising who are more alert to the waning of the Ego's desires and ambitions after fifty. Risk takers by nature, they wonder what's next; they're excited about the Unknown Future. They may be altruistic and/or develop an interest in spirituality; become Seekers on the path to Wholeness, Enlightenment or Realization. These are people who respond to the *esoteric Sun.*

People who listen and respond to the Higher Self will soon find themselves using their talents and skills on behalf of others. Like Henri Matisse who created a chapel with colorful stained glass windows for a community of nuns. He saw a need; he had the talents, the time and the resources to meet it.[19]

The talent is the one that brings you the greatest joy. When Henri Matisse saw a palette of colors for the first time as a child, he knew instantly that he'd become an artist. When Sting found a guitar left behind by an uncle who emigrated to Canada, he, too, had found his path.

---

19 Peter Schjeldahl, "Art As Life: The Matisse We Never Knew," *The New Yorker,* August 29, 2005, 78-82. He told his biographer, Francoise Gilot, that he was more a Buddhist than a Christian, but he wanted to do the chapel for his friend.

In the same way, in the Second Half of Life, opportunities come to us and we have the time to pursue them. We'll recognize the *right* one as coming from the Soul, the Higher Self. The task not only has our name on it, but doing it makes us happy. There are no "shoulds" or "oughts" involved.

There are tangents, though, from the esoteric path. Even Edgar Cayce, a man with a generous heart who received his gift and his guidance early in life[20] can sometimes drift off course.

Edgar Cayce was born with Leo Rising, Uranus (in Detriment) on the Ascendant, Pluto in his Tenth House closely squared his Ascendant and an Exalted Taurus Moon at the Zenith of his horoscope. The Sun, ruler of Leo Rising, was in his Eighth House, in Pisces, a Water Sign.

A psychic Water House esoterically, the Eighth House is also strong at the mundane level. It represents others' financial resources (investor's money) immovable property (minerals, commodities, stocks, and so forth.) So, Cayce was blessed with both spiritual potential and potential for mundane success.

In addition to the Moon, Mars and Venus were also in their Signs of Exaltation: he would consistently draw what he needed, opportunities and supporters would abound. His challenge was to discern *which* people and *which* projects to take on. Turning people away is difficult for Mutable Pisces. Discrimination is also a challenge for Pisces especially when the planet of logic, Mercury, is in Detriment as Cayce's was.

With Jupiter in the Sign of its Fall, three Exalted planets, and two Detriments, a total of six planets are Dignified by Sign placement. In addition, with the Sun in the Eight House ruling his Leo Mask, Cayce's is a fascinating story about a collaboration between the mundane Sun (Ego) and the Higher Sun (Self); between the esoteric and the mundane.

Like many Pisceans, Edgar Cayce grew up in a religious environment.[21] He had tremendous faith in God and in Life, but his Piscean Nature needed to develop a consistent belief *in itself*.

Uranus on the Ascendant accentuated his Leo Rising restlessness and enhanced his

---

20 Edgar was twelve when he received an answer to his prayer-question: "does God answer prayers?" He saw a figure in a bright light, which "may have been an angel," and heard a voice, "You will have your wish. Remain faithful. Be true to yourself. You will help the sick and the afflicted." Sidney D. Kirkpatrick, *Edgar Cayce: An American Prophet*, (NY: Riverhead-Penguin,) 2000, 37.

21 Cayce was a lifelong member of the Disciples of Christ and taught Sunday School. Believing in Atlantis and reincarnation distinguished him from most Fundamentalist Christians, however, as did his trance diagnoses.

optimism. It also symbolized his openness to unusual people; their techniques, ideas, and goals.

It was his practice to read the Bible through once for every year of his life, a good practice for staying centered. Born in the small town of Hopkinsville, Kentucky, Cayce's formal education ended with the ninth grade.[22] He worked in a bookstore and a dry goods shop on Main Street.

At the turn of the Twentieth Century he tried to sell insurance in partnership with his father but got such a severe case of laryngitis he was unable to speak at all. A traveling hypnotist cured him temporarily but the post-hypnotic suggestion failed to take; the condition returned.

Doctor Al Layne, a local hypnotist had better success with an initial session and follow-ups when relapses occurred. His diagnosis, "psychological paralysis," made me smile. Several Pisces clients have developed unusual and recurring symptoms which prevented them from doing something "psyche" didn't want to do, usually something recommended by a family member or career counselor. While the ego would like to please dad or the counselor, the Higher Self knows it's the wrong direction, so the unconscious responds with symptoms affecting the body part involved. For Cayce, it was the vocal chords. It's impossible to sell insurance when you can't speak.

He could, however, apprentice himself to the local photographer and wander from town-to-town practicing his craft until he found a place to settle.

Dr. Layne, fascinated with the theories of Franz Mesmer, found Cayce an unusual subject. In the hypnotic trance he spoke of himself as "we," not "I," or referred to "the body."

Layne asked Cayce, when in trance, about Layne's symptoms and received diagnostic advice. He next suggested that Edgar begin a trance-diagnostic practice and charge fees. Layne was certain that Cayce could soon afford to leave home and be independent. And Cayce, with Leo Rising and Uranus on his Ascendant wanted his independence. Yet he was certain that he was "not supposed to charge" for his gift. He could ask for donations, but he couldn't charge patients. He was adamant about it.

Layne then suggested Cayce offer free sessions to the public. As soon as he did, word spread in the press about "the miracle worker." Soon letters began to arrive and Cayce, by then able to put himself into a light trance on his couch, discovered that he could diagnose at a distance. (He needed the exact address though, otherwise he found himself diagnosing the letter-writer's neighbor instead.)

---

22 Cayce was born in 1877. This was common at the time for children of working-class parents.

He also discovered that he could not only access the diagnosis but the remedy as well. The archive[23] he accessed included prescriptions. However, certain ingredients proved difficult to locate; he sometimes needed to ask The Source for a substitute available where the patient lived. But on the whole, Cayce's practice was going smoothly. His clients were being healed and his reputation was growing.

His wife and eventually his son managed the record-keeping and correspondence. As the volume of patients increased, he hired a secretary, Gladys Davis, who remained loyal to him for the rest of her life. She recorded the trance readings in shorthand.[24]

By the 1920's Leo Rising Cayce had reached the peak of his fame. A cotton merchant offered him a hundred dollars a day just to watch the cotton market. He refused, though he regretted losing the security. The Cayces often wished Edgar had a salary.

Treasure hunters appeared, and gamblers wanted to know the outcome of sports events. He refused them. (When he experimented, The Source did not cooperate. His accuracy as a prophet was no better than random odds.) It was clear his gift was intended only for healing purposes.

One day a philosophical client, Arthur Lammers, asked The Source several questions through Cayce. When he was later shown the transcription of Lammers' reading, including the validity of reincarnation, Cayce suffered confusion and depression: a crisis of conscience. He was shocked that The Source had validated reincarnation. Cayce believed The Source to be The Lord, Jesus Christ.

It was clearly not Cayce who came up with this heresy! He had no memory at all of that session or any of the others. Afterwards, when the topic came up again in readings, Cayce felt he had to accept The Source at His word.

Then, in 1915, The Source gave Cayce a personal message: "Move to Virginia Beach." By that time, however, he was inundated by clients who had projects of their own: Wall Street brokers interested in commodities, Texas oil men looking to find new wells. If he found the wells, the Texans would finance his move to Virginia Beach and the healing facility he dreamed of founding. Surely if he helped others first, his own plans would soon fall into place.

There were also several interesting puzzles to solve: Could he find Amelia Earhart or a missing ship, the Lusitania? Amelia's husband George Putnam asked for Cayce's help. The Source found the latitude and longitude of the plane crash, and indicated that she had made it out of the plane alive and lived for a short time. An airplane and bones were

---

23 known as the Akashic records.
24 She started in 1923. Her records are still available. The total number of diagnostic readings that survived (in the vault) is 14,256. See Sidney D. Kirkpatrick, cited above, 525.

found at the coordinates, an anthropologist identified the bones as Amelia's and said it appeared that she *had* lived to walk some distance from the plane. The Source located the Lusitania[25] off the coast of Ireland and found that no munitions were stored on it, contrary to the allegations. Though quite pleased with The Source's accuracy, it seems Edgar went without a monetary reward.

Edgar thought perhaps he could find the Lindbergh baby; the reward offered would solve his financial problems. But he discovered that The Source would only cooperate if someone in the family had asked him to find a loved one. Unlike Amelia's husband, the Lingberghs hadn't asked his help. The Source did not cooperate.

Time passed. Edgar was caught up in others' problems and the mysteries of his period. In 1924, nine years after The Source had told Edgar to move to Virginia Beach, he and his son Hugh Lane went there to look at property. But the small, inexpensive village The Source had recommended in 1915 was becoming a very expensive resort during the Roaring Twenties! Stunned at the prices, they went ahead with Edgar's dream: the Cayces persuaded the Blumenthals and other wealthy clients to help them buy the land.

It was 1927 before Gladys and the Cayces moved to Virginia Beach. Morton Blumenthal helped organize the group that funded the hospital. Construction was underway in 1929, the year of the Great Depression.

Blumenthal and the other major other donors lost everything. Cayce was fifty-four when the property went into receivership, the equipment was sold and his family evicted. After moving across town, their utilities were shut off during the unusually cold winter of 1932. Bewildered and depressed, Edgar's laryngitis returned along with abdominal pain. The Cayces joined a prayer group. Gladys, his secretary, wrote the members of Blumenthal's foundation, by then called the A.R.E.[26] A generous response helped them survive the Depression.

In addition to finances, Cayce worried about his son, Hugh Lynn, in the military. In spite of advice from The Source and his family. Edgar increased the number of readings. The Source also told him to quit smoking, (he smoked two packs a day) eating pork and other high-fat food; to return to his daily walks along the beach. But Cayce's habits didn't

---

25 However, all the other sources consulted still consider her missing in spite of the anthropologist's findings. For the reading on the Lusitania, see the Internet link: <u>Cayce's Treasures and Ghosties of Lusitania,</u> available as of October 13, 2009. On Earhart, see Kirkpatrick, cited above, 485. Putnam had Amelia declared legally dead in 1939 and remarried the same year.

26 Association for Research and Enlightenment. Kirkpatrick, cited above, pp. 172-174. Today Cayce's work is studied in 34 countries. His dream was realized in 2006 when the A.R.E. established the Edgar Cayce Hospital in Virginia Beach, Virginia. (There is a photo of it in the Wikipedia article, "Edgar Cayce.")

change. By the time of his second heart attack in 1944, The Source was asking, *"how will you make him follow this diet?"* Nobody in the room had an answer.

The year that Edgar was sixty (his Jupiter Return year) the Source finally revealed who, among Jesus' disciples, Edgar had been. answering a question he'd had from the time he accepted reincarnation. As soon as he woke, the others told him he was Lucius (Luke) of Cyrene. Surprisingly, he was the author of the *Gospel* and *Acts,* not Luke the physician. He said it was his best birthday present ever.

Fortunately, Cayce lived long enough to finish his book, *There is a River.* (1943). He died in January 1945 at the age of sixty-eight. The day before his death he asked his wife, Gertrude, if she knew he loved her. She said she did. He told her that he'd never really sacrificed anything for her, and love usually involves sacrifice.[27]

His son Hugh Lynn helped organize and publish many of the readings as *The Search of God.* Many famous individuals, Elizabeth Kubler-Ross, Steven Spielberg and Elvis Pressley among them, have been influenced by the material. Edgar Cayce's work lives on.[28]

Two other esoteric horoscopes should be noted: the charts of Sri Aurobindo Ghosh (a double Leo) and Paramahansa Yogananda (Sun in Capricorn.) Both have Leo Rising when calculated with the Tropical Placidus formula.

So often when clients with Leo Rising and planets in Water Signs or Water Houses (4, 8, and 12) come to readings, they're already aware they have a psychic gift. Some discovered it in early childhood, as Cayce did at twelve. They may also know what the Higher Self has in mind for them as Cayce was told to help the sick and afflicted. And that there are certain limits placed upon its use. (Like Cayce, Water Sign clients will tell me that The Source, the Lord, The Holy Spirit, or their Guru "wouldn't want me to use my gift" for mundane purposes.)

If like Cayce's, the Sun is in Pisces, they tend to believe that their mundane needs will be automatically taken care of as long as they use their gift properly. Something ugly like bankruptcy will never happen to them: they're protected through their link to the Higher Self. They pray; they read the *Bible* or the *Bhagvad Gita.* They believe that in due time, the way will open for them, probably through the people they've helped. Several of their friends and clients are wealthy and successful. (Leo Rising often draws celebrities.)

As most Pisceans see it, there's a very thin membrane between themselves and others. Pisceans usually see themselves as cells in the larger Cosmic Organism. And Pisces senses that the Organism will feed every cell if we all simply do our part.

---

27 Neptune, the planet associated with sacrifice, rules Pisces at the mundane level.
28 Three million people have read *In Search of God.* Volumes I-II are now available as CD.

Since they know this already, I sometimes wonder why they're in my office, and then I remember my role in their process. The Oracle's role, as they see it, is to validate the direction they're about to take. Is it a tangent, a one-way-street, or the road to success?

And I think of Edgar Cayce, "maybe I'll solve my financial problems by finding the Lindbergh baby; there's a reward. Oops, that didn't work." And then, "Oh! I know, I'll find the Texan his oil well, then he'll have the money to help me! Oh. That didn't work, either. But oil wells have nothing to do with the gift of diagnosis. *Which, of course I already knew!*" And time passes.

And I'll remind the client, "time is passing. Perhaps your Source sees a more *direct* route to your goal than you do. It seems your goal is contingent on the success of your celebrity friend or a family member. Maybe there's an alternative here in *your own* timing, a *more direct* path to success. Why not ask the grateful friend to help you *now?*" And Pisces says, "Oh! I couldn't do *that.*" I point out that the *Leo Rising* lifetime is a good lifetime to try! And then I tell them what Cayce learned: the Blumenthals and his other clients were better able to help him in 1915 than in 1929. It's important to act on the inner guidance.

Creating the Mask of Success
Leo Rising in Youth

How does Leo Rising go about Mask-building? I want to be a famous Olympian skater. "I'll get up every day at 4 am and find an adult to take me to the skating rink," says the athletic Leo Rising child. If he perseveres—and Leo Rising is a stubborn, determined child—and if the adult continues to be supportive, Leo has a shot at achieving his goal.

"I want to be a ballerina," says the Leo Rising child. "but Mom (or Dad) can't afford lessons, so I'll ask Grandma." "This is how I want to be seen; this is the way I'll draw others to me," says the Leo Mask. The Leo *persona* is a tremendous help to the Sun Sign. And Leo is ruled *by the Sun,* the Natal Sun's House, Sign and aspects come into play, just as the Moon's do for Cancer. They give the Mask its color and texture.

In youth, Leo Rising usually seizes his opportunity to create a life for himself, a life he can live on his own terms. Zelda, the "wild and reckless" debutante daughter of the socially prominent Judge Sayre, loved to dance. She met a handsome young soldier, F. Scott Fitzgerald, at a ball in her hometown, Montgomery, Alabama. Her father didn't like him. Scott was from the wrong religion and the wrong social class. He'd dropped out of Princeton to write and travel. If she married him, Zelda would leave Alabama. And how could Fitzgerald support her?

To Leo Rising Zelda, the marriage proposal was an exciting opportunity and Scott a kindred spirit. With him, she could realize her dreams; develop her talents, see the world and meet interesting people. She had wealthier suitors than Fitzgerald, but he shared her sense of adventure.

A double Leo, Zelda had stamina, vitality, courage, confidence, zest for life and a very strong will. A spontaneous young woman, Zelda married Scott in spite of her father's views.

My California practice brought me many clients with Leo Rising, who like Zelda and Sting left their "boring" region of the country in search of fame. Like Sting, they were constantly updating their techniques and re-furbishing their Masks. Like Zelda and Sting, they usually had the courage to find a fearless, adventurous, optimistic spouse.

They were doubly blessed if their mate had business sense. Sting's first wife Frances had it but Scott Fitzgerald did not. (Alas, his Exalted Taurus Moon, completely invested in his work, was his only Earth.) We could say, because his Moon was in the home (House Four) that it symbolized his ideal Goddess, but Zelda was no Earth Mother. Their daughter, Patricia Scott Fitzgerald was raised by a series of nannies.[29]

The Leo Mask Over Fifty
Individuation and Wholeness

Zelda Fitzgerald said later in life (after she left Scott and returned to Montgomery,) that as a young woman she saw him as sophisticated and herself as provincial. She also said that he turned out to be less reliable than she'd expected. To Zelda, with a Void in the Earth Element, Scott's Fourth House Taurus Moon must have felt very solid. His alcoholism and philandering may have come as a shock, even in Paris during the Roaring Twenties.

The Leo Mask may seem similar to Terry Cole-Whittaker's Aries *persona*, ("what you think of me is none of my business,") because like the Aries Mask, the Leo Mask will also shrug off pain by pretending it doesn't matter. Sadly, the pretense goes on for years in unhappy marriages. So much energy goes into preserving the Mask of Success, energy which could be put to more creative purposes.

For Zelda, the price of individuation was leaving Scott. At the end of her life, back in her family home with a servant to care for her, she still spoke with Scott on the phone

---

29 Though Maud Gonne and Lady Gregory disliked each other, Yeat's patron gave Maud a piece of good advice about her fiance, John MacBride: keep your income separately from his. She did, fortunately. As a result, Maud was able to leave him when he became physically abusive.

almost every day. Though they couldn't live together compatibly, they missed each other. Scott once remarked that he'd known a great many women, but he'd never met anyone else like Zelda.[30]

In her old age, Zelda's stories of her years in Paris as Queen of Jazz held young men spellbound. Later, some of them couldn't recall *which* famous writer she'd been married to ("was it was Hemingway?") but they loved to come to the house and listen while Zelda talked.

As a young man, Henri Matisse, had told his fiancee that though he loved her, he would always love art more. He lived to eighty-four with the same joy in and commitment to art. During his last years on earth he developed a new process for his book, *Jazz*. He used a scissors and made cutouts, creating "a union of color and shape." And he designed a chapel with brightly colored windows, financing the project himself.[31]

Sting is getting older too, he'll be fifty-eight in October 2009, beginning his Second Saturn Return, a period of introspection and change similar to Saturn's First Return at twenty-eight, but this time Saturn's cycle will be followed at sixty by the Jupiter Return, a wisdom cycle that may include pilgrimage travel.

Sting seems to have mastered many Saturn lessons already. According to his memoir, *Broken Music* published at fifty-four, he has learned more from his failures than his "gigantic successes," and he's aware of the similarities between his mother's restlessness and his own. He also recognizes how his public *persona* shields him from pain.

Jupiter also symbolizes rituals, so perhaps a fitting memorial to his parents, whose funerals he missed will happen around the time of Sting's sixtieth birthday. Fortunately, he was able to say goodbye while they were still alive.

The Leo Mask, more than any other takes energy to maintain. Leo is constantly designing, updating, polishing and re-inventing the Mask.

Professional success has resulted in several Leo Rising clients and their spouses becoming ships that pass in the night, busily keeping to their own schedules. That can be changed on the Jupiter cycle. It's a good time to re-define "success" for the Second Half of Life; and to let the Mask reflect the new definition.

The Fifth House is analogous to the Fifth Sign, Leo, symbolizing of creativity: body, mind, and spirit. When Leo Rising has good relationships with them, Leo's children often turn out to be his most important creations, his greatest blessing and his source of happiness in later years.

30 Mitford, cited above, 81.

31 He did it for a former model who had become a nun. The other nuns were shocked when they first saw it. Peter Schjeldahl, cited above, 78-82.

Playfulness helps to keep body and soul together longer. Though Leo Rising may not have had time to play when his children were young, he often makes up for lost time with his grandchildren.

In honor of my Leo Rising friends and clients who love to dance; in appreciation to Henri Matisse, who created "Dance I" and "Dance II," and in memory of Zelda Fitzgerald, "princess" and debutante, this story was selected for Leo Rising:

The Ruined Dancing Shoes

This type of fairy tale about a king in his later years is a good one for Leo Rising during the Second Half of Life. There are many stories about old kings in poor health who have marriageable daughters. In this one, too, the king's vitality is waning. However, he seems more concerned about his daughter's health and happiness than his own.

As the story unfolds and we leave the castle we'll see that the kingdom's security and prosperity have already begun to decline; things have been getting worse for a long time; the daughter's dilemma must be resolved quickly.

This king did not hang on to his power by designing impossible tasks for the suitors as kings have done in similar tales. Nothing would have made him happier than for a suitor to heal the princess, marry her and take over the kingdom.

But the suitors had stopped coming. It's not that she was ugly or looking for the perfect mate; it was as if she'd been bewitched. The princess was very pale and growing weaker; she slept all day long. Though the king locked her in her room at night, she somehow managed to escape. Where did she go?

Her father's only clue was that she loved to dance. Every morning, he found twelve pairs of ruined dancing shoes in the corner of her bedroom. In the past, he had assigned the suitors to watch her at night, follow her and stop the compulsive dancing that consumed her energy. But none succeeded. The next morning he found them sound asleep in her chair. So, he had them executed. After all, they had spent the night with his daughter and claimed they couldn't remember what had transpired. They all failed to save her.

Finally, a new suitor arrived. He gained the king's respect and approval quickly, Perhaps the king intuited that this one was wiser.

The king was not aware the young man had encountered a mysterious stranger who had provided him a magic wand of invisibility and a large, magical sack.

Because he liked this young man, the king changed the rules slightly. "The other suitors had only one night—one chance—to rescue her; you will have three nights. But I must warn you that if you fail, I'll have to kill you. So try to stay awake."

Conscious awareness is essential!

As soon as he walked through the bedroom door, the suitor knew that room was a dangerous place. He could feel a spell, yet he was unable to resist it. No matter how hard he tried to stay awake, the first two nights he fell soundly asleep.

The king was angry and impatient in the mornings as he pointed out the twelve pair of newly-shredded shoes.

The third night the suitor was drowsy when suddenly he saw a girl in a white dress by the bed. He heard her whisper to the princess, "I'll make sure he's fast asleep, then we'll go."

He feigned sleep as the girl-in-white stuck a golden needle into his heel. He managed not to wince as he watched the two young women shove back the bed and leave through a hidden door behind it.

He got up quickly, put the needle in his pocket and followed them down the steps behind the bedroom into a dark forest.

He could hear the ghost-white-girl from a distance. "She looks like a foggy cloud," he thought.

"It's only the wind," she was saying to the princess, *"No one is following us."*

On the outskirts of the castle they passed through three eerie forests. The inhabitants of the villages had been petrified into trees of diamonds, silver and gold; their farms overgrown with foliage. He stopped long enough to pick a twig from each forest as evidence.

He saw a lake ahead. He hurried to catch up with them as the cloud-like-girl and the princess climbed into a rowboat. He lifted his invisibility wand. They neither saw nor felt him climb in.

The cloud-girl rowed them to the other side of the lake, where the Troll lived in his big, dark mansion. Still invisible, he followed them inside.

They entered the dining room, where the princess joined her host. Soon they were served on golden plates and using golden silverware. The Troll asked the princess why she was late. She told him she kept stopping to look behind her, she had felt someone following them.

"Ridiculous!" said the Troll, thinking, "nobody could resist that spell I put on the bedroom."

As soon as the princess had eaten, the suitor put her plate and utensils into his magical bag. At first the others looked for them, but soon it was time for dancing and they gave up.

As usual, the princess became caught up in the motion. She went thought the twelve pair of slippers quickly. At the end, she always saved the last dance for the Troll. She picked up the twelve pair of ruined shoes and left.

Back in the castle, the suitor fell asleep in his chair, wondering what the ruined shoes meant. "They're somehow connected to her pale skin and loss of vitality," he thought, "but *how?*"

The next thing he knew, the king arrived and woke him, demanding to know what transpired the night before; demanding he heal the princess. But the suitor remembered nothing.

"Well, then, you'll meet the same fate as the others," said the king. "I'll have my servant summon the executioner."

"No! Wait!" shouted the suitor, looking down at his magic sack which neither the king nor the servant could see. And the others watched, astonished, as he pulled out the items one-by-one: the twigs from the trees, the golden plates and the utensils. His evidence, together with the magical sack and the ruined shoes now made sense to the king.

Relived at his daughter's cure, the king decided to schedule the wedding right away. Soon he would share his responsibility for the kingdom with the bridegroom. For a moment he was blissfully happy.

But then the suitor said, "Wait, Your Majesty. *First she must give me her thimble.*"

This is the crucial moment in the story. Leo is about will power, free will, and conscious intent. She must agree to give him something he needs. The princess cannot be redeemed without her consent.

For the princess, her father, the inhabitants of the kingdom and the suitor to move on, she must first give up the King of the Underworld who flattered her; who served her on gold utensils, danced so seductively and made her feel so special. She must not only stop dancing with the Troll but also give up the atmosphere he created to seduce her: the life-style and the perquisites.

Will she be as intrigued with her new husband and her new life as she was with the seductive Troll and his mansion on the lake? Or would the young man seem boring after the fantasy?

Sometimes the lifestyle around the Troll is more seductive than the Troll himself. The suitor knew that as long as the Troll was still at large, she wouldn't be safe and their life together wouldn't be secure.

But she made her choice; she gave the suitor her thimble. In doing so, she chose waking-state-reality over the dream world. With her thimble and the gold needle, still in his pocket from the night before, the suitor went forth. He stabbed the seductive Troll and poured Troll blood into the thimble. On his way back, he sprinkled blood in the three forests. As soon as he saw the frozen people thawing out, he knew the princess would be safe.

And sure enough! When he sprinkled her with Troll blood, the anemic dreamer became a lively, rosy-cheeked vital young woman. Her humanity had been restored.

And of course they married. They ruled the neglected lands for awhile. Eventually, the old king died and the young couple inherited the kingdom.

After reading this story in Marie-Louise von Franz's *Archetypal Patterns in Fairy Tales*, I dreamed of a room full of whirling dervishes trance-dancing, though I hadn't done Sufi dancing since the 1970's. Dance is a wonderful metaphor for an altered state of consciousness. It's a sacred ritual in many cultures. When Margaret Mead observed trance-dancing in the Pacific Islands, she felt that village harmony was somehow restored after antagonists had come together in a community dance, losing themselves in the motion.

But the princess had taken things a bit too far.

Von Franz[32] sees the story as linked to the diurnal motion of the Earth on its axis which gives us day and night. The twelve pair of shoes are the twelve nocturnal hours, though we don't actually spend twelve hours sleeping. I like to think, myself, that the princess danced her way through the twelve Signs of the Zodiac every night.

Astrologers will recognize it as a Solar story from the gold utensils and the needle. Gold is the Sun's metal. It's also about *doing, being in motion*. Sleep bored the princess. But her blind spot was lack of confidence in her Lunar side. Though she did stop several times and look behind her, she disregarded the signals from her intuition. She was easily convinced by the Troll's representative that she'd imagined it; that nobody was following her. She heard what she wanted to hear, "It's nothing dear, go enjoy dinner and dancing in the lovely lakeside mansion."

While keeping her enthralled, the Troll was stealing her vitality with his spell. He thought he had everything under control; nobody could break his spell. Proud and arrogant, The Troll knew she bought into his drama and his dance; she'd protect his secrets.

If we apply this to life, what are the atmosphere and the spell? It depends on the Troll. For Leo Rising. Aquarius is on the Seventh House Cusp. Symbolically, this means he's somewhat glib. He seems to have life under control. Though he may be a high-functioning alcoholic, people say, he "just a social drinker; he does well at work." If he's a cheating

---

32 Daryl Sharp, ed., (Toronto: Inner City Books,) 1977, pp. 9-73.

spouse, everyone says he's "just a flirt" while he tells the ladies that he and his wife "have an arrangement; she doesn't care if I see other women."

The Troll is so charming that his girl friends want to believe him about "the arrangement." That way they're not embarrassed when they encounter his wife at a party. Once his spell is cast, it seems difficult for everyone to give up the fantasy.

The Leo Rising Progression

People born with an early degree of Leo Rising, like Zelda Fitzgerald, have nearly thirty years to build a strong Leo Mask. Zelda assimilated Mercury (communication, humor) into the Mask in early childhood. She was no doubt a precocious child.

During Zelda's childhood, the progressed Ascendant[33] contacted her Sagittarian planets in the Creative Fifth House. Her Mask was zany, reckless and fun-loving.

She loved Scott wholeheartedly and saw their life together as an adventure. When she was hurt, angry or felt neglected, she shrugged off her pain and wore the Mask of Happy Wife and Member of the Perfect Couple, though everyone knew Scott was an alcoholic and a "womanizer."

Sting was born with ten degrees of Leo on his Ascendant, close to the middle of the Sign. His Mask had twenty years to develop. His assertive public *persona* included Mars (competitive edge) and Pluto (power) in Leo. Though he attended parochial school, he had no qualms about cutting class to pursue music. His Mask was courageous, he was willing to take risks. Like most of my Leo Rising clients, he seems to have hidden his fears, guilt, anxiety and personal pain behind it.

Maya Angelou was born in a late degree of Leo Rising. With Neptune conjunct her Ascendant, she's a born story-teller. Living in the segregated South, Maya's Leo Ascendant was constantly on the defensive in her youth. However, she developed a useful Mask for her era and her circumstances: The Mask of Bravado, ideal for a civil rights activist and head of the Northern California S.C.L.C.

The Virgo Progression

Zelda, who never wanted to grow old, had a prolonged adolescence. She began to study

---

33 her Progressed Sun, also in early Leo.

ballet at twenty-seven, very late for a woman who aspired to perform. Close to the same time she progressed into Virgo, she went through the (disciplined) Saturn Return transit. She went at ballet with great determination in spite of a total lack of encouragement from her husband and her doctor. She performed in Southern France.

Zelda told a therapist her perfect day would include exercise, (tennis or swimming) ballet, painting and writing, but *not* reading. She "hated to read." (She pretended she never read her husband's books, though from her conversation it was clear that she had.)

Reading is usually a source of enjoyment during the Virgo progression. However, in Zelda's case, Mercury (Virgo's ruler) close to her Natal Ascendant came out as manic bursts of writing.

Zelda wrote a play which her husband claimed would require 13 hours to perform! She suffered from stress and nervous tension and was hospitalized several times. Institutional life provided Zelda the routine she needed to write six short stories and her novel, *Save Me The Waltz.* At home, she seemed lonely and looked forward to entertaining.

Maya Angelou became a progressed Virgo at the age of eight. She won a scholarship to study dance and drama at thirteen. Maya read everything from Shakespeare to the Russian novelists.

She became pregnant at 16. She and her son Guy grew up together. With no financial assistance from his father and sporadic help from her own family, she determined to pay his tuition through college.

Maya's Natal Leo Mask wanted to be glamorous. Meanwhile, the practical Virgo progressed Mask wanted to study acting, dance and (eventually) foreign languages while working full time and raising her son alone.

Virgo is a Mutable cycle. The thirty-year Virgo Progression usually develops resilience and resourcefulness through humble, low-paying jobs (Zelda Fitzgerald is the exception to the rule!) Maya cooked at fast food and Creole restaurants; briefly became a Madam for two lesbians, was a San Francisco Street Car conductor and a Calypso-style nightclub performer. As she gained experience, she discovered she had both stage presence and star power. Her Progressed Ascendant sextiled Natal Pluto in 1951.

By the 1950's, about halfway through the Virgo Progression, Maya had become a professional dancer, touring in *Porgy and Bess.* She was also in Jean Genet's play, *The Blacks,* with James Earl Jones.

Ten years later, in the last decate of Virgo Rising, the progressed Ascendant opposed Natal Venus-in-Pisces (Exalted.) She fell in love and married. She and her son moved to

Cairo with her husband, an African politician who didn't want his wife to work.[34] She quickly learned two African languages.

His entertainment budget left them almost nothing for household expenses; creditors were knocking at her door. Maya took a job with the newspaper despite her husband's views. He lost face. It was the end of their marriage.

They left Cairo for Ghana, where her son enrolled in college. Maya managed to pay his tuition from her meager salary as an university administrative assistant and part time work at a local newspaper.

In 1965 she heard that an old friend, Malcolm X needed an organizer. Her son was settled in school; his tuition was paid. It seemed time to go home. While she visited her mother in San Francisco, planning to continue on to New York to Malcolm, he was assassinated.

As Sting progresses through the Earth Sign Virgo, responsibilities have steadily increased. He now has four children and a large house. But he hasn't lost his Leo Rising edge to Virgo caution or financial fear; he still takes risks with new styles.

In 2010 Sting enters the last ten years of the Mercury-ruled cycle, which favors songwriting. In 2021 his progressed Mask will conjunct Natal Mercury; the thirty-year cycle may end with another award-winning song as memorable as "Roxanne." Around that time he's likely to be asked to write for a media project involving education or the environment. And travel is also indicated as his Jupiter Return includes a trine to Natal Leo Rising the same year.

The Libra Progression

At the end of her life, Zelda Fitzgerald entertained Montgomery, Alabama youth in her family home with anecdotes about life in Paris during the Roaring Twenties: Scott Fitzgerald, herself, Gertrude Stein and Picasso's circle. She spoke with Scott almost every day by phone.

Zelda outlived most of their old friends, the "creative set" who had avoided the Eighteenth Amendment (Prohibition of Alcohol) by living in Europe.

Maya Angelou's Ascendant progressed into Libra in 1972; she was forty-four. Libra is

34 Maya has a close Venus-Saturn square in the Natal chart, the progressed Ascendant brought out Saturn too. She was living in an unfamiliar patriarchal society, though at first it seemed a romantic adventure, it was difficult to understand African men. She got on much better with African women.

an easier cycle than Virgo. It's a calmer, more relaxed Mask. After her return to the US, Maya wrote, "Ghana softened my sassiness."[35] The long Virgo progression has its effect as well; Leo becomes less stubborn and more cooperative.

Symbolically, it's the sextile to their Natal Leo Ascendant, bringing opportunity and recognition. Natal Leo likes to be acknowledged. Maya received honorary degrees and literary awards; requests to work on network television projects "Blacks, Blacks, Blacks," and programs for the BBC.

Libra also means a balancing-out in relationships with family and spouse. (Venus rules the Libra progression.) Maya and her son had argued in Africa, but later, during Libra, she was proud of his rank in the corporate hierarchy of a major airline. She got on better with her mother; her African ex-husband no longer tried to persuade her to move "home" with him.

Maya's adventurous past is the stuff of poetry; her Eighth House Pisces planets represent talent. But when her friend James Baldwin referred her to Random House, they wanted autobiography instead. She wrote a series of short memoirs for them in the 1970's.[36] She wrote and directed the play, *All Day Long.*

But the pinnacle of fame, the Poet Laureate title, came in 1993 with President Bill Clinton's inauguration and her lovely poem, written for the occasion.

Maya's Ascendant progresses into Scorpio, the deepest of the Water Signs, in 2009. We anticipate more wonderful poetry!

Henri Matisse expressed joy and optimism through his art with the exception of one piece, which revealed his frustration at living in the body of an invalid, "The Sadness of the King."

He produced his masterpiece, *Jazz,* at the age of seventy-eight. There was an exact Sextile between his progressed Ascendant degree and his Natal Ascendant that year. Though his red "lion's mane"[37] had turned white, his posture had not changed. His friend and biographer Francoise Gilot wrote of Matisse in old age,

> he always stood with his back very straight, his movements showed good coordination, and because he had great grace and dignity, he did not appear to

35 Maya Angelou, *Collected Autobiographies of Maya Angelou, All God's Children Need Traveling Shoes,* (NY: Modern Library,) 2004, p. 1004.

36 The most famous is *I Know Why the Caged Bird Sings.*

37 He was known as a Fauvist. "In French, fauve is the reddish color of a lion's mane, though it also means a wild animal." Matisse believed in letting loose "the wildness from the Unconscious" by contrasting colors designed to raise the blood pressure with soothing colors. Francioise Gilot, *Matisse and Picasso* (NY: Doubleday,) 1990, p. 59 and footnote.

be heavy. His regal bearing conveyed the same huge feeling as that of an opera singer.[38]

After *Jazz,* art became play. Matisse would hold up the paper in his right hand; wind and twist it into a shape, then turn it as his left hand cut out pieces. All sorts of figures could be seen in the little scraps that dropped away in the process. Matisse assembled them to form miniature pictures. He lived to the age of eighty-three. Reproductions of his designs are still popular at museum gift shops today.

---

38 Gilot, cited above, 79-80. The book contains illustrations of Matisse at work on the charcoal drawings in the chapel at Vence, making the cutouts, and some of his earlier pieces as well.

Leo Rising Bibliography

Angelou, Maya, *Collected Autobiographies of Maya Angelou: I Know Why the Caged Bird Sings, Gather Together, All God's Children Need Traveling Shoes, A Song Flung up to Heaven,* (NY: Modern Library,) 2004.

—— *Wouldn't Take Nothing for My Journey Now,* (NY: Random House,) 1993.

Bryer, Jackson R. and Cathy W. Barks, "*Dear Scott, Dearest Zelda,*" *The Love Letters of F. Scott and Zelda Fitzgerald,* (NY: St. Martin's Press,) 2002.

Dumas, Alexander Senior, *The Count of Monte Christo,* (NY: Penguin,) 2004.

—— *The Three Musketeers,* (NY: Barnes and Noble,) 2004.

Eco, Umberto, *The Name of the Rose,* (NY: Harvest,) 1994.

Fitzgerald, Zelda, *Save Me the Waltz,* (Carbondale: Southern Illinois University Press,) 1967.

Gilot, Francoise, *Matisse and Picasso, A Friendship in Art,* (NY: Doubleday,) 1990.

Gonne, Maud, *Autobiography of Maud Gonne, A Servant of the Queen,* A. Norman Jeffares, ed., (Chicago: University of Chicago Press,) 1995.

Heehs, Peter, *The Lives of Sri Aurobindo, (*NY: Columbia University Press,) 2008.

Kirkpatrick, Sidney D., *Edgar Cayce, An American Prophet,* (NY: Riverhead Books,) 2000.

Mitford, Nancy, *Zelda: A Biography,* (NY: Harper and Row,) 1970.

Schjeldahl, Peter, "Art as Life: The Matisse We Never Knew," *The New Yorker,* pp. 78-83.

Sting, *Broken Music,* (NY: Dial Press,) 2003.

von Franz, Marie-Louise, *Archetypal Patterns in Fairy Tales,* "The Princess with Twelve Pairs of Shoes," Daryl Sharp, ed.,(Toronto: Inner City Books,) 1997.

White, Anna MacBride, (Maud Gonne's granddaughter) *The Love Story of W.B. Yeats and Maud Gonne,* (Bladrock, Cork: Mercier Press,) 2004.

Yogananda, Paramahansa, *Autobiography of a Yogi,* (NY: Philosophical Library,) 1946.

CHAPTER SIX

Virgo Rising - Solving the Riddle of Life

Paul Mc Cartney, "Nothing pleases me more than to go into a room and come out with a piece of music."

—— "I've got to admit it's getting better. It's a little better all the time."

Oprah Winfrey, "I know for sure that what we dwell on is who we become."

—— "I finally realized that being grateful to my body was key to giving more love to myself."

Louisa May Alcott, "Have regular hours for work and play; make each day both useful and pleasant, and prove that you understand the worth of time by employing it well. Then youth will be delightful, old age will bring few regrets, and life will become a beautiful success."

Paul Simon, "I'm more interested in what I discover than what I invent."

Dolly Parton, "The way I see it, if you want the rainbow, you gotta put up with the rain."

—— "We cannot direct the wind, but we can adjust the sails."

Ernest Hemingway, "For a long time now I have tried simply to write the best I can. Sometimes I have good luck and write better than I can."

Bob Woodward, "The legislator learns that when you talk a lot, you get in trouble. You have to listen a lot to make deals."

Madonna, "I'm a workaholic. I have insomnia. And I'm a control freak. That's why I'm not married. Who could stand me?"

—— "There are moments when I can't believe I'm as old as I am. But I feel better physically than I did 10 years ago."

—— "I became an overachiever to get approval from the world."

Oscar Wilde, "If one cannot enjoy reading a book over and over again, there is no use in reading it at all."

Charles Dickens, "A loving heart is the truest wisdom."

Virgo Rising

I'm the Virgo Rising Mask. When I ask, "how may I be of help?" I really mean it! I enjoy researching; finding the exact information you need. However, when you don't use it, my feelings are hurt. To my logical mind, this simply doesn't compute.

I feel even worse when you take the advice of someone less intelligent than I. After I've listened patiently to you for hours and provided a *practical* solution, you'll still make your decision in the heat of the moment.

What to me is precise and methodical may seem nit-picky to you. But who do you call when you need an editor; a medical specialist, an expert, or an efficient, industrious co-author? Who do you call at the last minute to fill in the gaps on your project? *Me.*

People may call me narrow-minded, literal-minded, critical or judgemental, but they're only describing my armor. Every Mask has its defenses. Usually raised by a strict parent (sometimes two) and often in a religion more rigid than my peers,' I absorbed parental ethics, even if Natal Uranus later rebelled.

Don't get me wrong, I love my parents. Tiger Woods[1] loved his father; so did Louisa May Alcott. Madonna loves hers, in spite of her song, "Papa Don't Preach." But there are reasons for my perfectionism. In my childhood results were important. Academic success was highly valued. Unlike creativity, it was measurable.

How to Recognize Virgo Rising

My favorite clue for recognizing Virgo Rising is the little verticle furrow between the eyebrows, the nervous wrinkle that usually develops by the age of twenty-eight. It results from cumulative anxiety: "will I pass the test? Will I/we win the game?" When Virgo is younger, the spark of intelligence in their eyes often gives them away. A bright child, Virgo Rising usually learns easily; enjoys school more than his or her siblings and reads all summer long. It's easy to see why parents tend to pin their hopes for success on the Virgo Rising child. But as their expectations grow, the child begins to feel the pressure.

There's another way to recognize Virgo Rising: they usually look ten years younger than others their age, an attribute they share with Gemini Rising.

By midlife, Virgo Rising usually has a large head to accommodate their "large brain," as Max and Augusta Heindel put it, and "a narrow face that tapers to a small chin. They tend

---

1 Virgo Rising Tiger Woods has an ambitious Capricorn Sun (he's double Earth) and seems to have really appreciated his father's mentoring. The title of the book they wrote together is interesting, *Training a Tiger: a Father's Guide to Raising a Champion in Golf and in Life,* by Earl Woods, Tiger Woods and Peter McDaniel, (NY: William Morrow,) 1997. Several Virgo Rising clients' fathers could have written books with similar titles.

to have light complexions and to be medium height to tall, 5'4" or taller."[2] I do find them, as a whole, paler than others in their ethnic group. However, Cancer and Pisces Rising also tend to need sunscreen.

Beginning astrology students sometimes say, "I *know* my new acquaintance has Virgo Rising; he won't give me his data but he's always complaining about his health!" While these complaints *can* become a major focus of Virgo Rising readings and hypochondria may be a clue to the Rising Sign—the Sixth Sign *is* also analogous to the Sixth House (Health) — you won't know till you get his birth data. Astrology is a helpful tool for understanding others but it's better not to pre-judge or categorize.

Also, many Virgo Rising people have been told by parents or teachers that the rest of us aren't interested in their allergies or minor aches and pains; that hospitals are filled with people who are *really* ill; "so, rise above it and think about something else. If you fuss about minor ailments, nobody will believe you or call an ambulance when you're *really* sick."

If brought up this way, Virgo Rising sometimes chooses medicine as a career, seeking answers to their questions (except for the Virgo-Pisces combination. They often faint at the sight of blood.) A nurse during the Civil War, Louisa May Alcott contracted typhoid at thirty. As a result, her health was impaired.[3]

On the whole my Virgo Rising clients have had excellent health, though a few do have Sixth House planets with challenging aspects. Sixth House symbols are to be taken seriously in *any* horoscope, regardless of Rising Sign.

However, if you know someone who pops an anti-acid tablet after every meal; avoids spicy foods and complains of gastric distress or mentions a peptic ulcer, the odds are good that they have Virgo Rising. The duodenum (small intestine) is associated with the Sign. Virgos who try to stay awake to study or finish a task may consume large amounts of diet soda or coffee, sometimes on an empty stomach. This will contribute to nervous system problems as they age. (See Mundane Ruler and Mutability, below.)

Other students have asked: "can we recognize this Rising Sign by the neatness of their

---

2 Max and Augusta Heindel, cited above, pp. 9-101. The Heindel couple used astrology in their healing practice, and seem to have drawn many Virgo Rising hypochondriacs. I notice the squeamishness they mention (inability to be around dead animals in labs) more when there are Pisces planets in the Sixth House.

3 Mary Jo Salter, "American Girls," a review of *Little Women, Little Men, and Jo's Boys*, (Library of America, in *New York Time Book Review*,) May 15, 2009, pp. 10-11. Around the age of 30, transiting Saturn crossed her Ascendant, passed through her T-square to Mercury and Jupiter and returned to its Natal degree in her First House.

desk and by their compulsive-obsessive approach to every detail of every step in the process?" Yes, they're meticulous. That's a clearer indicator of Virgo Rising than minor health complaints.

Keep in mind, though, the exceptions to the rule: *not all Virgos are neat.* Some, to the exasperation of the spouse, have stacks of books and magazines piled around gathering dust. Someday Virgo Rising intends to collect the tidbits of information from them. Meanwhile, the office may look messy, but Virgo's *mind* is organized. Because Virgo knows where everything is, nobody is allowed to move things.

Then there are those who go to the Dionysian polarity, Virgo Rising people who escape into alcohol and drugs: Betty Ford, Hugh Heffner and others with planets in Pisces in the Sixth and Seventh Houses. Or billionaire-recluse Howard Hughes, whose only Water Planet was Neptune-in-Cancer, sextiling Virgo Rising. Addicted to cocaine and valium, Hughes died at sixty-one, leaving his fortune to a hospital.

Most Virgo Rising people are masters of detail. In literature, Harper Lee (*To Kill a Mockingbird*) and Isak Dennison (*Out of Africa*) used detail beautifully. After reading their novels, the reader feels as if he's been to Alabama and Kenya.

On the other hand, people who usually provide more examples or details than you require may have Virgo Rising.

The Mode - Mutability

While the Fixed Rising Signs are strong-willed, stubborn and persevering and the Cardinal Rising Signs have natural authority and leadership potential, the Mutable Signs are flexible, pliable and good communicators. Their ability to compromise is an asset in working with others both in personal relationships and in their careers. They seem to have an affinity for journalism, where the focus is not on themselves but the other person's story.

Good listeners Oprah Winfrey and Bob Woodward exemplify the Virgo Rising talent for being good listeners. (Oprah began as a local television journalist in Baltimore and makes use of her skills in her role of talk show host.) Serious-minded, both Winfrey and Woodward convey genuine interest *in the person,* as well as the topic. They excel at asking tough questions in a respectful, concerned way. People from all walks of life trust Oprah. Supreme Court Justices; President George W. Bush, the anonymous source, Watergate's "Deep Throat" and Judith (Mrs. John) Belushi[4] all trusted Woodward to tell their stories.

---

4 However, in her recent biography of her husband, *Belushi*, (NY: Rugged Land,) 2005, Judith alleged that Woodward hid his intentions from her during the interviews. He didn't reveal that

The other Mutable Rising Signs, particularly Gemini tend to interrupt others with a witticism or change the subject when the interviewee has more to say, but not Winfrey or Woodward. Oprah goes to commercial while her subjects collect their thoughts; Woodward sits patiently and listens while his subjects ramble, knowing that he can replay the tapes and find the best quotes later.

Mutable Signs are suggestible; subjects sometimes mislead the Virgo Rising interviewer in an effort to sell their book or their war. Virgo Rising may be angry for a short time, but is likely to give the person a chance to explain himself in a second book or on a later show. Mutability will usually compromise.

Virgo Rising journalists will rarely give up access to a celebrity, or someone in a position of power. Woodward has published four books (and counting) about "W." *All The President's Men,* his eye-witness story about Deep Throat and the scandal that brought down Richard Nixon became a movie. People born after 1975 seemed to have learned more about the period from the film than the classroom. Woodward and Winfrey both impact American culture in powerful ways.[5]

Because they're impressionable, early childhood influences are particularly important for the Mutable Signs. Oscar Wilde, with Virgo Rising was fortunate to make valuable literary contacts through his mother's London salon and draw attention to his plays.

Most of my successful friends and clients with Virgo Rising grew up in homes with a strong work ethic, though none of them had a father as committed to their success as Tiger Woods. Louisa May Alcott's father, Bronson, educator and founder of an experimental community, asked her to write "edifying children's books;" her novels *Little Women* and *Little Women* are still enjoyed today.

Artist Francoise Gilot's father wanted her to become an attorney. Determined to avoid his "commitment to facts" and follow an imaginative path, she cut law school classes to study art. Confident in her talent, she left home in her early twenties to devote herself to painting. Francoise lived with Pablo Picasso for ten years; they have two children, Claude and Paloma.

Francoise Gilot, Bob Woodward, Paul Simon, Dolly Parton, Tiger Woods and Ernest Hemingway have something in common: their horoscopes all combine Virgo Rising with

---

he already had a contract and a format for the book. She'd wanted him to investigate the circumstances around John's death more fully. If true, this "Hermes approach" of revealing only part of the plot is reminiscent of Virgil and Chaucer's *Mercury.*

5 Even now television pundits are still discussing whether or not Woodward lost his objectivity while writing about the Bush Administration.

a Cardinal Sun Sign. Oprah Winfrey and Madonna and Charles Dickens have Fixed Suns. Rainer Marie Rilke, Paul McCartney and Woody Allen are "double Mutable."

The Element - Earth

Virgo Rising's industriousness is associated with the Earth Element, and with the Sixth House in the Natural Zodiac. The Sixth House has been mentioned above in connection with health, its most common meaning. But our daily routine is also a Sixth House matter, and Virgo Rising is routine-driven. For example, if exercise is on the day planner it will happen; if not, it usually won't. Madonna's statement about being a workaholic (above) is one that most of my Virgo Rising clients will appreciate.

We associate the Sixth House with "paying your dues" at work. Virgo Rising may have an unusually long apprenticeship with an employer who makes Virgo feel indispensable. As a result, Virgo Rising may stay longer than other interns, "helping out the boss" instead of moving onward and upward. Many Virgo Rising clients take longer than their co-workers to ask for raises or promotion; they take to heart the boss's fears of "possible budget cuts." Others have "helped him" by not listing all their overtime hours because "they enjoy the work."

Whether they're in the arts; sciences, media, health care, or education, Virgo Rising people tend to lose track of time. Once the workday begins they go with the flow. Their new spouse soon learns he or she will be scheduling his time with Virgo Rising carefully. Like Madonna, Virgo Rising women tend to delay having children till their careers are well-established.

Since most people with this Ascendant have a Gemini at the Zenith of the horoscope, they're likely to have more than one ongoing project. Oprah acted in *The Color Purple;* has a book club; a magazine, her T.V. show, and takes side trips to Africa to visit the girls' school she founded. She also volunteered in Obama campaign and went to Denmark in hopes of bringing the 2012 Olympics to Chicago.

Woodward wrote fifteen books in thirty-five years. Dickens was even more prolific with fifteen long novels. (some overlapped—he began his next before finishing his current book) essays, reviews, newspaper articles, acting, public speaking and philanthropy.

He never forgot his fourteen months of hard labor in a factory that made "blacking" for ovens and boots the year his father served a term in debtor's prison. Charles was twelve at the time but the experience stayed with him.

Fortunately, he was able to return to school. After graduating, he worked as a clerk, then became a journalist. With Jupiter-in-Gemini (Detriment) in his Tenth House, Dickens achieved fame as a novelist by twenty-five. He also found time for correspondence; his letters were published in twelve volumes. Dickens organized "home theatricals" and was known to take fifteen-mile-walks in preparation for acting.[6]

Many of his planets were Dignified by Sign or House placement: in addition to Jupiter-in-Detriment: Venus (Exalted) Saturn and Mars (Rulership) and the Moon by house position, (in the Fourth House, which it rules in the Natural Zodiac.)

A lifelong advocate for the poor, particularly poor children, through his books, articles and speeches, Dickens seemed to represent the social conscience of Victorian England.

How hard it must have been to find time for his wife and ten children! He eventually left and married an actress.

Dickens also had another Virgo Rising characteristic, he was a perfectionist. According to the latest biography, he went over the proofs of his writing so many times they "resembled an inky fishing net."[7]

Virgo Earth has a strong Sensate Function. They're often the first clients to notice a new picture or item of furniture in my office.

The Mundane Ruler - Mercury Finds His Niche

Mercury (the Roman Hermes) rules two of the four Mutable Signs, Gemini and Virgo. Symbolically, Mercury is associated with their language and communication skills and beyond that, their impulse to get the message out. Just as Mercury transmitted his message to the protagonists in Virgil, Chaucer and Boccaccio; Virgo Rising Woodward and Winfrey bring theirs to modern readers and television viewers.

Both Mercury-ruled Rising Signs include prolific writers, George Bernard Shaw, for example, had Gemini Rising and Charles Dickens had Virgo Rising. Virgo Rising singer-songwriter Paul Simon (see above quote) said that he enjoys discovering more than he enjoys inventing. I've found that to be generally true of Virgo Rising. Research seems to appeal more to Virgo than to Gemini Rising, unless Gemini has Mercury Retrograde.[8]

Some Virgos enjoy working with slides in laboratories while others, like poets and

---

6 David Grylls' review of *Charles Dickens: A Life Defined by Writing*, by Michael Slater, (New Haven: Yale University Press,) *Financial Times*, Saturday October 17, 2009.

7 David Grylls, cited above, October 17, 2009.

8 Geminis and others who didn't like research in the past but suddenly *do* enjoy it might check their progressed Mercury and see if changed directions.

memoirists, enjoy delving into their experiences in hopes of discovering something new. Whatever their interests, Virgo Rising's methodical approach is well-suited to research. Mercury as mundane ruler of Virgo likes to fact-check and edit as he goes along. But perfectionism sometimes slows him down. It was rumored that when "O" magazine first appeared, Oprah would "okay" every page personally. Eventually, she found it overwhelming to do the show, micromanage "O" *and* select a new book for her club every month.[9]

Though Virgo Rising may seem very efficient, he may be wasting his energy and fraying his nerves by filling his day with tasks that others could perform. Though Virgo Rising wants to stay on top of the details, as Virgo grows older it's important to have a good staff and delegate. What Madonna said (above) is true, Virgo may not feel any older or look older to others. There are still plenty of projects to keep the mind engaged and the spirit young. However, chronological aging does affect the body, and as Hemingway discovered at the end of his life, it affects the brain as well.

Dickens, Hemingway, Oprah and Madonna have all influenced the culture of their times. I have many talented clients with Virgo Rising. Most of them have found their niches by helping others or contributing to knowledge. Sometimes they instinctively discover and fill a gap that nobody else notices. (Yoga for carpel-tunnel-syndrome, for instance.)

In literature there are many examples of Virgo Rising writers who have found their specific audience: Woody Allen is popular on campuses and with urban intellectuals, particularly New Yorkers. Dolly Parton,[10] who has written over 3,000 songs, including "I Will Always Love You," is extremely popular with Country and Western audiences.

Paul Simon's eclectic journey of discovery has its fans. Older people like "the Garfunkel period," some love "Graceland" and others enjoy the Ladysmith group. According to radio disc jockeys, his "Bridge Over Troubled Waters" is among the most frequently requested songs.

Oscar Wilde's *Picture of Dorian Gray,* a serious novel by an otherwise lighthearted playwright, is now considered a classic. More recent authors like F. Scott Fitzgerald (Aquarius Rising) have taken the theme in new directions.[11] Jack Kerouac, a wanderer

---

9 Like Charles Dickens, Oprah has Jupiter in Gemini in her Tenth House squared the Ascendant. Jupiter sees the Big Picture while Mercury, the mundane ruler, focuses on the details. The Detriment position(Gemini) takes on *a lot* at once.

10 Whitney Houston sang "I Will Always Love You." Dolly is known to mainstream audiences from television Christmas specials and the movie "Nine to Five."

11 *The Curious Case of Benjamin Button,* his short story about a boy who is born old and becomes younger every year till adulthood, then begins to reverse the aging process, became a movie.

with a restless Mutable T-square, still appeals to young people who take off for California, slipping *On the Road* into their backpacks.

However successful Virgo Rising becomes by midlife— and I find that this to be helpful Mask for ambitious Sun Signs—it does get lonely living entirely through and for one's work.

Ernest Hemingway, who once said that Man can be destroyed but not defeated, shot himself when he could no longer write. He had told his friend and biographer A. E. Hotchner that others understand when old soldiers, prize-fighters and matadors can no longer fight. But people keep asking (old) authors, "what are you working on now?" and added, "a champion goes out at his peak."[12]

When the Sun Sign's ambitions wane, the esoteric ruler of the Rising Sign takes us beyond the mundane ruler's limited perspective.

The Esoteric Ruler
Lunar Wisdom Nurturing Self and Others

The mundane ruler often describes how the Rising Sign survives, using its talents and instincts. It also seeks to make life interesting and pleasurable while living from paycheck-to-paycheck. At the survival level, Virgo Rising has an analytical guide in Mercury. (*Logos*, or the Thinking Function, in Jung's Typology.) As a result of analyzing past mistakes, particularly in relationships, Virgo Rising may become more discriminating and make better choices in the future.

The esoteric ruler opens us to a world beyond the ego. It points us towards Wholeness. Charles Dickens supposedly said, "a loving heart is the truest wisdom." This is the meaning of the Moon as Esoteric ruler of Virgo. In the First Half of Life, the Mercury Signs are so busy thinking, communicating and learning to make wise choices; so caught up in their daily routines that the lunar, feeling side is often neglected.[13]

The Moon refers to the very first relationship, Virgo Rising's relationship with Mother. While Hemingway seemed to have a very good relationship with his father, who taught him to fish and shoot birds, he had a difficult time with his mother. An aspiring opera singer, she wanted him study music and learn to play the cello. He left home after graduating

---

12 A. E. Hotchner, *Papa Hemingway: A Personal Memoir,* (NY: Random House,) 1966, 298-300.
13 The feeling planet, Venus, is the esoteric ruler of the other Mercury-ruled Sign, Gemini.

from high school. (His Moon was in Detriment in Capricorn. He had Mars in his First House and Saturn in his Fourth.)[14]

Madonna, with both the Moon and Mercury conjunct her Virgo Ascendant, decided to take time off after *Evita* to attend to her personal life, according to the author of her biography, *Goddess*.[15] Most of the reviews were negative. Though she received a million dollars for the role, Madonna was disappointed and discouraged.

Sometimes those moods end in self-pity. But sometimes when the ego experiences a sense of failure, the Soul opens to new possibilities. Madonna developed a serious interest in Kabbalah and practiced yoga, In the end, the direction she chose was not mercurial, but lunar.

Madonna decided she wanted to remarry, have a second child and raise her family in England. Several years later, in 1998, a mutual friend introduced her to Guy Ritchie. For Madonna, it was love at first sight; Guy, though drawn to her, was in another relationship at the time.

Madonna had needed time out when she bought her home in London and moved her daughter, Lourdes there. She'd struggled for survival since the age of five when her mother died of inoperable cancer. A pragmatist, Madonna was talented at creating images and illusions, at giving form to her fantasies.

She cast herself in the role of Cinderella when her father remarried. Though she didn't mind "raising her younger siblings." (She was one of eight children, the "smartest and most verbal.")[16] But she did object to a stepmother replacing the loving mother she remembered. Her grandmother told her of the beautiful Madonna for whom she was named; her talented woman who could sing and dance, the mother she resembled.

Determined to succeed, Madonna left Bay City, Michigan for New York City at the age of eighteen. Alone in the city, she became her own "stage mother," encouraging and mothering herself. She was certain she could make it in the music industry. Five years later she was on television singing "Like a Virgin" in a transparent wedding dress.

With Pluto conjunct Mercury, she found a series of lovers to help her along the way, as Eva Peron ("Evita") had done when she arrived in Buenos Aires from the countryside. Like Eva's, Madonna's dream was to be seriously as an actress. She told a friend the goal was to become so successful that she would never again depend upon anyone for anything. The Pluto-Mercury conjunction symbolized a need to control her life and relationships.

Her videos, "Material Girl," "Boy Toy" and the title of her coffee table book, *Sex*, were

---

14 Hotchner, cited above, his stormy relationship with her made his home life "chaotic," 5.
15 It was a ten year hiatus from the stage, Goddess, 364.
16 *Goddess*, cited above, 80.

like signposts marking her journey. Unless there's a high percentage of Water, Virgo Rising doesn't need metaphors.[17] She was a centerfold in both *Playboy* and *Penthouse* Magazines; she wrote lyrics and melodies based on her life experience. Her song titles appeared on the Top Ten list through the 1980s. Around the time of her marriage to Sean Penn in 1985 it seemed Madonna had reached the pinnacle of success.

Acting was her first experience of failure. She'd worked very hard on *Evita*. She'd fought for the role. Over dinner, she convinced Carlos Menom, Argentina's President, to let the American production company film in Buenos Aires, protestors notwithstanding.[18] She took lessons to strengthen her voice; she researched her character and became Eva's double. She sang the theme song beautifully; she'd measured up to her own perfectionist standards. Though Madonna received a Golden Globe award, most of the critics were unimpressed. Even her fans seemed to prefer Madonna playing herself on the videos.

Lourdes, her daughter with Carlos Leon, her physical trainer was born when she was in her late thirties. Though her father was furious that Lourdes was born out-of-wedlock, Madonna said she loved and understood her father more after becoming a parent herself.[19]

Her Mask held firm, even when there was no Oscar nomination. "I cannot be a brush stroke in someone else's painting," she said, "I need my own film company and writers." It was bravado; behind the Mask she was devastated. Madonna believed that she had risked her reputation on *Evita* and failed. She was thirty-five years old and she "had nobody." She told a friend, a former priest, that in England actresses could work longer. Madonna would reinvent herself in London.

Winning acceptance in England proved difficult. She invested in a recording studio. Though she dressed the part of a thirty-something English woman, worked on her accent and added colloquialisms to her speech, she seemed brazen to the English. She was not invited to parties. But she received a piece of good advice, "do not pursue men when they don't call you back." She stepped back and quit pushing.

This Yin approach must have felt strange after nearly four decades of the Yang struggle for survival. She considered her daughter's needs ahead of her own fears.[20] Madonna knew

---

17 Madonna's only water planet is Neptune-in-Scorpio.

18 Many people in Buenos Aires remembered Eva Peron as a saint who distributed food to the poor; they didn't want an American who had written a "pornographic book" and "appeared on stage in her underwear" portraying her; there were local actresses available.

19 "even though he was stubborn and narrow-minded." Her Saturn is in the Fourth, square her Moon on the Ascendant.

20 Madonna had been stalked while living in the Hollywood Hills and though the stalker, Robert Dewey Hoskins was in prison, she still felt safer in London. *Goddess*, 342.

that Lourdes missed her father and her grandparents, so she bought a house in California. She brought Lourdes to see Carlos Leon and her Cuban-America cousins.

Madonna was eleven years older than Guy Ritchie, a film producer busy with his own creative projects. His mother, Lady Amber Leighton, urged him to marry someone from his own social class. But he eventually broke up with his girlfriend and called Madonna as she was leaving for a yoga retreat. They soon married and had a son, Rocco.

By midlife, Madonna had progressed from a "material girl" who wanted total control of her life to a mature woman, a mother who wrote children's books. She had found her niche in music and discovered the ego's limitations, as most of us do by fifty. She learned to make wiser choices along the way. Her esoteric ruler, the Moon, created *different* images and gave them form. At fifty, when Madonna performed for Al Gore's International Global Warming concert, she seemed content. More recently, Madonna expanded her family again. She adopted a child in Malawi and is attempting to adopt a second.

Few of us can afford to take several years off when we feel our lives are out-of-balance the way Madonna did. But the new Yin direction worked for her. She slowed down, relaxed with yoga, made peace with her father and concentrated on relationships.

The Moon on her Ascendant came to symbolize more than her mother or the Media; (she'd replaced her mother's love with the love of her fans,) she now had a personal life. After accepting with her vulnerable lunar side, she became comfortable with it. Her fans' love and approval was no longer as necessary.

The Virgo Mask and the First Half of Life
Mercury's Choices - Experience Leads to Wisdom

Oprah Winfrey once said that she knew for certain *we become what we dwell on.* That's very true. In graduate school one of my apartment mates was a young woman who was very thin and ate very little. She shivered with every spring breeze. We weren't familiar with the word anorexia then but we did encourage her to see a counselor. And, of course, we encouraged her to eat.

One day, tiring of friends piling her plate with food, she said, "I used to weigh nearly 200 pounds. I'm terrified of gaining weight!" We stared at her in disbelief. To convince us, she had her mother send her high school yearbook with the "fat" pictures. "But that was *then,* this is *now!*" we said. *"Look at yourself!"* However, she still thought of herself as obese. Every morning as she passed the hall mirror, she'd stop and checked her reflection to make certain she was still thin. As William Blake (see Cancer Rising) put it, she "armed her fears."

Her survival struggle continued in her own mind. After she left campus we heard a rumor that she was seeing a therapist. We hoped she did. Virgo Rising often puts off asking for help because they believe they can—or should- find the answers on their own. It seems to them "a matter of research," or of "mind-over-matter," "I can go cold turkey and change my habits any time I want."

Sometimes that works, but in severe cases, like my friend's, Sri Aurobindo was right, "the human mind trying to understand itself *by itself* is like a man trying to leap over his own shoulders."[21]

As Oprah said, we need to be grateful to our bodies. We also need to relax about them as we grow older. But like precocious Hermes in the Greek myths, Virgo doesn't want to age.

The First Half of Life involves acquiring academic or vocational credentials; gaining experience, "paying our dues" in a profession, taking on a mortgage. Virgo Rising's mundane ruler is very good, in fact, better than most instinctual rulers, at all of this. Earth is pragmatic and industrious; Mutability adapts. Virgo's bad choices or so-called mistakes tend to occur not in career but in relationships, unless Venus and the Moon are very well aspected. Virgo Rising is very pragmatic in its support of the Sun Sign's ambitions.

Many Virgo Rising women choose the unattainable (married) lover, or like Madonna, the "bad boys." Like Madonna with Sean Penn, there's a built-in excuse to leave the "bad boy" later: physical or emotional abuse. Or someone a great deal older, or younger. Madonna is eleven years older than Guy Ritchie. There was a forty-year age difference between Pablo Picasso and Francoise Gilot. Had they stayed together, he would not have lived on as her companion in old age.

Virgo men may choose wealthy women who try to control them. Or choose their polar opposite: psychic-but-fragile women, intuitives who appear very "spiritual" but are really needy and/or demanding. Either sex may choose an alcoholic in the First Half of Life. (Pisces is on Virgo's Marriage House Cusp.) Everyone will sympathize when Virgo Rising eventually leaves the marriage. Francoise Gilot's friends all knew that Pablo could be cruel.

Regardless of gender, Virgo Rising tends to focus on their work. If the horoscope is low in Water, they may put off the lunar part of life, one-on-one relationships, and/or having children. And, like Scarlett O'Hara, Virgo Rising may compartmentalize their emotional

21 Quoted by Dr. Haridas Chaudhuri, in a talk in 1975. Dr. Chaudhuri was the Founder of the California Institute of Integral Studies which is based on Sri Aurobinso's philosophy.

pain. Too busy to cry today, they'll wait and cry tomorrow. Or, like Madonna, they'll write songs about their suffering; others will identify with the lyrics.

The perfectionism and compulsive behavior (the Virgo workaholic: see Madonna's quote, above) tend to abate a little after midlife; the Ego seems to tire of it. Still, for Virgo, the devil remains in the details. Virgo's mind tries to fill in all the gaps; Virgo worries about what's missing from that perfect summer day. Meditation techniques are useful tools to catch the mind at its tricks, as it replays old tapes.

"We are what we dwell on." After fifty, Virgo usually makes wiser choices about that, and about relationships.

The Virgo Mask After Fifty
Solving the Riddle of Life

"When will you have a little pity for/every soft thing/that walks through the world,/yourself included?" Mary Oliver asks in her poem "At Blackwater Pond." I haven't yet come across her horoscope so I don't know her Rising Sign. However, Mary was born on September 10 (1935.) A Virgo Sun Sign, she has a deep understanding of Virgo's journey. Morning walks through natural settings around Cape Cod inspire her poetry. Her appreciation of beauty and sense of wonder at the marvel of Nature led to experiences that border on religious ecstasy. Though they usually want to be productive as long as possible, Virgo Rising clients have found sitting in tranquil gardens, like the Self Realization Fellowship grounds in Encinitas, California, or the Murakami Gardens in Delray, Florida have a salutary effect on the nervous system; tension and worry seem to dissolve away.

Some older Virgo Rising clients have found that the advice one traveler, Candide, received at the end of his journey, "cultivate your garden,"[22] works for them, too. After retirement, they relax by planting seeds and weeding their flowers or vegetables. In the sunshine and fresh air, digging in the earth, (their Element,) they spend hours watching new life blossom as the years pass.

Contentment needn't always come through Mercury: learning, writing, conversing, or improving one's golf game. It can also come from simply being present with, and amazed by, the world around us.

After fifty, few of us would choose to walk fifteen miles like Dickens, or get up at four

---

22 In Francois-Marie Arouet Voltaire's novel *Candide,* the protagonist had one misadventure after another as he crossed Europe during tumultuous times. At the end of his journey, he was happy at home working in his garden.

a.m. to exercise as Madonna did when playing Eva Peron. By seventy, most Virgo Rising people have shortened their five mile walk to a mile or two; few are still running marathons or doing long hikes in the mountains. Virgo Rising clients sometimes look back on their compulsive younger selves and smile.

The lunar side of life, friendships and family relationships become more important as Virgo Rising ages. Psychiatrist George Vaillant has a question in his study on aging, "when your old friends die, do you replace them with new friends?" He found that the men who answered, "yes" seemed much more contented than those who said, "no."[23]

Because Virgo Rising is inquisitive and accomplished at finding solutions to life's riddles, *The Green Face* seems a fitting tale. Written by Gustav Meyrink,[24] an imaginative novelist who lived and wrote between the two World Wars, felt the tension built around him as Europe veered towards World War II. The story's atmosphere is foreboding.

The protagonist, Fortunatus, feels an urgency about solving the mystery, his search gives his life meaning.

The Green Face

Young Fortunatus had been wandering around Europe for a several years, adrift in a changing world. One day he reached the city of Amsterdam. His last stop had been the Netherlands, and he was still captivated by a painting in the Leyden Museum. He began to dream about the Green Face in the painting; it was the most peaceful and beautiful face he had ever seen. Perhaps it was the Buddha!

Who would know? Who could tell him more about it? When he met a man about to leave for Leyden on business, Fortunatus insisted his new acquaintance go to the Museum and find the curator. "Ask for everything he knows about the painting," he insisted.

Walking around Amsterdam, Fortunatus wondered if someday his own face could become radiant like that one. He looked at himself in the mirror and tried to visualize the Face in his dreams.

---

23 Dr. Vaillant's study followed a group of Harvard graduates (John F. Kennedy's class) through their lives, asking them all the same series of questions. They were all men. Later, studies that included women and people from less privileged backgrounds were added. His questionnaires are reprinted as appendices. *Aging Well,* (NY: Little, Brown and Co.,) 2003.

24 Meyrink, had Gemini Rising, a Mercury-Ruled Ascendant. The color green is associated with the Egyptian Hermes, "Thoth of the Emerald Tablets." Meyrink referred to, "the Face of Memphis in The Green," likely a reference to Memphis, Egypt and Hermes-Thoth.

One day he came upon a shop. There was a green sign above the door: "House of Riddles, Chidher Green, proprietor." Surely they would have his answer! He hurried up the steps and into the store. At first he was disappointed; they seemed to stock only magic tricks and sex toys.

But then he was drawn towards the counter by the sight of an old man with a ledger, in the corner doing the bookkeeping. This, then was the owner. If he didn't know about the Face—Fortunatus was beginning to have his doubts— perhaps Chidher Green could direct Fortunatus to someone who did. He looked wise and strangely out-of-place here. But as he reached the counter, Fortunatus suddenly became shy. The owner was very busy. His question deserved Mr. Green's full attention; he would return another day.

In the weeks that followed, Fortunatus met several people who had seen the Green Face, but they each thought it was someone different, confusing Fortunatus. A learned rabbi smiled and told him the Face he described was definitely the prophet Elijah. His wife had claimed to have seen Elijah on the streets of Amsterdam, but when she pointed "Elijah" out to the rabbi, it was just an old Jewish man like himself. His wife was confused sometimes, he said.

The rabbi eagerly attempted to persuade Fortunatus to come to Brazil. His Kabbalah group had purchased land and would be leaving soon. The omens predicted that Amsterdam would flood and everyone would drown in a storm. Fortunatus couldn't see himself as part of a Kabbalah community in Brazil.

He met a dockworker from Africa who had seen the Face in a Vision. But *his* Face was on the head of a green snake, the tribal god, who if he chose could confer a great treasure. The dockworker would be rich and would never need to work again. A snake god was not what Foruntatus had in mind, either. He met a beautiful girl named Eva whose father was dying, and spent some time with them both. Her father knew a lot, but nothing about finding the Green Face. Eva fell in love with him but he didn't notice; the Green Face occupied his thoughts.

In his hotel room Fortunatus wrote down his experiences, from Leyden to his visualizations, to the dock worker's snake to Elijah. He noted that twice he thought he had seen Chidher Green in a restaurant, but it was an old professor, angry at being twice mistaken for a mere shopkeeper.

As he wandered the streets of Amsterdam, he came to the spot where the House of Riddles used to be, but it was gone. Apparently it had gone out of business and been torn down. Had his search come to an end?

Meanwhile, the businessman returned from Leyden furious with Fortunatus. He had demanded to see the museum's curator; he had described the Green Face in detail and insisted Fortunatus had seen it there. The curator had laughed at him. Having spent his entire career in Leyden, the man was certain that such a painting had never existed.

Feeling bereft, Fortunatus set out an a walk, then looked up to see that the House of Riddles was back exactly where it had been before! He glanced at the sign: "House of Riddles: Chidher Green proprietor." He rushed up the stairs. This time no matter how busy the man seemed, he would ask his question. Fortunatus interrupted the shop girl and demanded to see the old man, Mr. Chidher Green.

"Which old man?" she asked. "Lots of old men come in here."

"No, no, no, I mean *the owner,* Mr. Green. The last time I came in, he was sitting right over there in the corner, working. His name is on the sign outside."

The shop girl looked at him as if he were mad: "Holy Mother of God," she shouted, "there's no one here by that name and *there never was,* as sure as I'm standing here."

Fortunatus refused to believe her. He *knew* he was right. "His name is on the sign outside, I just read it."

"And what sign would that be? Not *our* sign. Because *our* Sign clearly says, Arpad Zitter, proprietor. *There's no Chidher Green!*"

Fortunatus hurried outside for another look at the sign. She was right, this time it read, "Arpad Zitter." An entirely different name, a name that shared only one letter with Chidher Green. What was happening? He looked through the store window at girl's reflection. She was tapping her head and gesturing outside at him as if to announce, "the man is crazy."

In his embarrassment Fortunatus hurried away, then realized he had forgotten his walking stick. It was still in their umbrella rack. "Oh well, leave it, then." He wandered through the labyrinth of canals and dark streets. Everything was deserted except for a few white angora cats sunning themselves on window sills. It felt like the end of the world.

Still, he felt a kind of excitement, as if he were an initiate in a new religion or a pilgrim in a new and very strange land. Who was the Face that haunted his dreams? He walked past old houses that seemed round-shouldered and bent over as if they were old men; rats scurried from the reeking canals, he sensed the River Styx.

He wrote for hours in his room. Through his window, he could see the water level rising. He would take his manuscript and bury it on the highest spot in the sinking city, a small rise, not quite a hill, where one green tree grew. Some future seeker might read his experiences and find meaning in them.

Suddenly, on the bridge crossing a canal he encountered an old man, a man who looked familiar. Could it be? Yes, it was! Chidher Green. He babbled to the old man about the store disappearing and reappearing with a new owner and the manuscript he was about to bury. Chidher Green told him they were on a thin line between the visible and the invisible worlds. As a result sometimes his store was on that street, and other times it was elsewhere. "I want to know about the Gr…" Fortunatus began.

But Chidher Green interrupted him. "I will now free you from all your fears," he said, and Fortunatus had an instant experience of immortality, he now knew that he would never really die. "And I will give you a boon: the ability to *really* love Eva. Now go quickly; get her, and take her to that high ground!"

And Chidher Green vanished. As Fortunatus hurried to get Eva, he encountered one of the few men who didn't think him insane. He quickly asked if Rabbi Safardy were safe. He learned that he and the Kabbalists had already left for Brazil; the rabbi had dreamed of Elijah, the Green Faced-prophet, who told him they should leave at once.

Eva was happy to see Fortunatus. Soon they stood under the tree on the little rise and watched the storm pound the city.

There's a liminal quality to the "House of Riddles. " The story is like a dream. Once the magic of Hermes is in play, things are never quite what they seem. Fortunatus didn't satisfy his curiosity about the Face, but he did experience his immortality; transcend his fears, and receive the only boon he needed, the ability to really love Eva. So often esoteric tales remind us that we may not always get what we want, but we always get what we need.

In workshops, a Mercurial participant will usually point out that it was more important for Fortunatus to *save Eva*, the lunar figure, *than the manuscript.*

Virgo Rising's Progression Through Libra

Libra Rising's warmth and charm are helpful assets for this workaholic Ascendant. Even when Virgo Rising has no Libran planets in the First House for the Mask to assimilate, during the Libran progression they may become more diplomatic and socialize more; they are concerned with and devote more attention to relationships.[25]

Most of my clients find Libra easier than the childhood years, especially with Natal Sun or Moon in Fire or Air. When there is a high percentage of these Elements in the

---

25 Socializing can require effort when Virgo's project awaits. There's an amusing anecdote about Bob Woodward in Adrian Havill's, *Deep Truth: The Lives of Bob Woodward and Carl Bernstein,* (NY: Carol Publishing,) 1993. Woodward once brought in Baskin Robbins ice cream to the staff at the *Post.* But instead of socializing with them, he went immediately to his office, closed the door and began typing.

horoscope, the Libran Mask forms many free-flowing trines and "opportunity sextiles," bringing out the qualities of the Natal planets.

During Libra, Life seems much easier to those Virgo Rising clients who were raised by strict parents and/or in strict religions. Many left the region where they were born for the East or West coast.

Bob Woodward and Ernest Hemingway had assimilated Puritan values, particularly the "work ethic," in Illinois. Both left the Midwest. Woodward attended college in the East, then decided not to attend law school. He talked the *Washington Post* into hiring him without any background in journalism. Cardinal Air (Libra) is persuasive when combined with Natal Sun in Cardinal Fire (Aries.)

Hemingway worked for the Red Cross in Europe; he stayed on in Paris to write *The Sun Also Rises.* He liked Scott Fitzgerald and Gertrude Stein, but left the "Lost Generation" for Key West, Florida.

Madonna went to parochial school in Bay City Michigan. She thought of the nuns as "superstars."[26] She rebelled against her stepmother and her father's "judgmentalism and narrowness." Her career took off quickly in New York. Her Fire Sign (Leo) Sun received a sextile from progressed Libra Rising.

Paul McCartney's father played in a jazz band and encouraged Paul to study music. Double Mutable (Gemini Sun) with Neptune on his Ascendant, Paul passed his A-levels in only one subject, art. He preferred playing-by-ear to formal study. With Mercury retrograde, Paul loves writing songs. (See his quote, in the beginning of the chapter.) He soon became the Beatles' most prolific songwriter.

Louisa May Alcott grew up in her father's utopian community, Fruitlands, where he corrected her journals and later, when she was in her twenties, encouraged Louisa to write "moral tales" for boys and girls. Double Mutable, with Saturn in her First House she was not a rebel even with Sun-in-Fire. (Sagittarius.) *Little Women* reached many generations of children through two movie versions and recently, a musical. Louisa never married. Though she didn't enjoy "didactic writing," she was good at it.

Her memorable characters. Jo, Meg, Beth, Amy and "Marmee" live on, like Woodward's book, *All the President's Men,* McCartney's songs, "Hey Jude" and "Yesterday," Paul Simon's "Bridge Over Troubled Waters," and Madonna's sensual body of work.

Multi-talented Oprah Winfrey began her career as a television journalist; acted in *The Color Purple,* introduced mainstream readers to African-American novelists they might

26 Her stepmother, with eight children to raise, dressed Madonna and two of her sisters in the same fabrics. So, in a sense Madonna was always in uniform, at home and at Catholic school.

never have otherwise discovered, and now encourages her book club members to read literary classics. Her career really took off after she moved to Chicago.

They all accomplished a great deal in the Libra progressed cycle, combining Natal Virgo industriousness with Libra's Cardinal Authority. The Libra Mask works well in music, entertainment, the visual arts and writing. Libra attracts people who recognize their talents and are in a position to open doors for them. Madonna and Woodward, neither of whom had formal training in their field and McCartney, who plays by ear, benefited from progressed Libra.

Still, for the previous two Rising Signs, (See Cancer and Leo Rising) the Libra period seemed an easier, and more mellow time. They were also older when they began the progression. Their careers established, they had more free time to focus on relationships than Virgo Rising

Paul McCartney and photographer Linda Eastman had a long, happy marriage from 1969 until her death in 1988. He said that she was a source of strength and courage after the Beatles' breakup. They were only apart one week during their entire marriage.

Oprah Winfrey and Steadman Graham have also enjoyed a long relationship.

Hemingway, with restless Mars in his First House, married four times. He was past the Libra progression when he met his last and seemingly most compatible wife, Mary.[27]

Madonna, with Mercury, Pluto and the Moon close to her Ascendant, Sun in Leo, and a Fixed Mars-Uranus square, sought to control her life and her relationships. After her daughter Lourdes was born she became more relaxed, more Yin. She and Guy Ritchie were married nine years, while Madonna divided her time between California and their home in London. In the entertainment industry, nine years is considered a *long* relationship.

Francoise Gilot, who had a late degree of Virgo Rising, progressed into Libra at the age of five. With four Libran Planets and the North Node in her First and Second Houses, she did not need to learn diplomacy, she came by it naturally. In fact, as a young woman, she was "a pleaser" in her relationships.

But she did break with her father, who valued "facts" so much, when the progressed Ascendant conjuncted her First House Jupiter. As soon as she knew she could make it as an artist, she left home and funded her studies herself. Older artists like Matisse and Picasso appreciated her beauty, enjoyed her company and valued her opinions.

Though she had her own approach to art—with her Natal Libra planets she was "a

---

27 She adapted to his structured routine: his door was closed until lunchtime while he wrote. In the afternoons he was available for fishing with guests. The night was for drinking, in Key West or Havana.

natural colorist"—she was very happy to learn from them. She accepted being called Picasso's muse and put up with his abuse. She moved in with him when the Progressed Ascendant conjuncted her Natal Moon in Libra in her Second House (personal resources and values.)

As the Mask conjuncted and brought out each Natal Libran planet, Francoise gradually grew into her Cardinality, her sense of personal authority and her artistic talent. She had two children, Claude and Paloma, with her lover.

The Scorpio Progression
Ascendant Sextile Natal Ascendant

Scorpio is more solitary. As it's a Fixed Sign, this is a more stubborn cycle than Libra. During this thirty-year-cycle my clients are generally less willing to compromise than in their romantic Libra years. (Venus rules Libra, but Scorpio is ruled by Mars and Pluto.) The first few years of the cycle seem restless, there's less patience with others until Virgo Rising becomes familiar with the new Mask.

The Scorpio Mask is less about "we" and more about "my needs" or "taking control of my life." (Pluto rulership.)

On the other hand, Scorpio is in symbolic sextile to Natal Virgo Rising, the Virgo tendencies, if set aside during Libra, come to the forefront. If there are Virgo planets in the First House, their attributes will come out again during the Scorpio cycle and with greater intensity.

A Water Sign, Scorpio is also about keeping secrets, one's own and other peoples' too. Woodward, who like Gilot progressed into Libra as a child (he was one year old) must have seemed an adult to his parents and teachers, the Libra Ascendant contacted Saturn, Uranus, Neptune and Mars. It moved into sextile with Pluto and the Moon; opposed his Aries Sun and squared his Exalted Jupiter at the Zenith *all before he was twenty*.[28]

The Scorpio cycle worked beautifully for Woodward as the progressed Ascendant moved through his Second House. He kept Deep Throat's secret while Deep Throat's information about Richard Nixon carried him to fame and fortune. His contacts at the Pentagon and on the Beltway gave him all the access he needed to get the story. He's still with the *Washington Post* today.

---

28 It inconjuncted his Venus in Rulership, (Taurus) too, but his Venus in the Eighth seems more focused on business than relationships.

Neptune on the Ascendant (in zero Libra) enhances his writing style. His non-fiction books are popular, though there has been criticism of his fact-checking. Neptune prefers a lively tale to a boring, accurate story.

Francoise Gilot was secretive during the Scorpio progression. Their friends had no idea she was planning to leave Picasso until she was gone. She inherited her grandmother's house, sold it and bought a home in Paris so her young children (ages four and six) could attend school in the city. She was thirty-two when she left him.

A gossipy woman had told Gilot that Picasso was having an affair, an "anecdote" she "had not asked to hear."[29] But she didn't mention it to him. She focused all her attention on her art, tried new techniques that intrigued him, and had two successful showings. Her armor hardened. When Picasso noticed, he asked her if he should purchase a can opener! Sea creatures with thick carapaces appeared in *his* paintings.

After she'd succeeded in intriguing him and, through art, in rekindling his passion, she left. But they remained good friends. Natal Libran planets excel at the Art of Relationship.

Paul McCartney, now 67, has progressed into Scorpio. In addition to songwriting, he's been spending more time painting, a solitary occupation, and has had several gallery shows. McCartney also does sound tracks for movies. Like Madonna, he's written a children's book.

Because Scorpio favors solitary projects, writers and artists usually benefit from the cycle. On the other hand, Extraverted Hollywood people who enjoy brainstorming sessions with other creative types (Art-by-Committee) have commented that at first they really missed the Libran cycle.

The Sagittarian Progression

During the Mutable Square to Virgo Rising, many of my clients relocated and several now live abroad. (Jupiter, the travel/relocation planet rules the Sign.)

Francoise Gilot is a good example. She married Dr. Jonas Salk, inventor of the polio vaccine, and lived in La Jolla, California until his death in 1995. In her late eighties now and based in Paris, Gilot still travels for international showings. Once known as a muse herself, she's now happy to be considered a muse for younger generations of artists.

---

29 It was "vulgar" of Madame Ramie to tell her. Gilot "armed" herself with her "belief that art was stronger than life's unwelcome anecdotal intrigues." Gilot, Matisse and Picasso, cited above, 274.

Philanthropy is a great blessing for Virgo Rising during the Sagittarian progression. Oprah Winfrey will feel tremendous joy when the graduates of her school in Africa make their adult contributions. The inner satisfaction of seeing the seeds she planted maturing and the world better off for her efforts should far exceed the fleeting joys of fame and material success. My older Virgo Rising clients enjoy this progression.

The Capricorn Progression

Cardinal Earth is the symbolic Trine to the Natal Ascendant. I know fewer clients in this cycle. Two have left the United States and returned to their natal place, near their extended family. Capricorn is the archetypal Matriarch or Patriarch. When Virgo Rising has developed harmonious family relationships, it's enjoyable to spend time with their adult children and grandchildren. Those who have developed the esoteric ruler seem content.

Psychiatrist George Vaillant asks an interesting two-part question: "what have you learned from your adult children and grandchildren? If you asked them, what would they say they had learned from you?" Former colleagues are sometimes viewed as extended family. Virgo Rising still enjoys being productive as they age, they like to keep in touch with their professional organizations even if they no longer practice their craft.

Though they may be too arthritic now to "cultivate their gardens" literally, Virgos usually enjoy having a window that opens on a park view or a well-tended golf course. I smile to think of the Egyptian Hermes with his Emerald Tablets! Green is a healing color.

Virgo Rising Bibliography

Brooks, Geraldine, "Orpheus at the Plough, the Father of Little Women," *The New Yorker,* January 10, 2005.

Faivre, Antoine, *The Eternal Hermes from Greek God to Alchemical Magus,* Joscelyn Godwin trans., (Grand Rapids: Phanes Press,) 1965, plates 1-38 on Hermes Trismegistes.

Farr, Florence, *Egyptian Magic,* (Wellingborough, UK: Aquarian Press,) 1982.

Gambaccini, Paul, *The McCartney Interviews After the* (Beatles,) *Breakup* (London: Omnibus,) 1975.

Gilot, Francoise, *Matisse and Picasso: A Friendship in Art,* (NY: Doubleday,) 1990.

Grylls, David, *Charles Dickens by David Slater,* (New Haven: Yale University Press,) 2009 *Financial Times,* book review, October 10, 2009.

Havill, Adrian, *Deep Truth: The Lives of Bob Woodward and Carl Bernstein,* (NY: Birch Lane Press,) 1994.

Hemingway, Ernest, *Hemingway on Writing,* ed. Larry W. Phillips, (NY: Barnes and Noble,) 1999.

—— *The Sun Also Rises,* (NY: Scribner,) 1986.

Hotchner, A.E., *Papa Hemingway: A Personal Memoir,* (NY: Random House,) 1966.

—— ed., *Dear Papa, Dear Hotch, The Correspondence of Ernest Hemingway and A.E. Hotchner,* (Kansas City: University of Missouri Press,) 2005.

Houston, Jean, *A Mythic Life: Learning to Live our Greater Story,* (San Francisco: HarperCollins,) 1996.

Kerenyi, Karl, *Hermes: Guide of Souls.* (Dallas: Spirit Publications,) 1990.

Meyrink, Gustav, *The Green Face,* (Atlanta: Daedalus,) 2004.

Shields, Charles J., *Mockingbird: A Portrait of Harper Lee,* (NY: Holt Paperbacks,) 2007.

Showalter, Ealine, "American Girls," Review of Library of America's *Collected Works of Louisa May Alcott, New York Times Magazine,* May 15, 2005.

Sperling, A. C., *Geoffrey Chaucer: The Knight's Tale from the Canterbury Tales,* (Cambridge: Cambridge University Press,) 1995.

Vaillant, George E., *Aging Well: Surprising Guideposts to a Happier Life,* (NY: Little, Brown and Company,) 2003.

Victor, Barbara, *Goddess: Inside Madonna,* (NY: Harper Collins,) 2001.

Virgil, *The Aeneid,* Robert Fagles trans., (New York: Viking,) 2006.

Woodward, Bob, *All The President's Men,* (NY: Simon and Schuster,) 1974.

VOLUME II: LIBRA - PISCES

CHAPTER ONE

Libra Rising - A Happy Life is Like an Art Form

Joseph Campbell, "Follow your bliss,"

T.S. Eliot, "You are the music while the music lasts."

Jimmy Buffet, "I just want to live happily ever after, every now and then."

—— "Whatever you think, be sure it's what *you* think; whatever you want, be sure that is what *you* want; whatever you feel, be sure that is what *you* feel."

—— "We shall not cease from exploration

And the end of all our exploring

Will be to arrive where we started

And know the place for the first time....

And all shall be well and

All manner of things shall be well." T.S. Eliot, *Four Quartets,* "Little Gidding"

Sidonie-Gabrielle Colette, "The true traveler is he who goes on foot, and even then, he sits down a lot of the time."

—— "I am going away with him to an unknown country where I shall have no past and no name, and where I shall be born again with a new face and an untried heart."

—— "We only do well the things we like doing."

Anais Nin, "Age does not protect you from love. But love, to some extent, protects you from age."

—— "How wrong it is for a woman to expect the man to build the world she wants, rather than to create it herself."

—— "My self is like the self of Proust, an instrument to connect life and myth."

—— "Life is a process of becoming, a combination of states we have to go through. Where people fail is that they wish to elect a state and remain in it. This is a kind of death."

—— "There is no separation between my life and my craft...my life is the form of my art."

—— "When you make a world tolerable for yourself, you make a world tolerable for others."

Albert Schweitzer, "The awareness that we are all human beings together has become lost in war and through politics."

—— "From naïve simplicity we arrive at more profound simplicity."

—— "There are two main refuges from the misery of life—music and cats."

—— "Constant kindness accomplishes much. As the sun makes ice melt, kindness causes mis-understanding, mistrust and hostility to evaporate."

—— "Humanitarianism consists in never sacrificing a human being to a purpose."

Jerry Garcia, "I don't know why, but you like some music and you don't like others. There's something about it that you like. Ultimately I don't find it's in my best interests to try and analyze it, since it's fundamentally emotional."

The Libra Rising Mask

I'm the Libran Mask. With my attractive appearance, charm and friendly smile, I make the best first impression of all the Masks! Decades later, my husband or wife is still telling people about the day we met, "I opened the door, there he (or she) stood, and I knew at once I'd met my future spouse!" How I love that romantic story!

I also love beautiful objects, so, like Paloma Picasso, I may be a jewelry or fashion designer, or interior decorator. Three Libra Rising women have perfumes named for them: Colette, Anais and Paloma. Cary Grant did advertisements for Fabrege. My taste is usually quite refined and very expensive.

However, I'm not just a pretty face; I'm also a good conversationalist. I'm popular partly because of my gift for finding a silver lining behind every storm cloud. As Colette once said, "hope costs nothing." I keep my sense of humor while those around me are losing theirs.

Like Sally Struthers and Sally Field, I often have comedic talent. Humor also comes through my art. When Yoko Ono met John Lennon at her exhibit, she was delighted that he shared her unusual (Venus-in-Aquarius) sense of humor.

A happy, love-filled life is my most important creation, my greatest ambition. Ideally, work is also play. Designing a comfortable lifestyle is itself an artistic process! Like Albert Schweitzer, George Harrison, Jerry Garcia and Jimmy Buffet, I may find music as essential as food and drink.

Several Venus-in-Pisces (Exalted) poets wear my Mask including T.S Eliot and Carl Sandburg, as well poets with Venus elsewhere, like Ralph W. Emerson. Some people consider me naïve and innocent, but others call me "the iron hand in the velvet glove" because my sweet appearance and tactful nature hide my strong competitive spirit. As Albert Schweitzer once said, "I see no reason to be unkind."

Unless I have a strong aspect from Saturn or Pluto to Venus, or several planets in Scorpio or the Eighth House, I believe, like Jimmy Carter, that more flies are caught with honey than vinegar.

I'm usually a peacemaker. However, if Mars is in my First House, I have no trouble whatsoever expressing my anger. Reporters who've interviewed Bill Clinton will confirm this! Anais Nin, Barbara Walters, Bill Clinton and Sonny Bono all have Mars-in-Libra (Detriment) in their First House.

Mars provides a competitive edge; Detriment Mars is often an asset in cutting through gullibility. Fairness and justice are vitally important to me. CNN television host Anderson Cooper, with Mars on his Ascendant, has a segment called, "Keeping Them Honest." Gracious and charming Barbara Walters asks her guests difficult personal questions, then passes them Kleenex tissues. The Dalai Lama, too, has a First House Mars. An apostle of peace, he's also adamant about Tibetan civil rights.

I know I seem indecisive. Sometimes I do fluctuate like a grocery store scales but I prefer to keep my options open until the last moment. A better offer might come along! However, once my decision is made, I'm adamant.

Astrologers are right, I want very much to be liked, so don't be too hard on me. And please don't share bad news with me unless it's absolutely necessary!

Remember, I'm *not* lazy, I'm simply lying fallow between projects. Colette was right, "we only do well the things we like doing."

How To Recognize Libra Rising

Librans are The Beautiful People—a great deal of time and effort goes into this Mask—but idealistic Libra is also about The Good and The True. Librans are, by nature, flirts; the Zodiac's romantics. The famous Libra Rising smile comes in many varieties from Stevie Wonder's to Suzanne Somers;' from Gary Cooper's to former president Jimmy Carter's (double Libran) toothy smile and John F. Kennedy's charming boyish grin.[1]

Unless Venus is afflicted to Saturn, Libra has a smooth, even complexion. They appear as Max Heindel said, "elegant."[2] Most Librans have a gift for choosing harmonious colors;

[1] Kennedy also had Libra Rising with Mars-in-Detriment, but his was in Taurus. As it was not part of his Mask it wasn't as visible. Detriment planets usually work harder than others.
[2] Max and Augusta Heindel, *The Message of the Stars,* (Oceanside: Rosicrucian Fellowship,) 1980, 101-03. Many of his Libra Rising clients had blue eyes, but my clients' were as likely to be hazel or brown. Heindel found Libra Rising "proud of their well-shaped heads and feet."

whether their eyes are dark, hazel or blue, they'll instinctively choose the right colors to accentuate them. Their eyes usually have a soft, gentle expression. Their other features, too, seem soft and blend well with each other, rather than standing out in a unique way.[3] Libra's face is usually symmetrical, like Anderson Cooper's (CNN) or Barbara Walters (20/20 and "The View.") Libra Rising is an attractive, photogenic Mask.

Libra Rising men will pull an unusual ensemble together with a colorful tie, and Libra Rising women with a shawl or scarf in ways that don't seem to work for the rest of us. The same necklace or watch that seems garish or ostentatious on someone else will look perfect on Libra Rising. Of course since most Librans have impeccable taste, they wouldn't own anything *really* gaudy.

Most of my Libra Rising clients are tall and slender in youth though a few are under 5'6." Ethnicity, of course, has an influence on height.

Many Librans instinctively rub their lower backs when standing after sitting a long time. The lower back, especially the kidney area, is problematic for Libra. In astrology we associate this with Saturn's Exaltation in the Sign.[4] Libra needs plenty of fluids, especially water, for electrolyte balance.

The Libran body type is on the whole, symmetrical. I've encountered very few that are either long or short-waisted. Because Libra really enjoys life's Good Things, including food and drink, by midlife most Librans have round abdomens. But even paunchiness doesn't seem as unattractive on Libra Rising as on the other Signs!

Apart from these physical characteristics, another important clue to recognizing Libra Rising, is their tendency to change the subject as soon as something unpleasant comes up in conversation. Even if they've had a bad day which left their Water planets sad or worried, Libra will "make nice" and attempt to keep social interaction on an even keel. Not only are they still well-groomed after a harrowing day, they're also gracious!

I once asked a client how she managed to keep her feelings hidden so well behind her Mask in spite of her pain. She replied, "Why would I want to dwell on a situation that I'm powerless to change? I only wish *others* would let *me* enjoy my evening out without venting!"

---

3 The smile alone is not enough to identify Libra. Before Barack Obama's mother provided his birth data, some astrologers expected to find Libra Rising because of his big smile. His *ears* however, are a stand-out feature, appreciated by political cartoonists! Those astrologers who guessed "Aquarius Rising" from his brilliant speeches and his cool demeanor were proven correct: "No Drama Obama" has Aquarius Rising.

4 Saturn is associated with the sacral area; the coccyx and tailbone. Yoga poses, particularly forward bends and Downward Facing Dog, are good to practice, especially after long airplane trips.

Unless there are strong adverse Saturn or Pluto aspects to Venus, or several planets in Scorpio or House Eight, the Libran Mask conveys optimism and positive expectations. Libra will remark at a party that "the economy will surely turn around in a few months" and "Susie (who has stage four cancer) will of course recover very soon."

However, if Libra has Scorpio or Eighth House planets, as soon as they leave the group they'll tell their spouse or close friend what they *really* think. This may contradict most of what they said earlier! ("Poor Susie looks dreadful" and "the economy will take at least a year to rebound.") With several First House Scorpio planets, Libra Rising may really be "a Scorpio with a smile," sardonic, sarcastic or even cynical.

With Gemini planets in trine to the Ascendant, Libra may later mimic other guests or gossip about them.[5] So if you meet someone new who tells you he or she has Libra Rising, someone who seems calm, gentle, peaceful and easygoing, remember that the entire horoscope must be considered, especially any First House planets and any other planets contacting the Ascendant.

There are other tendencies that enable us to recognize Libra Rising: they attempt to fashion a comfortable lifestyle around their talents and interests. Jimmy Buffet, George Harrison, Jerry Garcia, poets T. S. Eliot and Carl Sandburg as well as many elegant, beautiful socialites, attractive TV journalists and handsome politicians have succeeded at this.

Libran procrastination, that waiting "until it feels right" to proceed, seems to annoy others more than it rebounds on Libra Rising. Libra calmly meets deadlines at the last minute, usually looking well-rested; not one hair out of place.

Libra Rising will probably be discussing romance—if not theirs, someone else's—as they're the zodiac's matchmakers. Constantly weighing and evaluating options, Libra often asks others' advice, but like Alice in Wonderland, Libra Rising seldom ever follows it.[6]

There's also a Libran mannerism which I associate with Saturn's Exaltation in their Sign, an unconscious attempt to establish Cosmic Order around them. Libra Rising, and occasionally the Sun Sign too, may instinctively straighten the pens, notebooks, and other

---

5 Fire Signs often become impatient with Libra's 'pleaser nature', finding them deceitful. Many Sagittarians, whose high standards for Truth sometimes preclude little white lies told to "make nice" and who demand the literal truth, are especially put off when they later hear what Libra Rising *really thought*.

6 This tendency aggravates Earth Signs, especially Virgos, who'll spend hours on the phone advising them and helping research their various options.

items on their desk. Sometimes they'll lean over and straighten yours, too. It's a unique ritual.

The Mundane Ruler - Venus

She was a child and I was a child in a kingdom by the sea

But we loved with a love that was more than a love,

I and my Annabel Lee…

With a love that the winged seraphs of heaven

coveted her and me…

Yes! that was the reason (as all men know,

 in this kingdom by the sea)

That the wind came out of the cloud by night,

Chilling and killing my Annabel Lee…

But our love it was stronger by far than the love

Of those who were older than we

Of many far wiser than we.

And neither the angels in heaven above,

Nor the demons down under the sea,

Can ever dissever my soul from the soul

Of the beautiful Annabel Lee.

Though his Ascendant Sign is unknown,[7] Edgar Allan Poe really captured Aphrodite-ruled Libra in his poem, "Annabel Lee" about young love that will surely last forever, love so strong that even the angels covet it. And, of course, the poem also captures the pain of loss, the Eros and Thanatos polarity of love and death, of Venus and Pluto. We're mortals, after all, and eventually everything comes to an end here on earth.

Mundane rulers are associated with survival needs. What does Libra Rising require for survival? Love. Libra Rising men and women both use the words "love" and "intimacy." However for the women, love means *romance*, which includes tenderness, affection and attention. In the words of a Libra Rising client, "I need him to listen to *me*; to look at *me*

7 It's possibly Scorpio; he lived a tumultuous life. He also wrote many macabre short stories. When he married his cousin she was only 13, but they waited two years to consummate the marriage.

and *not* look around at other women! I don't like feeling neglected. And I certainly don't want him looking at pornography; *I'm* his Aphrodite! *I'm* beautiful and sexy enough for any man!" For the women, love means expressing appreciation: Aphrodite wants to hear, "you look beautiful tonight. Is that a new outfit?" She seeks kindness, loyalty, mutual support. She wants to establish a happy, lasting relationship.[8]

Libra Rising men are romantic in youth—finding their mate seems quite important to them as well—but soon after marriage they tend to delegate "all that relationship stuff" to their wives and devote themselves to music, their art form or their career. This comes as a surprise, and often a shock to their wives because during courtship many of them, especially the men with Venus-in-Pisces, wrote songs or poetry and arranged candlelight dinners. The spouse will remark, "I thought he was so different, so romantic, but now he's behaving just like my first husband!" Romance wanes after marriage for Libra Rising as for the other Signs. Their fantasy life seems to be channeled elsewhere, according to the Sign and Houses where Venus and the other imaginative planets[9] are located.

As ruler of Libra Rising, Aphrodite attempts to create a lifestyle where her desires and fantasies are likely to be fulfilled. Like Joseph Campbell (Venus-in-Pisces) she follows her bliss, usually in a graceful and dignified manner,[10] with her sweet, sometimes enigmatic "Mona Lisa" smile.

Helen of Troy's smile launched a thousand ships filled with warriors setting out to defend her honor and bring her home. She, no doubt, had Libra Rising! Aphrodite herself was said to envy Helen's beauty.

The Femme Fatal Archetype, personified by movie stars, looms large in our culture today. Aphrodite seems to share her Femme Fatale allure (she was the married lover of Hermes, Ares and Poseidon) with many Libra Rising women. When men first see her across a crowded room, they're seduced by her radiant beauty, her dazzling smile. Bored with the role of wife and mother, (just as young Adonis is often bored with the role of husband and father,) the Femme Fatale casts her romantic spell, causing a yearning, a longing for Beauty. Men of all ages, smitten by her, have told me, "I was certain my luck

---

8 A student once asked, "but don't *all* women want these things, not just Libra Rising women?" It's true that everyone has Aphrodite (Venus) somewhere in their horoscope but a good relationship is as necessary as food, sunlight and shelter to Libra. When they're unhappy, they tend to look outside the marriage for romance.

9 The Moon and Neptune.

10 There are a few exceptions now in the film industry; young women with Libra Rising who are rather coarse and dress almost like prostitutes. When we discussed this modern trend during a Santa Fe workshop, psychologist and playwright Marcie Teleander reminded me that they're "*sacred* skanks" in the ancient tradition of temple prostitutes dedicated to the Goddesses.

would change once we were married!" It did, but not in the way they expected. They often lost their house, their savings and the custody of their children over her. Older men were usually devastated when she left them, though one remarked philosophically, "(it was) better to have loved and lost than never loved at all."

As mundane ruler, Aphrodite is consistent in her own way, She always promotes romance! Libra Rising has an instinct for matchmaking, which sometimes works for her friends.

In folklore, the Muses and the Graces accompany Aphrodite; three of the Muses are associated with poetry alone. Many poets have Exalted Venus-in-Pisces ruling their Libra Ascendant. Exalted Venus signifies talent, and seems to draw success in the arts.

In music, the Exalted Venus short list includes Andrei Segovia, Sergei Prokofiev, Jon Bon Jovi, George Harrison, Rod Stewart and Seventies' idol Alice Cooper.[11] Authors Colette, Anais Nin, Carl Sandburg and Joseph Campbell have Venus-in-Pisces. Sardonic comedian Bill Maher of the TV show, *Politically Correct* has Venus-in-Pisces trine his *Neptune-in-Scorpio* in the middle of the First House.

Poets Arthur Rimbaud and T.S. Eliot had Venus-in-Libra (Rulership.) Libra. Eliot's Venus was on his Libran Ascendant; Rimbaud's was loosely conjunct his Libran Moon in the Twelfth House. Rimbaud needed solitude so badly that he moved to North Africa to escape his older lover, Paul Verlaine. Rimbaud, known for his beautiful imagery, died young.[12]

One of T.S. Eliot's favorite authors, Ralph Waldo Emerson had Libra Rising, with Venus-in-Detriment. (Aries.)[13]

American author T.S. Eliot (quoted above, "you are the music while the music lasts") created a life for himself in London. In fact, he became so comfortable, he became a British citizen. Hearing his accent was shocking to visiting American readers; they'd thought him a British author.

His sad, unstable wife was institutionalized several times. Emily Hale, his muse and mistress of many years, had expected to marry him after his wife died. But Eliot surprised

---

11 Stevie Wonder, Cat Stevens, Courtney Love and many others have Libra Rising with Venus in other Signs.

12 He wrote all his poetry between the ages of 15 and 21. Anais Nin loved his writing; images came to her while she read and some of his sentences inspired her short stories.

13 He once happily told a friend that Emerson would have approved of his muse, Emily, because she was a "true New England woman. She taught at prestigious Smith College.

her by marrying a secretary he'd only known a short time. Friends said, "poor Emily was never the same."[14]

Several Libra Rising men have requested that we spend the entire astrology session on the problem of finding a mate: "When will she appear? What will she be like? Because I'll know I'll be happy after I meet my soul mate. My life will take off as soon she comes; I'm (intuitively) certain of it! I need my anchor, my life partner, before I can do anything else."

Like Eliot, they're looking for a muse to inspire them. I used to think they were waiting to "delegate their Venus"—their ability to create a happy relationship—to the Soul Mate so they could move on to learning a skill or profession. Meanwhile, they ushered at the church, "checking out" the newly-arrived women, worked part time and attended talks on spirituality or lethargically strummed their guitars.

But one day after a sad session with a Libra Rising man—he'd once again thought he'd met "the one" but hadn't—I left the disappointed, enervated fellow to attend a talk by Jungian analyst, Robert Johnson.

Robert's topic was the romance of Tristan and Isolde, the central theme of his new book, *We*, on the topic of Relationship. He mentioned that the name of the knight, the protagonist in the tale, was Tristan. And that Tristan comes from the French word *triste*, or sad. And I thought, "that's amazing." A knight who's *sad about his love life*; I've just left someone like that!

Will Tristan, the sad knight in the tale, find his soul mate, get his energy back and begin to enjoy life? If he does find her, will he then try to delegate his Venus—the full responsibility of "relating"—*to her*? Will she stay with him? Or will they separate, as happens with so many "modern knights." Each time they're sure she's "the right one," yet the fair maiden will disappears or, after a short time, the knight becomes disappointed in her and becomes entranced by someone new.

So I sat on the edge of my hard folding chair and listened intently to the story. As Robert's talk progressed, I realized I'd been using the wrong language; that the "Tristans" I knew weren't consciously delegating their inner Aphrodite, but unconsciously *projecting*

---

14 Biographer Lyndall Gordon says Eliot believed a muse necessary to a poet. He also believed that the wife and the muse couldn't be the same woman. With Saturn in his Tenth House, Eliot attempted to create the perfect lifestyle for a writer; he was frustrated at falling short of his goal. (It's impossible to keep The Scales in perfect balance!) Gordon's title, *T. S. Eliot, An Imperfect Life*, comes from Eliot's attempts at perfection. See *An Imperfect Life*, (NY: WW Norton & Co) 1998, ix; on the muse, pp 71 and 82. Eliot's efforts, (except for the muse,) are similar to those of many Libra Rising clients in the arts and music to create "a lifestyle that works."

her on prospective partners. Regardless of vocabulary, though, the situation is the same. Like Tristan, the Libra Rising men were seeking completion; they'd correctly intuited that Love (Aphrodite) would make them Whole.

They were confusing a spiritual quest for Divine Love with their romantic search for a wife. They expected a human woman to fulfill them, to confer Wholeness, when only the Divine can accomplish that. They sought something in the outer world which can only be found within. No wonder they were sad, disappointed and lethargic.

This is a beautiful but complicated story in the Celtic tradition. There are often two of something in Celtic tales—two Grail cups or two disappearing castles. In this story, there are two Isoldes: Isolde the Fair, and Isolde of the White Hands.

Isolde the Fair was a healer. The daughter of a sorceress, Isolde herself was quite talented at casting spells. When the story began, her marriage had already been arranged to Tristan's uncle, the King of Cornwall. Tristan knew that. He had, in fact, been dispatched to escort Isolde across the sea from Ireland to marry King Mark. Bringing the future bride safely to his uncle was his first diplomatic mission.

It was challenging, too, because he had a history with Isolde. The last time Tristan saw her, Isolde said she hated him and raised her dagger against him! This happened after he had washed up on shore near her castle, wounded from battle. While cleansing his wound and applying healing herbs to it, she discovered a sword shard, which she matched to the missing piece in her brother Morholt's sword. She had just saved her brother's murderer! Would she agree to sail with him? His mission would require finesse.

Meanwhile the second Isolde, was sitting calmly in Normandy, sewing her trousseau in hopes of a normal marriage. Unlike Isolde the Fair, Isolde of the White Hands was an ordinary, *available* young noblewoman. She had no mysterious powers and no past history with Tristan. They had yet to meet.

When Tristan arrived at the Irish castle, he was again struck by the unusual beauty of Isolde the Fair. He thought, "this is no ordinary human woman!" And he was right. He convinced her to sail with him, in spite of her grievance about Morholt.

Then, the night before they left for Cornwall, Isolde's sorceress- mother gave her a vial, a potion, to drink with Tristan on the ship. "Guard this carefully," she told her daughter, *"for it contains both Life and Death."* Eros and Thanatos, the unavailable love and death mix together in the potion.

Isolde's mother may have thought, "one day handsome young Tristan will inherit the throne; Isolde should be with *him,* not the old uncle." Or she may have hated the man who killed her son in battle. Whatever she thought, she mixed love with death.

The two young people were soon "at sea" and drinking from the vial. As they drank, they immediately fell in love in the charmed Neptunean atmosphere.[15] They embraced and sated their passion. Before the ship docked, Tristan vowed that Isolde was henceforth *his only love,* that he would never make love to another woman. And she vowed that in spite of her future wedding to King Mark, she would never be sexually intimate with anyone but Tristan.

They arrived in Cornwall; Isolde quickly married King Mark and became his Queen. She was now even more unattainable! But on her wedding night she cast a spell on her maid, Branigan which sent her to King Mark's bed and caused him to mistake Branigan for Isolde. The two young lovers enjoyed their nightly trysts for awhile, but were finally observed by a jealous baron. And the baron told the King about them.

The next evening, King Mark looked out his balcony window and saw Isolde pacing in the courtyard below. But she felt his eyes on her. As soon as her lover arrived, she quickly gave Tristan a signal to leave. Instead, he dropped to his knees and said, "I am truly sorry, my lady, that an evil baron has started malicious rumors about us." When the king observed Tristan humbly kneeling before his wife, he decided to have the baron arrested.

After several such narrow escapes, Isolde convinced Tristan to run away with her. One night, after three years in the woods, they fell asleep fully clothed with Tristan's sword between them. On that night, the King finally found them. However, He did not wake them, preferring to believe that they lay together as brother and sister.

During their fourth year in the woods— the number four symbolizes Completion— they decided to return to the castle. They approached a wise hermit and told him of their plight. Tristan blamed it entirely on the potion. "Love just happens," he explained, *"we didn't plan it that way."*

That much was true, nobody plans to fall in love, it's one of the few things in modern society that we *don't* plan!

However, the hermit was not impressed with his argument. It had been a long time since they drank that potion. He pointed out that its effects had worn off; and they now had their free will back, and with it their responsibilities. Never mind romance; Tristan was guilty of treason to his feudal lord, and Isolde was an adulteress. So he sent them back to the King, though he promised to write a letter on their behalf.

---

15 It feels somewhat like the kingdom by the sea in Poe's poem, "Annabel Lee, " (see the beginning of this chapter) where the young couple "loved with a love that was more than a love." That, too, is like a charmed, illusory setting. The reader feels after the first few verses that something is very wrong; the story will have a sad ending. Neptune is represented by the spell and the potion.

Tristan sought and expected reinstatement as a knight of the realm. However, the hermit's letter suggested that if King Mark chose to take Isolde back, he should also deport Tristan. Clearly the two could not resist each other, the knight should not remain in Cornwall!

King Mark agreed with the hermit, Tristan would have to leave.

But Isolde gave him a jade ring and told him, if ever you need me, send it as a sign."

Tristan traveled to Normandy where he met Isolde of the White Hands, who was innocent, loving and very *human*. She had no potions or spells. She didn't lead him into an enchanted forest. He grew fond of Isolde of the White Hands, and after some time had passed, he agreed to marry her.

However, on his wedding night he remembered his vow to Isolde the Fair, his "once and forever love." He didn't tell his new wife the real reason for not consummating the marriage, only that he had made a solemn vow which he could not break.

Eventually, the young bride told her brother the situation. And he convinced Tristan to tell him the entire story of the vow.

"You need to journey back to Cornwell," he said, "you'll find Queen Isolde quite happy by now. *She's forgotten you, Tristan.* When you see that, you'll return to Normandy and all will be well between you and my sister."

So Tristan returned to Cornwall in disguise. As soon as he sent the jade ring to Isolde; she appeared and rushed into his arms. It was as if he'd never left her! Still, they could not be together.

In a short time, Tristan's vitality began to wane. He felt as if he'd made a pact with death when he drank the potion and made his vow! He knew he'd have to leave her again. His energy would return once he was back with Isolde of the White Hands.[16]

But Queen Isolde the Fair told him, "if you ever need me, send me the jade ring."

Many years passed, Tristan was again wounded in battle, this time fatally. He sent the ring to Isolde the Fair and asked her to come to him. She sent back word that she would try. She would sail for France; if he saw white sails she could dock; black sails would mean it was impossible for her.

Tristan sat at his window every day and watched for Isolde. Finally, a ship came into view; its sails were white. By then Tristan was too weak to sit; he asked his wife if she could see the color of the sails on the ship. "Why yes," said Isolde of the White Hands, (she who

---

16 In the Leo chapter of *Beyond the Mask, Part I*, there's a similar story about a Princess who must, of her own volition, give up the illusion of happiness in the Troll's castle if she wants a human husband. As soon as she does, her vitality returns and she's healed.

was only human,) "I see a ship passing, its sails are black as night." When Isolde reached him, Tristan was dead; she collapsed on his body and they were reunited in death.

Over the years I've encountered Tristan's naivety, sadness and lethargy (loss of vitality) in several Libra Rising clients, more men than women, although women with aspects from Neptune-in-Libra to their Venus or their Moon have also suffered from addiction to the Unattainable Love.

Like Tristan, they suffered disappointment each time they passed through the drama of separation and reunion, "we tried again and failed; somehow it never happens." With Aries Fire on the Seventh House cusp (the House of Marriage and other long-term relationships) Libra Rising seems *temporarily* stimulated by their heroic efforts to "make it work" with the Unattainable love, but cumulatively the situation is draining; enervating.

Often there's even an "Isolde of the White Hands" waiting in the wings, an ordinary, available woman who really loves them; a mortal with no other agenda, no life as Queen of Cornwall to defend. Most of Libra's friends and relatives wonder why they don't see the beauty of the "ordinary mortal."

Part of the addiction, though, is not to the person but to the drama, the intrigue of secret assignations; the risk of being caught, the larger-than life mystery of the Unattainable Love. Like Tristan, they feel caught up in a situation like the one Poe described in "Annabel Lee;" "we loved with a love *that was more than a love…*" a love that made other, powerful people envious: barons, the King; in Poe's poem, even the angels.

When like Tristan, Libra Rising falls in love with his boss's wife, this can cause a serious strain on his health, perhaps even open the door to Thanatos. Though today's bosses lack the power that King Mark had to disinherit and deport their vassals, they do have the power to fire Libra and/or like the barons in the story, spread rumors about his lack of loyalty throughout the land. Even today, he may find it easier to leave the area and start over.

And there are also cases where one of the lovers did become ill, like Tristan; lost his vitality and will to live.

Venus, the Feeling Function, Aesthetics, and Individual Taste

When it comes to taste, especially color and decorating, unless Venus is afflicted to Saturn, the partner is often better off letting Libra make the choices. In this Aphrodite area, Libra is usually quite talented.

While on the subject of music, Jerry Garcia of the *Grateful Dead* explained the Feeling Function perhaps better than anyone else:

> I don't know why, but you like some music and you don't like others. There's something about it that you like. Ultimately I don't find it's in my best interests to try and analyze it, since it's fundamentally emotional.

Most Librans have a confidence in their taste that seems to be missing in their Thinking Function friends, relatives and spouses. In my experience, this "Aphrodite confidence" is usually justified!

Neptune-in-Libra (1943-1957)

Neptune-in-Libra seems to intensify Aphrodite's influence on Libra's romantic nature. In my practice, I've encountered more Baby Boomers with Neptune in the First or Twelfth House who were addicted to love or "in love with (the idea of) Love" than Boomers with alcohol or drug addictions.[17] A First House Neptune aspecting Venus-in-Libra is highly susceptible to the addiction to romance. Neptune also has its own seductive, sensuous allure.

Fortunately, there are many positive outlets for Neptune in a Venus-ruled horoscope as the two planets work well together.[18] Neptune is a visionary planet. As ruler of Pisces, highly imaginative Neptune is gifted in working with images and symbols. Symbolically, Neptune-Poseidon rules the waters of the Creative Unconscious, from which our dreams and visions arise.

With Neptune-in-Libra near the Ascendant, the Baby Boomer may be an intuitive psychologist with a rich fantasy life. If a Jungian, he or she may enjoy Active Imagination. However, if Neptune is close to the Ascendant, rather than in the middle or the bottom of the First House, others may also receive mixed signals from the counselor's Neptune.

While Libra Rising intends to be pleasant and charming, Neptune easily takes on others' projections, so maintaining boundaries with clients or patients of the opposite sex may be a challenge. It helps that Libra is an *Air Sign*. (See below, The Element.)

---

17 The latter two addictions are usually the more common Dionysian pattern when Neptune is in the First House or the Seventh House.
18 Traditionally, the planet that rules the Rising Sign is considered the ruler of the horoscope.

In mythology, Aphrodite is surrounded by the Muses. And they can be helpful for all of us, not only for Libra Rising. When we think of the Muses, music, art and poetry usually come to mind. And there are many famous Libra Rising poets, musicians and songwriters. But we may have forgotten that drama (comedy and tragedy), history, and astronomy have their muses, too. Venus-Neptune aspects may reveal a hidden talent in one of these areas. Libra's esoteric ruler may have an interest in astrology or astronomy.

The visual arts, prophecy (especially through Tarot cards), television, the film industry, photography, fashion design and decorating are all Venus-Neptune fields. Though the Baby Boomer generation is known for colorful tie-dyed fabrics, psychedelics, disco dancing under flashing lights, they also designed computer software and developed technology that eventually led to the Internet. A horoscope with an angular Neptune (in Houses 1, 4, 7 or 10) can imagine and design almost anything.

The Esoteric Ruler
Uranus Impersonal (Unselfish) Divine Love

Uranus, Libra's esoteric ruler, takes Libra Rising on a journey beyond Aphrodite's self-absorption. For every Rising Sign, the esoteric (spiritual) ruler symbolizes a way of growing beyond the mundane ruler's survival skills. (Many Libra Rising clients have told me they couldn't survive a day without love.)

Yet, Aphrodite represents a personal, subjective love. Caught up in her own desires, Venus has very strong likes and dislikes. If you value (attach feeling and emotion to) the same things Aphrodite does, she'll like you. She may even fall in love with you and anticipate a long, happy life (or at least create a comfortable lifestyle) with you.

But romance wanes after courtship. Venus is vain, fickle, and sometimes superficial. "Do you remember my first love, my high school sweetheart?" Libra's inner Aphrodite asks. "He (or she) was a wonderful person. But, then, somehow I outgrew him (or her). I lost interest right around the time I met my second spouse. What timing! Isn't fate amazing?"

We may sometimes wonder if Libra Rising saw her "ex" as a *person,* apart from the role he or she played in Libra's life story. And we understand why Tristan's wife told him that the ship had *black sails* when they were really white! She was very human.

How does Libra Rising's spouse keep Aphrodite interested once the bloom is off the rose of romance? It helps if there's a common "Uranus interest," a desire to make the world a better place in some way. It can come through the arts, political organizing, the media, philosophy or medicine.

Ideally, the "Uranus interest" will not only bond the couple together but will also bring in new people and intellectual stimulation. (Uranus rules the Air Sign Aquarius, which involves groups and friendship.) With a "Uranus interest," Libra's inner Aphrodite is less likely to become bored and sulky; to expect the impossible of the spouse or of marriage itself, to feel "disappointed" and "unfulfilled." With an ever-expanding circle of friends some of the pressure is removed from what Carl G. Jung called the "container" that is marriage.

Libra Rising has Aries on the Seventh House cusp. Libra often looks to the spouse to bring excitement and drama to their cool, calm and collected Ascendant.

The long marriages of Carl Sandburg, Joseph Campbell, Albert Schweitzer and Jimmy Carter[19] centered around common interests, mutual idealism and the constant stimulation of their circle of friends. Helga Sandburg, daughter of the poet and biographer, wrote about her parents' marriage in *A Great and Glorious Romance, The Story of Carl Sandburg and Lilian Steichen.*[20] The Sandburgs met as young, enthusiastic organizers for the Social Democratic Party. Carl was very restless prior to his marriage. Unable to find work, he'd hopped freight trains to see the country during the Great Depression. Lilian's life as a housewife was not what she'd expected as a young political activist, she expected a more adventurous life. But she loved Carl deeply and was always supportive.

Jimmy Carter's wife Rosalynn gave birth to three of her four children in different states while her husband was in the Navy. As one of his closest political advisors, Rosalyn sat in on Cabinet meetings at the White House. She worked on behalf of mental health as First Lady in Georgia and Washington D.C. Interviewed by Larry King on CNN several years ago, she joked that she was delighted to see Jimmy's paintings selling on E-bay because "he's' done so many that we're running out of space." She was very supportive of his Habitat for Humanity project.

The William J. Clinton Foundation, established by the former president, is dedicated to

---

19 Dr. Albert Schweitzer and his wife built their own clinic in Africa, (the former French colony that is now Gabon.) She worked with him as an anesthetist. Long lines of patients, who walked miles to see them, arrived every day. He disliked preparing sermons; his happiest hours were spent playing the organ which his friends in Germany had shipped to him to assemble, piece-by-piece. Because Gabon belonged to France and they were German nationals, they were deported to Europe during World War II. He returned with another assistant after the war and rebuilt the clinic. His wife, however, preferred to stay home.
20 (n.p: Eastern National,) 2002.

eradicating disease worldwide. Though his wife Hillary, the current U.S. Secretary of State is not involved with it.

One of the Twentieth Century's most innovative thinkers was Joseph Campbell, whose books on mythology intrigued so many of us. In the 1940's he married Jean Erdman, a Sarah Lawrence student. After studying with Martha Graham, Jean became a professional dancer. Joseph accompanied her on her tour across India and Japan in the mid 1950s.[21] Together they explored psychology, mythology, and the role of the arts, dance and music in personal growth. Jean choreographed Broadway plays; she founded her own dance theater. After her husband's death, she established the Joseph Campbell Foundation to carry on their work. Uranus' instinct toward the widespread sharing of knowledge permeates the couple's life and work.

I could cite many more examples of happy marriages among my Libra Rising friends and clients. For nearly all of them, Uranus plays a part in enhancing their lives. A couple working together on a project or for a cause that interests them both are often able to make a contribution far beyond what either of them could achieve alone.

Anima and Animus
The Venus Rulership and Exalted Saturn

Addiction to romance is often a problem for Venus-ruled Libra Rising, especially when Natal Neptune aspects Venus.[22] In his book *We*, Robert Johnson explains how this addiction became deeply entrenched in the Western psyche. Over the centuries, from the seed of the medieval Courtly Love tradition, a deeply-rooted tree grew very tall and spread its branches wide. We now live underneath its leafy umbrella.

It can be tempting to avoid or escape the monotonous reality of daily life with the same person as Tristan did after his marriage to Isolde of the White Hands, fanaticizing and pining away for his "One True Love," Isolde the Fair.

As a culture, we've fallen in love with the idea (or the ideal) of the perfect love. Romance novels and romantic movies are ubiquitous. In the Middle Ages, however, the Lady was a symbol of Divine Love to the troubadours who wrote lyrical poems and songs devoted to the Fair Maiden.

---

21 Joseph Campbell, *Baksheesh and Brahman, Indian Journal, 1954-1955,* (San Francisco: HarperCollins) 1955.
22 Moon-in-Libra conjunct Neptune is often addicted to romance as well, especially in the Fourth or Seventh Houses.

As Robert Johnson describes it, Courtly Love may have been a medieval technique like Active Imagination. It was a technique through which a "selfish young knight like Tristan" could, while absorbed in his Lady, transcend his ego and learn Unselfish Love.

Through lyrical songs, stories and poetry, the knight transcended his own personal desires, fantasies and concerns about what the beloved could do *for him* or fulfill in *him*. In Courtly Love, *the* focus was on *her*.

Because in medieval times, the noble lady of the song, *roman*, or poem was already married or betrothed *to someone other than the knight*, he never actually expected to marry her. The knight knew and accepted that she was unattainable. It was a fantasy relationship. He wasn't keeping his options open awaiting the arrival of the Perfect Maiden,[23] nor did he attempt to take a 'sacred vow' of celibacy.[24] He married a suitable noblewoman and led a normal family life.

Isolde the Fair is the *anima figure*, the knight's soul projected outward, on a beautiful, otherworldly maiden while Isolde of the White Hands is, of course, his human partner in the "real" world. In the Courtly Love tradition, Tristan really had no need to give up one in order to possess the other. But the love potion (Neptune) confused everything for him and resulted in his "sacred vow."

According to Jungian analyst Robert Johnson, our challenge lies in respecting the *inner anima* (Aphrodite) and in doing our own inner work, rather than projecting it upon the lover or spouse. However, that seems more accurate for Libra Rising men than Libra Rising women. The women, generally speaking, seem to have an easier relationship with Aphrodite. They seem to work with their Neptune fantasies in a more constructive way.

If Saturn is strong by House position or aspects, Libra Rising women are more likely to have such *animus* issues as judgmentalism, ("why are other people so irresponsible?")

---

23 A Libra Rising client once referred to her as "She Who is To Come."

24 Several of my Libran clients have joked that there were many days when they wished they could take one! Libra Rising T.S. Eliot told a friend that he wished *he* could when his wife Vivienne was institutionalized and on morphine. Eliot's horoscope was 70% Air. He was drawn to her "excitable, eager nature, her quick fire." Gordon, cited above, 113. With Aries is on the cusp of the Marriage House for Libra Rising, the partner often brings drama, but Vivienne was excessive!

rigid opinions, addiction to perfection or spiritual dryness than to project their spirituality or artistic side on someone else.[25]

Symbolically, Saturn is Exalted in Libra. Libra Rising women with Saturn *literally* in Libra in the First House, especially when conjunct the *Ascendant degree,* tend to wear black or navy blue business suits, uniforms or lab coats.

Saturn in square, opposition or inconjunct (150 degrees) to the Ascendant degree tends to work the same way as in the First House but is not as obvious. Though "animus women" may wear a pleasant Libra smile, many have a sadness in their eyes as ambition wanes after Midlife.

Status and financial security are high on their list of expectations for marriage; romance, sexual intimacy and companionship usually rank lower. When Venus is in positive aspect to Saturn, "love of duty" shines through career and family relationships. Many take care of their elderly parents.However, those who attune to Venus and the muses after Midlife seem more contented; some saturnine Librans even seem younger and less serious-minded after midlife than in youth.

The Element - Air

Aphrodite's strong emotional nature is kept in balance by the Air Element. When we first encounter the "calm, cool and collected Mask" of Libra Rising, it's the aloof Air Element that we feel.

Libra's mundane ruler is subjective; her world is personal. Libra Rising Anais Nin considered the subjective view as important as the objective.[26] Her point is well taken, in fact, it seems *more* important to some artists. Many clients with Libra Rising constantly reference events in the outer world to their inner lives: how do political and economic changes impact soul growth? What symbolic messages lay behind new a challenge, like unemployment? What is Libra *personally* to learn from the situation?

---

25 "Addiction to perfection" tendencies may surface with Saturn-in-the-First-House, regardless of Rising Sign. For people with Natal Saturn-in-Libra approaching 60, though, 2010-12 is the Second Saturn Return cycle. As we grow older, Saturn tends towards vain regrets "I should have…" "If *only* I had…" or to odious comparisons like, "my friend sold his home during the Boom for a very high price. There was *no way* I could have moved then. Still, it seems so unfair that my friend was able to do it and I couldn't!"

26 Wendy M. DuBow, *Conversation with Anais Nin 1965-1972,* (Jacksonville: University of Mississippi Press,) 1994, 41.

However, Venus *is* self-absorbed. In youth, Libra's interests are usually limited to those shared by their circle of friends. The Air Element contributes objectivity and a broader perspective. Air is concerned with ideas and ideals. As Librans mature, their interests broaden.

Restlessness is an Air quality. The right partner helps to anchor Libra as Lilian Sandburg anchored Carl, the former vagabond.[27] It's important to keep the Airy mind occupied with new ideas and shared interests. Otherwise, the waning of romance after marriage usually feels like T.S. Eliot's desolate Waste Land to Librans. There are many healing options: reading, writing, blogging, playing an instrument, so many life-enriching ways to honor the muses.

Unless there's a high percentage of Air planets in the horoscope,[28] Libra Rising is not as detached as the other Air Ascendants. Unlike Gemini and Aquarius, 'Aphrodite people' are less able to compartmentalize their personal and professional lives. It's extremely difficult for Libra to conduct business-as-usual while going through a divorce. Eventually, when they feel ready for romance again, their energy and vitality return to normal.

An extraverted Element, Air works well with Aphrodite's charm and magnetism and with Uranus' humanitarian instinct to share their knowledge and experience with others.

If there are many Air planets, including Mercury, aspecting the Ascendant Libra has a quick mind and highly effective verbal skills. There are many brilliant Libra Rising people, among them Dr. Albert Schweitzer, Joseph Campbell, Juan Ramon Jimenez and T.S. Eliot. Bill Clinton and John Kennedy are considered among American's most intelligent presidents.

With very little formal education, Anais Nin and Colette achieved literary success.

Humor is another attribute of Air.[29] Fortunately, Librans are able to laugh at themselves

---

27 He remembered his "hobo" days nostalgically. Sandburg lived in three different states, ending his days in North Carolina. One of Colette's most acclaimed books was *The Vagabond,* written after three years touring music halls. Erica Jong called it, "a rare thing, one of the first and best feminist novels every written."

28 Colette was born at the New Moon in Aquarius, with the Sun-Moon conjunction in trine to Libra Rising. She was Triple Air, it's no wonder that Andre Gide praised her intelligence! She once said that people thought her sentimental (Venus-in- Pisces), but she didn't see herself that way at all. Phelps, cited above, introduction.

29 George Vaillant, cited above, 63 and 81. He sees the ability to laugh at oneself even in painful situations as a major asset in the aging process; it's an antidote to "depressive and paranoid thoughts that make many older people unhappy."

on days when life is *just plain unfair.* Humor helps on days when, after naively vowing never to let someone into their lives again, Libra discovers that the person is back and, of course, hasn't changed at all. When a friend or relative is outraged on Libra's behalf, Libra usually laughs. "Yes," Libra will say, "but I'm so much happier naïve than I would be cynical."

Librans often ask themselves, "Why must life be such a struggle? Why can't I just relax and be comfortable?" Jimmy Buffet put it well, "I just want to live happily ever after, every now and then." My Libra Rising clients agree with him; many have expressed the same sentiment.

And there are happy times, too. In a playful mood, T.S. Eliot, the same poet who wrote "The Waste Land" after the destruction of World War II and "Sweeney Agonistes,"[30] also wrote "Old Possum's Book of Practical Cats." So many audiences have enjoyed its musical version, "CATS!"

Eliot's late-in-life philosophical writing is altogether different from his postwar poetry. Each section of "Four Quartets," written at the end of his life, is about a different Element. In the last section, "Little Gidding," he wrote these beautiful lines.

> We shall not cease from exploration
>
> And the end of all our exploring
>
> Will be to arrive where we started
>
> And know the place for the first time…
>
> And all shall be well/and all manner of things shall be well.[31]

He must have been happy the day he wrote: "We are the music till the music stops."

Libra Rising poets and songwriters are similar. Stevie Wonder throws himself completely into his music in the same way. And Joseph Campbell was no ordinary academic. Campbell taught a generation the difference between religiosity (dogma, accepting others' beliefs)

---

30 Eliot's plays "Sweeney Agonistes" and "Family Reunion " were not well received by audiences or critics. He seems to have processed his marriage through the characters, especially the wife who refused to let go of her husband. On the other hand, audiences liked his play "Murder in the Cathedral."

31 T.S. Eliot, *Collected Poems, 1909-62, Four Quartets,* "Little Gidding," (NY: Harcourt Brace,) 1963. Some say there 's also a loose correlation to the four seasons. I sometimes like to close yoga classes with the last two lines of this stanza. "Little Gidding," his the last poem, was written the year before he died, (1942) the *Quartets* (written over six years) were first published together in 1943. Dante, Christian theology, the *Bhagavat Gita* and the *Mahabharatha* all come through the *Quartets.*

and spirituality (personal spiritual experience through which we become truly conscious, truly alive.)

Best known as the philosopher who told his readers and the PBS television audience to *follow their bliss,* Campbell's intuitive grasp of mythology and his clear writing style helped a generation of students to see value of mythology, East and West. His "Mask" series was a major influence on filmmaker George Lucas' *Star Wars* series. Campbell's *Skeleton Key to Finnigan's Wake* serves as a Rosetta Stone, enabling readers to decipher James Joyce's words.

The Mode - Cardinality

Cardinality is about leadership qualities, management skills, the ability to organize ourselves and our projects. Cardinality is also associated with the impulse to compete and win. (There's more information about it in the FAQ section as well.)

At first glance it appears that calm, charming Libran Rising, the Sign of sweet smiles and diplomatic finesse would be the ideal *employee,* not the office manager. However, that's not the case. Most of my Libra Rising clients are self-employed.

Because Libra seems so willing to please, Mothers of Libran children are often surprised to learn that this is Cardinal Sign.

"Really? You mean Libra is like Aries and Capricorn? Because I'm sure my teenage daughter would rather be voted Miss Congeniality by the other contestants than win the Miss America crown," one mom remarked, laughing. I told her to wait and observe. Watch her daughter when she's playing a video game with another teenager, or a card game with Grandma. The competitive drive is hidden well behind the Mask. Libra is known as the "iron hand in the velvet glove"[32] because the competition sees only the Mask and underestimates Libra time and again.

"They thought I was just a dumb-blonde-Valley-Girl when I first arrived at Radcliffe," a beautiful young Libran said with a smile.

"Oh. And how long did that work for you?" I asked, knowing she'd soon have felt a need to participate in class discussions. "About three weeks," she said, "the teachers were slower to catch on when I changed high schools. Others seem to like me better when they don't see me as a threat."

---

32 Wendy du Bois, who interviewed Anais Nin wrote, "behind the luminous eyes and slender, plucked eyebrows is a thread of steel." Cited above, 41.

Librans hate being subjected to bad management. Those in authority learn that Libra is uncomfortable with their current boss and also notice Libra's skills at gaining others' cooperation. Thus, "ready or not," Libra soon finds himself promoted to project leader.

As diplomacy comes naturally and Libra is a natural mediator, many choose law. Though the profession appeals to their youthful idealism, it seems to frustrate Librans by midlife. "The system" is not as fair as they had hoped. Some leave to become judges or politicians. This attractive, extraverted Mask does well in politics if Saturn (Exalted) is strong by aspect or House (1.4.7.10) or Mars is in Capricorn (Exalted) or Aries (Rulership) and they have the ambition. One client left his law firm for the city council, then served several terms as mayor. Others with a high percentage of Earth planets leave law to establish their own businesses.

With many planets in Fire and Water, this Mask does well in sales or consulting, where Libra's verbal skills shine. Several professional clients began to sell real estate during the property boom, and more recently, to sell health insurance. Sales offers Libra Rising freedom to organize their day, taking on as much or as little as they choose.

Libra's peacemaker side works well in counseling, particularly couples' therapy and leading groups, though by midlife most seem to have burned out on listening to others' problems. Libra Rising often finds, "there's too much negativity; the therapy sessions remind me of things I'd like to change about my own marriage."

Libra Rising is, in my experience, the Zodiac's best coordinator. At midlife Librans have become everything from personal shoppers to wedding planners to corporate facilitators (helping egos in one department work with egos in another, where the department heads had protected their own turf.)

Whatever their midlife career change, most Librans seem to tire of the responsibility by their mid-fifties. Like Colette, they discover they don't really want another career after all.

After sixty,[33] Libra Rising often applies their social and coordinating skills in starting new groups like book clubs, based upon their hobbies. Through these activities, former co-workers are replaced with new friends. One Libra client invites her favorite authors to local libraries for lectures; two others have organized yoga and tai chi classes at senior centers. Another is the "social chairman" of her gated community. She organizes museum and concert outings; trips to sports events, water aerobics, card parties, day cruises to the Bahamas, activities for both sexes and every age group.

Most Libra Rising clients tell me that they find it's much easier to follow their bliss in

---

33 Age sixty is an expansive Jupiter Return year for all of us, following the Second Saturn Return at 58.

retirement than during the years of the "day job." "It's wonderful to get up in the morning relaxed. Now, no one expects me to set the world on fire!" said a former salesman.[34]

In the first half of life Cardinality is goal-oriented. But later in life as the ego's self-importance wanes, Cardinal Signs are challenged to enjoy the *sociability* of competition; to enjoy playing golf, tennis or poker without being as concerned about winning, or even improving their skills. Here, Libra has an advantage over the other Cardinal Signs because most Librans excel at sociability. However, with several planets in Cardinality or a prominent Mars, after sixty, Librans may still be very frustrated at losing.

In their mid-to-late seventies, Libra Rising enjoys finding new ways to have fun with the spouse or partner, now their best friend. Libra widows and widowers are still very interested in finding new partners. One woman, 75, brought me a cruise ship brochure with photos of older couples dancing. "Crew members dance with the passengers," she said brightly, "do you think I'll meet another nice man on this cruise?" I told her I thought she'd have a very good time (like Anais Nin and Colette, she once danced professionally) but that a shipboard romance probably wouldn't last beyond the cruise. "Oh," she said wistfully. "Still… even for ten days… *it's worth it!*"

An octogenarian client is taking piano lessons again. She hasn't played in twenty years. For her "later years," she's chosen a nursing home with a piano in the dining room. She visualizes herself playing Christmas carols after dinner while everyone, including a handsome white haired gentleman, is gathered around the piano, singing. Romance lives on for Libra.

The Mask in Youth
From "Pleaser" to Knowing Your Own Mind

Adonis and Aphrodite are handsome and beautiful, respectively. Some are born into affluent families, others get by on their looks and their wits.

A mother-of-six once told me she was most concerned about the Libra Rising daughter because of her "pleaser" nature. "She needs to form her own opinions, not just echo the views of her clique, the shallow, popular girls at school." Eventually Libra Rising found her muse in the form of computer graphics. She's now a film animator.

The mother of an Adonis son once said that she was concerned he'd become a politician.

---

34 George Vaillant's *Aging Well*, cited above, 270. He says one benefit of retirement is the "absence of performance anxiety;" that as a result of decreased stress many people feel healthier in their sixties than they did during their working years.

At age four, regardless of the weather, he would hand the neighbor woman her newspaper every morning in return for a hug. Little girls began to follow him home from school when he was ten.

There was once a naïve, beautiful young Libra Rising girl named Gabriellie-Sidonie Colette who loved the sunlight and fragrant breezes of her parents' garden in southern France, which she described as "an Earthly Paradise."[35]She adored her mother. All was well until the day her father's comrade from the war, Andre Gauthier-Villars visited the family. He neglected to tell her parents that he collected, wrote and published pornography in Paris. He presented himself as a well-established, respectable suitor.

The fifteen year age difference troubled her parents at first. But Villars was a family friend, an educated man, a professional. And he seemed impressed with Colette's education at the all-girls' school. How many opportunities like this marriage would come along for her at nearly twenty years old?

Before leaving home with her new husband, she wrote in her diary:

> I am going away with him to an unknown country where I shall have no past and
> no name, and where I shall be born again with a new face and an untried heart.

After her small village in Burgandy, Paris seemed like a foreign country, though she didn't see much of the metropolis at first. Her new husband locked her in her room until she'd written enough pages each day to the satisfy him.

Villars rejected Colette's initial attempts at writing about the girls' school; he insisted that she write something lurid and "shocking"[36] instead, something he could sell. She told him she had nothing lurid to write about! Nothing unsavory had happened to her. He showed her samples of what he wanted and told her to use her imagination. The result was a series of stories about a "precocious" girl named Claudine. He signed his pseudonym, Willy, to her stories and sold them.

Her husband went off to his mistress in the afternoons, returning late at night. Colette slowly came to realize that she was supporting her husband *and* the mistress. Still, things seemed to improve financially after Claudine was staged (with a young actress, a new love interest, in Colette's role.) Villars bought his wife a country house and returned to Paris, leaving her alone to write. She "clung to the illusion of domesticity and the beauty of the

---

35 Robert Phelps, *Colette (Sidonie-Gabrielle), An Autobiography Drawn from her Lifetime Writings,* (NY: Farrar, Straus and Gibroux,)1966. The quote is from her stepson, Bernard de Jouvenal. Colette's descriptions of her mother's garden are more lyrical poetry than prose.
36 Though her parents would have been horrified at the time they're not shocking today. The stories are now considered "charming." See Wikipedia, "Colette."

countryside." At least he had stopped locking her up! She said she had "as much freedom as a person who is ill and confined."

When she was thirty, Villars forced her to read his new love's poems on stage and told her their marriage was over. She was angry that she hadn't left him first, that she'd only fanaticized about it. She was thirty-seven when the divorce was final. Her husband owned the rights to *Claudine* and the later Cheri novels, about the relationship between a beautiful courtesan who was approaching midlife and a much younger man.

How would a naive "provincial" woman support herself in Paris?[37] Where would she live? One day, she saw a circus billboard; she copied the design, made herself a harlequin tuxedo costume and became a mime. Later, she danced in music halls. Eventually she found an apartment near the *Bois* (woods) where she could smell the catalpa petals in spring.

Like many of my Libra Rising clients who feel their talents are unappreciated, it hurt Colette when people said, "she's *on the stage*," not "she's *an actress*." She wondered, "why is it that *others act* but *I perform?*"

By their late twenties (Saturn Return), Libra Rising women often complain of being considered "just a pretty face." It *is* unfair. And in her forties when her beauty had begun to fade, Colette overheard someone ask, "who is that woman?" (meaning Colette) and someone else reply, "they say she's a woman of letters who turned out badly." They ridiculed her "trousers" and capes, calling her unfeminine.[38]

Colette met her second husband while acting; she was forty when their child was born. She found English nannies for little Colette "Bel Ganzou" Juvenal so mama could continue writing. Her lifestyle was more affluent with him, but she didn't receive enough attention. She felt like 'a stick of furniture.'

The second half of life was happier. She became the most important woman writer in Paris. Colette had found herself through writing, and she'd finally been discovered by Parisian society.

Libra Rising songwriter Jimmy Buffet expressed the Libran journey well:

> Whatever you think, be sure it's what *you* think; whatever you want, be sure that
> is what *you* want, whatever you feel, be sure that is what *you* feel.

This seems to be Libra's challenge for the first half of life.

37 In fact she stayed for a time with an American woman who had a salon in Paris, Natalie Barney, with whom she had an affair. She may have also been romantically involved with Josephine Baker. She flaunted lesbian affairs, but married twice more after leaving Villars.
38 Phelps, cited above, 137-8.

When Anais Nin was eleven, her father, a concert pianist, abandoned his family in Paris and moved to Spain. That same year her progressed Ascendant contacted Natal Mars. Anais began a diary, a series of letters to her father intended to help him catch up on everything he was missing. "How happy he'll be to read it when he comes home!"[39] she thought. And even after she knew he wasn't coming back, Anais kept writing. Eventually, she realized that the diary was really for her. The Progressed Ascendant conjuncted the Life Direction Point (North Node) in her Identity House at twelve, Anais was very young when she found her way through journaling.

Like music and the arts, writing is a path to Individuation. Anais Nin and Colette not only committed their private feelings to their diaries, they went further, they courageously shared them with the rest of the world!

Two Thinking Type friends who liked Nin's diaries told me that they'd *never* publish their journals. In fact, both planned to destroy them. They were in awe of Feeling Type diarists who "publish the raw material." "Sometimes I select a sentence or a metaphor from my journals for an article or a lecture but I could never expose myself like that," said the first Thinking type. "I've read a few of the poems in my journal to the writing group, but *nothing really personal.* I'd feel much too vulnerable," said the second.

In touch with their 'inner Aphrodite,' Nin and Colette also had the gift of language we associate with the Air Element.[40] Though neither was well educated, after practicing their craft in the diaries they went on to novels and stage plays (Colette's *Gigi*, began as a novel, became a stage play and finally a musical. Her *Cheri* novels became plays and films.) Nin's most famous novel, *Henry and June,* the erotic story about Henry Miller taken from her diary later became a movie, too. Feminists loved *Under the Glass Dome,* her book of short stories.

Renowned authors after midlife, both women earned their living doing what they enjoyed.[41] It seems Libra Rising poets, songwriters, artists and musicians have their own path to Individuation! For artistic temperaments, the Writing Cure, the Painting Cure or

---

39 Nin had Sun-Jupiter conjunct in Pisces, as well as Venus, Libra Rising's ruler. She and Colette were both survivors, but Nin, wtih Mars-in-the-First House was more shrewd while Colette was more gullible. In the diaries Nin speaks of wanting to be independent yet seductive, courted, and feminine too! To retain her identity and not lose herself entirely in the Relationship "we."

40 Andre Gide praised Colette's intelligence. Robert Phelps, cited above, *Autobiography*, xix.
41 Nin also became a celebrated feminist and lectured to her fans around the world.

the Music Cure may be better paths to confidence and self-knowledge than the Talking Cure (psychotherapy.)[42]

The Mask After Fifty

Aphrodite and Adonis were so beautiful and so handsome in youth! Libra Rising laments physical aging as much, *if not more* than the other Rising Signs. Anyone who doubts this might want to re-read T.S. Eliot's "Love Song of J. Alfred Prufrock," the lines where he debates with himself about whether to turn around and go home instead of continuing on to the party, where the lovely young women, the "mermaids," who "go to and fro, speaking of Michaelangelo" will probably not be interested in singing to an old man with thinning hair.

Yet the decades between fifty and seventy can be a happy, even exciting time for those Librans who've matured; transcended the "pleaser" tendencies of their youth and are, as a result, less vulnerable to others' opinions of them. Those who, like Colette after fifty, no longer care as much what others think of their "trousers and their cape."

Libra Rising may also receive recognition from their peers in art, literature, or music as happened for Colette, Nin, T.S. Eliot and others. Or, be honored by the organizations where they and their partner volunteer.

When Librans with long marriages suffer the loss of the spouse, it's heartbreaking. Though this is very painful for anyone, it seems even harder for Libra Rising. Fortunately, most Librans are surrounded by people who care about them. The love and energy they gave to others returns to them in their time of need. Friends and children are usually there for them in times of crisis.[43]

When Libran Rising people "know their own minds" as individuals, when they're no longer limited to the "we" viewpoint shared with the marriage partner, they may find themselves playing a role in the larger community, the "all of us." George Vaillant, M.D.

---

42 Carl Jung seems to be in agreement. He wrote, "the personal psychology of the artist may explain many aspects of the work, but not the work itself. And if *ever* it did explain the work successfully, the artist's creativity would be revealed as a mere symptom. This would be detrimental both to the work of art and to its repute." *The Spirit in Man, Art and Literature*, CW, XV, (Princeton: Bollingen,) 1966. In the same essay he says that the artist is engaged, like Prometheus, in seizing the sacred fire, a process that *requires a great deal of energy!* Curing the artist's symptoms might interfere with the creative process.
43 If Libra has several grumpy Scorpio planets in the First, fewer people may appear.

discovered in researching his *Study of Aging* that extraversion tends to become altruism in old age.[44] If this is true of any Sign, it's certainly true of those who are attuned in to Uranus, Libra's esoteric ruler.

My clients have served on boards and contributed their knowledge of art, healing, literature and music to younger generations. Some of them mentor; others encourage young artists by providing scholarships and grants.

Many, like Colette, have attempted a midlife career change. That sometimes works, but often Libra will tire of the responsibility as Colette did with her beauty salons. After a rest, they tend to follow their bliss in the same creative direction discovered in youth; most find that it still excites them. In 1932, Paris' leading literary figure opened her *Salon de Beaute* in Paris at the age of fifty-nine. To her fellow authors, it was a shocking career move. And it lasted only two years.[45] She'd begun to think of "aging women's faces, the faces of women my own age," as "landscapes." She mixed her potions and blended her perfumes like an alchemist.[46]

"In all the time since I began giving beauty treatments to so many women my age I have never yet encountered a fifty-year-old woman who has lost heart or a sixty-year-old suffering from nerves…I am to be envied; I reap such fine rewards when the makeup is at last applied, the sigh of hope, the astonishment, the budding pride, and that impatient glance toward the door, into the street toward the effect it will make; toward the risks to come!"[47]

Colette's mid-fifties through her sixties were probably her most creatively fertile and happiest years.[48] Though she watched her weight, exercised and had massages, Colette's secret was "to be surrounded by young friends whose stars were on the rise; too many older people envied or criticized the young."

---

44 It was one of his hypotheses that proved true. Humor and altruism are "behavior adaptations" that work well for older people. Anger at not having something they want or need can be sublimated into volunteering. It can be energizing to help younger people suffering from the same issues and needs as the elderly person, such as loneliness; an alcoholic parent, childhood neglect or abuse, illness or a disability.

45 She opened a second in St. Tropez, nearer the camp where her third husband was held during the war.

46 Venus was in her Sixth House, the healing House. Nin's was also in the Sixth. She practiced as a therapist a short time.

47 Phelps, cited above, 302-303.

48 Judith Thurman, *The Secret of Colette,* (NY: Balantine Reader's Circle,) 2002.

At the end of her long life, (she lived to 81) Colette said, "Freud recommended love and work, but I would add, watch, look and observe!"[49]

Albert Schweitzer,[50] was right, "from naïve simplicity we arrive at a more profound simplicity." It's true that when a person is open and receptive to life, he has an easier time seeing his way out of a situation. He's able to reach a new and deeper understanding of the problem than he could if he complicated things with the cynicism or skepticism, saying, "nothing will change; I'm stuck in this quandary forever." If we think we're stuck, we are!

However, when Librans naively approaches Life in a *totally* Yin way, they find themselves repeating old behavior patterns that haven't worked. They're like Tristan accepting the jade ring from the Unattainable Lover instead of moving on to start over with his new love, Isolde of the White Hands.

Libra Rising has Aries on the Seventh House cusp. By fifty, many but not all Libra Rising people have learned to look before leaping into a new romance. They've already experienced what happens when they leap too quickly! Still, they feel so vulnerable after the loss of their spouse. And how wonderful it seems to be loved again!

The Progressed Mask

As he progressed through Scorpio, T.S. Eliot (70% Air, without a single planet in Water or Earth for the progressed Mask to contact)[51] kept his charming Libra Mask intact, though his friends knew he was unhappy.[52] His Muse's (Emily Hale's) sabbatical visits to him in London reminded Eliot of everything he missed about America. When she took nine months away from her new position in California to spend with him, thinking they would marry and be happy, Eliot didn't propose. The university didn't hold her job either, though the students loved her. She returned to America and, fortunately, was hired at Smith College.

---

49 Phelps, xvii! "Regarde!" She and T.S. Eliot were both very observant.

50 My information about Dr. Albert Schweitzer comes from *Out of My Life and Thought, an Auto-biography,* Antje B. Lemke trans., (Baltimore: Johns Hopkins University Press,)1988.

51 Though the North and South Nodes were in Cancer and Capricorn at the Midheaven and Nadir.

52 Lyndall Gordon, cited above, 207-291. He described his marriage as "a bad Dostoevsky novel," 252.He worried about finances. His wife, Vivienne, when not institutionalized, wanted him to participate in vendettas against literary figures like Marianne Moore and Edith Sitwell, or appeared at his poetry readings dressed head-to-foot in black "like a fascist," and embarrassing him during World War II.

Eliot seemed to feel that his poetry benefited from "love-in-separation." He re-read the story of Dante and Beatrice; he greatly admired the Courtly Love poets' idealism and their worship of the distant maiden, the *impersonal* goddess, Beauty. He began many poems with invocations to Beauty and ended them with the voice of God. Meanwhile, Ezra Pound cut nearly half of his poem "The Waste Land," reducing it to the form we have now.

Anais Nin had an early degree of Libra Rising (5.01.) Scorpio became her progressed Mask at age 33 and remained for forty-three years, until 1980, when the Mask shifted to Sagittarius for the rest of her life.

In her thirties she experimented with a surrealist approach, closing her eyes, letting the images flow, then writing. This imaginative Water progression works well with the Creative Unconscious.

During the long, introspective Scorpio cycle, her diary was a good friend. Critics sometimes complain about the number of times she used the world 'self' (or, in capital letters: SELF.) They see this as narcissism.

However, many who undergo the long Scorpio progression also find the inner world more interesting than the outer. Like Nin after meeting her absent father, they turn for awhile to therapy, seeking clarity about themselves. Like Nin's, theirs is a Cardinal approach to therapy ("how *dare* Otto Rank expect me to give up my diary, even for a short time! I chose him because he wrote a book on artists and therapy, so he should understand my creative process. I'm quitting!") Like Nin, several Libra Rising clients have decided to study psychology in the Scorpio cycle, though few have become therapists. They're happy, though, that they took time to analyze their 'pleaser tendencies' and relationship patterns.[53]

Colette, like Nin, kept writing in her diaries. By her fifties, the literary world recognized her; music hall fans had always enjoyed her performances and her novels. Though an impartial observer—she advised young writers, "Regarde!"—her feelings come through powerfully. When it comes to style, she and Rimbaud are two of the best Exalted Venus authors.

With 20 degrees Libra Rising, Joseph Campbell progressed into Scorpio during his

---

53 "As a child I created a persona, the little Anais everyone would like." "How did you get past it?" the interviewer asked. "I analyzed the fear and self-doubt behind it. I asked why I took time from my own work to help Henry Miller, even gave him my typewriter, which he pawned to buy alcohol. I learned I could merge with a man but not submerge or lose myself. I wanted to stop blaming other people for my problems. And to get energy back from the archetypes." Nalbandian, cited above, 122.

childhood. A university student, he returned from Europe, where he'd been researching his thesis on King Arthur, just as the stock market crashed. Unable to find a job, Campbell took off for a cabin in Woodstock, where he spent five years reading Freud, Jung, James Joyce, and Thomas Mann, as well as reading the Upanisads and learning Sanskrit.

Though he was unable to finish his thesis, the topic took off in a new, vast direction. *Skeleton Key to Finnegan's Wake* and later the "Masks" series resulted from his ever-expanding research. In 1934 he was hired by Sarah Lawrence College.[54] While bringing literature to life for his students, he continued to read mythology nine hours every day. In 1934 he became engaged to Jean Erdman, a dance student,[55] an artist on a parallel path to his. From then on, all actions and decisions were made by the couple. The "I" had become "we." They were married almost fifty years.

Progressed Ascendant in Sagittarius

Sagittarius is a fire sign; it symbolizes honesty; courage, risk-taking and seizing opportunities. In his youth, Eliot had "expected greatness to come through sublimity," but by his mid-forties, it seemed to require "savage honesty." Though it was difficult for Eliot to find the "right words to express (his) feelings," he now found it necessary. *His progressed Ascendant had entered Sagittarius,* the "straight-as-an-arrow" communicator. He said he "learned more from the ordinary people he met in air raid shelters than from the intellectuals at Hogarth Press."

At the same time, his sense of humor had returned; he seemed more playful and less fearful of taking risks. In 1933, with the progressed Sagittarius Ascendant applying to Natal Jupiter in 2 degrees Sagittarius, (Rulership) Eliot read his humorous poems about cats over the radio. The Mask was changing, shifting from introversion to extraversion. He began to draw attention.

His play "Murder in the Cathedral," about four "heretical" writers, (Aldous Huxley, Bertrand Russell, D.H. Lawrence and himself) was performed in air raid shelters, seminaries and schools. The world was still a wasteland—England was still at war and

54 Campbell didn't know if he wanted the job at first. He still had savings left from playing jazz as a student at Columbia. But then he saw all the pretty girls on campus and decided he *definitely did!* "In the presence of Beauty, all my psychological problems seemed to disappear!" *The Hero's Journey: Joseph Campbell on His Life and Work,* (Novato: New World Library) 2003, pp. 1-70.
55 According to *A Fire in the Mind,* by Stephen and Robin Larsen (cited above) the campus flags flew at half mast when his engagement was announced! The students were so disappointed their handsome professor was 'taken.

his muse unable to visit—yet Eliot seemed much happier in the early 1930's than in the Scorpio cycle.

During his late fifties, his wife became very ill. She died on his Second Saturn Return (age 58,) as his progressed Ascendant conjuncted Natal Mars. While executor of his wife's estate, Eliot diligently wrote Emily over 1,000 letters. After Vivienne's death, Eliot was in poor health for ten years.[56] He saw the cycle as a decade "of penance."

At 68, Eliot finally gave up the medieval "love and separation" tradition to marry his secretary, Valerie, much to the surprise of Emily and others who'd expected, or hoped, to become his second wife. He and Valerie seemed to be a contented couple.

The "Four Quartets," first published in series form during the war, were collected and released in 1947. They were considered his best work. In 1948 Eliot was honored by the British government and received the Nobel Prize in Literature.

Sagittarius is also the archetype of higher education, publishing, and travel, ways to expand beyond the limits of ego and culture. Anais Nin traveled widely. She usually connected with an intellectual audience, lecturing on campuses during the late Scorpio and early Sagittarian Progressed Ascendant cycles. (Her Pisces Venus was in 22 degrees, so, the end of the Scorpio progression brought increased magnetism and recognition on Progressed Ascendant trine Natal Venus.) Like many with Mars-in-the-First-House, Nin was controversial. "Militant feminists sought to claim her," but Libra Rising is a man's woman![57]

After the long progressed cycle through Scorpio, several Libra Rising clients commented that they trusted their intuition more and found less need of validation from others in making choices. A dear Libra Rising friend, Joyce Brady, told me that she realized she "now knew intuitively when the needle was at the middle. There is no yesterday and

---

56 A religious man, he attributed his illness to the sin of loving Emily while married to Vivienne. Saturn crossed his four Libran planets, his Ascendant, and aspected his two Sagittarian planets during that time.

57 For "a man's woman," see Nalbandian, cited above, 40. Venus-in-Pisces sometimes experiments with bisexuality, Pisces is a dual Sign. Venus is sometimes curious about lesbian experiences, but tends to return to heterosexuality in the end.

no tomorrow, there's only this moment." It's *in the moment* that the Scales come into balance."[58]

Some Librans acquire a new perspective during Sagittarius, the philosophical (Ninth House) archetype. Extraverted Sagittarius, in symbolic sextile to Libra, flows better with their Natal Ascendant than introspective Scorpio. Busy with traveling and speaking, Nin told her interviewer that at seventy-two she no longer wrote in her diary every day, and she'd gotten past feeling guilty about it. Apparently Otto Rank was right after all when he said, *"you* keep the diary, *it* doesn't keep *you.*"[59]

Just before Joseph Campbell had progressed into Sagittarius Rising he traveled with his wife Jean on her tour to India and Japan.[60] During Sagittarius, doors often open suddenly and unexpectedly, like this trip. In the 1950's it was rare to see an academic husband accompanying his wife on *her* tour but Campbell happily accepted the opportunity. The mythology of Hinduism and Buddhism became important to him personally, as well as to his work.[61] He began to teach seminars at Esalen, in California, where participants were older and very different from his East Coast students. He honored his teacher Heinrich Zimmler by editing and publishing twelve volumes of his lectures. He also edited the Eranos lecture series.

In 1972 Campbell retired from Sarah Lawrence. He and Jean traveled around the world. Travel, and distance, helped him to gain perspective on a "crisis" in his career, as well as on American culture. Hippies were beginning to take LSD while reading his 1949 book,[62] *The Hero with a Thousand Faces,* which had suddenly become quite popular. Campbell "didn't

---

58 Joyce quoted Yeats' poem, "An Irish Airman Forsees His Death," as an example of fully living in the moment. It's interesting that she had her experience of "the needle on the middle" during a long-awaited trip to Egypt, which coincided with her progressed Ascendant in Sagittarius applying to a sextile with Natal Libra Rising. Egypt is associated with (her former progression through Scorpio,) Death and Rebirth, the alchemical mystery of the Eighth House, Sagittarius with travel and higher knowledge.

59 It had become a ritual she was afraid to stop, Nalbandian, 227.

60 The tour was 1955-56. His progressed Ascendant changed in 1957, based on the time of birth in the Rodden database. A friend had given Campbell a copy of Jiddu Krishnamurti's *Upanishads* in the 1940's. Later, he met Swami Nikhilananda and they worked together on translations of Indian texts.

61 Larsen, *Fire in the Mind,* cited above, 559. He said that he liked the Buddhist concept of Sunyata, the Void, but he came to appreciate the *Gita* more at the end of his life, reading from it every day.

62 *The Hero's Journey,* cited above, 143. It had been difficult to find a publisher for *The Hero with a Thousand Faces,* in 1949, it was rejected twice before he found Bollingen, but in the 1970's and 80's *Heros* was tremendously popular.

know how (he) felt about that." He liked Jerry Garcia personally, had been to a Grateful Dead concert and understood the Woodstock phenomenon as "a cultural reaction to the bomb." Yet it still seemed odd to him that his book had become part of the "hippie scene." As he once remarked, "the ego always wants to fit in," we like to be popular. But sometimes it isn't a comfortable fit.

Campbell was lecturing the week he died, in 1987. In his eighties he had learned to use the computer; enjoyed a celebratory dinner, introduced by George Lucas, was thanked by Steven Spielberg for his impact on filmmaking, made a documentary on Plains Indians' sand paintings, and best of all, his wife, Jean was there to share everything with him. Strangers remarked that they still seemed like honeymooners. Campbell spoke as if his happy marriage was his most important accomplishment.[63]

Libra Rising Bibliography

Campbell, Joseph, *The Flight of the Wild Gander: Explorations of the Mythological Dimensions of Fairy Tales, Legends and Symbols,* (New York: Harper Perennial,) 1990.

—— *An Open Life: Joseph Campbell in Conversation with Michael Toms,* (New York: Larson Publications,) 1988.

—— *The Inner Reaches of Outer Space,* (New York: Harper Perennial,) 1988.

—— *The Hero's Journey: Joseph Campbell on his Life and Work,* Centennial ed. with preface by Phil Cousineau, (Novato: New World Library,) 2003.

DuBow, Wendy M., ed., *Conversations with Anais Nin.* Literary Conversations Series, (Jackson: University of Mississippi Press,) 1994.

Eliot, T.S., *Collected Poems 1909-1962,* "Love Song of J. Alfred Prufrock," "Four Quartets: Little Gidding," (New York: Harcourt Brace,) 1963.

—— *On Poetry and Poets,*(London: Faber & Faber Ltd,) 1957.

Friedrich, Paul, *The Meaning of Aphrodite,* (Chicago: University of Chicago Press,) 1978.

---

63 He said that a happy marriage wasn't a matter of one partner making sacrifices for the other, but both sacrificing at different times for the Relationship, "the We."

Gordon, Lyndall, *T.S. Eliot: An Imperfect Life*, (New York: W.W. Norton,) 1998.

Harrison, George, *I, Me, Mine*, (New York: Simon and Schuster,) 1980.

Johnson, Robert, *We: Understanding the Psychology of Romantic Love*, (New York: Harper & Row,) 1983.

Jimenez, Juan Ramon, *Time and Space: A Poetic Autobiography*, trans. Antonio J. De Nicolas, (Lincoln Nebraska: iUniverse.com,) 1998-2000. (Posthumous work by the Libra Rising Nobel laureate; remarks on Jimenez' emphasis on joy and beauty.)

Kinsey, David, "Radha," in *Hindu Goddesses*: *Visions of the Divine Feminine in the Hindu Religious Tradition*, (Berkeley: University of California Press,) 1988. (On the Divine Romance, "love and separation" in India. In Vaishnavite devotional practice, every soul seeks to love God as Radha loved Krishna.)

Larsen, Stephen and Robin, *Joseph Campbell: A Fire in the Mind: the Authorized Biography*, (Rochester: Inner Traditions,) 2002.

Nalbandian, Suzanne, ed., *Aesthetic Autobiographies: from Life to Art in Marcel Proust, James Joyce Virginia Wolfe and Anais Nin*, (New York: St. Martin's Press,) 1994.

Paglia, Camille, *Break, Blow, Burn*, (New York: Pantheon Books,) 2005. She not only includes the usual poets, but discusses Joni Mitchell as an important contemporary *poet*. A neo-pagan philosopher and anti-feminist, Paglia has Libra Rising with Uranus in close trine to her Ascendant.

Phelps, Robert, *Colette Sidonie Gabrielle: Autobiography Drawn from her Lifetime Writings*, (New York: Farrar, Straus & Gibroux,) 1966.

Sandburg, Helga, *A Great and Glorious Romance: The Story of Carl Sandburg and Lilian Steichen*, (n.p: Eastern National,) 2002.

—— *Where Love Begins: A Portrait of Carl Sandburg and His Family as Seen by His Youngest Daughter*, (n.p: Eastern National,) 2002.

Schweitzer, Albert, *Out of My Life and Thought: an Autobiography*, Antje B. Lemke trans, (Baltimore: Johns Hopkins University Press,) 1988.

Vaillant, George E, MD, *Aging Well*, (Boston: Little Brown & Co,) 2002.

CHAPTER TWO

Scorpio Rising - The Passion for Life

Mohandas Gandhi, "Action expresses priorities….be the change that you want to see in the world."

—— "A 'No' uttered from the deepest conviction is better than a 'Yes' merely uttered to please, or worse, to avoid trouble."

Martin Luther King, Jr., "Change does not roll in on the wheels of inevitability, but comes through continuous struggle. And so we must straighten our backs and work for our freedom. A man can't ride you unless your back is bent."

Sigmund Freud, "I am nothing by temperament but a conquistador - an adventurer, if you want to translate."

—— Dreams are often the most profound when they seem the most crazy."

Johann von Goethe, "We must always change, renew, rejuvenate ourselves; otherwise we harden."

—— "He who is plenteously provided for from within needs but little from without."

—— "Life belongs to the living, and he who lives must be prepared for changes. Let us live, while we are alive!"

"What you can do, or dream you can do, begin it; boldness has genius, power and magic in it."

—— In the realm of ideas, everything depends on enthusiasm; in the real world, all rests on perseverance."

Simone de Beauvoir, "Change your life today. Don't gamble on the future, act now, without delay."

—— "When I was tormented by what was happening in the world, it was the world I wanted to change, not my place in it."

—— "Life is occupied in both perpetuating itself and in surpassing itself; if all it does is maintain itself, then living is only not dying."

—— "Since I was 21, I have never been lonely. The opportunities granted to me at the beginning helped me not only to lead a happy life but to be happy in the life I led. I have been aware of my shortcomings and my limits, but I have made the best of them."

—— "In the face of an obstacle which is impossible to overcome, stubbornness is stupid."

Victor Hugo, "Each man should frame life so that at some future hour, fact and his dreaming meet."

—— "There is one spectacle grander than the sea, that is the sky; there is one spectacle grander than the sky, that is the interior of the soul."

Jacqueline Kennedy Onassis, "One must not let oneself be overwhelmed by sadness."

Friedrich Nietzsche, "And if you gaze for long into an abyss, the abyss gazes also into you."

—— "There is more wisdom in your body than in your deepest philosophy."

—— "When marrying, ask yourself this question: Do you believe that you will be able to converse well with this person into your old age? Everything else in marriage is transitory."

—— "A friend should be a master at guessing and keeping still. We must not want to see everything."

—— "One has to pay dearly for immortality; one has to die several times while one is still alive."

—— "That which does not destroy me makes me stronger."

—— "The individual has always had to struggle to keep from being overwhelmed by the tribe. If you do this, you may be frightened and sometimes lonely. But no price is too high to pay for the privilege of owning yourself."

Martha Stewart, "My new motto is: When you're through changing, you're through."

Daniel P. Berrigan, S.J. (to Robert Coles, M.D.), "I realized back in 1965 that I was missing something without being able to define it. I now realize that my spirit was simply dying. I craved escape from a self-congratulatory life-a life without any challenges. I was extraordinarily isolated. Isolated, smug, and full of slogans."

Gore Vidal, "A good deed never goes unpunished."

—— "Many writers who choose to be active in the world lose not virtue but time, and that stillness without which literature cannot be made."

D.H. Lawrence, "Be still when you have nothing to say; when genuine passion moves you, say what you've got to say, and say it hot."

—— "One never can know the whys and the wherefores of one's passionate changes."

—— "For man, as for flower and beast and bird, the supreme triumph is to be most vividly, most perfectly alive."

—— "The mind can assert anything and pretend it has proved it. My beliefs I test on my body, on my intuitional consciousness, and when I get a response there, then I accept."

—— "The cruelest thing a man can do to a woman is to portray her as perfection."

—— "The only history is a mere question of one's struggle inside oneself. But that is the joy of it. One need neither discover Americas nor conquer nations, and yet one has as great a work as Columbus or Alexander, to do."

Gloria Steinem, "I have yet to hear a man ask for advice on how to combine marriage and a career."

—— "Some of us are becoming the men we wanted to marry."

—— "Without leaps of imagination, or dreaming, we lose the excitement of new possibilities. Dreaming is a form of planning."

The Scorpio Rising Mask

I'm the mysterious, magnetic Scorpio Mask. With Water planets in my horoscope, especially Scorpio Water, I have a seductive, often hypnotic, *presence.* I'm as sensual as Milan Kundera's film, *The Incredible Lightness of Being.* Even when Fire and Air—the more straightforward Elements—predominate, some will say I have "hidden depths."

Like Oliver Stone, my work often results from my convictions.

While Libra Rising overtly flirts and Leo Rising is surrounded by fans, *I* am more subtle. From my perch in the corner, I'll make an occasional ironic or sarcastic remark and, like Gore Vidal, attract *my* crowd. I have an unusual sense of humor like Tracey Ullman, Robin Williams and Groucho Marx.

The opposite sex is drawn to my powerful libido, sensing my restless, often turbulent, emotional nature. In youth, this may result in envy and strained friendships with same-sex peers. Unless, of course, I'm gay.

If my horoscope is low in Air with high percentages in Earth and Water, I may be perceived as the strong, silent type. Because I seldom reveal personal information, people are intrigued; they want to know my secrets.

With a high percentage of Earth, I'm more patient and likely to be successful, but may have intermittent bouts of depression. When Earth mixes with my watery Mask, muddy moods result. However, whether I'm grieving or simply in a funk, please don't try to cheer me up, I can handle it. As Jacqueline Onassis said, "one must not let oneself be overwhelmed by sadness." And, as Gore Vidal put it, "creative work is done in stillness." Solitude and privacy are important to me.

Unless I have several Libran planets, I won't be considered easygoing or mellow. I can be either a good friend or a formidable enemy. A word to the wise: do *not* attempt to come between me and my spouse, partner or lover. If you do, you'll soon feel my sting!

Would Scorpio Rising Jacqueline Kennedy Onassis give up her first husband to

Marilyn Monroe or her second to Maria Callas? Certainly not! When Jean Paul Sartre tired of his mistresses, he asked his longtime love, Scorpio Rising Simone de Beauvoir, to get rid of them. Simone explained, "I was tough and Sartre wasn't."

Like Katharine Hepburn, Bette Davis and Joan Crawford, my Mask is forceful and intense. Like Sigmund Freud, D.H. Lawrence, and Simone de Beauvoir I set my own standards and seek to live life on my own terms.

With the Sun in Aries, like Gloria Steinem and Diana Ross, I'm a trailblazer. Some may think me selfish or controlling. But why should I care what they think?

With Sun, Moon, or Mars in Fire, I may enjoy the battle more than the victory celebration.

For an esoteric Scorpio, the journey is as intriguing as the destination. Because I know what I want and have a very strong will, I usually get my way. But I'm introspective too. Once I've fulfilled a desire, I usually wonder why it was so important to me. Like Martha Stewart, I learn from my mistakes,

My nest seems to go up in flames every-so-often like the mythical Phoenix. This seems to happen when I resist changes I'm powerless to prevent. But as soon as the ashes settle, I rebuild. I'm a survivor.

How To Recognize Scorpio Rising

Scorpio Rising's distinguishing characteristic is intensity; we see it immediately in their expressive eyes. The song, "Bette Davis Eyes," was inspired by an actress with Scorpio Rising! Aldous Huxley endowed one of his characters with D.H. Lawrence's 'striking' blue eyes. Whether violet, like singer Edith Piaf's, dark and luminous like Simone de Beauvoir's or blue-gray like many of my California clients, Scorpio's eyes reflect their intense personality. Sitting across the desk from them, I'm often reminded of the stanza in Longfellow's poem, "A Psalm of Life:" "Life is real! Life is earnest! /And the grave is not its goal,/Dust thou art, to dust returnest,/Was not spoken of the soul."

The strong, silent Scorpio is often skeptical at the first session. Capable of sitting silently for ninety minutes without giving the astrologer any feedback, his eyes usually reveal his hopes and expectations. In fact, the astrologer may need to break eye contact, detach from the emotional message, and center himself. This prevents being drawn into Scorpio's wishful thinking, especially if Neptune is near his Ascendant.

While the skeptic usually has several planets in Scorpio in the First House, the "strong, silent type" tends towards a high percentage of Earth and Water, the slower, more patient Elements.

On the other hand, the "double Mars" personality, with Sun or Moon in Aries, fidgets while his flashing eyes convey, "get to the point, I have a busy day ahead." Double Mars is usually thin and wiry. Mars is associated with digestive fire. Even in the second half of life, without a rigorous exercise program, he metabolizes calories efficiently.

If Water planets enhance Scorpio Rising's Water, his eyes communicate, "I hope this woman is psychic enough to see my spirituality;" "I hope she'll validate my talents." Or, (with many Scorpio planets,) "I hope she won't tell me to forgive my 'ex', who was so mean to me, for I have no intention of doing that! I hope his house burns down in the Santa Ana winds!"

Air is a lighter, sociable Element. With a high percentage of Air, intelligence shines through Scorpio's eyes. With Aquarian or Libran planets (in the Eleventh House,) there will likely be a *verbal* dialogue, and less sardonic humor. Air is rarely sarcastic. With Air planets, Scorpio Rising interrupts with questions and asks for clarification. With Gemini Air in the Eighth House, Scorpios may be interested in how astrology ties in with their dreams. Many have some background in psychology; a few are analysts. The Eighth is a serious placement for otherwise lighthearted Gemini planets.

Scorpios are also likely to have secrets which they probably won't bring up themselves. They're hoping, though, that *the astrologer* will bring them up so they can discuss the situation's outcome. Will they be caught at Insider Trading? Will their (often much younger) lover be free to marry? If so, will he or she marry *them? Before discussing the secret, they'll often ask that the CD be set on "pause," lest someone else find it later. Privacy is extremely important.

After their intensity, and their eyes which communicate so well, Scorpio Rising is known for having a strong, firm jaw. When that jaw is set, the discussion is over; Scorpio will not be imposed upon further.[1]

Max and Augusta Heindel found Scorpio Rising to have a long "eagle's nose," rather like a beak, (or like Mahatma Gandhi's,) but this is not common with my clients,[2] many of whom have smaller, rounder noses. I do agree that with them that on the whole Scorpio Rising people are short. Two exceptions to the rule are Katharine Hepburn, who was taller

---

1 At the end of the day, or the yoga class, it's good to open the mouth wide and then slowly close it. Doing this several times releases the tension that accumulates from "setting the jaw" repeatedly.
2 Max Heindel and Augusta Foss Heindel, *The Message of the Stars,* (Oceanside: Rosicrucian fellowship,) 1973, 104.

than many of the "leading men" in her movies, and Simone de Beauvoir, who was taller than her lover, Jean Paul Sartre.

Aries is usually on the cusp of their Sixth House (health.) The ruler of Aries, Mars, is associated with the male reproductive organs. In youth, sexually-transmitted diseases are a concern, and after sixty, hernias. If Mars is in a Fire Sign, older Scorpios tend to quickly lift suitcases or other heavy objects; seemingly unaware that their bodies are no longer as strong now.

Mars is also associated with accidents. If there are hard aspects from Natal Mars to Mercury, the Ascendant or the Moon, accidents may occur on eclipses within three degrees of one of these points.

Because Mars-in-Fire so often likes to drive at high speeds, it's important that older people with Mars-in-Fire or Aries on their Sixth House cusp have their vision checked annually. As they age, they also need to be more attentive in traffic because their reflexes and coordination, so reliable in youth, may become slower.

Like Aries Rising, Scorpio Rising can be recognized by their tremendous courage, which remains to their last breath.

Though passion and restlessness may bring Scorpio Rising marriages to an end, they seldom interfere with friendship. Unless, of course, a friend becomes romantically involved with Scorpio's lover, spouse or partner! Taurus is on the cusp of the Seventh House; (Marriage) monogamy is an important ideal for Scorpio Rising. Loyalty is expected *of the partner,* though Scorpio may not live up to the ideal. An advocate of free love, D.H. Lawrence was very unhappy when his wife, Frieda, left for Italy to see her lover.[3]

The Mundane Rulers - Mars and Pluto

Mundane rulers are associated with survival instincts. Mars' glyph is the biological symbol for the male sex. Active, restless, and courageous, *Mars is about change.* As seen in Part I, (Aries Rising,) Mars also signifies a heroic, energetic, and often pioneering impulse. This is true of Scorpio Rising as well. As ruler of both Signs, Mars is assertive and confrontational, too, though Scorpio is usually more subtle when he chooses to be.

Intuitive Scorpio Rising counselors also have that built-in bullshit detector that Monika Wikman describe so well in *The Pregnant Darkness.* This saves time. The astrologer, analyst

---

3 Frieda von Richthofen Lawrence, *Not I But the Wind that Blows Through Me and Other Autobiographical Writings, (San Francisco: Pandora) 1994.*

or healer gains respect by using it confrontationally, coming right to the point. Clients or patients usually feel relieved afterwards!

In the 1970's, several clients with Scorpio Rising were attracted to political movements, or spiritual communities where, as they put it, they "could make a difference." This impulse was shared by poet Daniel Patrick Berrigan, S.J., a leader of the anti-war Underground in the 1970's. He became a Jesuit because, "historically, the Order has played an influential role; it has made a difference." He saw his role as "raising (national) awareness of moral issues.[4]" His opinions haven't changed over time. He protested the 2003 invasion of Iraq.

The 'purposeful impulse' wasn't limited to the Twentieth Century, of course! Novelist Victor Hugo, who left us a fascinating account of his times in *Les Miserables*, also wrote "Les Chatiments," a long, polemical poem (over a thousand verses) to further his cause, the overthrow of Emperor Napoleon III. He announced that he would not return to France until liberty was restored, and kept his word. After the Emperor's death, Hugo was greeted at the train station by a large crowd of Parisians chanting lines from "Chatiments."[5] In the Twenty First Century, too, many Scorpios will continue to push for change, for progress as each new generation understands it.

The list of Scorpio Rising pioneers includes such major cultural influences as feminist authors Simone de Beauvoir and Gloria Steinem;[6] Rudolph Steiner, founder of Anthroposophy, Sigmund Freud, founder of clinical psychology, novelist and artist D.H. Lawrence, advocate of women's right to sexual fulfillment,[7] Johann von Goethe,[8] explorer of humanity's dark side (*Faust,*) and Friedrich Nietzsche, who contributed the Superman Ideal to modern culture. We associate Nietzsche's philosophy more with Pluto (will power, or Will-to-Power) than Mars. See below, the story from his *Prologue to Zarathustra*.

---

4 He also lived and worked in Mississippi during the Civil Rights movement. See Robert Coles M.D, *The Geography of Faith: Conversations Between Daniel Berrigan while Underground and Robert Coles,* (Boston: Boston Press,)1971, p 71. He spoke throughout the interviews of a need to courageously live "on the edge," (beyond polite academic debates and forums,) in order to bring about change.

5 Victor Hugo, poems, bilingual edition, *Chansons du Crepuscule,* "Les Chantiments," (Chicago: University of Chicago Press,) 2001. In *Chatiments* Hugo scolds the Emperor. See also, Samuel Edwards, *Victor Hugo: a Tumultuous Life,* (NY: David McKay Co.,) 1971. He had Pluto-in-Water (Pisces) trine the Ascendant from the Fourth.

6 A political activist for fifty years, her most recent works are *Doing Sixty and Seventy, Moving Beyond Words,* and *Revolution from Within.* She was a journalist with New York Magazine. Pluto is in her Ninth House (publication) in Cancer.

7 Like (Aries Rising) Henry Miller, Lawrence effected cultural change by breaking literary taboos in his novels. Lawrence had Pluto in his creative Fifth House (Aries) inconjunct the Ascendanr.

8 He had Pluto in his First House in Scorpio.

Though Scorpio Rising has pioneering spirit in abundance, Mars (unless in Fire or Houses 1,4,7 or 10) usually comes through in a quieter, more subtle way than when ruling Aries. At meetings, others are often aware of where Scorpio Rising stands on the subject under discussion without his needing to verbalize it.

In general, Mars as ruler of Scorpio is introspective. In Earth or Water, Mars is often sublimated into creativity or causes. With Mars-in-Pisces, Simone de Beauvoir was content to let John Paul Sartre have the limelight while she wrote afternoons in her favorites café. She avoided the political rallies he attended. Gloria Steinem, on the other hand, has Mars-in-Aries conjunct the Sun and is known for publicly voicing her opinions.

As ruler of Aries Rising, the Mars' fight-or-flight-response usually opts out of a political movement, spiritual community or other group if his input or leadership talents go unrecognized. Aries Rising is happy to make his or her contribution elsewhere! Ruling a Fixed Sign, Mars is likely to stay put and try to bring about change from within, even if health symptoms develop.

Sublimated Mars may opt for political activism. Daniel P. Berrigan's Underground struggle;[9] (he was chased from campus-to-campus by the F.B.I,) Victor Hugo's battle with his nemesis, the Emperor are examples. *Or,* Scorpio may sublimate his energy into creative pursuits, but as Gore Vidal pointed out, *it's extremely difficult to do both.* He expressed this well, "…there is a stillness without which literature cannot be made, and activists lack that stillness." (See above list, for the full quote.)

Berrigan sitting in the courtroom writing poems while awaiting his sentence comes to mind. That could not have been easy![10]

Over the years, several Scorpio Sun Sign *and* Scorpio Rising clients have quoted Parmahansa Yogananda, "seclusion is the price of real greatness," and "solitude time is a key to happiness."[11]

In astrology, the Eighth Sign is analogous to the Eighth House in the Natural Zodiac, a psychic house. We associate Houses Eight and Twelve in particular with solitude, stillness and depth.

---

9 Berrigan, with Mars-in-Gemini inconjunct the Ascendant was an anti-war speaker at Teach-Ins.

10 The poetry he reads now on PBS seems so much deeper. A professor emeritus at Fordham University, he's of course older and wiser. Gore Vidal's body of work is an important contribution to American culture as well.

11 See Parmahansa Yogananada, *Inner Peace: How to be Calmly Active and Actively Calm,* (Los Angeles: SRF Publications) 57, and *How to Be Happy all the Time,* (Nevada City, Ca: Crystal Clarity Press,) 2006, p. 67.

As ruler of Scorpio, Mars dives into the Underworld and emerges with new insights that lead to change for the individual and sometimes for society. In reading through the list of quotations at the beginning of Scorpio, a pattern emerges; many Scorpio Rising people have written *about change* and/or tried to make it happen.

In addition to the Political Underworld with its causes, and the Underworld of the Creative Unconscious, there's a third, psychological underworld. If, like the ancients, we interpret *psyche* as soul or spirit, this Underworld extends beyond the Talking Cure (psychotherapy,) and beyond pathology to guidance received in dreams. Dream interpretation was a highly valued spiritual gift in Old Testament times. An intuitive Jungian Analyst, Marie-Louise von Franz (Scorpio Rising) had this gift.[12] Robert Johnson and others have shared many wonderful stories about her insights into their dreams, insights which brought an entirely new perspective on life.

In youth, Scorpio Rising often seeks to change society or change *other people*. However, by midlife, many Scorpio Rising people discover that the key to happiness lies *in changing oneself.*

Pluto, the Greek Hades - Will and Power
Sturm und Drang

Pluto, the other mundane ruler, was discovered in 1931 around the time the Lindbergh baby was kidnapped and public attention was focused on the Mafia. *Cosa Nostra* was involved with alcoholic beverages, illegal between 1920 and 1933, prostitution and drugs. So, the newly discovered planet became associated with the criminal underworld.

Psychology, too, was an major topic of discussion. In 1932 Freud received the celebrated Goethe Prize. Then a year later, the tide turned; the Nazis came to power in Austria and his books were burned.

Many of my Scorpio Rising clients are psychologists, majored in psychology, or found

12 von Franz had Exalted Mars-in-Capricorn and Pluto in the Eighth House, which it rules in the Natural Zodiac. Her Mars was in a very loose opposition to Pluto-in-Cancer. (Mars in her Third House, and Pluto near the cusp of her Ninth.) Both rulers were well-placed for psychology and the inner alchemy. The square from Uranus-in-Rulership (Aquarius) was the closest aspect to her Ascendant. She was comfortable allying herself with Jung, an original thinker (Aquarius Rising) when Toni Wolff chose to opt out of the alchemy research. Unlike Wolff, von Franz didn't care that medical doctors found alchemy bizarre and thought Jung odd for wasting his time on it. (Deirdre Bair, cited above, 371) Von Franz was nineteen when they met; she changed her major to classics to aid in his research.

therapy helpful during times of upheaval. There's a definite connection between the field and Scorpio Rising.

Thirdly, Pluto is associated with power. In the early 1930's, thirty years after Nietzsche's death, there was widespread interest in the philosopher's theory of human motivation, "the will to power."

Nietzsche had observed that, like animals, individuals and nations will risk their lives to *defend or extend their power;* that in ancient Greece a hero didn't live very long. He saw Mankind as a bridge, a rope over the Abyss that connects the present Human Race to a better future, the Age of Supermen. Pluto inconjuncted Nietzsche's Ascendant from Aries, in his Fifth House, and Mars made a close sextile to the Ascendant from Virgo.

According to Nietzsche, the ancients believed that there was a slave-morality which kept people powerless and poor. There was also a master-morality of heroes who were powerful, affluent, and free.

There are many modern variations on Nietzsche's theme. A client recently remarked that she was "in bondage to credit card banks." She called it "a type of hell." The bank's money is an Eighth House issue. When media celebrity and entrepreneur Martha Stewart went to prison for insider trading, she, too, experienced the dark side of the Pluto/Eighth House archetype.[13]

Pluto is associated with compulsive and sometimes with cruel or destructive behavior.[14] Emotionally, we may experience Hades when a strong desire, seemingly impossible to give up, becomes an obsession. It's as if we've fallen into a pit of misery. This happened to *Faust,* Johann von Goethe's character, in a story transmitted through many different media and retold in many versions. *Faust* is a powerful story about the Shadow Side. A restless man with many unfulfilled desires, Faust suffered through humanity's inner struggles.

The devil, Mephistopheles, appeared to him, offering to satisfy his desires in exchange for his soul.

Succumbing to the "seven deadly sins," anger (or hatred,) lust, greed, pride, jealousy (or

---

13 This is another meaning of the Eighth House (Other People's Money.) The Eighth is opposite the Second House (Our Money and Other Resources.) When we borrow more (in the Eighth) than we can repay (from the Second House,) we feel as if we've fallen into the Abyss. The Eighth includes casinos; the stock market, the lottery, IRS, joint property we own with others and investment property (not including our home, which belongs to House Four.)

14 The Marquis de Sade had Pluto on his Scorpio Ascendant. Johann von Goethe had it in Scorpio in the middle of his First House. A theater director as well as a poet and playwright, Goethe held a position of power in the government of his German principality, Weimar.

envy), gluttony (food, drink, drugs) and sloth has serious repercussions and may involve more than one meaning of House Eight.

For instance, a politician or a sports' figure may lose not only his lucrative television endorsements, but also visitation rights with his children as a result of alchoholism or lust. Gluttony will take years off a person's life.

Hades does not always have prison walls as it did for Mahatma Gandhi,[15] D.P. Berrigan[16] and Martha Stewart.[17] This process of moving from Thanatos (death) to Eros (renewed energy and returning libido,) is associated with the Eighth House journey (Death and Rebirth.)

It may be a state of prolonged depression after a serious illness, a divorce or the death of a loved one. Formerly passionate Scorpio may become lethargic and seem to lack interest in life. Or, Scorpio's time in Hades might be the result of addictive behavior. While in downward free-fall, the Abyss seems bottomless. Fortunately however, most of my clients eventually "bottom out" and seek recovery programs. Just as grieving is a longer process for some people than others, some recovering addicts take longer; they may be in and out of rehab for years. As a result, friends and family often lose patience with them. When family possessions are sold to purchase drugs, parents or spouses practice "tough love" and change the locks.

But when the alchemical process of "death and rebirth" is successful, when Scorpio will and the Higher Power prevail, passion for life replaces lethargy and the soul emerges energized from the Abyss.[18] Scorpio begins the work of restoring trust and, if possible, repairing relationships.

In my astrology practice, vengefulness is one of the most difficult Hades states. It's like an eighth deadly sin! Anger, though it sometimes causes irreparable damage, usually flares up and dies away quickly. Vengeance endures. William Blake's (Cancer Rising) poem,

---

15 Imprisoned in Transvaal, Africa as a young man for leading immigrants in nonviolent marches, Gandhi chose to spend his days making sandals for the guards and his adversary, General Jan Smuts. Later, he was again imprisoned in (British) India. He had Pluto in the Sixth house, probably near the cusp of the Seventh. Though married, he tried to remain celibate, sublimating his energy into the Independence movement.

16 Daniel P. Barrigan, S.J, has Pluto-in-Water trine his Ascendant from the Eighth House.

17 Martha Stewart, media mogul and entrepreneur, has Mars inconjunct the Ascendant from Aries and Pluto square it from Leo.

18 There is a great deal of wisdom on the subject of moving from Thanatos to Eros in Monika Wikman's excellent book, *The Pregnant Darkness*, (Berwick: Nicholas-Hays) 2004. I've found, too, that family and friends often go through a period of readjustment learning to trust the process and accept the individual back into their lives.

"The Poison Tree," is an imaginative description of what happens when a person dwells on the desire for revenge: his thoughts water and nurture a poisonous tree within himself.

Those who constantly wish others ill seldom draw mature, mentally-balanced people into their live. Negativity and cynicism tend to draw more negativity and attract more experiences which reinforce the cynicism. Gore Vidal captured the lower Scorpio attitude well in these lines, "it's not enough to succeed, others must fail," and "every time a friend succeeds, I die a little." If the mundane rulers of the Ascendant, Pluto and Mars, are in Square to each other or Pluto squares the Rising Sign, Scorpio Rising will find himself engaged in an *inner* battle. (The theme of this conflict will be indicated by the House where Natal Mars or Pluto is located.) If Mars opposes Pluto or the Rising Sign, conflicts take place with other power people.[19] There's a sense of spiritual maturity, of rising from Eight House struggles in St. Paul's lines, "I die daily;"[20] "I will put aside the things of a child"[21] and in exhorting the congregation to "lay aside the old man corrupted in the lusts of deceit and... be renewed in the spirit of your mind... put on the new man, created in the holiness of the truth."[22]

Fortunately, we're not limited to the person we used to be. Our present capacity grows; our future self opens up far beyond what our present self believes possible. This is the meaning of death and rebirth.

In taking risks, living on the edge, spending time in solitude,[23] through all his struggles, St. Paul exemplified the archetype of Death and Rebirth.

---

19 Freud had Pluto opposite his Ascendant. It was in the Sixth House, conjunct the cusp of the Seventh. His friendship with Jung suffered when he refused to let Jung interpret his dream, preferring to keep it secret, (it pointed to his longtime affair with his sister-in-law.) He insisted he remain the Authority Figure: it would be "inappropriate" for Jung to interpret *his* dream, but Freud could interpret Jung's! He also demanded that Jung support him in his view that human behavior must be explained in terms of sexuality. He also expected Jung to give up his interest in poltergeists and other phenomena.

20 I Corinthians, 15:32. Some Christian theologians see this as referring to Paul's perilous life, pursued by Roman soldiers; living on the edge of martyrdom. Yogis interpret it as having reached the breathless state, the ability to suspend bodily functions and enter into Samadhi (union) at will.

21 I Corinthians, 13:11.

22 I Ephesians, 4, 14-21

23 Some of his solitude time was spent in prison, paralleling the experience of Berrigan and other 1970's activists who were also dedicated to their beliefs and lived on the edge.

Pluto in Scorpio (1983-1995)

Pluto was in Scorpio for about twelve years. Traveling along its irregular orbit, Pluto passed through the Sign more quickly than it did in, for instance, Leo. "Pluto-in-Leo" came to symbolize the generation famous for political activism. Twelve years is not quite long enough to be considered a generation, so astrologers don't usually think in terms of a Pluto-in-Scorpio generation. (Fortunately, very few girls today give birth at age twelve or become grandmothers at age twenty-four!) Still, Pluto-in-Rulership makes a powerful impression.

Pluto-in-the-First House is an *intensifier.* It strengthens the attributes and tendencies of *any* Ascendant Sign. Pluto conjunct the Ascendant in Cancer intensifies worrying, especially about family; Pluto-in-Virgo enhances perfectionism and dissatisfaction with self, Pluto-in-Libra accentuates the "We" approach to life.[24]

Pluto-in-Scorpio on the Ascendant or in the middle of the First House intensifies the willful, demanding, controlling, obsessive, or seductive and manipulative attributes of Scorpio. (Pluto close to the Ascendant degree, can be almost hypnotic.)

If Mars-in-Scorpio (Rulership) conjuncts Pluto or there's a close square from Mars-in-Leo, the person may be ruthless. This is similar to Nietzsche's will-to-power as German propagandists later interpreted it.

The karate teacher or sports coach is often an important childhood mentor, if there are adverse aspects to Scorpio Rising from Mars or Pluto.

Positive aspects to Venus and the Moon will strengthen the feminine side of the personality. Fourth House benefic planets (Venus or Jupiter) may indicate a happy childhood in which little Superman or Superwoman received affection along with discipline and learned to *give* as well as take.

Otherwise, Pluto conjunct Scorpio Rising may be alone at the end of his life. Perhaps, though, like people with five or six planets in Scorpio, he prefers it that way. Clients in their seventies with a stellium of planets in Scorpio have said that "the trade-off of solitude for sexual intimacy" ceases to be worth it, even with Viagra! With several planets in sociable Air, Scorpio Rising is motivated to compromise with others; he's not reclusive in old age.

---

24 Pluto conjunct Libra Rising will phone a co-worker, insisting she attend an event with him. After the third time that the person, the very last name on Libra's phone list, says, " Sorry, I'm not interested," Pluto-in-Libra will reply sadly, "but I *really* want to go to the concert and I don't want to go *by myself.*"

The Esoteric Ruler - Mars as Spiritual Warrior
Life on the Inner Battlefield

In Leo, the Sun rules the Sign at two different levels, mundane and esoteric. (See Part I, Leo). In Scorpio Mars rules both levels of the Sign as well. At both levels Scorpio goes at life with passion; symbolically, red is associated with passion and Mars is the red planet. The most important difference between the levels is that esoteric Mars is unselfish.

Scorpio Rising includes the depths and heights, the best and worse of human nature.[25] The Marquis de Sade and Mahatma Gandhi share this Ascendant, with most Scorpio Rising people falling somewhere in between.

Many of us are familiar with the Chinese folktale about the Scorpion that wanted to cross a river but couldn't swim. The Scorpion convinced a frog to take him across, after promising not to sting him. The frog decided to let the scorpion ride across on his head. Once they were across, there would be no *reason* whatsoever for him to sting his benefactor! But as soon as they reached the other side, the Scorpion stung the frog!

The wounded frog cried out, "Why did you sting me? I did what you wanted!" And the Scorpion replied, "because it's my nature." As Gore Vidal supposedly said, "no good deed goes unpunished." At his worst, Scorpio Rising behaves like the scorpion in this folktale; he acts according to his lower nature. He does things *because he can and he wants to*, regardless of the consequences for others.

There's also a higher level, more conscious level called *serpens*. At this level, Scorpio Rising doesn't act *entirely* on instincts, but he takes everything literally. Abstract reasoning (Air) and the imaginative side of the Water Element seem missing. At this level *serpens'* actions follow upon information provided by the five senses, the only data he trusts. And he may be mistaken because his senses sometimes mislead him.

At this level, Scorpio is very much like the man in the Indian tale who saw a rope at twilight, was convinced it was a dangerous snake and attempted to kill it. If they cannot measure something quantitatively and/or sell it, then the item has no value.

Serpens is very restless. They seldom think for themselves; their opinions and ethics are derived from those of their role models, whose codes they absorb. For instance, they may be very loyal to a street gang, preferring prison to revealing its secrets to the police. Early environment makes a strong impression. Once an opinion is formed, it tends to stick.

---

25 In *Esoteric Astrology,* Alice Bailey says that St. Paul had Scorpio Rising. His was certainly a tumultuous life.

Serpens may also come from a environment where he's expected to become a stockbroker, doctor or attorney because that's what his father and grandfather did.

The next level is named for Zeus' Eagle, (Aquila) who carried his messages and thunderbolts. Most Scorpio Rising people fly high. Some soar like eagles! (The Air Element represents consciousness; clarity, perspective, and the ability to form their own opinions.) But Aquila was also sent to Hades to taunt Prometheus, he isn't limited to Sky and Earth.

Eagles set their sights high, yet also descend to eat carrion. We see all of this in Gustave Flaubert. He wanted to work on his play, "The Temptation of St. Anthony," about the desert hermit. His friends laughed and told him it was a dreadful idea; it would never sell and he needed to support himself. He still lived with his mother, after all!

So he wrote a satire about a frivolous middle class woman named Emma, a bored housewife married to a doctor. Emma went restlessly from affair to affair. Though she had poor taste, Emma wasted her husband's money on useless possessions, driving him into bankruptcy. The novel, *Madame Bovary* made Flaubert's reputation,[26] but he was not content. His satire was highly acclaimed, but success sometimes leaves Scorpio with an empty feeling.

However, with success the eagle was free to soar! Flaubert returned to "St. Anthony." Through the taunting questions he wrote for the devil and St. Anthony's responses, he did his inner work. "Temptation" was a thirty-year project, as Flaubert pondered the enigmas and mysteries of human nature and his times.[27] When he finished, Sigmund Freud was impressed enough to write a blurb for the first edition (1874.)

It was as if there were two Flaubert's, the author of *Bovary*, and the author of "The Last Temptation," a philosophical play with poetic imagery, supposedly impossible to perform. The eagle is often complex.

Jean Paul Sartre was fascinated with Flaubert; the philosopher wrote a five volume biography of the novelist, much to Simone de Beauvoir's chagrin.[28]

---

26 A professor once said that anyone who writes a novel about an adulterous woman today is really rewriting either *Madame Bovary* or *Anna Karenina*. We now live in the era of the TV show called, "Desperate Housewives." It's doubtful that today's Emma or Anna would commit suicide.
27 The scene where he's tempted by the Queen of Sheba inspired a famous painting by Lovis Corinth, "The Temptation of St. Anthony by Gustave Flaubert." Salvador Dali later chose the same theme.
28 Bored with hearing about Sartre's project, she said that she'd enjoyed reading Flaubert too, but five volumes seemed excessive. My information about Beauvoir comes from Deirdre Bair, *Simone de Beauvoir: a Biography*, (Simon and Schuster/Touchstone,) 1990, based on interviews with the subject.

The third level is the Phoenix, a sacrificial bird who lives a life of upheaval, his nest constantly catching on fire. A bird of great faith and boundless energy, he keeps rebuilding it from the ashes.

Phoenixes are extremely rare. The Phoenix is very generous and helpful to others; he seems to anticipate the Jupiter Rulership of the next Sign. With the Phoenix, there is no manipulation involved, no strings are attached to his gifts. While doing his Eighth House work, it's as if he's preparing for the Vision that comes in the Ninth House, represented by the Ninth Sign, Sagittarius.[29]

The creative process is one good way to get in touch with the subtle body, which, symbolically, is ruled by esoteric Mars.[30] Dream work, yoga and meditation are others. Once in touch with the subtle body, Scorpio is able to reenergize and renew himself in times of crisis, much like the Phoenix.

The Ouroboros, or snake that bites its own tail, is a symbol of Wholeness. By biting it's tail, it revitalizes the human race. Viewed as a continuous circle of energy, the Ouroboros also symbolizes the physical body connecting with the subtle body and receiving nourishment from it.

Any enjoyable activity in which Scorpio Rising loses track of time, becomes absorbed in his project and is one with the process will take him there. The hours will pass unnoticed and Scorpio will be content.

It needn't be necessarily writing, music or the arts, those are just examples. Many mid-life changes involve themes, projects or occupations set aside in young adulthood that he's really missed. But it's not necessarily an old talent from the past; it could be a new, progressed Sagittarius interest. Scorpio's own version of the "Last Temptation of St. Anthony" might be coaching a little league team. It's whatever brings Scorpio joy, satisfaction and contentment.

The process will keep Scorpio occupied. It will keep him from gazing into the Abyss, because, as Nietzsche said, if we do that too long, it'll gaze back at us!

---

29 Mahatma Gandhi was possibly a Phoenix.

30 Alice Bailey, *Esoteric Astrology*, (NY: Lucis Publishing,) 1971, 209-210. At the mundane level, Mars rules the physical body, but for the initiate, the spiritual seeker, the tasks and struggles of the subtle body are ruled by esoteric Mars.

The Element
The Turbulent or Swampy Waters of Scorpio

Water is the most imaginative Element. It's also a feminine Element. In dream work, we speak of the Waters of the Unconscious, where the archetypes visit us in our sleep. In astrology too, Water is a useful metaphor for the creative imagination, a world we may enter like artists, through visualization. A world we describe with metaphor and imagery.

Water was discussed in Part I, (Cancer Rising,) the section on William Blake, poet and artist, who saw Imagination as the Second Person of the Christian Trinity. In the Natural Zodiac, the Water Houses (4, 8 and 12) are psychic houses. The Eighth House is a lot like The Hermit card or the Abyss card[31] in Tarot. In astrology, the Eighth House is more like the muddy waters of marshland than the ocean. These waters are not like a clear lake where people catch trout on a sunny day. The Eighth House is foggy, like the moor where Catherine and Heathcliffe met in Emily Bronte's *Wuthering Heights*. Swamps are dark and murky. There are alligators.

Quicksand is sometimes found on swampy land. Clients with Eighth House transits often feel as if they're sinking in it, particularly when lab tests come back unclear and have to be repeated. There's anxiety, then relief when the news, good or bad, finally arrives and they're back on terra firma. They're so happy to know "where they stand!" And, if necessary, logical steps can now be taken to deal with the medical issue.[32]

While in the swamp, there were no steps to take and no plans to make. Waiting can be very difficult for a Sign that feels a need to act (Mars) and take control (Pluto.) Once out of the swamp, Scorpio's desire for control is restored.

Like Hercules facing the hydra in the swamps of Lerna, his eighth task in Alice Bailey's *Labours of Hercules,*[33] we sometimes feel alone in the swamp. Our spouse or partner, children and friends are also processing *their* fears of losing a loved one; they can sympathize; do

---

31 The Abyss card in the Aleister Crowley deck is the Hermit Card in other decks. It represents solitude, where new realizations come. These insights are later assimilated as *behavior change,* without which there is no permanent Eighth House breakthrough.

32 Of course if the test comes out well, no steps need be taken. Many clients have had surgery when Mars transited their Eighth House.

33 The story is taken from Bailey, *Labours of Hercules,* VIII, (NY: Lucis,) 1977. "Destroying the Lernian Hydra," 67-75. There are many versions of the tale. Bailey's has a ninth, immortal head which Hercules couldn't kill. He placed a boulder on top of it. She interprets this to mean *Desire will always be with us,* our will power (the rock) can only submerge or sublimate cravings.

internet research and give well-meaning advice, but cannot really *empathize*. In a way, when it's a life-or-death situation like cancer, the entire family is groping around in the marsh, each member feeling alone.

Illness is one concrete example. But there are many different kinds of swamp creatures and swampy situations! When Hercules grappled with the (eight-headed) hydra, he first approached it in a logical way. But that rarely succeeds in a watery environment. (While in crisis, people are seldom amenable to logic.) When Hercules lopped off one hydra head at a time, *two* new heads grew back to replace it.

Finally, in exhaustion Hercules lifted the hydra out of the murky water into the sunlight and air, the world of logical clarity, objectivity and perspective. Then he dropped it on the ground where Earth, Reality, dried it out. Without water, the hydra died.

The heads multiplied faster than he could destroy them. There's seemingly no limit to the human desire nature! (Unlike cats, humans will seldom walk away from a dish that's half full.)

Poor Hercules exhausted himself. It's hard enough to control *one* strong desire, let alone eight, sixteen, thirty-two, and on to infinity. His struggle reminds me of people who try to give up smoking and alcohol while attempting to lose forty pounds![34] When the logical approach, removing one "vice"—one head at a time—didn't work with the monster, Hercules realized he must also contend with the swamp, *the environment itself.* This takes the courage, fortitude and superhuman strength of esoteric Mars.

As soon as he lifted the hydra out into the daylight, it lost its monstrous power, just as Scorpio or Eighth House secrets do when we bring them into the open. This may be difficult for Scorpio but may result in others opening up to him. Scorpio discovers that others have peculiar secrets, too.

Not only is our inner hydra not a unique monster, but it turns out that *everyone* has an inner hydra.

Gluttony is usually more obvious than other "deadly sins." In the current recession we're contending with greed, previously considered practically a virtue! Bankers, though at least as greedy as everyone else, used to represent Groundedness, or Reality. Like the gigantic Lernian hydra, property speculators became overextended, believing the Boom would never end. Some said, "if it the Bust does come, it won't affect *me, I'll* survive."[35]

---

34 I once had a client who tried very hard to lose weight but found herself going out to lunch with co-workers who loved fried food. It was only after transferring to a department where she met people who went to salad bars or brought healthy food from home that she was able to meet her goal. Habits feed on the "swampy waters " around us.

35 One realtor client owned seven houses at the peak of the Boom.

Pride that "goes before a fall" is yet another hydra head. Many proud, formerly successful people now humbly present their revised, pared-down budgets to bankers in hopes of keeping their homes. Whether or not they succeed, the Eight House struggle—*the sturm und drang*—has its impact. Longer recessions result in insights that change behavior patterns.

Many years ago, a young astrologer friend with Scorpio Rising would call me whenever he passed through California. And I was always glad to see him. We'd have lunch; I'd ask him how things were going. And he would usually answer, "(I'm) going through changes, Kathleen, going through changes again." One day he responded, "another divorce is underway." As I started to say, "I'm so sorry," he shrugged and added, "*but I'm used to it now.*"

That's an important breakthrough for Scorpio Rising, because in one area of life or another, change keeps happening. A Scorpio Rising friend once told me it had been the only constant in her life. There are respites from it, some of which last for years, with Scorpio on solid ground. But then, circumstances change. Several very spiritual Scorpio Rising people have told me, "it's a challenge to absorb the insights from the last cycle of change before going into the next one!"

Finally, Water is a psychic Element. The Gift of Prophecy is associated with Scorpio Rising and Eighth House planets.[36] This Scorpio gift comes through in everything from predictive astrology to dream interpretation to the prediction of stock market cycles. It's even there in Martha Stewart's intuitions about which designs will appeal next to customers. Whether used for mundane or esoteric purposes, Scorpio/Eighth House prophets are usually quite accurate. The more we honor our intuition, the stronger and more accurate it becomes.

The Mode - Fixity
Will Power, Stubbornness, Perseverance, Spiritual Potential

The Fixed Ascendants (Taurus, Leo Scorpio and Aquarius) all have *presence.* Each Fixed Sign has its unique type of charisma. This Mode is stubborn, opinionated, willful and persuasive. Hard aspects from Saturn or low Mutability may indicate mental rigidity, though Mars-ruled Scorpio is less likely to remain stuck in a rut than, for instance, Taurus. Water broods, but unless it's in a Fixed Sign, Mars tends to move on.

---

36 Edgar Cayce, who had Leo Rising, had his Sun in the Water Sign Pisces, in the Eighth House. His prophetic work is described in Part I, Leo Rising.

Pluto's influence on this Fixed Ascendant (mysterious, intense, and powerful) is palpable; Pluto subtly suggests hidden depths and, perhaps, hidden agendas. The Fixed Ascendants often attract other "power people."[37]

Fixity has a stabilizing function, This facilitates the alchemical process of changing one's inner 'base metals' into gold. As C.G. Jung observed, marriage is an alchemical container for a couple's growth. Scorpio, however, craves solitude and privacy. As a result, Scorpio's willingness to compromise for the sake of marriage (the Libran "we" of the last chapter) is problematical.[38]

If one of the ruling planets, Mars or Pluto, is in Mutability, compromise comes more easily to stubborn Scorpio. If Venus, ruler of the marriage archetype, is in Libra, Scorpio will be more motivated to contain that tremendous passion in one relationship.

Otherwise, monogamy can be challenging as an ideal. Many of my clients have, like Mary McCarthy (*The Group, The Groves of Academe*), experienced four marriages and numerous affairs. None to my knowledge, though, can compete with Victor Hugo's record. He had affairs with over two hundred women and kept notes on them all. His wife eventually chose to live in Paris while he lived and wrote on the Isle of Guernsey.

Unless there's a high percentage of Mutable planets, Scorpio will hold out longer in a battle of wills than anyone else, even Taurus Rising! Simone de Beauvoir described herself as "tough" in defending her lover, Sartre. Several of my Scorpio Rising clients have described themselves similarly. Recently, a client remarked, "when it's time to give a patient bad news, I'm the one the staff calls upon. I've gotten used to it."[39]

As Johann von Goethe said, "in the realm of ideas, everything depends on enthusiasm; in the real world, all rests on perseverance." Fixity is the persevering Mode. It helps *most* Scorpios establish stability in youth; overcome Mars' restlessness, (temporarily, at least), prepare for a profession or learn a skill, and commit to a long-term relationship. Because Scorpio usually excels at follow-through, this Mask is an asset in furthering the Sun Sign's goals.

As a young woman, Simone de Beauvoir loved her fellow philosophy student, Jean Paul Sartre, deeply but freedom mattered more. They shared a common philosophy,

---

37 Unless there's an intercept, Fixity will be on the four angles of the horoscope (1,4,7, and 10) the points of interaction with the outside world.

38 I was unable to find playwright Samuel Beckett's (*Waiting For Godot)* exact time of birth, but I suspect he has Scorpio Rising. He loved his privacy; he and his wife lived in adjoining apartments in Paris. He also writes of the importance of stillness and solitude for the writer. See *Collected Short Prose* of Samuel Beckett (London: Calder) 1986).

39 Pisces' Mutability in the horoscope will soften Scorpio, however.

Existentialism. As university students she and Sartre became a couple though they never married; they both had other lovers and their work.[40] They kept separate apartments but spent mornings at their desks together, just as she'd imagined herself and her husband when she was a small child. For Simone, theirs was a "marriage of two minds." The relationship served as an anchor for fifty years.

It wasn't until she met Chicago novelist Nelson Algren (*Man With the Golden Arm*) that sparks flew for Beauvoir; she found sexual compatibility and satisfaction. But Algren didn't understand her commitment to Sartre, or the fact that she "belonged in Paris." He broke up with her.

Most Scorpios are adept at keeping the vows they made to themselves in their youth. Several of my clients remained single until past midlife. Like Beauvoir, who vowed as a young woman never to marry because "the institution has nothing to offer women," Scorpios value their freedom.

Among my clients are several former monks, priests and nuns who in youth preferred like Daniel P. Berrigan, S.J, to "make a difference" by devoting themselves to religion and/or political activism rather than take on householder responsibilities. (Berrigan himself never married.)

Others choose to sublimate their passion in the arts, like Gustave Flaubert, author of *Madame Bovary,* who lived with his mother and visited his mistresses at their apartments.

Johann von Goethe (*Faust; The Sorrows of Young Werner*) finally convinced Christiane Vulpuis, the mother of his children, to marry him in perilous times. He was impressed with her courage when Napoleon's army sacked Weimar; she helped him defend his house, shouting and rattling pots and pans.[41]

Several Scorpio Rising clients have long, intense, passionate marriages like D.H. Lawrence's to Frieda. Around the time of an eclipse, I'll often receive a frantic phone call from Scorpio Rising, "we've just had the worst fight in our entire marriage! I'm *definitely* filing for divorce *this* time!" And sometimes he or she will. However, if the passion is still

---

40 When she declined his proposal of marriage, Simone knew he'd keep seeing other women anyway. Sartre applied Existentialism to political movements, she applied it to novel writing (where she explored the desire nature, particularly in *She Came to Stay)* and her memoir *The Second Sex.* After fans in the Feminist Movement claimed her, she was as much in demand as a speaker as Sartre.

41 A woman of "unsuitable lower class background," Christiane told Goethe she preferred their eighteen year relationship the way it was. She knew, of course, she wasn't his only mistress. He was fifty-seven when they married.

there, Scorpios tend to reunite with the spouse. They'll insist they're tired of the *sturm and drang,* but once they separate, life seems flat without it.

In discussing the Scorpio archetype, so often we focus on sex or on the dark side of the Sign: betrayal, vengeance, anger, resentment bitterness and cynicism. Yet, of all the Rising Signs, passionate Scorpio may have the greatest potential for spiritual growth.

Time and again, I've observed Scorpio's indomitable will engage in battle against incomprehensible obstacles and overcome. Several Scorpio Rising friends and clients have emerged triumphant and strong after doctors had given them only a few months to live. When former spouses moved Scorpio's children out-of-state, long protracted battles were fought and won. When school boards threatened Scorpio's tenure, and, recently, banks attempted to take their homes Scorpio Rising has won its battles.

The Eagle and the Phoenix are loyal, dependable friends in time of need. Anyone who has such a friend is very fortunate.

The Mask in Youth
The Search for Meaning and Purpose

Nietzsche gave good advice in his later years, "when you choose someone to marry, ask yourself this question. "Do you think that you will be able to converse well with this person into old age?"

But this advice seldom resonates when passionate Scorpio is young. Very few young adults think that far ahead. Simone de Beauvoir seems to be the exception to this rule. A Capricorn Sun Sign[42](long-term planner,) she seems to have intuitively done as Nietzsche suggested, establishing her "marriage of the minds" as a student. But she's the exception. I rarely encounter a *young* Scorpio Rising client who puts conversation first! He or she would have to have a *lot* of Air!

Early in life, Scorpio's partnership choices are more likely to echo an earlier Nietzsche observation, "there is more wisdom in your body than in your deepest philosophy;" to reflect Freud's views on the primary importance of the sex drive,[43] or D.H. Lawrence's

---

42 Like many Capricorns, she considered herself "old" in her thirties and began to feel younger as she grew older.

43 C.G. Jung, *Memories, Dreams, Reflections,* ed Aniela Jaffe (NY: Vintage Books,) 1965. Jung wrote that Freud's " tone became urgent, almost anxious" in speaking of his theory about sex, and a deeply moved expression came over his face." Clearly, "he was emotionally involved with the

statement that there's more to life than the brain and the nervous system.[44] Some of Scorpio Rising's early choices resemble those of characters in D.H. Lawrence's and Gustave Flaubert's novels; they speak of "grand, passionate love affairs." And sometimes, like Lady Chatterley and Emma Bovary, they and/or their lovers are married to other people. When acting from libido alone, Scorpio Rising can behave quite selfishly

Later in life most Scorpio Rising clients remark that short-term relationships, however passionate, intense and exciting (the intrigue and secret assignations), failed to bring long-term happiness. The progression through Sagittarius helps them integrate flexibility and willingness to compromise, required traits for long-term relationships, *without losing their passion.*

Activism is another First Half of Life theme. Many will work for social or political change like Berrigan, Steinem, and Beauvoir (through her Existentialist novels and *Les Temps Modernes).* As mentioned above, in youth, many with Scorpio Rising have identified with a cause or purpose— something larger than themselves— and made an effort to change the culture.

Others have sought to change society through a religious group or an ideal community like those that proliferated in the 1970's, some of which still exist today. Whatever their chosen direction, Scorpio Rising is persuasive about their convictions; others admire them and are often drawn to their ideals.

By midlife, though, spirituals seekers and other highly conscious Scorpios will discover that the Ego is still there. Hydra-heads they'd thought they'd severed long ago pop up from the swamp again on Mars transits, transits of the outer planets,[45] and/or eclipses. Sublimating energy into a movement for political change or an attempt to create an ideal society may simply result in a new, charismatic spiritual or political Mask, with the hydra heads popping up behind it.

What's next, Scorpio wonders, now that I've failed to change *everyone else,* my spouse, my children, my community and the culture around me? Several Scorpio Rising people have told me that society seems as much at odds with their values now as it was forty years ago. Much inner work remains to be done.

theory." Jung had "a strong intuition that for him (Freud) sexuality was some sort of *numinosum.*" 150.

44 D.H. Lawrence viewed sex in an almost sacramental way. Through it resentments were healed; anger and violent urges transcended, forgiveness came more easily. His friend Henry T. Moore explains this in *The Priest of Love: a Biography of D.H. Lawrence.* The title comes from a letter of Lawrence's to Sallie Hopkins, on Christmas Day 1912. "I will always be a priest of love." (NY: Farrar Straus & Giroux,) 1974

45 Saturn and the trans-Saturnian planets, Uranus Neptune and Pluto.

The Mask after Midlife
The Path to Spiritual Maturity

Martha Stewart remarked at midlife, "my new motto is, when you're done changing, you're done." After the tumultuous first half of life concludes; after numerous battles, both outer and inner, most Scorpio Rising people have seen the need for flexibility and accepted the need for compromise. And because it's impossible to win every battle, Scorpio has learned to prioritize its battles and adjust to change.

For example Simone de Beauvoir saw no need for compromise as a child. When she was denied something she wanted, she threw a tantrum. Her father stayed out late every night "playing bridge," his euphemism for time with his mistresses, and her mother was unable to handle Simone's strong will. Simone held her breath until she fainted, then got her own way. This worked for a long time.

At sixteen, she met her first serious obstacle. She decided to marry her older cousin Jacques, who'd loaned her his Robert Louis Stevenson books. She had enjoyed his company since childhood. Her mother supported her plan. However, Jacques' mother had arranged his marriage to a wealthy young woman whose dowry would cover his law school expenses.

Devastated, Simone knew she couldn't change the situation by the sheer force of her will.[46] She vowed never to marry. She didn't want an absent husband like her father or a life like her mother's.

Meanwhile, her father had told Simone that she was ugly; that she had "a mind like a man's"[47] and, unfortunately, no dowry. While her lovely sister Helene would easily find a husband, clearly Simone must study very hard to prepare for a profession. He suggested teaching, a career that wouldn't "embarrass" her upper middle class (haut bourgeois) parents.

Simone didn't mind; she enjoyed school. Ambitious, like most people with the Scorpio/Capricorn combination of Ascendant and Sun, Simone worked hard. And, by the time she enrolled in the Sorbonne and met Sartre, she was much more attractive.[48] Having failed

---

46 After *The Second Sex* brought her international fame, Jacques, dressed like a homeless person, approached her for money. An alcoholic, he had run through his wife's dowry.

47 At first she took the remark, "a mind like a man's" as a compliment, but later Simone realized he didn't intend it that way. He considered her mind an impediment in finding a husband.

48 Sartre gave her the nickname "the beaver" (Castor) because she was so industrious, the best -prepared student in their study group for the exams. Their school friends called her that the rest

his exams for lack of preparation, Sartre joined a study group with younger students, including Beauvoir. She considered him "more creative in philosophy" than she.

Simone merged her life and interests with his. She became Sartre's editor, sounding board, collaborator; and ghost writer when he was too busy for his column. She set aside her novel writing to accompany him on lecture tours abroad. They dedicated themselves to a common cause, enlightening the culture by disseminating their philosophy. Seventeen years would pass before she began her memoir, *The Second Sex*, and, through the writing process, *she found herself.* Her inner work had begun.[49]

During her thirties, Simone discovered that her Existentialist novels didn't appeal to readers; very few, it seemed, could identify with her characters. But she attained unexpected fame with the *Second Sex*, which appealed to women as far away as America and Australia. This was her first success independent of Sartre. For decades, The Great Man had had his intellectual groupies then, suddenly, Simone had fans of her own.

Through speaking engagements—which she'd declined before *The Second Sex*— she met novelist Nelson Algren in Chicago[50] and he became her lover. Their passionate connection was quite a contrast to her "marriage of minds" with Sartre. It was a tremendous change for Simone, who wore Algren's silver ring for the rest of her life. Without sacrificing her freedom, Beauvoir enjoyed two intense but very different relationships.

And she had changed. More fashion-conscious after her travels abroad, Simone was no longer viewed as Sartre's "dowdy, spinsterish collaborator." She became known for her turbans. They still spent mornings working together. Though Simone was not pleased when Sartre asked a younger woman to be his executor and "literary heir," at the end of his life his several mistresses helped her with his care. She outlived Sartre by eight years.

Simone was still in demand for blurbs, prefaces and public appearances at seventy-eight, the year she died. According to her biographer she would not have changed much about her life. She had only two regrets; she wished that she'd been kinder to her mother and that Sartre had not weakened in his Existentialist convictions under the influence of a younger generation of students.[51]

Journalist and editor (*Ms. Magazine*) Gloria Steinem's timing was the reverse of

---

of her life. Sartre was shorter than she, overweight, and wore thick glasses. Still, like a modern rock star, he was followed by women groupies into his old age.

49 Beauvoir's Mars-Pluto-square, an indicator that she felt a need to be in control of her life, comes through in the memoir.

50 She was thirty-nine.

51 They were Maoists. Sartre wanted above all to be relevant; to be called upon for his opinion by the leading thinkers of his time. By the end of his life Levi Strauss was being quoted instead.

Simone's in many ways. A public speaker as a young woman, Gloria wrote her memoir, *Revolution from Within,* at 69. While Simone had hated politics and attended rallies only to support Sartre, Steinem was active in feminist causes and supported Shirley Chisholm's campaign for the presidency. Like most of my clients and unlike Simone de Beauvoir, Gloria experienced passion early in life.

Branded a radical in her youth,[52] many of Steinem's ideas seem fairly commonplace now that Feminism has attained so many of its goals. Gloria's efforts not only helped make career women socially acceptable[53] but brought working mothers tangible benefits. There are now day care centers and paid maternity leave. Much remains to be done by younger feminists; equal pay for equal work (the Equal Rights Amendment) failed to pass, and Planned Parenthood clinics are fighting for survival, but on the whole Gloria's cause was a success.

Asked about life after fifty, she said, "I'm not obsessed with sex anymore. It's not a loss, it's just different…the brain cells obsessed with it can now be devoted to other things;" "I don't regret not having children," and, "the bad news is that I find myself doing things over again, the good news is that I *can.*"[54]

In her two essays, "Doing Sixty and Seventy," she wrote that at first it was a shock to be invisible; to realize nobody cared what she thought anymore, "but then, on second thought, it was liberating. It was a new type of freedom."

During her late sixties, Steinem decided to write a book on self-esteem. In researching the topic, she discovered that her life had, in fact, centered around developing her own! She discarded her notes and began her memoir, *Revolution from Within.* Both Steinem and Beauvoir gained self-knowledge from memoir writing. Who knows where Scorpio's projects will lead?

---

52 In a 1973 *New York Times* op ed, she said that she saw gender as "probably the most restricting force in American life." Quoted in *St. Petersburg Times,* March 6, 2008. Steinem, then 73, was interviewed during Hillary Clinton's presidential race.

53 Prior to the late 1960's, career women were often gossiped about. Many people thought something must be wrong with "spinsters:" "Not *all* of them are too ugly to find husbands, after all! Why aren't they married? Perhaps they're all lesbians!" The Feminist movement brought unmarried career women respect.

54 Leonora Epstein, "Feminist Missteps in front of Gloria Steinem," Quoted from thefrisky.com/ post, June 2, 2009. Article still posted as of March 4, 2010.

Bridging the Abyss - The Scorpio Rising Story

Nietzsche's story is fascinating in a similar way to the tale about the Hundredth Monkey.[55] Both are based on the concept that it only takes one member of a species, one individual, to make a leap in consciousness. Not only does he instantly acquire a new ability, (power) but his leap may bring about an evolutionary change for his entire species.

Just as only *one* macaque among the hundred made a major breakthrough that quickly spread to the other ninety-nine, Nietszche's story proposed that *one* human genius could make a such a leap for Mankind. Then, geniuses would appear and proliferate in the arts and sciences.

The story in the *Prologue to Zarathustra* begins with a strong-willed philosopher-poet who thinks he has all the answers. Though he soon discovers his limitations, his Phoenix-like compassion and generosity are revealed. As it involves major themes and attributes of both Signs, the story begins in Scorpio and concludes in Sagittarius (Chapter Nine.)

It's tempting to identify with the philosopher-poet, especially when we've recently "come down from the mountaintop" ourselves, having taken a respite from our own fast-paced lives.[56] However, he's not the hero.

The hero is the tightrope walker, the spiritual warrior who lives on the edge and who takes on a seemingly impossible challenge. If he succeeds, he becomes a Superman. This Archetype has had a strong impact on Western culture. Batman, Spiderman and Superman all began as comic book heroes and ended up with their own movies.[57]

---

55 This Japanese research was discussed in Lawrence Blair's *Rhythms of Vision* (1995.) When one monkey learned to wash sweet potatoes, the other ninety-nine picked up the skill almost instantly. Macaque mothers began teaching it to their babies. Authors like Ken Keyes theorize that the skill spread quickly to nearby islands whose macaques had never observed the original monkey. However, some scientists say there's insufficient evidence to substantiate this.

56 Many of us have returned home full of insights after writers' retreats, yoga retreats or retreat weekends with people in our professions. When we've attempted to share the insights, we've met with similar reactions to those the philosopher received in this story. Perhaps some insights are not meant to be shared.

57 In politics, the theory of vesting absolute power in a supreme ruler—a kind of Superman—has been tempting as well, especially during economic downturns like the Great Depression. While legislatures seem too slow in responding, a Superman might "save" the country quickly.

The Philosopher, the Tightrope Walker, and the Crowd

The philosopher-poet is still in the tower but intuitively he knows that his ten years of solitude have come to an end. It's time now to rejoin society and share his insights. He takes one last look through the window-slits in the stone wall, at the mountain in the far distance. Suddenly, he realizes that the mountain he's now on is the Past and the other one is the Unknown Future.

He leaves the tower and slowly starts his downhill climb. As he descends, he wonders where the villagers have gone. Perhaps there's a festival in the town. Gradually, he becomes aware that the edge of the cliff is now a sheer ledge there's a steep drop if he loses his footing. Still, he stands at the edge and looks down. He stares into a pit that's larger and deeper than the Grand Canyon. It seems bottomless. "Oh," he mutters to himself, "that's the Abyss." He shrugs, "I'll deal with it later."

Eventually he reaches terra firma, the flat land at the outskirts of the town. Suddenly, he realizes he's also in the Present, that noisy, crowded, hectic place where civilization happens. But he's ready for it. A crowd of villagers and townsmen have gathered; they're standing near the Abyss and they're staring upward. They've probably been watching him climb down. That's it! They're waiting *for him!* He's not worried, though because he's enlightened, after all! He'll share whatever wisdom they require.

Drawing closer to them now, he attempts to get their attention. He shouts out questions to them, "do you know how to get past the beast, the part of yourselves that has no will power and cannot focus? The lower self? *I have the answer!*"

Someone shouts back, *"who cares about that? Shut up!"*

And someone else shouts, *"we're waiting for the acrobat!"*

"What acrobat?" asks the philosopher, who has now reached the gathering.

"The tightrope walker who accepted our challenge! See those two mountaintops? There's a rope strung between them, right over the Abyss!"

"Right," says another voice in the crowd. "Maybe he'll make it and maybe he'll fall. Either way, it'll be a damn good show!"

The philosopher thinks, "a tightrope. What a marvelous metaphor to illustrate my point." He shouts, "do you know what the rope is made of? That rope is *our imagination!*" It's a very strong rope, but it takes will power and focus to hang on! "Ha!" says a loud voice followed by a guffaw, "that acrobat better hope the rope is *real*. What good's an imaginary rope?"

Tired of talk, the restless crowd wants action.

Finally, the acrobat appears. They see him halfway up the mountain, his pole in hand, starting off across the Abyss on the rope. They turn their backs to the philosopher-poet, tilt back their heads and begin to watch the show.

"What discipline he has, what will power, what concentration!" shouts the philosopher.

"*Shut up,*" the crowd yells in unison.

"The Abyss is full of his past mistakes, his shame, his fears, and his embarrassment if he falls. And death awaits him down there. Do you see those shadows around the edge of the pit?" the philosopher asks.

"*Shut UP!*"

"The rope—the imagination—that he clings to, that's his safety net as he moves towards the Unknown Future. How brave he is to face his fears!"

"*QUIET!*" shouts the crowd in chorus.

"*What safety net? There's no net under him!*" someone yells.

A mighty gasp sweeps through the crowd. The acrobat slips, grips the rope with his toes, and regains his balance. He's now two-thirds of the way across the Abyss. Every eye is now glued to him, even the philosopher has stopped talking to observe his living, breathing metaphor.

Suddenly, from a crevice in the mountainside, nearly invisible in the clouds, a figure in a harlequin suit emerges from the Future side of the Abyss. He has a malicious smirk which only the tightrope walker can see. And the acrobat from the Future leaps out onto the rope. He quickly does a handstand, then vaults over the tightrope walker to do a headstand behind him. As he springs off and lands back on the rope, it bounces.

Each time the acrobat from the Future lands, the tightrope walker loses focus. In panic, he looks behind him, judging the distance he's already come. Is it better, safer to turn around and go back? No. He's two-thirds of the way across; he can only go forward. As the distracted man panics, the malicious acrobat lands hard on the rope.

The acrobat falls, but not into the Abyss. He lands on the ground between the Abyss and the crowd. Again, they release a collective gasp.

"Is he dead?" a short man yells from the rear.

"Almost," shouts a man in the front.

"Too bad," someone mutters.

"Well, it was exciting, anyhow. Let's go," says someone else.

The crowd disperses, leaving the philosopher-poet to attend to the fallen acrobat.

"Your life was well and bravely lived with discipline and effort," he tells the dying man.

"Thank you," whispers the acrobat.

"I'll bury you," the philosopher-poet promises.

He lifts him up and carries him for miles, stopping to rest at nightfall. He continues on, walking uphill for several days, but finds no suitable place to bury the hero. Finally he comes to a forest. His arms and back ache as he places the acrobat's body into a hole in a tree. "It's as good a place as I can find," he sighed. "The spirit of a brave man will live on in this living tree."

A few years later, an old woodcutter named Gepetto went to the forest in search of material to make a puppet. He saw several suitable trees but one in particular called out to him. "This tree has a good spirt," Gepetto said aloud. "It's exactly what I need. I'll cut a branch for my puppet."

He named the puppet Pinocchio (pine wood.) The story of this fearless, restless and somewhat prickly spirit continues in Chapter Nine.

The Sagittarius Progression
Inspiration, Flexibility, Freedom

The progression through Mutable Fire is particularly important for Scorpio Rising if Scorpio's Fixity is enhanced by a Fixed Natal Sun and/or Moon or if there's a high percentage of planets in the Fixed Mode. During this cycle Scorpios are challenged to compromise their desire to live life on their own terms with others' desires. The give-and-take of Mutability; the *Yin of yielding* is essential for lasting friendships and marriage; this long progression aids stubborn Scorpio in developing some Mutable traits.

Sagittarius' Element (Fire,) is usually much easier for Scorpio to work with than its Mode (Mutability). It's easier for the Mask to assimilate qualities when Natal planets are "in their Element" with the progressed Ascendant. The progressed Ascendant will form trines to Natal planets in Fire.

When, like journalist Gloria Steinem, a person has *no* planets in the First House (Identity) the progressed Ascendant fills in for them. Gloria's progressed Ascendant gradually moved into a Grand Trine with her Aries and Leo planets. Symbolically, her First House was no longer empty as she began to identify with causes.

Gloria returned from her studies in India inspired to bring about change. She became an activist for liberal politics and women's rights. In the late 1960's, as Progressed Sagittarius trined her Natal Sun/Mars conjunction in Aries, she campaigned for Democratic candidates. In 1972, the year her progressed Ascendant trined her Leo Moon (Ninth House) she founded *MS Magazine*.[58]

When there are Sagittarian First House planets for the progressed Ascendant to conjunct, Scorpio's Mask assimilates their extraversion. With Natal Sagittarian planets in the *Second* House, there's a tendency to speculate during the progressed conjunction. Because this usually occurs between Scorpio's late fifties and his seventies, it usually causes his family anxiety. They fear that funds lost later in life will be more difficult to replenish. However, if Scorpio's Natal Second is well-aspected, the risk may have a favorable outcome.

If the Natal Sun is in Sagittarius, Scorpio Rising may have a special project in mind for retirement, like Flaubert's[59] St. Anthony play. With Sun or Moon in Fire, the progressed trine is usually enjoyable. Fire planets are playful; Leo and Aries are involved in outdoor sports or yoga. Though they keep themselves in shape physically, they may tend to become overextended financially.

If there's a "singleton planet" in the Fire Element, it can seem to take over one's life for awhile. If Natal Mars, for instance, is the *only* Fire planet in the horoscope, Scorpio Rising's latent spirit of adventure may lack an outlet. In that case, on its trine to Mars, the Sagittarius Ascendant seems to encourage playful Natal Mars to find one! Rock climbing, mountain biking or bungee jumping may suddenly appeal. Or, Scorpio Rising may purchase a red convertible. Sextiles to Libra and Aquarius (Air) Natal planets usually bring opportunities, often in the arts or public speaking. Air planets work well with the progressed Mask.

The Sagittarian Ascendant will *square or oppose* Mutable planets in the horoscope. We feel the squares within us and we experience the oppositions in relating to the outside world. Scorpio, for instance, feels its Pisces or Virgo planets on the squares from the progressed Sagittarius Rising. Virgo clients sometimes feel dissatisfied with themselves under the square, wishing that they could accomplish more.

D.H. Lawrence had several Natal planets, including the Sun, in the late degrees of Virgo. He suffered health challenges (tuberculosis) and financial frustrations but he learned to adapt. He spent time abroad in dry, sunny climates like Mexico and Santa Fe. He used the settings in his novels.

---

58 Like Steinem, Simone de Beauvoir had no planets in her First House, but she had only one Natal Fire planet, Jupiter.

59 Flaubert had Sun-in-Sagittarius trined Saturn and Jupiter, but didn't live long enough for the progressed Ascendant to conjunct his Sun in the Second. His reputation achieved during the Scorpio cycle, he enjoyed his freedom during Sagittarius.

Sagittarius Rising is about freedom. During the progression, Scorpio Rising may feel he needs more of it for Individuation. Simone de Beauvoir traveled abroad without Sartre for the first time during the last five years of her Sagittarian progression. When the Ascendant was in square to her Natal Mars and Moon-in-Pisces, she met Algren, her lover, and flew back and forth to Chicago to be with him.

As Simone's Ascendant was changing from Sagittarius to Capricorn, Algren visited her in Paris. He hoped she'd marry him but instead he discovered that she was still seeing Sartre every day. He was very angry when they ended the affair. Simone decided that she "belonged in Paris;" that her long "marriage of-the-minds," her history with Sartre, mattered most.

Travel is one area where Scorpio's perspective seems to broaden, and may even open up in surprising ways during the Sagittarian progression. D.H. Lawrence is a good example. However, if, like Sigmund Freud, Scorpio Rising has several Fixed planets (Freud had the Sun and three others in Taurus), when the progressed Ascendant aspects them, there may be resistance to travel. Some find it uncomfortable. If Mutability is low, Scorpios tend to miss their familiar language, food and beverage.

In 1910, when Freud was fifty-four, he was invited to travel outside Europe for the first time. He wrote Jung that he didn't plan to attend the conference, citing his preconceptions about America as excuses to stay home: Americans were too materialistic. Further, they hadn't offered him enough money to cover his trip; he'd be better off financially staying home. Americans were also much too prudish for his theory of sexuality. After being persuaded to attend, Freud found most of his expectations confirmed.[60]

The more Fixity in the horoscope, the more difficult it is for Scorpio to see beyond his preconceived opinions. Most of my Scorpio Rising clients, however, enjoy traveling during the Sagittarian progression. Those involved in the Peace Corps or humanitarian work abroad (Sagittarius is a generous Sign) return with an understanding of other cultures and different perspectives. Two close friends purchased property abroad during the cycle.

Spouses and partners of the Strong Silent type of Scorpio, Scorpios with a lot of Earth and Water but who also have some *Natal Gemini planets* may receive a shock when progressed Sagittarius opposes their partner's restless Gemini nature.[61] Not only will the

---

60 Jung, who had Sun, Moon and Ascendant in Fixity and had Fixed *Air* Rising, was very interested in the theories of the *other* psychologists at the conference. He wrote his wife that he was returning with "about a thousand new ideas," but that Freud seemed interested *only in his own theories*, and would end the conversation if others wanted to discuss something else. Sagittarius is in hard aspect, the inconjunct, to Taurus. See Deirdra Bair, cited above, 153-166.
61 Simone de Beauvoir had Pluto-in-Gemini in the Seventh, close to the cusp of her Eighth House.

Scorpio Rising partner become more talkative, but he or she may also become interested in the Talking Cure (psychotherapy) either as a patient or as a student, and end a long marriage.

Because Gemini planets thrive on novelty and variety, previously loyal and monogamous Scorpios sometimes decide to separate from their partner to experience new relationships. Sagittarius Rising may bring out other facets of the personality hidden away in the Eighth House. For instance, the inconjunct from the progressed Ascendant to Cancer planets in the Eighth sometimes coincides with the desire to have or to adopt a child at midlife.

Many astrologers associate Natal Sagittarius Rising with bachelorhood. I first heard this in the early 1970's at a talk by Katherine de Jersey and have found it true of many male clients.[62] There's a similar freedom impulse during the Sagittarius progression. It's interesting that Johann von Goethe's seventeen-year-relationship ended with marriage just after his Sagittarius progressed Ascendant *had finished* all its contacts to his Natal planets. Void-of-Course, it was losing steam in the adventurous Fire Sign. Three years later, his Rising Sign progressed into Capricorn, Sign of stability and commitment.

The chaotic circumstances at the time of his proposal—his home in Weimar under siege by Napoleon's soldiers—no doubt accelerated the couple's decision to marry. Both he and Christiane were ready to commit.

In sum, Mutability is about *direct* verbal communication in relationships as well as sharing ideas through travel; teaching, lecturing or publishing. During the cycle, Scorpio becomes more involved in sharing his or her political, spiritual or philosophical perspective and may discover new ways of being as well as doing. This thirty-year cycle offers potential for positive change, both inner *and* outer.

Capricorn Rising - Groundedness

Few of the creative people in this chapter lived long enough to don the Capricorn Mask. Four exceptions are authors Simone de Beauvoir, who had worn the Sagittarian progressed Mask since the age of four and progressed into Capricorn at age forty-eight (1954); Sigmund Freud, who progressed into Capricorn in 1934 and died in England five

---

She had brief affairs, including one with Arthur Koestler, before meeting Algren, but seemingly only two intense relationships, Sartre and Algren.

62 Though several married at midlife. A brilliant and compassionate astrologer, she wrote *Destiny Times Six* (1970) and *Appointment with Destiny.* (1995.) There's a Memorial Page about her on the Internet.

years later; Gloria Steinem, who progressed into Capricorn at the turn of the Twenty-First Century, (2001) and Daniel Berrigan S.J., who became a progressed Capricorn in 1997. The last two are still progressed Capricorns.

As Capricorn stands in symbolic sextile to Scorpio, (Water and Earth are compatible Elements) this is usually an easier cycle for Scorpio Rising. It's a slower paced, more cautious Earth cycle that accords well with Scorpio's retirement years. Most are ready to settle into a slower paced-routine, though in Capricorn they like to feel productive.

In earlier developmental cycles, will power has been applied; in youth to establishing a career and at midlife, independence. Adaptability and communication skills were (one hopes) developed during Sagittarius, and the Scorpio Eagle has likely expanded his horizons to include the world beyond himself and his culture. All four examples lived by their philosophy and each, from his or her own perspective, attempted to make the world a better place.

The two women examined their lives in the memoir-writing process. Steinem, formerly skeptical of the Talking Cure, went into therapy following a cancer scare in 1986. She sold *Ms Magazine* in 1987, freeing her schedule for longer writing projects. D.P. Berrigan traveled to France and spent time with Vietnamese Buddhist monk Thich Nhat Hanh discussing the Vietnam War. He still appears at anti-war demonstrations.

Their lives parallel those of my "Eagle clients" in different ways. Several were volunteers or social activists back in the 1960's and 1970's. Several are therapists and/or retired professors like Berrigan. Some are writing memoirs in the Capricorn cycle, while others, like Berrigan, write poetry.

In late Sagittarius and Capricorn, symbolically the Zenith of the Natural Zodiac,) there have been awards and recognition. Simone received two from the French government, which must have pleased her. She had three Natal planets in ambitious Capricorn for the progressed Ascendant to conjunct! While working for Hillary Clinton in 2008, with the Cardinal progressed Ascendant squaring her Mars-in-Aries, Steinem was in the limelight with frequent interviews.

Sigmund Freud's story is exceptional in that it presents a graphic example of what occurs when an individual's developmental cycle like Old Age intersects with a period of upheaval in the outer world. Freud had lived for seventy-nine years in Vienna, but in his eighty-second year he was forced to leave. Seriously ill, he packed and left shortly after his daughter's overnight interrogation by the Gestapo.[63]

Capricorn Earth is suited to peacefully staying home and "cultivating our garden,"

---

63 Robert Coles, *Anna Freud: The Dream of Psychoanalysis,* (NY: Addison-Wesley,) 1992, appendix, 186.

but the world around us doesn't always cooperate. Though few stories are as dramatic as Freud's, his comes to mind when, in the current recession, clients lament the loss of the comfortable retirement that they'd anticipated. As their property and equities lose value, their "working years" seem to stretch into the distant future. Scorpio Rising seems to deal with this better than most of the other Signs. The strong will developed through Eighth House struggles can be a real advantage.

Only Freud, among the above examples, had children and grandchildren. (Simone de Beauvoir did adopt an "heir" who lived and traveled with her, but the woman was an adult, a teacher.)

Most of my Scorpio Rising clients have children (though seldom large families) and some now have grandchildren. But unless the Cancer Archetype is present, I've found that while they enjoy their visits with grandchildren none to my knowledge has adopted them; helped raise them on a daily basis, happily coached their sports team or served as their girl scout den mother as other Rising Signs have done. As they grow older, Scorpio Rising seems to value privacy and solitude ("alone time") more than ever.

Aquarius Rising
Friendship and Sociability in Old Age

Simone de Beauvoir progressed into Aquarius two years before her partner of fifty years, John Paul Sartre, died. She outlived him by eight years. Simone was fortunate in her friendships, some of which dated from student days at the Sorbonne. In addition to the young woman she adopted, and with whom she traveled, there were several friends who dined and drank with her in the cafes. Propping her up by the elbows, they helped her home. She told her biographer, Deidre Bair, how important they were to her.

I have as yet no Scorpio Rising clients who've progressed into Aquarius. As most of my clients are very loyal to their friends, it seems their friendships will endure into old age.

Scorpio Rising Bibliography

Bailey, Alice A, *Esoteric Astrology, A Treatise on the Seven Rays,* (New York: Lucis Press,) 1997.

—— *The Labours of Hercules, The Lernian Hydra,* (New York: Lucis Press,) 1977.

Bair, Deirdre, *Simone de Beauvoir: A Biography.* (New York: Simon & Schuster/Touchstone,) 1991.

Beauvoir, Simone de, *The Second Sex, H.M. Parshley trans,* (New York: Knopf,) 1993.

Berrigan, Daniel P, with Robert Coles, *The Geography of Faith: Conversations between Daniel Berrigan when Underground and Robert Coles,* (Boston: Beacon Press,) 1971.

Edwards, Samuel, *Victor Hugo: A Tumultuous Life,* (New York: David Mc Kay Co.,) 1971.

Freud, Sigmund, *Diary of Sigmund Freud: A Record of his Final Decade,* (New York: Scribners,) 1992.

—— *Letters of Sigmund Freud,* by Ernst and S. Freud, (New York: Dover,) 1992. Includes Letters to C.G. Jung, Thomas Mann, Einstein, H.G. Wells.

—— *Letters of Sigmund Freud and Lou Andreas Salome,* ed, Ernst Pfeiffer, (New York: WW Norton & Co.,) 1995.

—— *The Freud Reader,* ed, Peter Gay, (London: Penguin,) 1905.

(Chronological presentation includes 50 texts; follows the development of his theories on the instincts through patients' cases.)

—— *Freud-Jung Letters: The Correspondence Between Sigmund Freud and C.G. Jung,* ed William Mc Guire, Bollingen Vol. 94, (Princeton: Princeton University Press,) 1974.

Hollis, James, *Swamplands of the Soul: New Life in Dismal Places,* (Toronto: Inner City Books,) 1996.

Hugo, Victor, *Les Miserables,* Fahnestock and MacAfee, eds. (New York: Signet Classics,) 1987.

—— *Les Chatiments,* satirical, polemical, romantic, metaphysical and religious poems. (Chicago: University of Chicago Press,) c2001.

Jones, Ernest, *Life and Work of Sigmund Freud,* (New York: Random House Anchor,) 1995.

Lawrence, David Henry, *Lady Chatterley's Lover, The Rainbow and Women in Love,* Lawrence, Frieda von Richthofen, *Not I but the Wind that Blows through Me and Other Autobiographical Writings,* (San Francisco: Pandora,) 1994.

McCarthy, Mary, *The Group,* (New York: Harvest Books,) 1991.

—— *Memoirs of a Catholic Girlhood,* (New York: Mariner's,) *1972.* Includes life with Protestant and Jewish relatives after the death of her parents; life before Vassar.

Maddox, Brenda, *D.H. Lawrence: The Story of a Marriage*, (N Y: W.W. Norton & Co.) 1996.

Moore, Harry T, *The Priest of Love: A Biography of D.H. Lawrence,* (New York: Farrar Strauss and Giroux,) 1974.

Mookherjee, Ajit, *Kali: The Feminine Force,* "Hymn to Kali," (London: Thames and Hudson,) 1988.

Parkes, Graham, *Composing the Soul: The Reaches of Nietzsche's Psychology,* (Chicago: University of Chicago Press,) 1994.

Ruskin, Jimmy, *The Prologue, the Poltergeist and the Hollow Tree, a retelling of the tightrope walker from Thus Spoke Zarathustra,* (New York: Foundation 2021,) 2005.

Salome, Lou Andreas, *Nietzsche,* Elise, Theo and Siegfried Mandel, ed. and trans., (Urbana: University of Illinois Press,) 2001.

Smith, Anne, *D.H. Lawrence and Women,* (New Jersey: Barnes & Noble/Vision,) 1980.

Steinem, Gloria, *Moving Beyond Words,* (New York: Simon & Schuster,) 1994.

—— *Revolution from Within: A Book of Self-Esteem,* (Boston: Little Brown & Co,) 1992.

—— *Road to the Heart: America as if Everyone Mattered,* work in progress.

von Goethe, Johann-Wolfgang, *Faust Part I and Part II*, trans, John Clifford, (London: N. Hern Books,) 2006.

Yogananda, Parmahansa, (Mukunda Lal Ghosh,) *How to Be Happy All the Time,* (Nevada City: Crystal Clarity Press,) 2006, Solitude time is a key to happiness.

—— *Inner Peace,* (Los Angeles: SRF,) Seclusion is the price of Greatness.

Wikman, Monika, *The Pregnant Darkness: Alchemy and the Rebirth of Consciousness,* (Berwick: Nicolas-Hays,) 2004.

CHAPTER THREE

Sagittarius Rising - Inspiration Comes From Helping Others

Dame Edith Sitwell, "I'm not eccentric. It's just that I'm more alive than most people."

—— "Hot water is my element. I was in it as a baby and have never seemed to get out of it since."

—— "The aim of flattery is to soothe and encourage us by assuring us of the truth of an opinion we have already formed about ourselves."

—— "My poems are hymns of praise to the glory of life."

—— "As for the *usefulness* of poetry, its uses are many…it is the deification of reality. It should make our days holy to us. The poet should speak to all men, for a moment, of that other life of theirs that they have smothered and forgotten."

Hans Christian Andersen, "Being born in a duck yard does not matter if only you are hatched from a swan's egg."

—— "Life itself is the most wonderful fairy tale."

—— "My life is a lovely story, happy and full of incident."

—— "Every man's life is a fairy tale written by God's fingers."

Jean-Paul Sartre, "As far as men go, it is not what they are that interests me, but what they can become."

—— "Freedom is what you do with what's been done to you."

—— "I cannot make liberty my aim unless I make that of others equally my aim."

—— "The best work is not what is most difficult for you; it is what you do best."

—— "We do not judge the people we love. In love, one and one are one."

—— "If you seek authenticity for authenticity's sake, you are no longer authentic."

Simone Weil, "I can, therefore I am."

—— "A science which does not bring us nearer to God is worthless."

—— "When a contradiction is impossible to resolve except by a lie, then we know that it is really a door.

—— "In struggling against anguish one never produces serenity; (the struggle) only produces new forms of anguish."

—— "The highest ecstasy is the attention at its fullest."

—— "To be rooted is perhaps the most important and least recognized need of the human soul."

—— "Two prisoners whose cells adjoin communicate with each other by knocking on the wall. The wall ...separates them but is also their means of communication. It is the same with us and God. Every separation is a link."

Mary Baker Eddy, "Happiness is spiritual, born of truth and love. It is unselfish, therefore it cannot exist alone, but requires all mankind to share it.

—— "To those leaning on the sustaining infinite, today is big with blessings."

Hermann Hesse, "Happiness is a how, not a what. A talent, not an object."

—— "Eternity is a mere moment, just long enough for a joke."

—— "Knowledge can be communicated, but not wisdom. One can find it, live it, be fortified through it, but not communicate it."

—— "One never reaches home, but wherever friendly paths intersect the whole world looks like home for a time."

—— "Only the ideas that we really live have any value. The truth is lived, not taught."

—— "Advance, mount higher, conquer yourself! For to be human is to suffer an incurable duality, to be drawn toward both good and evil. And we can achieve harmony and peace only when we have killed the selfishness within us.

—— "The marvel of the *Bhagavad-Gita* is its truly beautiful revelation of life's wisdom which enables philosophy to blossom into religion."

—— "You're only afraid if you're not in harmony with yourself. People are afraid because they have never owned up to themselves."

Dr. Hunter "Patch" Adams, "I'm about doing. I'm a raging doer. I think inherent in the doing is the energy for the doing."

—— "Can I look at injustice and do nothing, or can I do something?" With that, Gesundheit! was born."

—— "It's the job of the clown and the doctor to walk towards suffering and not be afraid to speak up. As soon as you stop being part of peace and justice and care, you're going to be lonely and your life isn't going to have meaning."

—— "If you want to prevent extinction, then you have to think it (peace justice and care) *for everybody.*"

—— "I clown 10-16 hours a day uninterruptedly. Blissfully. But it's not the thing to say in an interview. The important thing in an interview is for a physician to say, look, our species is going to be extinct if we don't convert to a society that puts the emphasis on compassion and generosity that we now put on money and power."

—— "As people came through onto the other side and transformed those complexes, huge creative energies began to emerge. Because the energy that had been located in the addiction, when transformed, became very creative and spiritually oriented."

Marion Woodman, "That naturally led into soul and spirit. I think there's a place where psychology and religion meet, and where religion becomes more essential than psychology. Healing is a coming to wholeness." Jungian analyst, author and inspiring speaker,

Betty Friedan, "It is easier to live through someone else than to become complete yourself."

—— "It is better for a woman to compete impersonally in society, as men do, than to compete for dominance in her own home with her husband, compete with her neighbors for empty status, and so smother her son that he cannot compete at all."

Bob Dylan, "A man is a success if he gets up in the morning and gets to bed at night, and in between he does what he wants to do."

—— "A lot of people can't stand touring but to me it's like breathing. I do it because I'm driven to do it."

—— "Don't matter how much money you got, there's only two kinds of people: there's saved people and there's lost people."

Helen Gurley Brown, "Beauty can't amuse you, but brainwork - reading, writing, thinking—can."

L. Ron Hubbard, "Boldness in itself is genius." "Never regret yesterday, life is in you today and you make your tomorrow." Author of *Dianetics* and founder of Scientology.

Robert Bly, "By the time a man is 35 he knows that the images of the right man, the tough man, the true man which he received in high school do not work in life." Poet, and publisher.

—— "I have risen to a body not yet born, existing like a light around a body through which the body moves like a sliding moon."

The Mask

I'm the Mask of Sagittarius. Unless there are First House Capricorn planets to weigh me down or serious Scorpio planets in my Twelfth House, I'm a cheerful, positive, playful Mask.

I'm more concerned with the future than the past, unless I have Sun or Moon in Water. With Gemini planets, I like to clown around. Dr. "Patch" Adams, (above) is literally a blissful clown!

I'll tell you my opinion frankly and directly. With many planets in Air and Fire, it's obvious that I'm outspoken. But in horoscopes where the quieter Elements (Earth and Water) predominate, people may not notice right away. So, when I blurt out my shockingly unpopular views—I'll praise a Democratic politician at a Republican gathering or *vice versa*—my hostess sometimes thinks I have foot-in-mouth disease.

Others may be Politically Correct but *I'm* no hypocrite! Like Dame Edith Sitwell (above) "I was in hot water as a baby and have been there all my life;" I'm used to it!

An idealist, I write or lecture from my own philosophical or religious perspective. Because I speak from personal experience, others often find my words inspiring. They know I'm sincere in my convictions.

Jean-Paul Sartre wore my Mask, Bob Dylan wears it, too. Dylan (above) believes that people "fall into one of two categories—the saved and the unsaved" while Sartre, an atheist, lived by his personal code of ethics and his philosophy of individual freedom.

Because I stand on principle, I'm usually respected and often admired. Helen Gurley Brown and Betty Friedan still draw readers who share their views.

I've been accused of being an Absolutist. I tend to see the world in black and white with no shades of gray, especially if I have Pisces or Sagittarian planets.

The least wishy-washy of the Mutable Signs, I'll take that "Absolutist" remark as a compliment! I'm outraged at injustice, but my bark is usually stronger than my bite.

Though I'll argue vehemently with you today, I'll still be your friend tomorrow. I might be a gifted Life Coach. I could help with your Mission Statement; let's discuss your goals! I can instill confidence if you're discouraged.

Friends seek me out when they want an honest opinion; I don't waste time "soothing or flattering." (See Edith Sitwell again). I may tell you that your new car is a horrible color. Or that I'd never choose anyone remotely like your new love! With several Libran planets, I'll be more tactful. Still, few who wear my Mask would bother competing for Ms. or Mr. Congeniality.

Life is too short, so I'll come right to the point! If I'm a therapist and you've been in denial about alcohol or drug abuse, I'm the right choice for you! I'll aim my archer's arrow at the complexes and neuroses behind the addictive behavior and release the Eros. Like Jungian analyst Marion Woodman (above) I enjoy helping people take back their energy from the archetypes; I find it exciting when creativity and spirituality emerge.

If there's a lot of Fire in my horoscope to enhance the Mask, I may be accused of being *self-righteous,* especially by people *low* in Fire. They seem to find my directness brash or rude. They seem *to me* to lack both passion for life and the courage of their convictions.

Some say I'm impatient, impetuous, even arrogant. Yet they call me for inspirational pep talks.

Unless Saturn is stronger than Jupiter in the horoscope by Sign (Rulership; Exaltation), aspects or house position (Houses 1,4,7,10,) I'm usually generous with my time and money on behalf of a needy friend or my favorite cause.(If I'm married, my spouse may complain I'm impulsive and *overly* generous!)

If Saturn is stronger than Jupiter, I'd like to contribute to friends and causes but may find myself short of funds and/or free time to volunteer.

When you're ready for an adventure, do call! But remember, I enjoy traveling so you may not find me at home. I'm energized and stimulated by new experiences, groups and friends. And I need my freedom, so please, please, *don't fence me in.*

How To Recognize Sagittarius Rising

Sagittarius Rising is usually medium height to very tall, though there are a few exceptions like Jean-Paul Sartre. Most Sagittarians are attractive, though a few, like Sartre, are not. Dame Edith Sitwell's nickname was "Stork." Hans Christian Anderson, too, was very tall. Hermann Hesse was tall, as is Robert Bly.

Though some of my clients have long, narrow faces, the "horse-head" shape described in older astrology books, others have rounder faces like Sartre's. Many have curly hair, particularly those with the Sun in Fire.

In mythology, Sagittarius means archer and is associated with horses. The legendary Centaurs, archers, half-man and half-horse, particularly fearless Chiron, adventurer and "wounded healer," have a lot in common with this Sign. Wild, restless and high-spirited, Centaurs seem to symbolize the unbridled passion of human nature in youth. In esoteric astrology they symbolize the impetuous desire nature, constantly racing ahead. The senses must be "reined in" by the Seeker. Otherwise, the Centaur's horse body will dominate his human head.

I've found Joan McEvers' observations about Sagittarius Rising having large front teeth; large hands and feet accurate for most of my clients. My Caucasian clients *have* tended towards blue eyes, "small but bright" as she says.[1] The eyes convey their enthusiasm; life is an adventure. My academic and professional clients often have large foreheads with a wide space between the eyebrows. Like Libra Rising, Sagittarius has a symmetrical face and a clear complexion, unless Saturn is in hard aspect to Venus.

Max Heindel wrote in *Message to the Stars,* "this tall Sign tends to stoop later in life," which I've also found to be true. He observed that they need rest because so much activity tires them out. My clients seem to work in spurts; meeting writing or (sales) bonus deadlines, or arranging speakers church or non-profit foundations. The "working in spurts" pattern is similar to that of their polar opposite, Gemini. Both Signs tend to run on nervous energy. (See Mutability, below.)

Heindel knew many Sagittarius Rising people with chestnut-colored hair, and many who were involved in sports. An esoteric healer, he believed that they should stay home more and "travel within."[2] This advice seems to me more appropriate for the Second Half of Life than the first fifty years.

Slender in youth, Sagittarians tend to gain weight around the abdomen after midlife, when the tendency to eat rich and/or sweet food catches up with them. The pancreas and the liver (the largest organ, analogous to Jupiter, the largest planet in the Solar System) begin to show the ill effects of over-indulgence in favorite foods and alcoholic beverages.

The thighs are also associated with the Sign; most Sagittarius Rising people have very strong thigh muscles. As beginning yoga students, Sagittarians seem able to hold the standing poses longer than other Rising Signs, even Sagittarians who list yoga as their only physical activity. Sciatica is a common complaint for both Sagittarius Sun and Sagittarius Rising.[3]

Aspects from Jupiter to Neptune (Dionysus) and Venus may describe alcohol, drug or dietary addictions, but sometimes strong Saturn (discipline) aspects offset them. Lack of exercise, (procrastination about going to the gym), is common by midlife. Friends who enjoy tennis, dancing or swimming are helpful to this extraverted Sign. Certain friends, however, are available for lavish lunches afterwards; the calories burned are immediately replaced.

---

1 Joan McEvers, *12 Times 12: 144 Sun/Ascendant Combinations,* (San Diego: ACS, Inc,) 1983, 180-83.

2 Heindel met some who were cruel to animals and people and some who were dishonest. Fortunately, I haven't encountered those! (Oceanside: Rosicrucian Fellowship,) 1973, 104-106.

3 Groin injuries sometimes occur in the practice of yoga. It's important to ease into the standing poses carefully, not rush into them. And, as a beginning student, not to hold them beyond your comfort zone.

With aspects between Mars and Jupiter, Sagittarius Rising tends to have a higher metabolic rate; "digestive fire" seems to burn more rapidly. Mars/Jupiter people also enjoy exercise. In Florida some still play golf in their eighties.

From youth through old age, Sagittarius is characterized by a restless, almost boundless enthusiasm. The freedom urge is perhaps the most impressive of their "wild-horse" traits. Even more than the Sun Sign, Sagittarius Rising resists being fenced in. They sense greener pastures in the distance. This restless urge to explore may last beyond midlife; sometimes until the Second Saturn Return (age 58-60. Saturn is an invitation to settle down.)

Astrologer Katherine de Jersey referred to Sagittarius Rising as "the bachelor Ascendant" during a talk in the early 1970's. I found this true in my astrology practice.[4] By the mid 1980's, however, it seemed to apply to career women as well as to men!

Even if young Sagittarius' work responsibilities keep him close to home, when his partner presses for a permanent commitment, he'll often express a need for "freedom to pick up and go."

"But you don't travel *now*," the partner will say, "you haven't any free time. Travel is just an excuse to remain single!"

"No! It's true that I can't travel *yet*," says Sagittarius, "but when the time comes, I need to be free to go. Maybe I'll live abroad for a year or two."

This can be difficult for the partner to accept where there's compatibility *between the planets* in the two horoscopes, but *not the Rising Signs*. The partner will list everything they have in common.

However, if she has Cancer Rising, she will likely want children; a house with a yard, relatives living nearby and a spouse who'll be around to participate in parenting duties.

Young Sagittarius, on the other hand, appreciates an adventurous partner. He feels fenced in when he thinks of mortgages, orthodontists, property taxes and his mother-in-law living down the street. During the relationship readings, Sagittarius Rising often seems to be champing at the bit and ready to move on to greener pastures. But he or she is a good friend or companion.

Sagittarians speak their mind directly, and, especially in youth, often spark controversy by setting others straight. An example would be Robert E. Bly's 1963 essay, "A Wrong Turning in American Poetry." Bly praised the direct speech of poets like Pablo Neruda

---

4 Author of *Destiny Times Twelve* and *Appointment with Destiny*. There were many bi-coastal marriages. After the mid 1990's, jobs began to be outsourced abroad and couples seemed to spend more time together. There is a memorial page on the internet about this excellent astrologer.

and Juan R. Jimenez, in contrast to Eliot, Pound, and Marianne Moore. The essay drew heated responses.

During the "modernizing" Vatican Council in 1964, a Belgian Trappist monk remarked that the world took a wrong turn after the Middle Ages, first towards Renaissance Humanism and then towards science. "Both tangents," he said, "led Western Civilization away from God."[5] Both Bly and Father Charles were fearless and outspoken in expressing controversial views.

Sagittarius, the Ninth Sign, is analogous to the Ninth House in the Natural Zodiac, known as the House of travel. Many, but not all Sagittarius Rising people have a strong travel desire. Publishing is another Ninth House theme. Some Sagittarians long to send out their message, their perspective on life, to a wider audience. Dame Edith Sitwell and Hans Christian Andersen both wanted to be heard.

Andersen, who'd hoped to become a successful novelist, was astonished at the end of his life to find that readers enjoyed his collection of folktales much more than his fiction. (It's still true today.) Fairy tales were his hobby but novel-writing was his passion.

From early childhood Hermann Hesse wanted to be a poet. However, his novels fared better than his poems, especially *Siddhartha* and *The Glass Bead Game*. Like Andersen, he adapted idealism to reality; they both focused on writing what their readers enjoyed.

Academics and Deans also reflect the Ninth House archetype. They're Ivory Tower philosophers who shape their students' thinking, or their universities' curriculum, according to their own values.

The Father of Existentialism, Jean-Paul Sartre, who taught at the Sorbonne and wrote articles for *Les Temps modernes*, is perhaps the archetypal example of the Sagittarius Rising philosopher and academic.

Several Sagittarius Rising clients love the Ivory Tower culture. A professor emeritus said, "my first day on campus as a freshman, I called home and told my parents that this would be my life! I wouldn't leave the academic world until I was a very old man." And he was right; he didn't.

Though Centaurs may be too busy to notice during the first half of life, there's another reason that Sagittarians guard their freedom. Early on, of course, they recognize the travel desire; the desire to publish the "message," or their love of Ivory Tower mental stimulation.

But there's something more: all these Ninth House environments *facilitate self-discovery.* They expand Sagittarius beyond the ego's pre-conceptions and expectations. Travel is an

---

5 Conversation with Father Charles Dumont, Abbey de Scourmont, 1971.

opportunity for Sagittarius to compare his culture's approach to life with other cultures.' The anthropologist or physicist delves deeply into his field of knowledge; immerses and loses himself in his work. Having expanded his vision beyond his limited ego, he emerges with a deeper understanding of human nature and/or Einstein's expansive perspective.

The Ninth House also includes spirituality and religion. (It's *not* the Zenith of fame, fortune and material success, that's the Tenth House.) Zarathustra, the philosopher-poet we met in the last chapter, was ten years finding the answers. He then descended the mountain to civilization to share his message with The Crowd.

After my Sagittarius Rising client told his Cancer Rising partner that he needed his freedom, (the Cancer moved on to someone who was ready for the mortgage, property taxes and children,) he went to India for two years and immersed himself in finding "the answers." Like Zarathustra in the story, he committed to his Vision Quest.

Sometimes the soul knows it cannot be encumbered "right now," as the Sagittarius Rising client put it. The soul knows when the time is near for the Philosopher's Journey up Ninth House mountain to the Tower, although everyone around him says it's an insane waste of time: "your peers are getting themselves established in life and you should be, too," he doesn't listen.

To him, becoming overextended in material possessions and the resulting debt feels wrong.

"Marriage seems a distraction to you?" I asked the client.

"It seems *much worse* than a distraction!" said Sagittarius Rising.[6] He felt as if he could "lose his soul" by marrying now instead of embarking on his journey.

Cancer Rising, who was an astrology student, was pointing out marvelous wedding dates during the relationship session; dates which worked unusually well for both their horoscopes. But the soul sometimes overrules the transits and others' well-intentioned advice. When this happens, we need to listen to the soul.

Zarathustra came down from the mountain filled with of enthusiasm. He thought his personal experience, his Vision and his answers were universal. He expected the crowd to be eager, even overjoyed to hear his news. But they were waiting to be entertained. They wanted him to leave. The philosopher learned that his vision was unique; intended for him alone.

---

6 I asked the Professor Emeritus in the earlier example, "what did your parents say when you called them on your first day of college and announced you were going to become a professor?" "My intuitive mother was delighted," he said. "My father, however, was a banker. He told me that PhDs, no matter how famous, make very little money. He hoped I'd change my mind and choose a different profession."

Hermann Hesse, the author of *Siddhartha,* knew this when he wrote, "knowledge can be communicated, but not wisdom. One can find it, live it, be fortified through it, but not communicate it." Sagittarius has more zeal than any other Rising Sign, but as Zarathustra discovered, "the crowd" will not always be receptive. The self-aware members of the crowd will go through the process of finding and living their own truth.

Sometimes, however, Sagittarius Rising makes an impression. Though their messages were quite different, Betty Friedan and Helen Gurley Brown both reached women whose background and life experiences were similar to their own. Friedan's message resonated with traditional stay-at-home mothers and Brown's reached career women like herself. Sagittarian outrage at injustice, real or perceived, comes through both authors: "I, and other women like me, have a right to our chosen way of life!"

The Ninth House is also the House of Religion and the ministry, that is, people with theological credentials, not Twelfth House mystics. (See Pisces Rising, particularly Thomas Merton, for that archetype.)

A missionary relative once wrote that she was returning to the United Sates after forty years in an African country. Her church had provided schools, hospitals, tractors and generators yet the local religion was still viewed as more prestigious than hers. In that culture, status lay in the ability to afford four wives and a dozen or more children. Local leaders with the most sons were best able to defend and hold their land.

So often the benefits that accompany the message are received better than the message itself! My relative's youthful idealism and her adult expectation that some day she'd be buried in the soil she'd come to love met with disappointment. No longer as zealous after fifty, she was open to "whatever the Lord had in mind" for her at home.

Unless hard aspects involving Saturn/Moon or Saturn/Mercury indicate otherwise, Sagittarius is seldom depressed for long. Of course, not everyone with this Ascendant will become a priest, minister, nun, rabbi, missionary, academic, philosopher, author, traveler or publisher.

A higher percentage of my Sagittarius Rising clients are salespeople, agents, or spokesmen for a product or service. Idealistic in youth, they seem to shrug off the obstacles they encounter. Sagittarians often express outrage or disillusionment at the "greedy" or "ineffectual" corporate hierarchy. They'll change companies and/or products but meet with the same conditions.

Instead of "the best way to take off weight and keep it off" (the "crowd" grew bored with the diet or refused to exercise) Sagittarius decides to promote "the best retirement savings plan." But the "crowd" seldom stays with it; the company may go under in a recession. Everything falls apart. And like Zarathustra, Sagittarius keeps moving along.

The Justice System is another Sagittarius theme. Several clients who combined the Libra and Sagittarian archetypes-doubling their interest in fairness and equal opportunity—idealistically went to law school in hopes of contributing to society and making the world a better place. By midlife, most seriously considered a career change. They feared they were becoming jaded; they wanted to follow their bliss elsewhere. Most decided that family responsibilities precluded a change until their children had finished college.

According to Herman Hesse, a descendant of missionaries on both sides of his family, "happiness is a talent, not an object; a how, not a what." (See above.) Sagittarius keeps heading onward and upward till, eventually, they find their way. Like Dr. Patch Adams, (above,) most are "raging doers," though Earth or Water in the horoscope tends to slow their pace.

Patch Adams found his bliss (see above) in clowning and in establishing his vision, the Gesundheit Clinic whose staff members, employed elsewhere, would all be volunteers. Though he's on the road most of the year earning money to support the clinic, he also loves the day job that enables his humanitarian vision.

Herman Hesse, whose novels were removed from German bookstores after he declared his support for the Allies, returned with his family to Basel, Switzerland. Friends paid their rent; they had nothing.

Eventually, Hesse connected with Carl Jung in Zurich at exactly the right moment. After his father's death, he experienced writer's block for the first time. He and his father had never gotten along. Hesse told Jung his dreams. When the analysis was over, he was able to finish his book.

When later asked about the war years Hesse, with Sagittarian optimism, focused on its positive outcome. Had there been no war, he'd never have corresponded with author Romain Rolland, who became a good friend, or worked with Rolland in getting messages about Allied victories to the discouraged troops behind enemy lines. Without the war, he'd never have moved to Switzerland, met Jung or had the opportunity of life-changing therapy.

Sagittarius Rising is often quicker than other Signs to see the silver lining. They believe that new opportunites are just ahead, waiting for them around the next bend. Their optimistic nature helps Sagittarians recognize opportunities that others miss. A well-aspected Jupiter symbolizes the potential to draw the right people at the right time; serendipitous events.

Zarathustra performed an act of kindness. He promised the dying tightrope walker a burial. He picked him up and carried him a long way over rocky ground. Exhausted, unable to find a place to bury him, the philosopher at last came upon a forest. He then did the next-best-thing, he found a young, healthy tree, (a magical tree common in German folklore) and gently placed the fallen hero into its bore. After explaining to the soul of the dead hero that he'd done the best he could for him, the philosopher moved onward, up the mountain into The Unknown Future.

Parents, teachers, spouses or friends who have, of necessity, broken a promise to Sagittarius and have then, like the philosopher-poet, done the "next best thing," have discovered that this Sign is prickly! Broken promises are not permitted, nor are they easily forgiven.

Consciously or unconsciously, Sagittarius is a Truth Seeker. Even little white lies are in direct conflict with their sense of justice, of "how the world should be." Ideally, people should communicate honestly and directly! People should always keep their promises, *no matter what!* We'll meet prickly Pinocchio, the puppet with attitude, later.

This was a sad moment for the philosopher, one that many idealists experience as they grow older. The tightrope walker was a metaphor for his dream of a glorious future for the human race. His Superman-prototype would make the great breakthrough. But his fearless hero, his symbol of unlimited, uninterrupted progress, failed to live up to his expectations.

Sometimes, like Zarathustra, Sagittarian idealists set the bar too high. Still, the fearless philosopher keeps moving on, like Jean-Paul Sartre in old age, updating Existentialism and reconsidering its role in politics; did his philosophy still have a role to play?

Sartre observed that *philosophers'* opinions were no longer sought; French political speechwriters had turned instead to *anthropologists* like Claude Levi-Strauss. At the Sorbonne, his former fans, the student radicals, were moving farther Left, to Mao-tse-Tung. The "Crowd," the culture, had stopped listening. Sartre sought to adapt his message for the new generation.

The Mundane Ruler - Jupiter/Zeus

Sagittarius and the Ninth House are ruled by all-Highest Jove, who presided over the Greek pantheon from Mount Olympus. Zeus came and went as he pleased. Though he enforced the law, he considered himself above it. In courtrooms, the ancient Greeks swore oaths "by Jove," or, they swore oaths on the waters of the River Styx.[7] Zeus sentenced convicted

---

7 His title *Zeus Horkios* means "Zeus of the Oaths." Hestia once swore an oath on Zeus' head. In Hesiod's *Works and Days*, Dike, the Goddess of Justice sits beside him.

perjurers to swallow polluted Styx-water or build statues of him. The latter sounds like the easier sentence, for those who could afford it!

In astronomy, Jupiter is the largest planet in the Solar System. In astrology, Jupiter is called the Great Benefic, not because he's entitled, grandiose or arrogant; certainly not because he's above the law or luckier than the other gods. Jupiter is called the Great Benefic because the Bountiful Father is associated with wisdom and generosity.

Zeus married Metis, Goddess of Wise Counsel, then swallowed her up in one gulp. But after assimilating Wisdom, his behavior didn't seem to improve! No less impetuous; Zeus was still a risk-taker and a philanderer. (Sagittarians who rely on good luck and become addicted to gambling are associated with this side of Zeus' personality.) And the moral arbiter never became monogamous. Ethically-challenged politicians who feel they're above the laws they enact and the moral law as well seem to take after him.

Jupiter presides over the Ninth House, where Big Dreams and visions take shape. The Ninth House is associated with those who seek bliss or, at least, happiness.[8] Dr. Patch Adams faces the challenge of establishing his Big Dream, Gesundheit clinic. Like most Sagittarians, he's talented at fund-raising, but the real challenge lies in finding others willing to volunteer at Gesundheit while earning their living elsewhere. With Natal Jupiter in Detriment (Virgo) at the zenith of his horoscope, Dr. Adams is a hard worker. But Jupiter is also Jove, from whom the word jovial is derived and Adams' day job is, fortunately, "blissful."

As we have seen with Andersen's[9] novels and Hesse's poetry, the outer world doesn't always appreciate the Big Dream, or cooperate in the manner Sagittarius had hoped or expected. The Crowd responds, "entertain us! Give us more folk tales, Anderson! Forget the poetry; give us more novels, Hesse!" the Crowd responds.

Or, the Big Dream may suddenly go out-of-style: "Sartre!" says the Crowd, "Existentialism is *so* outdated! It's so World War II. This is *1970!* Give us a more modern vision!"

The key to serendipity, (meeting the right person at the right moment,) is sharing the Big Dream and generously including others in it. And when we find ourselves temporarily lacking a vision, volunteering may be the answer. In helping other fulfill their dreams, our own inspiration often returns.

At the end of his life Sartre sat cross-legged on the floor with the "dirty hippies" as

---

8 Poet Robert Bly, with Sagittarius Rising, edited and wrote the introduction to *The Soul is Here for Its Own Joy: Sacred Poems from Many Cultures,* (NY: HarperCollins,) 1955, in which there are many poems on the soul's hunger and longing for God, from Dante's love for Beatrice through Rumi and Emily Dickenson. Several Sagittarius Rising clients have sent me this book as a gift.
9 Hans Christian Andersen had Jupiter in Rulership in the Twelfth House.

Simone de Beauvoir called them. He wanted to keep up with the younger generation; to see the future through their eyes and help them if he could. (His Jupiter was in Taurus, a neutral Sign, and a practical Element.)

Hermann Hesse had Jupiter-in-Rulership. He began his *Pictorial Autobiograph*[10] with the words, "I was born with the Sign of the Archer Ascending and Jupiter rising on the horizon,"[11](in his First House.) Though he was totally without financial resources because of his stand against the Nazi government, Hesse was generous with his time. He believed that one's convictions must be lived, regardless of cost.

In the course of his volunteer work, Hesse began corresponding with Thomas Mann, who visited him in Switzerland and later nominated him for the Nobel Prize.

Born into a family of writers, Dame Edith Sitwell was also generous. She'd inherited a small stipend for living expenses but she was quite frugal, too. She gave up her secretary in order to help her protégés financially. With Jupiter-in-Detriment in Virgo, she wrote in bed to save on her heating bill.

My friend of many years, astrologer Catalina O'Brien Ely was extremely generous with her time. She organized the annual visit of a group of Tibetan monks to her small town in Northern California, where they played music and designed sand paintings. A few months before her death, she cooked them dinner at her home.

Wearing her travel agent hat, she brought many groups to John of God, the Brazilian healer. In her role as real estate agent, Catalina went beyond the job description in helping clients relocate to her small town. She also volunteered at her meditation group and Sunday services. I, too, benefited from her generosity. She invited me as a guest lecturer on several occasions, and contributed a photograph for the cover of my book, *Beyond the Mask, Part I*. Catalina's Jupiter was in Gemini, (Detriment.)[12] Her only regret was running out of time to finish her numerous art projects and her design degree.

To summarize: many Sagittarians have what Hesse described as "a talent for happiness;" they seem to draw exactly what they need when they need it. They're also very generous with time, energy, inspiring words, and monetary resources too, if they have them. Ever

---

10 "Speech to the Nobel Prize Committee," (1946.) In a very brief speech due to ill health, he mentions his love of the countryside and natural beauty. See Nobelprize.org/Herman Hesse.
11 "Speech to the Nobel Prize Committee," (1946.) In a very brief speech due to ill health, he mentions his love of the countryside and natural beauty. See Nobelprize.org/Herman Hesse.
12 This is perhaps more difficult than the other Detriment position (Virgo,) because Jupiter-in-Gemini is more extraverted. Quicker to volunteer, it indicates that the person may spread himself too thin. Erica Jong has Jupiter-in-Gemini on the Ascendant. (See *BTM*, Part I.)

ready to help others with projects, they often remind me of the philosopher who carried the acrobat over very rough terrain to his final destination.

Sagittarius instinctively pursues happiness, firm in the conviction that it can be found.

The Esoteric Ruler - The (Arabic) Part of Earth
Practical Idealism - Grounding the Vision

The Arabic "Part of Earth" is located 180 degrees from the *Sun Sign.* It's in the House and Sign opposite the Sun, in the same degree as the Sun. For example, consider a Sagittarius Rising horoscope with the Sun in Virgo at the Zenith, (House Ten,) and the Part of Earth in Pisces (Water) near the Nadir. This person may feel comfortable walking by a river, a lake shore or along the ocean thinking about an important decision.

Now, consider the reverse. Suppose Sagittarius Rising has the Sun in Pisces at the Nadir and the Part of Earth at the Zenith. Pisces Sun may seek out a busy coffee shop. Though people come and go around them, which is distracting, *nothing is expected of Pisces.* There's no laundry basket waiting in the coffee shop. A few people are quietly reading; it's a Virgo environment. So Sagittarius Rising/Pisces Sun sits with her laptop to work out the pros and cons of her decision, away from everything that needs doing at home.

The opposite House offers the Sun a different perspective. If the Part of Earth conjuncts a planet, then that planet helps in the grounding process, according to its nature. If that planet is Mars, then going to the gym will raise the spirits (most people have clearer heads and feel better after exercise.) If the Part of Earth aspects Neptune, the Sun seeks relaxation. This may be more of a challenge; Dionysus likes to wind down by having a glass of wine while watching a mindless TV show. While this does release the day, it's not exactly *grounding!* Reading or writing a poem; attending a meditation or chant group, doing yoga in silence, these are way of working with Neptune, too.

Ideally, the Part of Earth environment will clear a person's head without putting him to sleep or leaving him with a hangover. He or she will emerge from the House opposite the Sun feeling less anxious and agitated over the decision. The problem itself no seems longer as mind boggling as it did earlier.

The more technology and gadgets we acquire; the busier we become. There seems to be less time available now to *find our center,* the Ground of our Being, from which we make decisions and from which Hesse's "happiness talent" unfolds. The Part of Earth can help all of us, not just Sagittarius Rising.

In the esoteric tradition, though, it's particularly important for Sagittarius Rising. Over the years, I've observed that with a high percentage of Earth (the grounded Element) and Water in the horoscope, Sagittarius Rising is usually quite practical about tax receipts, retirement plans, and their duty to an elderly parent. But they may become mired in their routine and responsibilities. Some have said that they've "lost touch with themselves" (with the Self) in the process of serving the community, the foundation or the church. By midlife, they've achieved many of their youthful ideals, but they've lost their sense of fun. They tell me that life seems flat.

A hiatus, time out to travel and/or study abroad, has helped several Sagittarius Rising clients who have a high percentage of Earth and Water regain their zest for life. Natal planets may aspect the Part of Earth, if so, transits to the Esoteric Ruler and its aspects may indicate a solution.

The Jupiter Return year (age 60), especially if it involves Houses 1,4,7,10, may bring opportunity for a change. Or, the progressed mask may form aspects to Jupiter, the Sun or the Part of Earth.

Grounding the Vision - Practical Idealism

Sagittarius Rising with Air and Fire as the predominant Elements will seldom tell the astrologer that life is dull or flat. They're more likely to consider burning their bridges behind them and moving on. A new person, or a new opportunity beckons. Sometimes, too, there's a physical symptom that troubles them. It might be sciatica, or, like Simone Weil,[13] they might have headaches. By midlife they've tried Eastern and Western treatments.

Simone, whose intellectual background was similar to Jean-Paul Sartre's (she was a year behind him in philosophy at the Sorbonne and the Ecole Normale) tried every possible treatment for "violent" headaches, but nothing worked.

Then, suddenly and serendipitously, she was cured. Though not a Catholic, (her parents were Jewish agnostics) she went to Assisi while on sick leave and attended a service in the chapel of St. Francis. She fell into ecstasy listening to the Gregorian chant and "St. Francis passion seemed to enter her body." A year later, on sick leave again, she experienced ecstasy while staying at the Benedictine Abbey of Solesmes. This time her headaches were permanently cured.

---

13 She preferred "Weil" pronounced "Vay" or "Veil." A member of the Free French, she hated the German pronunciation. See her poem, "The Red Virgin, A Poem of Simone Weil," (Madison: University of Wisconsin Press.) 1993.

She then turned to fasting and the spiritual techniques of such austere Catholic saints as Julianna of Norwich.[14]

As a result, she lost so much weight that some thought her anorexic. Anna Freud, however, said it wasn't true. Simone didn't care at all about clothes or sex; anorectics are obsessed with their appearance. She refused to eat or rest. For nourishment, she preferred reading St. John of the Cross and George Herbert's poetry, particularly his poem, "Love." They were her food; she had no interest in her body.[15]

Weil held absolutist views like those astrologers sometimes observe when Sagittarius masks a brilliant Air Sun Sign. (Hers was in Aquarius.) After graduating from the Ecole Normale Superieure, (teachers' training) she worked in a factory to better understand the lives and needs of working class people. It seemed unfair to her that she, a doctor's daughter, should enjoy a quality of life denied to them.

Esoteric Sagittarians are like Weil, in a sense. When they speak of justice and fairness, it's not to complain about *their* "rights" being violated or assert society's obligations *to them.* They're more altruistic than mundane Archers. They focus on the rights of those society has left behind and the obligation to promote a more equitable society. Because the focus is not on themselves, esoteric Sagittarians are less likely to blame others for their problems.

Jean-Paul Sartre, whose Existentialist philosophy was based on individual freedom, said, "I cannot make liberty my aim unless I make that of others equally my aim." He worked towards this goal in politics and in the classroom. Because the archer's arrow is a projectile, it's interesting to observe where Sagittarians aim it.

To Weil as well, focusing exclusively upon one's own rights seemed selfish and motivated by envy. After the factory job, she went to Spain to participate in the civil war. She left after her ankle was badly burned in a camp fire, but her hopes for a socialist Spain were dashed by the atrocities of both Right and Left.

When the Germans occupied Paris, Simone was teaching in a *lycee.* One day, she received notice that she was being terminated. When she demanded to know the reason for her dismissal, she learned it was her Jewish surname. She told the authorities how ridiculous that was; neither she nor her parents had ever been inside a synogogue. They replied that it didn't matter whether she and her family *thought of themselves* as Jewish or not; by definition, *they were!*

She was outraged. How could the government define her, or anybody else? Her parents,

14 It's interesting that Juliana, a Fifteenth Century recluse, also suffered a serious health problem, nearly died, and after her recovery had several visions of Christ and the Trinity.
15 Coles, cited above, Simone Weil, 117-118, for Anna Freud's opinion of Simone.

then living in Manhattan, begged her to leave Paris and join them. She visited, but left immediately for London to join the Free French in exile. As she was leaving, she told her parents she was no coward, "I'd rather be an object of persecution in France than an object of philanthropy in New York."[16]

She volunteered to return to France as a spy, but was told that was not appropriate work for a woman *or* an intellectual, and she was both. She was assigned instead to write summaries of reports from field agents. In the margins, she wrote poetry and non-fiction. And she fasted in sympathy with people at home in Vichy France who probably had little to eat. How could she eat when they had nothing?

As she became thinner and thinner, Simone worked on the essays that later became her famous work, *The Need For Roots. (L'enracinement.)*[17] Her biographer, psychiatrist Robert Coles, said she "loved talking about roots!" She wrote that too many people were leaving the land. Rural communities suffered while in cities, uprooted people were lonely, confused and vulnerable to the slogans of charismatic leaders.

From Weil's body of work, it's clear that she saw roots as both inner (our souls) *and* outer, (the community around her.) She seemed to be seeking an equilibrium between social activism and the inner life of spirituality and ethical choices. Her horoscope was about equally divided between Air and Fire (Yang Elements) on the one hand and Earth and Water (Yin Elements) on the other.[18]

After World War II she became more religious. Weil believed governments needed to address rootlessness by encouraging people to return to the land. In the future, she said, Europe would be more concerned with growing food, with the "greening" of the earth. She remarked that the human soul, too, has a need for roots; for spiritual nourishment. It has a thirst for justice which cannot be satisfied in "the World of Necessity." In the "world of appearances," people are too often exhausted just surviving to challenge power-hungry politicians.

Albert Camus, among the most respected literary figure of Simone's time, called her

---

16 Robert Coles, *Simone Weil: A Modern Pilgrimage* (Woodstock: Skylight Paths,) 2001, p. 27. Scorpio Rising activist D.P. Berrigan (Chapter Eight) and others wondered why it had to be one extreme or the other for her. Why couldn't she have taught philosophy in a university? Pursued a third option? But Sagittarius and Pisces, Jupiter's children, are often inclined to absolutist extremes. See also, Robert Coles, *Anna Freud and the Dream of Psychotherapy*, (NY: Addison-Wesley Inc.) 142-52 on Weil, idealism and altruism.

17 T.S. Eliot wrote the introduction to the first English translation. He said of Weil, "we simply must expose ourselves to the personality of a woman of genius, of a kind of genius akin to that of a saint."

18 She had two oppositions involving Cancer and Capricorn, and Jupiter-in-Virgo.

early works, "remarkable for a young woman of her age," and encouraged everyone to read them.[19]

Her highly acclaimed work, *Waiting for God*, and the *Notebooks,* in which she'd written daily, were published posthumously. She died of tuberculosis with cardiac complications at thirty-four. On the sanitarium's admittance form, she wrote "none" after "religion." Weil saw no need for churches or dogma; she took exception to Catholic disparagement of her favorite "pagan "philosophers.[20] Content to be an outsider, she was happy in her personal relationship with Christ and the saints.

Weil is now taken very seriously; some rank her among the greatest Twentieth Century philosophers. During her lifetime, though, people thought her odd; a religious eccentric or even a madwoman. Camus said that after she "became so religious," she was "a scold."

Edith Sitwell, was called a scold, too. This mask's inner certainty may seem, as Coles said of Weil, "intimidating." Friends, spouses, relatives and co-workers often remark of Sagittarius Rising, "he (or she) is so morally *righteous,*" sometimes adding that they wish the person would "lighten up."

Weil liked to quote the line from the Beatitudes, "blessed are those who hunger and thirst for righteousness, for theirs is the kingdom of heaven."[21] After testing her philosophy in the fire of experience during the Spanish Civil War, Simone abandoned her youthful Marxist ideals. She discovered that they didn't work.[22] Weil grounded her vision of the future through her writing; her practical idealism attracted readers. Her Jupiter was in Detriment (Virgo). Jupiter and the Part of Earth (Leo) were both in her Eighth House.

The Element - The Fire of Inspiration

By midlife, most Sagittarians know that moderation is important to balanced living, health and contentment. When it comes to entrenched habits, though, it can be difficult to persevere, to put this knowledge into action.

---

19 Camus later called her "a saint for outsiders," and "the most spiritual writer of the Twentieth Century." When he received news of receiving the Nobel Prize, he chose to spend the day with Simone.

20 She loved Plato, Pythagorus and the stoics. Later, she read the *Bhagvat Gita.* Some say she also studied Sanskrit. Her mention of the "world of appearances" and "non-attachment" reflect Asian philosophy.

21 Sometimes righteousness is translated as "justice."

22 and when Trotsky, whom she'd previously admired, began defending Stalin to her.

Fire Rising is usually confident, even dynamic; Fire Masks make strong first impressions. A Fire mask is usually an asset to the horoscope's Sun Sign, whatever its agenda. Even with a high percentage of planets in cautious Earth and Water, Sagittarian extraversion is palpable at job interviews, committee meetings and social events. The mask's overall impression is positive.

However, on days when Sagittarius Rising feels emotionally low, he or she may reschedule the interview. Because Sagittarians want to be perceived as energetic, optimistic, enthusiastic and eager to help, they intuitively wait for a better biorhythm day.

Most days, though, Sagittarius Rising, whether young or old, is good at giving pep talks. Fire inspires others to keep moving ever onward and upward. Whatever his calling, life coach, sports coach, physical therapist, personal trainer, evangelical clergyman, nun, priest or rabbi, agent, salesman, teacher or publisher, Sagittarius excels at motivating others.

Unless Saturn in in hard aspect to the Ascendant, Sagittarius makes a positive impression. Saturn in the First House, however, if badly aspected to Venus, the Moon, Mars, or Jupiter tends to modify the extraversion; he may not be as exuberant.

Compared to the other three Elements, (Earth, Air and Water) Fire's energy-level remains high later in life. This is true of Sagittarius *unless he loses his inspiration.* He needs a reason to get up in the morning! Air "lights Fire," as we know from watching the breeze reignite a campfire's embers. If Sagittarius is temporarily without a creative outlet, his Air Sign friend or relative may have one that excites.

Jean-Paul Sartre put this well, "the best work is not what is most difficult for you, it's what you do best." It's also what you enjoy doing! Jupiter (Jove) is all about joy or bliss. When Sagittarius Rising has a strong, responsible Saturn, others' most difficult duties or clients might be passed along to him. It might be time to do things differently. He or she may want to move on during the Jupiter Return year, age 48, 60 or even 72 (let someone else invite the family for the holidays.) Good fortune is with us then.

The Ninth House theme of humanitarian service, which may involve a spiritual or religious group, a non-profit, or a project of Sagittarian's own devising, is also energizing. For that matter, *any* project that Sagittarius believes in is uplifting. On the other hand, continuing to work in an environment where others' beliefs are at cross-purposes to his convictions is enervating. Sagittarius may feel like a prisoner "doing his time" in jail.

In general, Fire Rising is eager to get on with life. As a child, Hesse was in a hurry to become a poet; as a young woman, Weil was quick to put her principles into action through trade union demonstrations and as a soldier in Spain. However, a natal Saturn/Moon or Saturn/Venus aspect will tend to slow the pace of life. It offsets risk-taking Fire.

With these Saturn aspects, Sagittarians find it easier to hold off on romantic commitments and impulsive purchases, but once they do commit, their relationships are likely to last *at least one* seven year cycle. And they'll tend to keep that car they carefully researched in *Consumer Digest* for a long time.

Gambling is an example of risk-taking; Jupiter's children who have a high percentage of Air and Fire especially enjoy it. They feel lucky. In hopes that "their ship will come in," they may see lottery as a way to finance their Big Dream.

However, if Sagittarius has the Sun or Moon in Earth or Water *and* a strongly-placed Saturn (Houses 1.4.7, 10), they're more cautious and less likely to spend their vacations gambling in Las Vegas.

Sagittarius Rising with forty percent Earth and Water might be a stock broker, especially with Cancer planets in the Eighth and/or Capricorn planets in the Second. Or, they may remodel old houses and resell them. To Cancer and Capricorn, this is investing, not gambling.

Whatever the retirement goal, it helps to think inclusively, as well as expansively. In youth, Fire is an impulse towards personal freedom. Fire on the cusp of the Identity House facilitates self-awareness and Individuation. But when, after midlife, Jupiter's children expand their Vision to include others, the later years become more satisfying.

Some find their bliss, as Dr. "Patch" did. A few client examples are given below, in the "Second Half of Life."

The Mode - Mutability

Sagittarius Rising's spontaneity and dramatic flair come from the Yang Element. Their adaptability derives from the Mutable Yin Mode. Astrologers sometimes compare Sagittarius to a flickering candle which burns as brightly, but not as steadily, as a Cardinal (Aries) or Fixed (Leo) candle.

This Mutable tendency towards procrastination ("flickering") may be offset by an angular Saturn (in Houses 1.4.7 or 10) or a high percentage of Fixed planets in the horoscope.

Early environment is very important for the Mutable Rising Signs. They're more suggestible than Fixed or Cardinal Signs. Parents or teachers who are firm in their views on politics and/or religion usually make a stronger impact on a Mutable Ascendant child than his Fixed or Cardinal Ascendant siblings.

When Sagittarians from small towns, especially those who've attended parochial schools, enroll in large, urban universities, they may be in for a shock. They usually discover that their professors and fellow students don't share their parents' convictions. Many become angry and accuse their parents and teachers of "misleading (them) about the way the world is."

Coaches, too, shape expectations about "how life should be." Poet and publisher Robert Bly, the author of *Iron Man: a Book for Men,* said, "by the time a man is 35 he knows that the images of the right man, the tough man, the true man which he received in high school do not work in life."

Bly's words, spoken with sincerity and conviction in 1990, meant so much to his readers that a men's movement was born. The discussion that *Iron Man* began, about the meaning of heroism in modern times, continues today.

Mutable Signs, especially Sagittarians, are talented at communicating insights; their message resonates with their audience.

Beginning astrology students are quick to notice a willingness to compromise in the *other* three Mutable Signs (Gemini, Virgo and Pisces) but are often slower to see it in Sagittarius Rising.

This Sign's outrage at perceived injustice; fierce arguments in defense of their views, "our department (or astrology organization) must take *this* direction, *no other* direction makes any sense," and tendency to leap to conclusions are, at first, confusing. ("He sounds like a leader; he must have Aries Rising," says one student. "He's an *adamant* Fire Sign! He probably has Leo Rising," says another.)

After students get to know Sagittarius Rising, though, they notice the adaptability. "He was so *vehement.* After his side was voted down, he left the meeting with smoke coming out his ears! I was sure we'd never see him again. Yet, a week later, there he was, all smiles, as if nothing had happened."

Another student added, "when his friend wasn't chosen as committee chairman, he thought she'd been slighted. Later, he discovered we'd sounded her out beforehand. We already knew she wasn't interested in the project."

Sagittarius' bark is usually worse than his bite; their Yang Fire masks their Yin Mutability.

Most Sagittarians learn by the Saturn Return (age 28-30) to check with those underdogs first and see if they want (or need) defending before rushing to their aid. Helping too many "ungrateful underdogs" may result in burnout. Several *pro bono* attorneys and social workers have expressed a sense of urgency about a midlife career change, usually on Uranus-opposition-Uranus, (ages 38-42.) Some have mentioned a fear of becoming "jaded" or "cynical."

With a high percentage of Air and Fire, Sagittarius Rising is more likely to move on at midlife than remain in his first career for money, status, or pension benefits. With a high percentage of Earth and Water, he's more likely to repress his desire for change or adventure.

There's wisdom in Robert Bly's anthology, *The Soul is Here for Its Own Joy,* and in the poems he selected. Ruled by Jove, Sagittarius seeks bliss.

In astrology, the nervous system is associated with Mutability. With a high percentage of planets in Mutable Signs and/or the Nodes in Mutability, it may be better not to resist that inner prompting to change career or work environments. Of course, the whole horoscope must be considered.

Conscious adaptation to life experience and changing times is usually an asset. Sometimes, though, it appears that Sagittarius is updating himself and compromising his convictions, aligning himself with the current trend. In that case, if his spouse or lover has a Fixed Sun or Rising Sign, he'll really surprise the person! He or might react with, "I've always admired you (Sagittarius) for your convictions; why are you now tossing them aside like yesterday's newspaper!"

Simone de Beauvoir (Scorpio Rising), for instance, was deeply shocked at her lover, Sartre's willingness to adapt the philosophy by which they'd both lived their lives to the views of student Marxists, "those dirty hippies who call the great philosopher by his first name!" But Sartre believed that for Existentialism to survive, it had to change. At the time, French politics was moving farther to the Left.

Hermann Hesse and Simone Weil, both Pacifists during World War I,[23] changed their views prior to World War II. Hitler, after all, was much worse than Kaiser Wilhelm; they adapted their views to a changing world. Hesse's philosophical change may not have been as shocking to his family as his giving up German citizenship and financial security, uprooting them and moving them to Switzerland.[24] Weil's parents were clearly more concerned about her health than her changing philosophical positions.

Some of my Sagittarian clients who were Leftist radicals in the Sixties became Reagan Democrats twenty years later, only to shift gears and vote for Obama in 2008. His idealism, especially his concern for the underdog (the uninsured) appealed to them. Firm in their convictions, Sagittarians can also be quite pragmatic about changing them.

---

23 Weil gave up sugar when it was rationed during World War I, allowing others to have her share.

24 He had become a naturalized German citizen in 1923.

As we grow older, Mutability is an asset. The Mutable Ascendants, for example, adjust more quickly and cheerfully to relocation than the other two Modes, even after sixty-five. Many couples relocate after downsizing or retirement. When asked about friends and family left behind, most Mutable Ascendants will shrug and say, "they visit me here and I visit them 'back home.' But that phase of life, that region, is my past. I used to think of myself as a Midwesterner, (or an East Coaster or a West Coaster) but my spouse wanted to move. And there are *many good things* about my new region."

One woman said, "nobody here knows me here, so I'm free to reinvent myself and develop different talents." Another said, "I've joined a different church than the one I was raised in; it has a choir and I'm singing again."

Finally, Mutability is also *receptivity.* One advantage of Yin vulnerability is spiritual openness; the ability to trust a power beyond the Ego. Simone Weil passed through a crisis, headaches with no known cure, by focusing all her attention—"the effort, in itself, was a prayer because I was in terrible pain"—and opening herself to God's grace, trusting that healing would come. While *Waiting for God,* (as she called her book) she sought out spiritual environments Assisi and the Abbey at Solesmes.

Weil seems to have succeeded in turning Mutability, "humble receptivity," into a spiritual technique. There's a Fixed phase in the healing process when will power shouts, *"I'm going to get well!"* That's the phase right after the doctor, unable to find a cure, makes his dire diagnosis. The "will power phase" sometimes goes on for a long time. But there's also a stage where Mutability is required. It comes after the patient has tried every possible remedy, Eastern and Western, and like Simone Weil, waits attentively for God's grace in the silence.[25]

Mask in Youth - Authenticity and Freedom
"I want to be all that I can be."

Idealistic and adventurous, the Fire Element is often more visible in the youthful *persona* than the Mutable Mode, especially when the Rising Sign is enhanced by the Sun in Air or Fire. Herman Hesse described himself as an "unmanageable child."[26] Like many young Sagittarians, he was impatient with the expectations of the adult world, especially all that

---

25 A student once asked, "is there a Cardinal phase, too?" Sometimes there is. For cancer survivors, it's the stage when the treatment comes to a successful end and they feel "back in control" again.

26 in his speech to the Nobel Prize Committee, see Nobelprize.org/Hesse.

extraneous study! He wanted to aim his arrow directly at his target, poetry, not waste his time.

Young Hermann rebelled more dramatically than most people with this Ascendant. His parents, who had met as missionaries in India, enrolled him in a secondary school to learn Latin, Greek and the other pre-Divinity School requirements. He liked classical poetry, but "not the rest of it." Determined to become a poet, not a Pietist[27] missionary, he was first impatient, then furious that nobody would listen to him.

Hermann ran away from the religious school twice. Finally, he acquired a rusty pawnshop pistol and wrote his father, threatening to shoot himself if forced to stay there. He was then allowed to leave and live with an uncle. At nineteen, he left school behind to work in bookstores; he began writing novels. On weekends he put his poetry notebook into his backpack and went hiking. As the outer world was of no help to him, he learned by doing, through the writing process itself.

Though they understood the need to live her socialist philosophy,[28] Simone Weil's parents worried when their brilliant daughter took a factory job in a rough part of town. At one point, her mother moved closer to Simone's workplace to keep an eye on her, but Simone soon left the area to experience a different type of factory.

Next, she enrolled as a soldier on the anti-fascist side of the Spanish Civil War. Both the factory and the wartime experience were grim and disillusioning. She hoped to make a difference by joining the Free French, but was given a boring desk job in London. Having tested her philosophical convictions through action, she eventually determined that the world cannot be changed through political activism. Her health suffered; she focused inward, became interested in pilgrimage places, and experienced ecstasy.

My Sagittarius Rising clients are also free spirits. Each in his own way, consciously or unconsciously, seeks authenticity. But as Jean-Paul Sartre, said, "if you seek authenticity for authenticity's sake, you are no longer authentic." Through the writing process Hesse learned what it was to be a poet. He stopped blaming his teachers for their inability to show him how to do it. He climbed the mountain with his poetry notebook.

Weil tried very hard to be an authentic socialist. However, her illusions were dispelled one-by-one. First, the factory workers were too tired at night to listen to her, then the Left

---

27 He saw Pietism as a narrow religion. Still, his parents had experience of foreign cultures. They printed the *Bible* and tracts in various Indian languages; they spoke Malayalam with visiting missionaries. Hermann learned about Indian philosophy by osmosis. This comes through in his novel, *Siddhartha*.

28 in the language of today's recovery movement, Weil "wanted to walk the walk, not just talk the talk" like a Leftist intellectual.

and Right were both guilty of atrocities in Spain, her side was not "pure," and finally, her work for the Free French was unsatisfying. Eventually, through her Chiron wound, the terrible headaches, she found her way. They were her "Existential anguish," her path to authenticity.

Sartre described this anguish in an article defending his philosophy against those who called it negative. (To him, Existentialism seemed extremely optimistic.) According to Sartre, we know that human beings exist and that they make moral choices. Our deeds, the results of our choices freely made, shape our biographies. To blame God (who may or may not exist,[29] according to Sartre) or to blame others, or to treat others as "objects designed to promote our own happiness, not as people" is to act in bad faith with ourselves. To act on illusions or wishful thinking about others instead of facing reality is to be inauthentic and dishonest with oneself. Honest choices often involve anguish.

In other words, Sartre focused his arrow, the Sagittarian projectile, inward rather than outward. He gave two examples of existential anguish, a state with which Weil, Hesse, and many of my young Sagittarian clients are familiar.

In the first example, a general makes a decision about battle tactics and sends the troops out. If the tactics fail and many die because he made the wrong choice, he has the full moral responsibility. There's nobody higher up in the chain of command to blame. (He could attempt to blame God, but for Sartre that would be cowardice.) What the general feels watching the troops leave for the battlefield, Sartre calls *Existential anguish*.

His second example is more nuanced and also more common, because few of us are generals. One of Sartre's students came to him with a dilemma. The young man's older brother had been killed early in the Second World War. After the occupation, his father became a collaborator, much to the disgust of their small town. Then, his father died. His mother was old and frail.

This student considered sneaking off to join the Free French. If he left, though, there would be nobody to take care of his mother. Would she get her rations? Would she survive without him? The townsfolk were not fond of the family, so there was nobody to help her.

On the other hand, if he joined the Free French he might be sent to Algiers where he could do some good, or he might be shuffling papers in London. Still, he would be *doing something* for the war effort. He quickly added that he would not be going because of what

---

29 Sartre said that as long as scientists are unable to prove the existence of God, humans are free to make their ethical choices in the here and now, without regard to rewards or punishments in the Hereafter. Not all Existentialists were atheists. Playwright Gabriel Marcel, for example, was a Christian Existentialist.

others thought of him; it wasn't about salvaging the family honor, but about doing his part. He knew Sartre disdained choices made based on *others'* opinions or *others'* dogmas.

Sartre was curious to know whether the student had consulted a priest, as many did, about the decision. If so, illusion had become part of the process. If the young man really wanted to join the Free French, he'd ask a Leftist priest who sympathized with them. But if he leaned towards staying home, the student would ask a priest who sided with the collaborators. Either way, the Existential anguish would soon be over because he'd *hear what he wanted to hear.* He'd also be "acting in bad faith with himself."

"No," the student answered, I didn't ask a priest, I'm asking *you!*

"Sartre replied that it wasn't *his* decision. He added that he wasn't going to set himself up for the blame if the student later decided he'd made the wrong choice. Conscious human beings have their share of moral anguish; these decisions are our responsibility as adults.[30]

Like Hesse and Weil, Sagittarius young people—consciously or unconsciously—learn about freedom and authenticity while attempting to live by their convictions. When Sagittarius Rising confront parents of teachers with, "I know I'm right about this and I'm going to do it," Existential anguish often results.

The Story of Pinocchio, who wanted to be a Real Boy

Benedetto Croce once said, "the wood from which Pinocchio was carved is humanity itself." In modern times, we meet the impudent, curious, and impatient puppet with the prickly attitude through Walt Disney's children's movie. Seen as an allegory, though, it's also a tale for adults. In the Italian story, Pinocchio is often in serious jeopardy. The original version might frighten younger children.

In the *Prologue to Zarathustra,* the philosopher-poet, having failed to interest the crowd in his metaphor, (the bridge to humanity's future evolution, the Superman) performed an act of kindness. Though he'd promised to bury the fallen tightrope walker, he was unable to find a suitable burial spot. He came upon a forest and chose a young, green tree,

30 Jean-Paul Sartre, "Existentialism is a Humanism," 1946, Walter Kaufman ed. (Meridian Idaho: Meridian Publishing,) 1989. The student's decision is unknown. Perhaps he left Paris without informing his professor. Sartre's own choice was to enlist. While a prisoner of war, he wrote *Being and Nothingness.* Due to problems with supply lines, the Germans were running out of food. Sartre was "allowed to escape" and hitchhiked back to Paris. In Austria, another famous man, Sigmund Freud was also allowed to leave quietly. (See Chapter Seven, Scorpio Rising.)

perhaps a symbol of the Tree of Life. He placed the acrobat's body into a hole in the tree and walked on.[31]

After "burying" the body, Zarathustra saw a serpent grasp an eagle by the neck. These are both Scorpio symbols; the magical tree may represent the tree of Death and Rebirth, Scorpio and the Eighth House.

The continuation of the story from Zarathustra to Pinocchio was beautifully done as an art exhibit by Jimmy Ruskin,[32] and I'm following Ruskin's interpretation here. Most of us remember Carlo Collodi's story about the old woodcutter who needed a new marionette for his act. He respectfully took only one branch of the Tree, enough to make his puppet. He wanted Pinocchio ("pine nut") to be lifelike; to jump and run like a normal boy, and Gepetto got his wish. What he didn't want was a *talkative* puppet, but he soon discovered that his magical creation was opinionated.

Pinocchio had a prickly attitude, similar to certain Sagittarius Rising children after their parents, of necessity, break a promise to them. It was as if Pinocchio resented the philosopher's broken promise and felt abandoned; as if he'd found Gepetto too slow in liberating him!

A courageous free spirit, Pinocchio was a lot like the acrobat. He didn't want to perform for Gepetto; he wanted adventures of his own. He wanted to play with "other" boys. He wanted to be independent. He *didn't* want to be nagged by Jiminy Cricket, the blue-haired fairy, Gepetto or anyone else. But most of all, he wanted to be real.

An inventive spirit, whenever his schemes failed and he was caught, he told lies to get out of trouble. But each time he told one, his nose grew longer.

In one of the stories,[33] Gepetto told him that "real boys" had to attend school, and enrolled Pinocchio. Gepetto knew Pinocchio would find it boring, and hoped he'd cooperate with the act instead. He was bored, but not enough to perform for the old woodcutter.

In a hurry to get on with life, Pinocchio ran away from home. At first, he was delighted to earn gold coins performing for an evil puppeteer, who later used his wooden feet to start the cooking fire. He ran away again.

Gullibly, Pinocchio fell vicitm to two greedy animals. He'd excitedly told them he had

---

31 In later chapters, Zarathustra saw himself as "part poet;" so perhaps he buried his metaphor along with the tightrope walker. The philosopher seemed changed as a result of the failed attempt to share his wisdom with the crowd.

32 See, Ruskin *The Prologue, the Poltergeist and the Hollow Tree,* (NY: Foundation 2021,) 2005.

33 They were written as a series for magazines, and then collected as, *The Adventures of Pinoc-chio.*

some coins for his "father" Gepetto, whom he now loved and missed. He'd saved a good retirement income for the old man.

They tricked him out of his gold coins with their get-rich-quick scheme. The thieves informed Pinocchio he could make those few paltry coins multiply. On their instructions, Pinocchio buried the coins in a field and watered them. He left, giving the coins time to grow. The animals, of course, had dug them up by the time he returned.

The blue fairy and Jiminy Cricket kept turning up magically, helping help him out of his predicaments. Eventually, Pinocchio learned not to take them or their advice for granted. And above all, never to lie to them.

He gradually came to see that to become real (authentic) meant being honest; telling the truth. To become real is to accept reality, whatever its consequences.

Gepetto, meanwhile, had gone off looking for his "boy." The old woodcutter had come to see Pinocchio as more than an unmanageable puppet; an object intended to help him survive in old age. He'd come to love him.

They each went looking for the other. Concerned for each other, they both wanted to help. While searching for Pinocchio, Gepetto fell into the ocean and was swallowed up by a whale; Pinocchio, was swallowed up by the same whale. They met at last! Together, they set a fire in the whale's stomach and escaped. Unselfish love triumphed.

Back at the woodcutter's house, Pinocchio looked into the mirror, and discovered that the puppet strings were gone. *A real boy* looked back at him.

The Sagittarian Mask Matures - Altruism and Inner Satisfaction

In youth, Sagittarius Rising has a passionate need to experience life. Though they seldom codify their moral philosophy like Jean-Paul Sartre, it's been forged in the fire of life experience. And, like Sartre, most find it impossible to live by "other people's dogma." Seldom is Sagittarius concerned with "what other people think (of them)."

From the mid thirties to fifty, many of these free spirits settle into a comfortable routine, which may involve long-distance travel through career, long vacations, or both. Like Hermann Hesse, most seek out beautiful spots that energize them, usually mountains, but sometimes lake country. Many of my clients have told me they're claustrophobic in office cubicles. If they live in cities, they prefer to eat lunch at a park or at an outdoor café.

Midlife changes, which set the tone for their later years, are usually made with the same zest for life that characterized their youth.[34] Few become cynical or jaded. Their prickly edges usually soften. Former classmates who meet them again at reunions have said, "he (or she) is not as brash as I remember from Back in the Day, (Sagittarius was) in a hurry to set the world on fire." Or, "(Sagittarius) has become more patient; he's (she's) accepted that the world isn't going to change the way they'd expected!"

Many Sagittarians begin a long, happy marriage in their late forties or their fifties. For about a third of my clients, it's the first marriage. One bachelor who married in his mid fifties said, "now that I know who I am, it's okay to get married. I wouldn't have wanted to mix my karma up with someone else's any sooner! Now I'm ready for a companion."

Most Sagittarians who married in their youth remark that the second marriage is happier; they're more relaxed and compatible with the second spouse.[35] As Mercury-ruled Gemini is on the cusp of the Marriage House (Number Seven), communication, in the sense of "being on the same wave length," is important. Most of my women clients praised the intelligence of their second husbands. Many married doctors, dentists and academics.

In my California practice, there were often *more* than two marriages by midlife. (Gemini symbolized Multiplicity instead of "The Twins.") Like Hermann Hesse, though, after fifty relationships tend to be happier.

When I asked if Ninth House religion and spirituality was important to them, most clients said, "yes." Those who said "no" would often pause for a moment, then add something like, "when my husband was young, though, his first degree was in *Divinity*. But he later changed fields and *he isn't at all dogmatic!* I'd say he's more scientific now and I really value his opinions and insights."

When Sagittarius stops to think about it, the Ninth House archetype is often there in the background, like the missionaries and the *Bible* tracts of Hermann Hesse's childhood.

I've met several mystical Sagittarians who enjoyed solitude and sometimes fasted like Simone Weil, though not to such an extreme. The influences of Scorpio and/or Capricorn planets add intensity, earnestness and self-discipline to an otherwise extraverted Ascendant. Most share Weil's outrage at injustice.

Psychiatrist George Vaillant *(Aging Well)* theorizes that extraversion has the potential to become altruism in old age, and that altruism makes life much more fulfilling. For

---

34 Jungian analyst, author and speaker Marion Woodman's first career was teaching. At fifty, she began her studying Jungian psychology. It became her Second Half of Life career. Dr. "Patch" Adams was a late bloomer, the oldest medical student in his program.

35 Robert E. Bly, for instance, had four children with his first wife, then divorced and remarried. He and his second wife have been married a long time.

Jupiter-ruled Sagittarius Rising, this theory seems to work. There's often a Big Dream that involves improving the quality of life for others. Like Dr. "Patch" Adams,' dream, theirs may involve healing.

Patricia Connolly, president of the Price-Pottenger Nutrition Foundation in San Diego, was inspired by Dr. Price in her mid thirties; she transcribed his lectures. Now, at the age of 82, (she has Sun-in-Taurus), she's still involved in disseminating his writings and helping others improve their diets.

The afternoon that Dr. Price called her to his office and asked her to take over the Foundation, Sagittarius was Rising. Her Ascendant and the Foundation's are the same, a synchronicity that's helped over the decades with timing speakers and events.

One of her sons lives in Italy; Patricia looks forward to his visits with the grandchildren. In old age, the world sometimes comes to Sagittarius; long-distance travel may become unnecessary.

Astrologer Catalina O'Brien Ely was also involved with healing. She traveled thirteen times to Brazil, bringing groups to the village of healer John of God, familiar to some of us from the *60 Minutes* television program. She also volunteered at her meditation group, sponsored speakers, and helped her husband, Haines Ely, introduce and interview new authors on his radio program. Her second marriage enabled her to travel to Europe, with John of God's group and on other occasions. Unable to fulfill the travel desire in the first half of life, Catalina "loved every minute of it" in her fifties.

Ken Flor, a CPA who volunteers at his meditation group and his church's annual class series in Los Angeles, realized his dream of studying in Europe in his fifties. He went to England and learned SOT (Sacral-occipital-therapy,) which he practices in a chiropractor's office. Though he'd traveled extensively in his younger days, he'd never before had a chance to live abroad.

Lastly, Susan Holmes, who'd done so much business travel she'd tired of it by midlife, spent several years meeting her love "half way" geographically between "his" city and "hers." The couple married and chose a city whose art, dance, theater, jazz music and cuisine fascinated them both.

She remarked, as have several Sagittarius Rising women clients, "my husband was better at saving money than I ever was. He was very supportive of my talents, and as a result, I was able to quit my job."

Susan left her consulting business in the health industry to study architectural design. She knew from the first seminar that it would be her Second Half of Life career. She began designing living space so that Altzheimers' patients could remain at home with their families.

Whenever the architects' business slows she's laid off, but now she can enjoy jewelry-making and sewing. There's no financial pressure.

Most of my Sagittarian clients seem content in the Second Half of Life; some are downright blissful! Several told me that their greatest joy lay in fulfilling a childhood dream.

Hermann Hesse, who'd always seen himself as a poet, was, no doubt, delighted to hear that critics considered the poems at the end of his novel, *The Glass Bead game,* to be among the best ever written in German.[36]

Hesse was astonished when students appeared from distant countries like Canada, the United States, and Australia. With *Siddharta* in their backpacks, they tracked down their favorite author at his lakeside retreat.

In old age, Sagittarians sometimes prefer to sit still and let the world come to them.

The Sagittarius Rising Progression

Poet, political activist and "father of the men's movement" Robert E. Bly was born in late Sagittarius (twenty degrees.) During his childhood, the progressed Mask formed Fire trines from Sagittarius, bringing out the heightened sensitivity of his Moon-Neptune conjunction in Leo. (The Natal conjunction is common to the horoscopes of poets, mystics, artists, designers, musicians and those who work with symbols and images.) Bly's Sagittarius progressed Mask also sextiled Jupiter-in-Aquarius (Air) when he was four years old. Jupiter is well-placed in the Sign of its esoteric ruler. Bly may have had a spontaneous spiritual experience around the age or four or five, in which he was One with the beauty of the natural world. Jupiter-in-Aquarius, if aspected in childhood, expands the awareness. The experience leaves a lasting impression; it may return in dreams or be captured on canvas, in a poem, a song, or a metaphor later in life.[37]

Bly's beautiful poem describing Minnesota in the snow may have flashed back to an early mystical experience. When Bly returned to writing nature poems after his years as

---

36 The book was written late in life, after his work with Carl Jung.

37 As Bly's Jupiter was in an intercept, (see Introduction, FAQs, Intercepted planets) it's likely that nobody around him noticed the impact of early childhood experiences on his personality. Intercepted planets indicate unique gifts; some of them are powerfully linked to that wellspring of imagination, the Creative Unconscious.

a political activist, he did, according to many critics, his best work. Nature is a powerful inspiration for Sagittarius Rising!

Around the same time the progressed Mask sextiled Jupiter, it squared Uranus-in-Pisces in his Third House, a "Mercury House," in the Natural Zodiac. This challenging aspect from the progressed Mask to Uranus, planet of upheaval, was unsettling. The outside world, in some way, no longer felt as stable or as secure. Fortunately, the Jupiter aspect at the same time eased the impact.

Uranus-in-the-Third symbolizes an independent, sometimes quixotic thinker. He was *very young* for the progressed Mask to bring out this facet of the personality! Now, in his 80's, with Uranus returning to the Third House and squaring the Ascendant degree, Bly may look back on his life narrative with satisfaction at having come "full circle."

The Capricorn Progression

Capricorn is Cardinal Earth. This long cycle is about settling into a profession, starting a family and gaining career experience; the "business" of life and responsibility. Though Bly was twelve years old when he progressed into Capricorn Rising, his Sagittarian Mask had already begun assimilating four planets.

In Capricorn, the progressed Mask immediately conjuncted the Sun at zero degrees in Bly's First House. Eight years later, when he was twenty, it conjuncted Venus-in-Capricorn. Like Hesse, he was aware of his life's work, the work that Venus loves, early in life.

The Capricorn progression puts Sagittarius Rising in touch with Earth and Water planets in a positive way through trines and sextiles. Progressed Capricorn trined Mars, putting him in touch with his sense of adventure, and also his sense of responsibility. (An Earth Trine) He spent two years in the navy.

If there are Cancer planets, the Progressed opposition from Capricorn offers them perspective. Around the time that the Progressed Ascendant opposed Bly's Natal Pluto-in-Cancer he went to Norway on a Fulbright grant. While his Minnesota friends and family were probably delighted at this opportunity to visit the land of his ancestors, the progressed opposition would open the world to him in unexpected ways. However, his time in Norway was not only an opportunity to translate Norwegian poetry and meet Norwegian poets, it put him in touch with the work of Mirabai, the mystical woman poet known as India's Nightingale, Rumi the Sufi poet, modern poets like Pablo Neruda, Juan Ramon Jimenez, and many others.

For Bly, the project was no longer about European poetry, but *world* poetry! At the time of his Saturn Return (ages 29-30) he decided to focus on translating, making many great but unfamiliar poets accessible to Americans.

His hard-working Natal Mercury (Detriment) -Pluto-trine began an enormous project that was to delight many English-speaking readers. Bly's career took a new direction in his thirties. The poet and translator became a publisher not only of classical poets like Kabir and Hafez, but of new, unknown poets as well. Their work appeared over the decades in his issues, *The Fifties, The Sixties* and *The Seventies.*

The Capricorn "business" Mask industriously applied itself to introducing the world to fine poets, both classical and modern.

The Capricorn opposition to Natal Pluto opened another vista, too. Bly began to see his own country's poetry differently after the Fulbright trip. When the Capricorn progression ended, he wrote his controversial essay about the wrong turn American poetry had taken during the time of Eliot and Pound.[38]

The Capricorn cycle usually develops patience and humility, two requirements of parenthood. Acquiring skills, or credentials, and establishing oneself in a career belong to this cycle. Sagittarius Rising, unhappy with suffering fools gladly, must patiently adjust to the process of earning a living. Groundedness usually happens during this long Earth progression.

Bly lived on the family farm while raising his children. Born in 1926, he was a generation older than the Baby Boomers, many of whom participated in the back-to-the-land movement, particularly the spiritual communities, during their Capricorn cycle.

Some Boomer stayed on in rural areas, while others tried taking the message to cities. Those who went to town, like Zarathustra found, too, that audiences prefer to be entertained.

Simone Weil was right, though, life in the countryside is grounding. Nature seems to put Sagittarius in touch with its esoteric ruler.

The Aquarian Progression

Aquarius is the symbolic (archetypal) sextile to Natal Sagittarius Rising. It's an easier developmental cycle because sextiles offer opportunity.

Aquarius is also associated with originality, and/or brilliance. Aquarius is ruled by

---

38 The essay was written in 1963. See above, "How to Recognize Sagittarius," direct speech.

Uranus, which, in Bly's horoscope squares Sagittarius Rising from the Third House. By midlife, Bly's ideas would challenge his culture.

As his progressed Mask reached zero Aquarius, Bly and his wife, Carol founded an organization called "American Writers Against the Vietnam War." Two years later, when he received the National Book Award for "The Light Around the Body,"[39] he donated the prize money to his resistance group. Until the mid 1970's he was active in the anti-war movement. However, he also wrote several books. Bly is definitely an exception to Gore Vidal's theory that political activism will divert a person's creative powers! In the late 1970's and early 80's, the Aquarian Ascendant opposed his imaginative Moon-Neptune conjunction and brought out their Natal talents. Jungian archetypal symbolism began to influence his work; he became interested in meditation, immersed himself in mythology and suddenly found himself involved in a new career as storyteller! Moon-Neptune in *Leo* lends dramatic flair. And Sagittarius' life is often serendipitous.

The Pisces Progression

One story, "Iron Hans," from the *Grimms* collection, particularly appealed to Bly. It was suited to the times, and he made it his own. Bly asked himself, "what does heroism mean to a man now? What does a man who goes off to work in a cubicle every day teach his son?"

As the progressed Pisces Ascendant squared his Natal Mercury-in-Sagittarius, (Twelfth House) Bly wrote and published *Iron Man,* based on "Iron Hans." The book stimulated discussions about the inner Wild Man as a source of energy and led to workshops and men's groups with drummers, poetry and storytelling. Eventually, a men's movement emerged from the workshops and Bly became known as it's founder. He also presented workshops with analysts Marion Woodman and James Hillman. In 1988, Bly wrote *A Little Book on the Shadow.*

The Aries Progression

At the turn of the Twenty-First Century, Bly progressed to Aries Rising, a Cardinal cycle, at the age of seventy-four. Cardinality is associated with authority; Bly is a frequently quoted source not only in literature, but in Jungian circles as well.

---

39 This coincided with the Uranus-opposite-Uranus transit.

As an archetype, Aries includes the themes of heroism and individual identify (the First House and the First Sign,) two themes that have interested Bly over the years. Recognition came to him in this progression; an archive was established for his manuscripts in 2006. In 2008 he was named Minnesota's first poet laureate. At 81, Bly still writes poetry and shares his wisdom in interviews.

Sagittarius Rising Bibliography

Adams, Hunter "Patch," M.D. and Maureen Mylander, *Gesundheit! Bringing Good Health to You, the Medical System and Society through Physical Service. Complementary Therapies, Humor and Joy,* (n.p: Healing Arts Press,) 1997.

—— *House Calls,* (n.p: Robert D. Reed Publications,) 1998.

—— *Patch Adams,* Movie based on Dr. Adams' life, with Robin William as Patch.

Bair, Deirdre, *Simone de Beauvoir: A Biography,* (New York: Touchstone,) 1991.

Bly, Robert, *Iron John: A Book About Men,* (New York: De Capo Press,) 2004.

—— ed, *The Soul is Here for Its Own Joy, Sacred Poems from Many Cultures,* (New York: HarperCollins) 1995.

—— *The Light Around the Body,* (New York: Harper and Row,) 1967.

—— *A Little Book on the Human Shadow,* with James Hillman and Michael Meade, (San Francisco, Harper and Row,) 1988. *The Rag and Bone Shop of the Heart: Poems for Men,* (New York: HarperCollins,) 1993.

—— *Silence of the Snowy Fields,* (Bloomington: Wesleyan,) 1962.

—— *A Wrong Turning in American Poetry,* 1963.

Collodi, Carlo, (Carlo Lorenzini) *Pinocchio: The Adventures of a Puppet,* E. Harden trans illus, (New York: Penguin-Puffin,) 1996.

Elborn, Geoffrey, *Edith Sitwell: A Biography,* (London: Sheldon Press,) 1981.

Finch, Henry Leroy, *Simone Weil and the Intellect of Grace,* Martin Andic ed., (New York: Continuum Publications,) 1999.

Freedman, Ralph, *Hermann Hesse: Pilgrim of Crisis,* (New York: Fromm International,) 1997.

Hesse, Hermann, *The Glass Bead Game,* (New York: Picador USA,) 2002.

—— *Soul of the Age, Selected Lettters of Hermann Hesse,* 1891-1962, trans, Theodore Ziolkowski, (New York: Noonday Press) 1991.

—— *Hermann Hesse: Pictorial Biography,* including Hermann Hesse's, Life Story Briefly Told, Denver Lindley, trans., (New York: Farrar, Straus & Giroux,) 1975.

—— *Siddharta,* Susan Bernofsky, trans, (NY: Modern Library,) 2006.

—— "Speech to the Nobel Prize Committee," 1946. Nobelprize.org/Hesse.

Sartre, Jean-Paul, *Being and Nothingness, (L'etre et le Neant),* Hazel E Barnes, trans, (New York: Philosophical Library,) 1950.

—— *L'imaginaire,* (Paris: Alcan,) 1936.

—— *No Exit, (Huis Clos,)* (Paris: Gallimard,) 1945.

—— *The Family Idiot, (L'idiot de la famille,)* play about Gustave Flaubert, (Chicago: University of Chicago Press,) 1981.

—— *Existentialism is a Humanism,* trans, Philippe Mairet as Existentialism and Humanism, (London: Methuen,) 1948.

—— *The Psychology of Imagination,* trans, Bernard Frechtman, (New York: Philosophical Library,) 1948.

—— *The Transcendence of the Ego*: an Existentialist Theory of Consciousness, trans, Forrest Williams, Robert Kirkpatrick, (New York: Noonday Press,) 1957.

Sitwell, Lady Edith, *The Collected Poems,* (New York: Vanguard,) 1968. "Still Falls the Rain; (set to music by Benjamen Britten;) "Street Songs," "Song of the Cold."

Vaillant, George E, M.D. *Aging Well: Surprising Guideposts to a Happier Life,* (Boston: Little Brown & Co,) 2003.

Weil, Simone, *Gravity and Grace, (La Pesenteur et la Grace,)* trans, Arthur Wills, (New York: Putnam,) 1952.

—— *The Need for Roots, (L'enracinement,)* trans, Arthur Wills, preface by T.S. Eliot, (Boston: Beacon Press,) 1962.

—— *Waiting for God, (L'attente de dieu),* trans, Emma Crawford, (New York: Harper and Row,) 1973.

—— *First and Last Notebooks,* trans Richard Rees, *(Cahiers),* 3 vols., (London: Oxford University Press,) 1970.

CHAPTER FOUR

Capricorn Rising - Productive Poet, Scientist, Mentor

Margaret Mead, "I learned the value of hard work by working hard."

—— "Sooner or later I'm going to die, but I'm not going to retire."

—— "The way to do fieldwork is never to come up for air until it is all over."

—— "Even though the ship may go down, the journey goes on."

—— "I must admit that I personally measure success in terms of the contributions an individual makes to her or his fellow human beings."

—— "Old age is like flying through a storm. Once you're aboard, there's nothing you can do."

—— "I was brought up to believe that the only thing worth doing was to add to the sum of accurate information in the world."

Colleen McCullough, "Once I've got the first draft down on paper then I do five or six more drafts, the last two of which will be polishing drafts. The ones in between will flesh out the characters and maybe I'll check my research." Author, *Thorn Birds* and scientist. (neurology)

—— "The lovely thing about being forty is that you can appreciate twenty-five-year-old men more."

James Joyce, "A man's errors are his portals of discovery."

—— "I've put in so many enigmas and puzzles that it will keep the professors busy for centuries arguing over what I meant, and that's the only way of insuring one's immortality." About *Finnegan's Wake.*

—— "Think you're escaping and you'll run into yourself. Longest way round is the shortest way home."

—— "... battles inspired me - not the obvious material battles but those that were fought and won behind your forehead."

—— "When I die, Dublin will be written in my heart."

Marie Curie, "I never see what has been done, I only see what remains to be done."

—— "I was taught that the way of progress is neither swift nor easy."

—— "We must believe that we are gifted for something, and that this thing, at whatever cost, must be attained."

—— "A scientist in his laboratory is not a mere technician: he is also a child confronting natural phenomena that impress him as though they were fairy tales."

—— "You cannot hope to build a better world without improving individuals…each of us must work for his own improvement and at the same time share a general responsibility for all humanity, our particular duty being to aid those to whom we can be most useful."

Albert Einstein, "Marie Curie is, of all celebrated beings, the only one whom fame has not corrupted."

William Butler Yeats, "In dreams begin responsibilities." *Responsibilities.*

—— "Every conquering of temptation represents a new fund of moral energy. Every trial endured and weathered in the right spirit makes a soul nobler and stronger than it was before."

—— "Happiness is neither virtue nor pleasure nor this thing nor that but simply growth. We are happy when we are growing."

Victoria (Vita) Sackville-West, "Growth is exciting; growth is dynamic and alarming. Growth of the soul, growth of the mind." Bloomsbury poet, novelist and world famous horticulturist.

Tennessee Williams, "All of us are guinea pigs in the laboratory of God. Humanity is just a work in progress." Playwright.

—— "Don't look forward to the day you stop suffering, because when it comes you'll know you're dead."

—— "I have always been pushed by the negative. The apparent failure of a play sends me back to my typewriter that very night, before the reviews are out. I am more compelled to get back to work than if I'd had a success."

Joseph Wambaugh, "I enjoy doing the research of nonfiction; that gives me some pleasure, being a detective again." Mystery writer and former policeman.

Dustin Hoffman, "A good review from the critics is just another stay of execution."

Ray Bradbury, "I know you've heard it a thousand times before. But it's true—hard work pays off. If you want to be good, you have to practice, practice, practice. If you don't love something, then don't do it." Novelist, playwright, and producer.

—— "I don't try to describe the future. I try to prevent it." (About his science fiction novels.)

—— "You must stay drunk on writing so reality cannot destroy you."

—— "We are the miracle of force and matter making itself over into imagination and will. Incredible. The Life Force experimenting with forms, You for one, Me for another. The Universe has shouted itself alive. We are the shouts."

—— "The best scientist is open to experience and begins with romance - the idea that anything is possible."

—— "I didn't notice that Maggie was unhappy until she asked me for a divorce in 1957 and again in 1959. I convinced her to stay for the good of the children. In those days, that worked." (About his wife of fifty-seven years.)

Art Buchwald, "I always wanted to get into politics, but I was never light enough to make the team." Critic and columnist.

—— "If you attack the Establishment long enough and hard enough, they'll make you a member of it."

—— "So far, things are going my way. I'm known in the hospice as The Man Who Wouldn't Die."

—— "Whether it's the best of times or the worst of times, it's the only time we've got."

—— "I had a wonderful time celebrating my 80th birthday. My wish was to be 65 again but they—Homeland Security—wouldn't let me."

John Dryden, "Beware the fury of a patient man." English Renaissance author.

—— "Boldness is a mask for fear, however great."

—— "He has not learned the first lesson of life who does not every day surmount a fear."

—— "We first make our habits, and then our habits make us."

—— "Jealousy is the jaundice of the soul."

John Greenleaf Whittier, "For all sad words of tongue and pen/ The saddest are these, 'It might have been.'" Poet ("Snowbound,") novelist and Abolitionist.

—— "The joy that you give to others is the joy that comes back to you."

Candice Bergen, "I got the role I loved the most at a point in my career when most women are being phased out."

—— "I realize I should be grateful that at age 54, people were still offering me film roles. …I've never felt more comfortable in my skin, I've never enjoyed life as much and I feel so lucky. At an age when most actresses are being phased out, I'm being phased in with a vengeance!"

Jane Fonda, "I don't want my wrinkles taken away—I don't want to look like everyone else."

—— "When you can't remember why you're hurt, that's when you're healed."

The Capricorn Mask

I'm the stoic Capricorn Rising Mask. Regardless of the Sun Sign's nature and the Moon Sign's moods, I project responsibility, reliability, and discipline. I make the Sun Sign look well-organized, practical, realistic, and ambitious.

Extremely competitive, I contribute a great deal to my department or organization. I put in the time and effort, I'm no "hanger-on."

I'm the Mask of the CEO; school superintendent, principal, administrator, broker, banker, dean, police commissioner, ambassador, fast food restaurant or property manager. I'm the Mask of politicians who exude *gravitas*; I demand and receive respect. I respect people who live life by the rules; people who also keep their cars washed, their shoes shined and their bills paid on time.

In childhood, parents and teachers consider me mature for my age. Rather than miss an examination or an athletic competition, I'll hide my flu symptoms and go to school. I'm attuned to adults' expectations. Dutiful and diligent, I pitch in whenever I can. Even before I have the vocabulary to express my feelings, I sense adults' anxiety and wish I could alleviate it.

A natural problem-solver, I feel frustrated when too young to help. In youth I usually work very hard, like Margaret Mead and Marie Curie. Like them, I may live on very little while learning my trade, paying my dues and climbing the ladder of success.

Unless, like Tennessee Williams, I have Uranus close to the Rising Sign I'm a traditionalist, cautious and conventional. With Mars (Exalted) near the Ascendant, like Margaret Mead and Jonas Salk, or Mars square it like Ray Bradbury, I'm an explorer who blasts through obstacles and makes discoveries.

Because I identify more with career than other Masks, meaningful work is essential. Like Dustin Hoffman and W.B. Yeats, I believe that a talent—a "gift"—demands a great deal of us and that "talented people cannot be expected to put as much effort into relationships as others."

It's quite possible that I'm an only child, like entrepreneur and oil millionaire John Paul Getty, or the oldest child like Mead and Yeats.

Like Marie Curie, whose father taught science at home, I may assist my father in his work. If I do and I'm a woman, by the time I'm thirty, dad may treat me more like a son than a daughter.

Or, perhaps, like Edward F. ("Teddy") Kennedy, I'm the youngest son. If so, by midlife I may take on responsibility for a parent and/or nieces and nephews as well as my own children. Like Teddy, I may eventually become "the Clan's" Patriarch (or Matriarch.) If I'm the youngest daughter, like journalist Eve Curie, I may live in the shadow of my highly accomplished parents and sibling(s.) Whether my parents are in business; skilled trades, the professions, or the arts and entertainment, like Jane Fonda's, Dustin Hoffman's, and W.B. Yeats,' I learn from them, but family relationships are seldom smooth or easy.

Many who wear my mask follow in their fathers' footsteps. Like Mead, Curie and Yeats, they identify with, and try to live by, his definition of success.

Unless Venus and/or the Moon are in strong houses (1,4,7, or 10) and/or well-aspected, one or both of my parents is a strict disciplinarian and taskmaster. If both my parents were too busy to spend time with me, I may be closer to a grandparent, like Mead, and Bradbury. If I was a lonely child, I may invent a world of my own, like Irish ex-patriot, James Joyce, who invented his own Dublin.

I love midlife. After forty, I feel much younger than I did in childhood. By fifty, the prime of life, there's no more pressure to add to my resume. There's nothing left to prove to others, *or even to myself.* Though more relaxed and contented, I still want to be productive. Like Hoffman, Bradbury, and Candice Bergen, I still take on interesting projects. Like novelist Alice Walker, I'm still willing to take on difficult topics.

W.B. Yeats was revising his poem, "Under Ben Bulben," the week before he died at seventy-four. Yeats (quoted, above) was right, "we are happiest when we're growing." I'm not content to rest on my laurels.

I like to challenge myself. Self-improvement is no less important in old age than in youth. Less driven now, I still work at improving my tennis backhand or my golf stroke. (If Supreme Court Justice Stevens plays tennis every day at ninety, so can I!)

Some say that mine is a melancholy or saturnine temperament. *I* think I'm a realist. I do set high standards for myself and, when I fall short of them, I sometimes get depressed.

Like Tennessee Williams with writing (see above,) I learn from my mistakes and my work improves.

Astrologers have called me judgmental, demanding, controlling and even ruthless (while climbing the ladder of success,) but I'm also known for stepping up to the plate in the ninth inning and saving the day when the game is all but lost.

I'm the teacher whose name students remember and whose work ethic they imitate. Whatever my chosen profession, as the poet Longfellow wrote in "Psalm of Life," I'll "leave behind/ Footsteps in the sands of time."

How to Recognize Capricorn Rising

Capricorn Rising can often be recognized by their businesslike manner and their stride. Jeanne Avery, *(The Rising Sign,)* and Joan McEvers (*12 Times 12, 144 Sun/Ascendant Combinations*) both noted Capricorn Rising's tendency to strut. I find this true of shorter Capricorns and horoscopes with the Sun and/or a high percentage of planets in Fire. Capricorn's gait conveys that the boss has arrived and is now in charge; "everything's in order, so let's get started."

Even when they're the job applicant, not the interviewer, Capricorn's firm handshake and serious demeanor sets a businesslike tone. Inwardly, they may be as nervous as the other candidates, especially if they have several planets in Mutability, but the Capricorn Mask projects confidence.

If the interviewer had planned to begin with small talk, once he meets Capricorn Rising, he'll usually change his mind and come right to the point, "this is what the job entails. I've read your resume and you seem a good fit. Tell me how you, as a manager, would develop the department." And having prepared in advance, Capricorn then takes over the interview.

Rarely will Capricorn Rising need a book on dressing for success. They're consummate professionals. Most wear business suits even in hot climates like Florida and Southern California where the dress code is casual and suit jackets are generally reserved for special occasions.

The Capricorn professional favors navy blue, black and gray apparel. One client, a corporate attorney (Libra Sun in the Tenth House) has an extensive collection of colorful shirts and ties to set off his dark suits.

If, however, like Tennessee Williams, Capricorn has Uranus close to the Ascendant degree, he or she will dress more flamboyantly. Artists dress appropriately for their careers, too. Though the artist's apparel may be more colorful than other Capricorns, it's always tasteful, never garish.

For dining out or corporate parties, most Capricorn women choose a little black dress, pearls, and an evening bag full of business cards.

Max Heindel noted in *Message of the Stars* that most have thin, shiny, dark hair which often turns prematurely gray. However, hair color and texture vary with ethnicity; several of my Capricorn Rising clients have curly hair. I've encountered very few blue-eyed blonds with this Ascendant.

Unless Jupiter, Venus or the Moon is in the First House or aspects the Ascendant degree,

Capricorn Rising is slender. (Moon/Ascendant indicates a tendency to retain fluids.) Like Margaret Mead, who had Jupiter on her Ascendant, Capricorn may become overextended and "too busy to exercise." He or she tends to gain weight at midife, especially during the Jupiter Return years, (36, 48, 60, and 72) unless Saturn's house position and aspects offset Jupiter's.

Mead, the Earth Mother, seemed comfortable with her weight. Actress Jane Fonda, on the other hand, struggled for twenty-three years with bulimia. Her Capricorn perfectionism fought a tendency to be rotund. (Jupiter-in-Fall in the First House.)

Jupiter, the Moon and Venus in, or aspecting, the First House indicate a warm, nurturing Mask. If Jupiter is stronger by house position than Saturn, (1,4, 7,or 10) Capricorn's cup of Life seems half full. If Saturn is stronger, Capricorn sees the cup as half empty. With Saturn-in-the-First or aspecting the Ascendant degree, the Mask is cool, distant, and may seem judgmental.

Though the horoscope may be shy or sensitive, this Mask hides fear, anxiety and insecurity well. Like a suit of armor, it provides a strong defense. It's also the Zodiac's best boundary-setter.

Heindel observed that Capricorn Rising people have thin necks. I find this is true until their forties or early fifties.

In Heindel's experience, Capricorn is a short Rising Sign. At five feet tall, Margaret Mead is an example. My own experience, however, has been more like Jeanne Avery's. She found that some Capricorn Rising people are tall with large feet and hands, like Sean Connery. A few are knock-kneed. But there are also many short Capricorns with small wrists, ankles, hands and feet. Both tall, rangy, Capricorns and shorter ones tend towards osteoarthritis or osteoporosis as they grow older.

Even Jane Fonda, known as "Queen of the Workout" after her famous exercise video, had a hip and knee replacement in her late sixties.[1] These are fairly common surgeries for Capricorn Sun and Ascendant.

After fifty, Capricorn Rising tends to stoop, as if the weight of the world is pressing down on their shoulders. Yoga stretches for both the upper and lower back are highly recommended.

This Rising Sign can also be recognized by its wry sense of humor, which resembles Scorpio's but isn't quite as dark. Capricorn humor is often self-deprecating. Some examples are Dustin Hoffman's performance as Benjamin in *The Graduate*, Alan Alda's as Hawkeye

---

1 "Body Talk," Deborah Soloman's interview with Jane Fonda, now 72 years old, in the *New York Times Magazine*, April 19, 2010. Fonda's original exercise video sold the most copies. She believes it started a trend.

in *Mash* and in Jane Fonda in *Barbarella*[2] though all three actors are remembered for their more serious roles.

Art Buchwald wrote satirical columns and speeches. He once gave a commencement address at Tulane University, wishing the graduating attorneys success in "defending those poor, unfortunate banks and corporations from the widows and orphans who persecute them." English Renaissance poet John Dryden was famous for his satirical couplets.

Ray Bradbury used sardonic humor against censorship, particularly book burning, in *Fahrenheit 451*. (The title derives from the temperature at which paper burns.) The anthology's short stories were first published during Senator Joseph McCarthy's Un-American Activities Committee hearings.[3]

Many highly-disciplined self-made men and women have this Ascendant. Successful artists, writers and entrepreneurs often mention strict parents who praised hard work and achievement but were not affectionate.

Several clients lost their mothers in childhood, as did Marie Sklowdowska (Curie,) Jane Fonda, and Art Buchwald.

An autodidact whose post-secondary education "consisted of ten years at the public library," Ray Bradbury joked that his mother, Esther, was "a stoic Swedish lady of the Victorian generation," and that "her girdle must have been too tight."

Before Ray was born, she'd lost one of her twin sons, Sam, to influenza. So, whenever little Ray played in the yard, Esther worried. She attached him to a tree by a long rope. But she took him to the movie theater every afternoon; it was cooler than the house in summer and warmer in wintertime. When Ray's infant sister died, he never saw Esther weep.

During the Depression, the family was very poor. His father moved them West twice, attempting to find work; then moved them back to Waukegan, Illinois.[4] Wherever they lived, until their late teens, Ray and his older brother Skip shared a sofa bed. Yet, his was one of the *happiest* Capricorn Rising childhoods in this chapter. He often looked back nostalgically at his early years in Illinois and some of his best work was set in the Midwest.

By midlife, some Capricorns come to understand their parents' inability to nurture.

---

2 directed by her first husband Roger Vadim.

3 This and other references to Ray Douglas Bradbury are taken from Sam Weller's *The Bradbury Chronicles: The Life of Ray Bradbury, Predicting the Past, Remembering the Future*, (NY: Harper-Collins,) 2005.

4 The third attempt, when Ray was thirteen, succeeded partly because other relatives were established in Los Angeles by then to help the family settle. Ray was happier once his grandmother and Aunt Neva joined them.

They realize that because one or both their parents may have lacked nurturing as children, their parent or parents were unable to provide it to their own children. It may take a long time, though, for Capricorn to move beyond intellectual understanding to forgiveness.

More often than other Rising Signs, Capricorn clients will volunteer information about their early childhood and/or mention their birth order in the family. (Their siblings, though raised by the same parents, seldom do so.)

Like Eve Curie (see above, "The Mask") they're usually quite accomplished, yet they'll often compare their success to others' in a self-deprecatory way. Jane Fonda, who received two Oscars and many nominations, is an example of Capricorn's tendency to keep proving themselves.[5]

Poet and playwright William Butler Yeats was an autodidact, like Ray Bradbury. Yeats' younger brother, Jack followed in their father's footsteps and became a painter. By choosing literature, young "Willie" differentiated himself from them and their aesthetic standards. He avoided any odious comparisons they might have made about his work.[6]

Eve Curie, daughter of scientist Marie Curie, had Mercury and Uranus conjunct her Ascendant. She chose journalism and public speaking over science, the family career.[7]

Astrologers associate Capricorn Rising with the survival instinct and longevity. Those who find fulfilling work seem happiest. They expect to live to a ripe old age. Like CNN

5 See Jane Fonda, *My Life So Far,* (NY: Random House) 2005. Adult Capricorn Rising clients often mention a parent who was physically or emotionally absent. Fonda's mother was hospitalized with mental problems; she killed herself when Jane was 13. Curie's mother died when she was ten. While researching her dissertation, Mead's mother took little Margaret along on her interviews. After the death of her infant sister, Katherine, Mead's father withdrew emotionally to avoid the pain of attachment and loss. Mead mothered her younger sisters and wrote plays to showcase their talents. She addressed her letters from Samoa to her grandmother, who'd always found time for her. Art Buchwald's father placed him in a Jewish orphanage, then confused him by visiting for two years. Art developed his sardonic humor in foster homes. He considered the Marines his first real family. Bradbury seemed closer to his grandparents and "creative" Aunt Neva than his parents. The last few years of his father's life, the two bonded.

6 Later, the father, John B. Yeats, distanced himself from the son by moving to New York, ostensibly to paint portraits for the wealthy. Instead, he enjoyed lecturing at the YMCA for small fees. "Willie" Yeats paid his father's bills whenever he passed through the city to lecture or read poetry. Distance seemed to improve their relationship; the father began to express his pride in and admiration for his son to others.

7 *Astrodienst* (www. astro.com) has a horoscope for her older sister Irene (9/12/1897) with Gemini Rising. I was unable to find an accurate horoscope for her father, Pierre, who died while Eve was very young.

host, Larry King and the examples in the quoted above, Capricorn Rising people who love their work seldom intend to retire. They remain productive well into old age.

The Mundane Ruler - Saturn

"Striving, ever striving! At last, behold the goal!"
Parmahansa Yogananda

In astrology and alchemy, Saturn's mineral is lead. Saturn endures. In Saturn's Natal House, regardless of our Rising Sign, we're rooted, grounded, and weighed down. Many challenges come to Capricorn in Saturn's Natal House, as well as in House Ten (career.) In youth, Capricorn learns to set boundaries and build defenses. Over the years, their armor grows thicker, like the scales of the mythical crocodile, Makara, a Capricorn symbol.[8]

A well aspected Saturn helps with timing—success may not take as long—but a badly aspected Saturn may result in the feeling that Capricorn is working very hard just to stay in the same place. But if, as Yogananda (Sun-in-Capricorn) recommended, they "keep on keeping on," they'll eventually succeed. (Saturn is the symbol for Father Time.) With Saturnine discipline and focus, they achieve their goals.

The secret to working with the mundane ruler seems to be, *don't struggle in Saturn's House.* Once Capricorn Rising relaxes about his desires, leaves room in his life and opens his heart, grace intervenes. Once his heart is open, he becomes more Yin. As Capricorns release their expectations and preconceptions, they become more receptive to Life; their timing improves.

But also important to let go of thoughts like, "I don't need any help, *I can make this happen by myself.*" And, "I have to do it perfectly." This becomes easier with the aid of a spiritual technique such as meditation, yoga, or journal writing; anything that increases self-awareness and offers "time-out" from the thoughts circling through his mind.

One day, Capricorn will observe that he's beginning to attract different, more congenial people. Or, he'll find that he appreciates the people who're *already* in his life and the success

---

8 See Alice A. Bailey, *Esoteric Astrology,* (NY: Lucis,) 1972, "Capricorn" on the three symbols for the three stages of Capricorn, the Goat, the Crocodile, and the Unicorn. Makara was the vehicle on which the Vedic god Varuna, who controlled the changing seasons, traveled. The same armor that may have been necessary for survival in youth becomes brittle after fifty. It's hard to live by Saturn's shoulds and oughts.

he's *already* achieved. He'll stop waiting for the perfect job or the perfect mate to appear on the doorstep.

Saturn also represents long-term planning. Margaret Mead chose her three husbands carefully, each for a different reason. With Jupiter on her Ascendant, she drew interesting men and generously helped get them grants. She nurtured their careers. But when Ruth Benedict, her friend and lover of thirty years died, Mead suddenly realized what the relationship had meant to her. She fell apart emotionally.

"I read everything she ever wrote; she read everything I've ever written. Neither of us could say that about anyone else," she wrote in her autobiography, *Blackberry Winter.* Her daughter, Catherine Bateson, wrote that though she'd known the two women were friends, her mother had *many* women friends. She was unable to understand Margaret's loss or the depth of her sorrow over Ruth.

Margaret and Ruth had kept quiet about their relationship. Capricorn Rising sacrifices a great deal for career. Because the Tenth Sign is analogous to the Tenth House, Capricorn is invested in success.

The Saturn Chakra is associated with anxiety, fear and self-doubt, those "Saturn worries" like, "what will people think of me? What will happen to my career if people find out about Ruth and me?"

The most common Saturn worries are failure in career; poor health, premature death, and fear of financial loss or outliving their money.

As they grow older, Capricorn men often remark, "one of my parents developed a certain illness at 58; *I'll* soon be 58! Will *I* be diagnosed with it?" The more he worries, the more certain Capricorn becomes that he has the parent's DNA and all the symptoms! Yoga, which works with the breath to release fear, anxiety and stress, can be really helpful.[9]

Finally, Saturn is associated with Father and male relatives. If Saturn is not well-aspected, Capricorn Rising's relationship with his or her father can be difficult.

Though it's usually Capricorn Rising, not the parent, who moves cross-country, Capricorn often comments, as Yeats did, on "the freedom that distance allows" in relating to "a difficult" parent.[10]

---

9 Poses like the pigeon and downward facing dog are recommended.

10 Yeats and his father became congenial correspondents. J.B. no longer knew about his son's important decisions until after they'd been made and carried out.

The Moon-Saturn Balance
Dreams, Imagination, the Writing process, Sensitivity, Nurturing, Support

Lunar Imagination is a powerful antidote to Saturn fears; it enables us to see beyond them. Imagination belongs to our Feminine, lunar nature. Integrating the lunar side is also important to balanced living. For Capricorn Rising, it's symbolized by Moon-ruled Cancer, the Sign located opposite the Ascendant, on the Seventh House cusp. (Marriage and other one-on-one relationships.) Whether in dreams or waking-state awareness, it's important to face our fears and find a way to transcend them.[11]

Prior to America's entry into World War II, Ray Bradbury dreamed of being chased by a large, black bulldog. The dog eventually caught and ate him; Bradbury died in the dream. He awoke terrified! He knew at once what it meant. In the coming war, his life would be cut off like that of his talented young uncle in World War I. Like his uncle, he'd never have an opportunity to realize his talents. He sat up in bed and said aloud, "I'm going to *live* for my country."[12]

He need not have worried. By the time World War II was declared, Ray's eyesight was so poor that he failed the army physical. And, in a sense, he did "live for his country." Through his imagination, Bradbury created a mythology for the Space Age. He wrote of aliens, rocket ships to Mars, and astronauts for whom space travel was as commonplace as driving a truck cross-country. He helped prepare a generation for what lay ahead. In the 1930's and 40's, he foresaw televisions hanging on walls and many electronic devices that were invented decades later.

Though Capricorn is the polar opposite of Cancer Rising, (the former is stoic and pragmatic; the latter feeling-oriented, often hypersensitive) both Signs have long memories and face similar issues around letting go of childhood misunderstandings and resentments.

Many adults still hurt from past wounds, from being victimized when they were too young to fight back against powerful adults. Anger and frustration are usually directed at

---

11 John Dryden (see above quote) and W.B. Yeats, in his *Memoirs,* both wrote about conquering fear.

12 A classmate told Bradbury's biographer that Ray wore the suit in which his uncle was shot under his graduation gown and showed classmates the bullet hole. Whether or not the anecdote is true, it's clear the story of the uncle's death left a strong impression on Ray. His classmate remembered it.

parents, though like James Joyce and the Jesuits, sometimes these emotions are directed at teachers.[13]

Jane Fonda put it well when she said, *"when you can't remember why you're hurt, that's when you're healed."*

Capricorn Rising, people of both sexes seek nurturing (the Cancer Archetype) in marriage. Margaret Mead loved her first husband, divinity student Luther Cressman, for his sensitivity; he was so unlike her father! He joined the Episcopal Church as she suggested, but a few years later he found that he lacked a religious vocation. For Mead, the marriage seemed to lose its purpose; as she would no longer be a minister's wife.[14]

Later, when Mead discovered she could conceive a child,[15] she chose her third husband, Gregory Bateson, in the belief that he'd be a more nurturing parent than Reo Fortune, her second husband and fieldwork companion.

Though pragmatic about her choices, sensitivity and emotional support mattered to Margaret. Her First House Moon was a powerful influence. (Her First House Venus, another feminine planet, added warmth to the Mask.)

However, with Mars and Saturn on the Ascendant, she also valued masculine strength. When they met on shipboard, Reo Fortune was finishing his degree in psychology. By the end of the voyage, he'd decided to prepare for Margaret's field, anthropology. More macho than her first husband, Mead thought the young New Zealander would be a good companion in remote villages, some of whose inhabitants were one generation removed from cannibalism.[16]

With Saturn-in-Rulership, Mars-in-Exaltation, and Jupiter-in-Fall lined up on her Ascendant, ages thirty and sixty, the Saturn and Jupiter years, were milestones in Margaret's life.

Exalted Mars played its role. She spoke of giving students and others "a transfusion of extra energy," which they appreciated when working "at the top of their capacity, but

---

13 Joyce later made his peace with his former teachers, admitting that without them he might have been a sloppy thinker.

14 Jane Howard, *Margaret Mead: A Life*, (NY: Ballantine,) 1984, 36. They were engaged five years, followed by what both later called their "student marriage." They lived in New York, then she left for Samoa and he left for London and Paris. Cressman eventually became an archeologist.

15 Because her uterus was tipped, a doctor told her it was unlikely she could become pregnant. After miscarrying twice in the field, she decided the doctor was wrong.

16 They were in New Guinea and the Admiralty Islands together.

seemed to resent when they weren't."[17]Gregory Bateson had considered suicide shortly before meeting Margaret. Her enthusiasm for his theories changed his mind. They fell in love doing fieldwork along the Sepik River, while Mead was still married to Fortune.

Jane Fonda, too, valued sensitivity in a husband. She found it in Tom Hayden, her second husband, who was gentle and respectful with her daughter, Vanessa. Both Fonda and Mead had very strict fathers and chose disciplined, ambitious husbands.

My women clients tend to follow the same pattern. However, a husband who goes beyond ambitious to *driven* will soon seem "too much like dad." Cancer on the Seventh House symbolizes a creative spouse, a spouse more sensitive than Dad. Yet, Natal Saturn appreciates ambition in a man!

Capricorn Rising men often choose an Earth Mother type, a woman like James Joyce's Nora Barnacle, the prototype for Molly Bloom in his novel, *Ulysses.* Their grandson, Steven, said that without Nora, Joyce "could not have written one book!"[18]

William Butler Yeats, who, like Mead had a First House Moon-in-Detriment, married Georgia Hyde Lees at fifty-one. She brought him the gift of automatic handwriting, a new source of metaphor. He gave up séances and mediums; he'd "found peace and harmony." When Georgia became seriously ill with influenza in 1918, Yeats' father wrote a friend that if she died, "Willie would fall to pieces."[19] His biographer Richard Ellmann believed that without her, Yeats would have been considered a minor poet.

Earth Mothers endure. Though her husband called her "the family intellectual,"[20] Marguerite McClure Bradbury was a supportive wife and devoted mother of four. Like Nora Joyce, the Earth Mother is often the stronger personality in the marriage. While

---

17 *Blackberry Winter,* cited above, 181. Many of us with Mars close to our Ascendant have had similar experiences with the "energy transfusion, though Mars-in-Exaltation has a particularly strong impact.

18 Brenda Maddox, *Nora: The Real Life of Molly Bloom,* (Boston: Houghton-Mifflin,) 1988. Steven's quote, 376. Joyce and Nora were together thirty-seven years, until his death from peritonitis. Like so many Capricorn Rising stoics, he diagnosed himself instead of visiting a doctor. He was certain he had stomach cancer. His ulcer was treatable in the early stages but became perforated.

19 Richard Ellmann, *Yeats: the Man and the Masks,* (London: W.W. Norton) 1979,114 and preface, ix.

20 Maggie said that marriage to Ray was like taking a vow of poverty. She spoke four languages and was re-reading Proust in French when Sam Weller, Ray's biographer, met her. She attended UCLA; she loved Proust and Yeats. Her husband was self-taught; he loved Buck Rogers comic strips, science fiction and fantasy novels. He wrote for the Alfred Hitchcock Show and the Twilight Zone.

James Joyce was vociferously anti-Catholic, Nora raised their two children and their grandson as Catholics.

Mead became anthropology's matriarch. (She was also called its "evangelist" for her recruiting efforts.)[21]

In summary, the Moon, ruler of the Seventh House for Capricorn Rising, represents the feminine, Mother, women relatives, feelings, intuition and imagination. Saturn, the mundane ruler, represents the masculine, Father, male relatives; focus, discipline, pragmatism, rationality. Even when Capricorn Rising has a prominent First House Moon like Mead and Yeats, it's quite a challenge to integrate Saturn and the Moon within.[22]

The Cancer Rising Chapter in *Beyond the Mask,* Part I, on William Blake, (the Creative Imagination theme,) and Christopher Isherwood, (on memoirs and the Writing Cure) might be interesting if you have Cancer on your Seventh House cusp. Memoir writing can be a healing process for both Cancer and Capricorn Rising. Both Signs have very long memories.

Eve Curie, with Capricorn Rising, also wrote a memoir.[23] Because Eve was only two years old when her father, Pierre, died, her sister's recollections filled many gaps in her memories. During the writing process, Eve came to understand her mother's close relationship with her older sister, Irene. Marie and Irene had gone to the lab together every day, leaving little Eve with a sitter. Irene eventually married Marie's most trusted lab assistant. Later, after Marie's death, the couple took over the Curies' work.

Catherine Bateson, the only child of Margaret Mead and Gregory Bateson, wrote an engaging memoir about her parents and her childhood. Her parents believed early childhood development was crucial, so they "found her an excellent English nanny." They

---

21 She once remarked at a conference, "we (anthropologists) are a family and we will not have differences of opinion before strangers.

22 However, it can be magical when the two planets— or the masculine and feminine sides—unite to create a literary work! Bradbury combined his sensate powers of observation with the lunar gift for metaphor. One evening he and his wife were walking on the beach near Venice pier, where the city had let nature reclaim an amusement park. The rollercoaster lay on its side in the sand. "Look! The bones of a dinosaur," Ray said to Maggie, pointing to it. Then, suddenly, a foghorn blew and the metaphor became a story. "The dinosaur's mate is calling to it from the depths of the ocean!" And later, as the story developed, a dinosaur heard the foghorn, awoke after millions of years and emerged from the sea in search of its lost mate. But the sight of the skeleton on the beach infuriated him! The dinosaur charged the lighthouse, the source of the foghorn sound.

23 *Madame Curie: A Biography by Eve Curie*, Vincent Sheean trans, (NY: Doubleday,) 1938.

once spent "an entire weekend" caring for little Cathy themselves "to see what it was like," but apparently they didn't repeat the experience![24]

The Moon and Intuition

Mead's "complex empathy and imagination," according to her daughter, was "capable of seeing possible futures" for others, futures that "eluded them." As a child, she'd seen her mother hurt when others called her domineering, so, at thirteen, Catherine decided to avoid a later quarrel with Margaret and future pain. She convinced Margaret to let her stay in Israel and learn Middle Eastern languages. She decided to find her own way lest her future, too, be set in motion by Margaret's "daydreams." If she became a linguist, not an anthropologist, neither parent would know the languages or the region in which she specialized. As an adult, Catherine considered that a pivotal decision in her life.[25]

Later, however, she became an anthropologist. When, after her mother's death, Bateson interviewed Mead's first and second husbands, her research validated her childhood impressions. They'd both come to resent Margaret's "complex empathy."

It helps if Capricorn Rising had a childhood influence who encouraged him or her to develop their intuition and imagination. Ray Bradbury had his granny, his "artistic Aunt Neva" and encouraging teachers.

Margaret Mead's grandmother assured her that a woman "could have it all," a fulfilling career and motherhood. Mead wrote poetry in college. Her prose style, devoid of social science jargon, reached mainstream America through *Redbook* magazine.

William B. Yeats developed his lunar, imaginative side as a child in his mother's kitchen in Sligo, Ireland, listening to stories of ghosts and fairies. Though an imaginative artist, WBY's father, John B. Yeats, preferred the Utilitarian philosophy. Father and son argued vehemently about that and other subjects. Once, in the course of an argument about John

---

24 In fairness to Mead and Gregory Bateson, they were both occupied with the war effort at the time. The British government loaned Bateson, who was OSS, to Washington. After Pearl Harbor, the American government put his knowledge of the Pacific to use. Margaret moved to Washington DC and also involved in classified projects around her teaching schedule and her work at the Natural History Museum.

25 Catherine Bateson, *With a Daughter's Eye: A Memoir of Margaret Mead and Gregory Bateson,* (NY: HarperCollins Perennial,) 1984, *passim.* Looking back on her decision at 13, it later seemed critical to her life development.

Ruskin, J.B. Yeats pushed young Willie against a wall so hard that he "broke the glass on a picture with the back of my head."[26]

His mother's folk stories nourished one side of the poet's Gemini (Sun Sign) personality; his father's skeptical philosophy influenced the other.

Later as an adult, the symbol of the two rotating gyres, (which came from the automatic writing,) seemed to help Yeats in reconciling the Gemini opposites. Writing and revising *A Vision* helped him reconcile his public and private personalities, especially the dialogue between the skeptical politician, "Owen Aherne," and the more mystical "Michael Robartes."[27]

The third symbol for Capricorn is the beautiful, pure white Unicorn with big blue eyes. In folklore, he stares into the Abyss of materialism.

Sure-footed, he stands at the edge of the pit and shines his horn, "the light of discrimination," downward, dispelling fear of death and the illusion of insufficiency. Alice Bailey tells us that "when the goat becomes the Unicorn, he "no longer wanders arid paths in fear of his unknown future."[28]

The Esoteric Ruler - Saturn as Dharma
Higher Self and Selfless Service - The Fearless Unicorn Gazes at the Stars

Saturn rules Capricorn at two different levels; the mundane, where the plucky, sure-footed mountain goat ascends to the pinnacle of material success at the Zenith of the horoscope,[29] and the esoteric, where the rare, fleet-footed Unicorn, a symbol of the Self, may appear in dreams or call out to Capricorn in some other way. Carl Jung associated the Unicorn with the alchemical *Spiritus Mercurius.*

---

26 Ellmann, cited above, 278. His sister told a friend that the house was much quieter "after Willie got his own place, without WIllie and father constantly shouting at each other." Their father had the children make up stories to develop their narrative skills. "How was today's trip to the mailbox different from yesterday's?" He taught them that the arts were as important as the sciences.

27 There is a sketch of the gyres in *A Vision*. (Gyres is pronounced with a hard "g.")

28 Scorpio Rising Friedrich Nietzsche warns not to stare too long into the Abyss, lest it stare back at us. See also Alice A. Bailey, cited above, "Capricorn," (NY: Lucis Press) 1972. The single horn symbolizes single-pointed concentration. The Unicorn's horn is located at its "third eye." Associated with the pineal gland, the third eye is said to control the endocrine system in esoteric healing.

29 The Zenith is the cusp of the Tenth House, analogous to the Tenth Sign, Capricorn. In numerology, the Number Ten is reduced to One, the number of Wholeness, by adding the digits, One and Zero.

Though most of us are familiar with the gentle Unicorn tamed by the innocent young girl,[30] Unicorns are also fierce. A client, chased by a unicorn in a dream, told me it felt like being pursued by the 'Hound of Heaven' in Francis Thompson's poem:

> I fled Him, down the nights and down the days/ I fled Him, down the arches of the years/ I fled Him, down the labyrinthine ways/ Of my own mind; and in the mist of tears/ I hid from Him/ and under running laughter/ Up vistaed hopes I sped/ And shot, precipitated, /down Titanic glooms of chasmèd fears/ From those strong Feet that followed, followed after/ But with unhurrying chase, And unperturbèd pace/ Deliberate speed, majestic instancy, They beat—and a Voice beat/More instant than the Feet—/"All things betray thee, who betrayest Me."

She interpreted the dream's message as, "he'll run me through with his sharp horn if I don't start paying attention to Psyche around my busy schedule!"

According to biographer Virginia Moore,[31] W.B. Yeats was captivated by a painting of two unicorns in side-by-side panels. One stands next to a Victorian maiden wearing an elaborate brocade dress, while the other, more libidinous unicorn,[32] has his head in a naked woman's lap. Yeats supposedly contemplated this painting for a long time. He chose the Unicorn as the symbol for his third initiation in the Golden Dawn Society, and took the name, *Monoceris de astris,* "Unicorn from the Stars."[33]

While fascinated with the symbol, Yeats wrote two plays, "The Unicorn from the Stars" and, (with his patroness, Lady Gregory,) "Where There is Nothing, There is God."[34] Reviewers and theater audiences alike were *un*impressed. Their verdict was that though

---

30 "La Dame a la Licorne" is on a series of 15th Century Belgian tapestries, representing the five senses. They're in the Musee de Cluny in Paris. Gentle and compassionate Quan Yin has a small, spotted unicorn. In Chinese folklore, the unicorn is the noblest of animals and said to live 1,000 years.

31 Virginia Moore, *The Unicorn: W.B. Yeats' Search for Reality,* (NY: Macmillan,) 1954.

32 Unicorn horn was considered an aphrodisiac during the Middle Ages; hunters hoped to trap them, using maidens as bait. It was also considered a magical cure for many ills and the antidote to poison.

33 Yeats wrote to his sister Elizabeth, "most people don't know that the Unicorn is a symbol of the soul. It's a personal symbol for me as it's the name of my grade level—level three-in the Golden Dawn. See Kathleen Worth, "Where There Is Nothing, There is God," (Washington DC: Catholic University of America Press,) 1987. Worth also states that the Paul character is modeled on his father, J.B. Yeats, "full of a hard passion and a mad reverie," according to his son. See her introduction.

34 "Where There is Nothing, There Is God," cited above.

symbolism "may enrich poetry and plays, it's a poor substitute for a plot." Yet, these plays were Yeats' personal favorites. He felt they belonged in the "canon" of his works.

What's it like when Capricorn removes his armor (defenses) at the end of the crocodile phase and leaves the arid path of materialism to follow the way of the Unicorn? Or, for that matter, what's it like for *any of us to* relax and make our peace with Saturn? We leave behind self-doubt; financial insecurity, fear of failure as professionals, scientists, writers or artists. Capricorn Rising also transcends the fear of being forgotten (not living on in others' memories, a type of immortality) and the fear of death.

Yeats once wrote of a fear that "this alchemist had been working for a long time with the wrong *prima materia*." That fear, too, had disappeared.

The Unicorn is fearless! As he gazing at the stars *(asters,)* he glimpses eternity.

Ray Bradbury wanted to be famous; his Leo Sun Sign's agenda and Capricorn Mask worked well together. As a young man, he tried acting first. Later, he hoped to be remembered like his heroes, science fiction and fantasy authors, H.G. Wells, Robert A. Heinlein, and Edgar Rice Burroughs. He kept on writing short stories. By midlife, he was happily surprised to discover that he was considered a mainstream author.

James Joyce sought to carve himself a niche in literature unoccupied by any other famous Irish writer. GB Shaw and JM Synge were the playwrights and Yeats the famous Irish poet, so young Joyce decided to become a novelist. He developed his "stream-of-consciousness" narrative style in *Ulysses*; the rhythm was similar to his wife Nora's Galway speech patterns.[35]

In the 1950's and early 60's, many American teachers encouraged students to imitate the stream-of-consciousness technique. Joyce also employed symbolism as a literary gimmick, "hoping to keep literature professors busy for three hundred years figuring out *Finnegan's Wake.*"

Yeats extolled his readers, future generations of "Irishry," to learn their craft well, polish their lines and live up to the standards of those who went before.[36] For Yeats and Joyce, literary immortality involved a great deal of effort.

But Capricorn's high standards aren't limited to the literary arts, the social sciences, or Madame Curie's lab. Actress Jane Fonda improved her performance with each movie. She won two Oscars; several of her films have become classics. Art Buchwald won a Pulitzer; Marie Curie and Yeats won Nobel Prizes.

---

35 His characters repeated the same phrase twice, as Galway people did, like, "I pray every day. I pray every day for rain," and often began conversations with the phrase, "do you think…?"

36 "Under Ben Bulben," V, "Irish poets, learn your trade/Sing whatever is well made./that we in coming days may be/Still the indomitable Irishry." *Collected Poems,* 327.

Margaret Mead became a household word and received the Congressional Medal of Freedom posthumously. Although she wasn't offered a cabinet post, Margaret achieved all her other goals. She's had her share of detractors but her work lives on.[37] Mountain goats do reach those lofty Tenth House peaks! Many students of my generation changed their majors to anthropology because of Mead's sense of urgency about documenting vanishing languages and "pre-industrial cultures."[38]

Yeats defined happiness as personal growth. "We're happiest when we're growing." (See above list of quotes.) To esoteric Capricorns, growth is more important than achievement.

As Paramahansa Yogananda (Sun-in- Capricorn) once said, "we don't want to become psychological antiques." Between forty and fifty, many mountain goats move beyond self-doubt and the need for approval, which comes across to others as defensiveness. They've come to realize that they, themselves, are the *prima materia*.

Margaret Mead loved to write poetry but gave it up "after his (Bateson's) criticism killed the impulse."[39] But she didn't give up writing! Her clear, simple, direct style reached a wide audience through *Redbook*.

In *My Life So Far*, Fonda looked back on bulimia and breast implants in wonderment and asked herself, "why did I care so much what others thought of me? Why did their approval seem so important?" Unlike most actresses, Fonda made peace with her "character lines," or wrinkles.

Breakthroughs occur at every level, emotional, spiritual and physical. After Yeats reconciled with his lost love, Maud Gonne, and they became "spiritual friends," he wrote, "When day begins to break/I count my good and bad/Being wakeful for her sake/ Remembering what she had/What eagle look still shows/ *While up from my heart's root/So great a sweetness flows/ I shake from head to foot*."

Jupiter is the antidote to Saturn' s work obsession. As the principle of limitation, Saturn excels at focus, discipline and boundary-setting. But when carried to extremes, Saturn's

---

37 A colleague once called her a "lady novelist." Because her first book, *Coming of Age in Samoa* was so well-written, it was read by many outside anthropology. A First House Moon may indicate that the general public will identify with the author's work.

38 As a graduate student, Mead once woke up thinking that the last old man on Rarotonga might die *that day,* before she had a chance to interview him! As it turned out, she worked mainly with women and children.

39 *With a Daughter's Eye,* cited above, 42. She did write a beautiful poem for her daughter, un-titled. It's in her memoir, *Blackberry Winter.* Cited above, pp 271-72. With the kind permission of the Institute for Intercultural Studies, I once read it at a Mother's Day workshop. Participants really enjoyed it.

dedication to career results in unbalanced living. As the principle of expansion, Jupiter opens wide the door of experience to those Capricorns willing to take risks.

As long as Ray Bradbury, who had a Sagittarian (Jupiter-ruled) Moon, sadly affirmed, "I'll *never* have enough money to travel to Europe," he limited himself. However, after he agreed to collaborate with John Huston, the world opened to him. He spent six months in Ireland, then visited other countries. Still, it wasn't easy. His phobias about flying and driving still restricted him.[40] He missed American hamburgers and other familiar food.

There's a Kafka short story about a mouse who lived in a wall which illustrates Saturn's narrowness as the Principle of Limitation. In this story, the mouse felt safe only in small spaces; he avoided the wide passages as he navigated his maze. Then, one day, moving along with his flanks securely pressed against the narrow passage, he saw light at the end of his tunnel.

However, as he came to the last stage of his journey to freedom, he saw a mousetrap blocking the exit. He stopped to stare at it, wondering, "what now?" Then he heard a sonorous voice say, "*you can do this*, you're almost out! I'll guide you; just back up a bit away from the trap and move slightly to the right, between the trap and the wall."

The frightened mouse did as suggested, edging himself slowly towards the right of the exit hole. Suddenly, a paw reached in and snagged him; the sonorous voice belonged to a purring cat! It's not wise to act in fear.

Like Scorpio, Capricorn Rising works well in solitude. However, it's possible to take austerity to extremes. During her student years at the Sorbonne, Marie Curie's sister and brother-in-law would have welcomed her into their comfortable Paris home. Marie, after all, had worked as a governess in Poland to pay for her sister's training.

Instead, Marie rented an attic apartment that was freezing cold in winter and insufferably hot in summer. When she fainted and was diagnosed with pneumonia and malnutrition, her sister insisted she come to live with them. But as soon as she recovered, Marie returned to the garret.

Even after she married Pierre, an older scientist with a salary from the Sorbonne, the couple lived austerely. Her vacations involved hiking in the mountains while discussing physics with her husband or Albert Einstein, when he joined them. Her mind was always on her work, and *it was never finished.* (See the list of quotes, above.)

As Assistant Curator, Margaret Mead enjoyed her solitude in her aerie on the top floor

---

40 I suspect his Moon was in the Twelfth, not the Eleventh, because the Twelfth, (opposite the Sixth,) is, in my experience, the more likely position for phobias. John Huston threatened to leave him in Ireland unless Bradbury would fly to England with him but Ray took a boat and met him there.

of the Museum of Natural History. She seldom went to lunch with her peers. A colleague once tracked her to her lair, remarking, "the staff downstairs weren't sure if you were even in the country. They haven't seen you in months; they thought perhaps you were off doing field- work." Mead smiled and told him she liked it that away; she accomplished so much more when everyone thought she was away.

Mead risked her health for her career. When her thesis advisor wanted her to work with Native Americans, Margaret insisted on the Pacific Islanders instead. Even after her return to the United States, Mead suffered from bouts of malaria. She needed quinine immediately after giving birth to her daughter. Curie's mysterious symptoms prior to her death are attributed by many biographers to working with radioactive elements without any protection, even gloves. (At the time, scientists didn't know protection was necessary.)

Solitude needn't mean privation. In contrast to Saturn, Jupiter is generous; Capricorns with a prominent or well-aspected Jupiter are generous *with themselves* as well as others. Esoteric Capricorns are known for generosity with their time and resources. Saturn may still whisper, "you shouldn't buy that; you'd better not take that trip! You might outlive your money," but Jupiter represents faith in Life, and in abundance.

Even if Jupiter is stronger by house and aspect than Saturn, Capricorn Rising is seldom extravagant. He or she *is,* however, more likely to believe that "God will provide" at the end of life; and all basic needs will be met.

Mead, with her widespread friends and acquaintances, experienced the world as a global village. With a prominent Jupiter, Capricorn Rising is often enriched by relationships with gifted and interesting people.

Capricorns who slow down and take an occasional vacation by midlife, who occasionally stop to smell the roses, will be healthier in old age.

Generosity includes *sharing the credit for one's achievements.* A major difference between the goat and the Unicorn is that the goat will seldom do that. The goat is constantly thinking about his resume.

It's good to be productive in our seventies and eighties like Buchwald, Yeats, Mead and Bradbury. But for the esoteric Capricorn, there's more to life than productivity. In 1941, Bradbury set himself the task of writing a complete short story *every week,* regardless of his other projects, the screenplays, anthologies, and film directing.

Ray completed a story every week for *six decades*, long after he needed the practice or the discipline. Meanwhile, he failed to notice that his wife, Maggie, was unhappy until she asked him for a divorce.

The art of balancing personal and professional life (Houses Ten and Four) is a lifelong challenge. No scales remain perfectly in balance for long.

Service to the community is also part of the dharma (duty) for esoteric Capricorns. The goat may volunteer because he was trained to do so in childhood; his religion expects it of him or his boss requires community service for promotion. Because he lacks the spirit of service, he finds volunteer working draining.[41]

The Unicorn, on the other hand, enjoys his time with the other volunteers in the Rotary, the Moose, the Kiwanis, the Knights of Columbus or the Red Cross. Energized by helping people, he doesn't isolate himself from them. It gets lonely at the top.

After volunteering, the esoteric Capricorn leaves happily, without a thought as to whether his presence or his efforts were noticed. He feels a glow of satisfaction; virtue is its own reward.

Esoteric Capricorns enjoy mentoring talented apprentices. More will be said about this below.

Finally, esoteric Capricorns are often prescient. Bradbury's science fiction visions became reality decades later. Curie's lab results exceeded her expectations, and Mead imagined or "daydreamed" her own and others' futures into being. When Capricorn is relaxed as well as industrious, the Moon and Saturn, the Feminine and Masculine, work together in amazing ways.

Because Moon-in-Detriment (Capricorn or Aquarius) in the First House, or in the psychic Houses (4, 8, and 12) is so powerful,[42] when Capricorn Rising sees the future and acts on that vision, others may be temporarily caught up in Capricorn's agenda. Later, though, they may feel manipulated or cheated.

Should intuitive people be more cautious when their visions include others? Can lunar prescience sometimes be harmful? Astrologers are often asked by Capricorn parents why a child seems resentful, rather than grateful, *after everything Capricorn Rising has done for them*. But "everything" may include pulling strings with Capricorn's contacts on behalf of the child.

After Mead "daydreamed" the future, "seeing" herself married (to Luther Cressman) and organizing church activities; married to "fellow anthropologist," (Reo Fortune, then

41 Some "goats" view volunteering as an opportunity to meet new business contacts.
42 Two contemporary Capricorn Rising authors with psychic abilities are Barbara Roberts, (Moon-in-Detriment in the Twelfth House) of Encinitas, California who's written two books on Face Reading and appears on The Tyra Banks Show, and author James Van Praagh, (Moon in the Twelfth) who writes for the show *Ghost Whisperer* and teaches "Mastering Mediumship" at Omega in Rhinebeck, NY.

planning to continue in psychology) and doing fieldwork with him; married to "sensitive" anthropologist (Gregory Bateson,) having a child and continuing with her work, all of it came to pass, temporarily.

But afterwards, her ex-husbands wondered, "how might my life have developed had I *not* met and married Margaret Mead?"

Mead's dissertation on Samoa became an overnight best seller. It brought her the unbelievable sum of $5,000 *during the Depression*. She had the funds for her next field trip with Reo. But two years later, when Reo's thesis was published as a trade book, he held it up and said sadly, "this is the last book that my name will be on *alone. Margaret's name* will be on everything else I publish for the rest of my life."

After the divorce, Mead wrote Reo's former professor in New Zealand, suggesting that Fortune needed a grant for a trip to China. Margaret didn't mention the divorce until A. R. Radcliffe-Brown replied, asking if she, too, needed funding for China. (He could help, but he needed to know the total amount.) He was surprised to learn that they were no longer married.[43]

After the divorce from Bateson, she also pulled strings on his behalf, angering his new wife. When told to stop manipulating, she expressed her concern about Cathy spending the summer with them. She thought Bateson impractical; she "wanted my daughter to have enough to eat."[44]

Mead's was an unusually dynamic horoscope with three Dignified planets on the Ascendant and Moon-in-Aquarius[45] (Detriment) in her Identity House. She was driven. It took the Museum of Natural History a decade to catalogue the 25,000 slides from the Bateson's field trip to Bali.

Back home, Mead enthusiastically planned an international conference for attendees from many different disciplines. She envisioned them all working together, studying a village that had a high percentage of schizophrenics. But World War II intervened and travel was restricted.

Gregory Bateson was exhausted; Bali was their last field trip together. After the divorce, Margaret said what she missed most was doing fieldwork with him.

---

43 Howard, cited above, pp 183-4.

44 In 1951 he married Betty Summer, a bishop's daughter and psychiatric nurse, in California.

45 The moon is in Detriment opposite *both* the Saturn-ruled Signs, Capricorn and Aquarius. In the Twelfth, First, or Second House, a Capricorn or Aquarius Moon will draw on the Creative Unconscious, (Twelfth,) Identity (First,) or means of earning a living and developing financial resources, (Second.)

The Element - Earth

Capricorn is the Zodiac's last Earth Sign. All the Earth Signs are practical, but Capricorn is the most pragmatic. Saturn's Rulership seems to accentuate the Element's patience. The other Earth Signs are hard-working too, but Capricorn endures in institutional settings. I once asked a Capricorn Rising administrator if she were the person who'd worked the longest in her department. "Yes, as a matter of fact," she said, "I am." She'd outlasted everyone else.

Capricorn's second home, the Institute, school, law firm, lab, corporation or committee is always in the back of their minds. In astrology sessions with them, I often think of Margaret Mead painstakingly collecting artifacts for her "museum home" on every field trip.

Capricorn is thorough. Mead's daughter, Catherine, remarked that hers was probably the best-documented childhood in the United States. Margaret had saved most of her childhood drawings!

Other Rising Signs also make contributions to knowledge, but this Ascendant seems to set higher personal standards. Influenced by her economist father, Edward Mead, who taught at the Wharton School of Finance and Commerce, Margaret believed the only worthwhile career was one in which she would "add to the world's sum of accurate information." She devoted herself to documenting cultures that were losing ground to trade, colonialism, missionary schools, and other modernizing influences.

But it wasn't simply about discovering "new, accurate facts." The knowledge should also be useful to Mead's own culture. She asked questions like, "what can *American women* learn from the way babies are delivered in the Pacific islands? How does marriage work in other cultures? Is monogamy really the best way; should it be the only standard? Does Western culture lose something by giving up religious rituals which bring communities together?" Her *Redbook* columns, which discussed many of these topics, reached a wider readership than academic conferences.

As a teacher, Mead was also extremely practical. She didn't care that other professors laughed at her "role playing" classes for students who were about to leave for fieldwork. She wanted them to know how to use their new cameras; preserve their film in the tropics and charge their batteries. She knew an anthropologist who'd left his lens cap on, losing an entire ceremony in the islands. Her students also left with lists of local people who could help them, should they need help thousands of miles from home.

Similarly, Marie Curie believed classroom lectures should be practical. After Pierre died, Marie took over his classes at the University of Paris, and reporters attended her first session. They expected to hear Mrs. Curie's tribute to her late husband, but they were surprised. She launched right into the lecture on physics. Afterwards, she told them that Pierre had already been eulogized; the students were not there for that purpose. She herself had sat through many tedious lectures at the Sorbonne, filled with useless information and speculation. Students deserved better!

Social scientists like Mead and physicists like Curie are noted for their keen powers of observation, but Capricorn's strong Sensate Function comes through in the arts as well. James Joyce, who professed a belief in free love but had never had an affair, decided to set the scene for one in his novel, *Ulysses.*

He rented a hotel room, bought a certain type of clock for the mantel, and rearranged the furniture. He then invited a young woman, who thought she was going to an actual tryst with him, to the room. He observed every move she made as she walked around it. Then, he made an excuse and left. Later, he returned to rapidly write down the description of her dress, the scent of her perfume, her attitude; her general reaction to him and to the hotel. He did all this research for *one* scene!

Vita Sackville-West and Colleen McCullough both had a scientist's eye for observation and detail. Before they were writers, West was a noted horticulturist and McCullough did research in neurology. Colleen is perhaps best known for her novel, *Thorn Birds,* (sometimes called Australia's *Gone with the Wind,*) which exemplifies Capricorn's talent for creating atmosphere by a layering on of details. Readers feel as if they're present in the scene along with her characters.

When the Sensate Earth Element combines with lunar imagination and memory for detail, the result can be magical. McCullough has Jupiter-in-Fall in her First House, Pisces Moon in her Second, and Saturn conjunct the Nadir.

Ray Bradbury's short stories are atmospheric, too. We can almost see the fireflies at twilight in summertime; taste the homemade dandelion wine in the ketchup bottles, smell the circus animals as they're unloaded from the train at five in the morning and hear the carnival eccentrics setting up their tents. We almost feel the cool mist over the ravines in Waukegan, Illinois.

Yeats gave a great deal of thought to his legacy, which poems would survive in his anthologies, and which would not. He was adamant that his various memoirs be called *Autobiographies,* in the plural. He polished every line of his poetry many times. The week before he died, Yeats was re-working *Under Ben Bulben* and *The Black Tower.*

The Earth Element is literal minded. Unless the Moon and Venus, the feminine planets, are strong by aspect and house position,[46] Capricorn can be quite judgmental. People who set high standards for themselves often wonder why others don't live up to those standards, too. They may, for example, resent paying taxes to help out fellow citizens who aren't as practical as they.

A high percentage of Air, for objectivity and humor, and Water planets for empathy and compassion, are helpful. Earth and Fire are a powerful combination, like a locomotive pulling a train down the track at top speed. Mead, Fonda and Bradbury had Sun-in-Fire; Yeats, Joyce and Mc Collough Sun-in-Air. Marie Curie had Sun-in-Water (Scorpio) and a Pisces Moon.

Capricorn Rising with five or more planets in Earth, including Mercury, or Capricorn Rising with difficult Saturn/Mercury or Saturn/Moon aspects, may indicate bouts of depression. Art Buchwald, Libra Sun with Saturn/Mercury conjunct, discussed his struggle with depression in print and on the Larry King show. Tipper Gore presented Buchwald with an award for his slogan, "don't commit suicide, because you might change your mind later."[47]

The Mode - Cardinality

Cardinal Masks contribute authority to the horoscope. Cardinality is a Yang, active Mode. The mode delegates work well, has organizing talent and helps in facilitating projects. Each of the four Cardinal Signs is associated with a different season; each is creative in a different way.[48] Capricorn is associated with professional and business creativity.

Because winter is "Capricorn's season," it's interesting that Margaret Mead chose *Blackberry Winter* for the title of her autobiography. "The colder the winter, the better the blackberries taste."

The Capricorn Mask, through its association with the Tenth House (the pinnacle of

---

46 In the First House or near the Ascendant, the Feminine planets convey an impression of warmth and empathy.

47 His mother was diagnosed with manic depression soon after his birth and hospitalized for thirty-five years. See, *Too Soon to Say Goodbye,* cited above, Chapter 7, "Depression." A sad consequence of Art's Earth/Air horoscope was that his friends misinterpreted his remarks about being suicidally depressed as "dark humor," not as a cry for help.

48 Capricorn and Cancer with the winter and summer Solstices; Aries and Libra with the spring and autumn Equinoxes. In the Western hemisphere, each Cardinal Sign coincides with a change in the weather.

success) and the steadfast Earth Element, is *particularly* authoritative. Capricorn's posture and gait (see "How to Recognize Capricorn," above) announce, "I'm in charge."

When Mead was a student at Barnard, teaching assistant Ruth Benedict informed her that others criticized the way she walked "with a spring in her step." A five-foot-tall woman preparing for a career in a man's field, Margaret wanted respect and intended to get it![49]

Leadership is a cardinal quality. As a child, Mead wrote plays to showcase her siblings' talents. Later, she took charge of her sisters' wardrobes before they left for college. She helped them to fit in at sororities. Margaret herself had designed her own college apparel, which drew laughter at De Pauw.[50] Rejected by two sororities, she spared her sisters that experience. Cardinal Rising leaders learn from their mistakes and make any needed adjustments. They seldom make the same mistake twice.

Yeats applied his organizing skills in the Irish nationalist movement and at the Abbey Theater, which he and his patroness, Lady Augusta Gregory, founded. Comfortable in his leadership role at the Abbey, Yeats had a unique was of soothing theatrical egos. He'd walk on stage during rehearsal and slowly, dramatically intone the name of an Irish hero, for instance, *"Charles. Stewart. Parnell."* Silenced, the cast and crew would stare at him, wondering, "what's this about Parnell?" Once Yeats had their attention, he proceeded to resolve the dispute, which had nothing at all to do with the beloved hero.

The most competitive Mode, Cardinality hates to fail. *Capricorn* Cardinality, though, is sometimes inspired by failure. Tennessee Williams would rush to his typewriter, energized by a bad review. When critics said his play "didn't work," he accepted their verdict, immediately responded to the challenge and fixed it. "A bad review can be more useful than a good one," he once remarked.

In the Master's program at the University of Chicago, one of my classmates received a B+ on a seminar paper. Furious because she'd never received anything less than an A as an undergraduate, she confronted the professor after class. She demanded to know what, besides "that unhelpful criticism at the top of the paper," she'd need to do to change her grade. The rest of us looked on in admiration as the professor became flustered, then made several suggestions.

---

49 *Blackberry Winter,* cited above, p.132. Her sisters married Leo Rosten, who wrote humorous stories about an immigrant's attempts to learn English, *(the Education of Hyman Kaplan),* and cartoonist William Steig.

50 Because her father had lost money on his investments, she didn't attend school on the East Coast. She went a year to his alma mater in the Midwest, De Pauw, where the students laughed at her East Coast pronunciation of "been" ("bean" instead of "bin.") Ser then transferred to Barnard, in the East.

An astrology student at the time, I calculated her chart and discovered she had Capricorn Rising with several Cardinal planets opposed and in square to the Ascendant. *She intended to succeed,* and she did. The next time our class met, she dropped her paper, including several rewritten pages, on the professor's desk.

Astrology teachers are sometimes asked if Cardinal Earth is ruthless, given its Saturnian discipline, focus, pragmatism and competitive nature. The answer is, *the entire horoscope must be considered.* In a chart with Saturn-in-Rulership *or* Mars Exalted, —and Margaret Mead had both— the Identity House (First) *does* seeks to control life, and the person may well be called "domineering" by his or her competition and former spouse.

However, if there's a First House Moon and/or a Mutable Sun Sign—Mead and Yeats had both— or, if Jupiter is strong—Mead's was conjunct her Ascendant—then empathy and generosity will counterbalance the problem-solving Mars or the ambitious Saturn. They're more generous; *they expand their ambitions to include others' success.*[51]

The more planets there are in the First House, the more complex the personality. Moon-in-Cancer or Pisces (like Marie Curie's) indicates sympathy and/or empathy.

The more aspects there are to the Ascendant degree, the more complex the personality. Though English astrologer, poet laureate, essayist, playwright and courtier John Dryden had no planets *in* his First House, five planets *aspected* Dryden's Ascendant degree. His was a complicated life. Successful under Oliver Cromwell, the Great Protector, Dryden changed religions when a Catholic dynasty came to power in 1680, (the "Glorious Revolution") then lost influence when it fell. The inventor of the "heroic couplet," Dryden may have left us the most practical essay in the English language about writing.[52]

Even without First House planets, the Capricorn Mask is authoritative. In fact, if there are no First House planets (or no Earth planets) in the horoscope, this Mask may overcompensate by trying even harder to achieve.

Cardinal Masks are more adaptable than Fixed but less flexible than Mutable. World War II and its aftermath affected several of the Capricorn Rising examples; it's interesting to observe how they coped.

Mead's plans for an interdisciplinary, international study of remote Pacific villages were interrupted and finally cancelled; social scientists lost interest in working with people outside their area of expertise. Her husband Gregory's life took off in a different direction during the War; they divorced afterwards. Divorce was more difficult for Mead this time, because *he* was the one who left. However, with Sun in Mutability (Sagittarius,) she quickly

---

51 "Who shall I have on my committee? Who shall I include in the grant proposal? It's interesting that Mead saw competitiveness as "based on envy."
52 It's in the introduction to his book, *Fables.*

adjusted, immersing herself in seminars, museum administration and government service. She wrote a beautiful poem[53] expressing her feelings about letting go.

World War II brought Art Buchwald to Paris, where he left his "Marine family" and began his career as a journalist. With Mutable (Sagittarius) Moon/Venus, he, too, adapted well to change.

Ireland became independent at the end of the War. In the new democracy, life changed for Yeats and his friends, the Anglo-Irish elite. Outnumbered by Roman Catholics, they lost power. Though Yeats had worked for Home Rule as a young man, some of the post-war changes saddened him. The poet wrote, "Ireland is a nation now, but I have lost my country."

After a series of sorrowful poems, he, too, adapted. Yeats became the "smiling public man of sixty," as he described himself in "Among School Children," while serving in the Senate. He had a Mutable (Gemini) Sun Sign.

The Mask in Youth
Lunar Imagination Helps Transcend Saturn's Sense of Limitation

In youth, Jane Fonda's conventional Mask stifled her Sagittarian Sun.

> I was brought up in such a restricted kind of way, you know, one doesn't raise one's voice, one never shows what one feels, one is always polite. If someone said something to me that I didn't like, I would never show it.

Like Fonda, many of my clients with the Sagittarius/Capricorn Rising combination had parents who used the rules of etiquette to distance themselves from their own feelings and their childrens' feelings, too. In her career as a method actress, where drawing on one's emotions is a major part of the process, Jane found her family's approach a liability.

At the age of thirty-three, after the Saturn Return, while researching her role in the movie, *Tall Story*, Jane discovered Freudian analysis. When she mentioned it to her father, Henry Fonda told her she "needed analysis like a hole in the head."[54] Yet, she learned from therapy that "an actor's performance is blocked by the same issues that block the actor as a human being." After analysis, her Leo Sun was able to speak out, regardless of

---

53 Untitled, it's at the end of *Blackberry Winter*.
54 He thought her too self-absorbed as it was and didn't see her insecurity.

social conventions. In her three marriages, however, Jane still found it difficult to tell her husbands what she needed from them. She was afraid of losing their love.

And, too, her Leo nature became caught up in the action, first in Tom Hayden's political career, then later, in giving parties and traveling from ranch to ranch and back to Atlanta with Ted Turner. Owning twenty houses left her "feeling rootless!" She missed her children, whom she saw only when they managed to connect along the Turners' travel route. While in Nebraska and New Mexico, she also missed her "energizing" volunteer work in Georgia.

Margaret Mead developed both her feminine side *and* her very ambitious masculine side. Her relationship with her father brought her a useful skill, *the ability to negotiate.* She used it throughout her career.

Whenever her father promised to attend a school performance, but *didn't*, her brother Dick and her grandmother were more upset than she. She knew that at the last minute he'd "beg off," but he always gave her a dollar the next day. She could *depend* on that dollar! "Only love," she said, "is irreplaceable; *everything else is negotiable.*[55]

Later, as a successful professional, whenever Mead wanted a grant for herself, a student or an ex-husband, she'd call an organization and negotiate. She'd promise to come and speak at their conference or to give lectures at their university if they, in turn, would help her candidate with his grant.

Her First Saturn Return was very difficult. She later wrote that she'd never in her life been as lonely or unhappy as she was on her thirtieth birthday, spent in a primitive village suffering from a broken ankle. Her husband, Reo Fortune, had gone away with the village men for several months. Shortly afterwards, she met Gregory Bateson.

In Ray Bradbury's childhood, every Fourth of July his grandfather was the "priest of the magical fireworks' ritual" and Ray was "his altar boy." Like Fonda, Bradbury had a Fire Sun Sign. Theater was also Ray's creative outlet in youth, though he began in radio. When his family lived for a short time, in Tucson, Arizona, Ray told the other boys that he'd soon be hired at the radio station. "What? That's stupid! *You're only twelve!*" they said. Ray then volunteered to run errands at the station, was accepted, and before long was doing voices on the "Katzenjammer Kids" radio program.

At thirteen, when his father found a job in Los Angeles, Ray roller-skated to Paramount Studio, met George Burns and wrote several jokes for the comedian. Next, he turned up at the Wiltshire Theater, in his thick glasses, long hair and shabby apparel, demanding a role. The woman in charge, who had her choice of attractive, fashionably dressed young

---

55 *Blackberry Winter*, 77.

people, including trained actors, said she had nothing for him. "Oh, but you *have to* hire me! I've already told my friends I'm working here," he said. And she did.

Though he always loved the theater—he'd own one later in life— Bradbury soon discovered his real talents lay in writing fantasy and science fiction.

Like many with Capricorn Rising, in his thirties, Ray took on a difficult project, the *Moby Dick* screenplay, with a difficult director, John Huston, known in Hollywood for ridiculing underlings and expecting the impossible. Like Bradbury, my Capricorn Rising clients often choose the most challenging degree programs, the most demanding professors, and the most difficult universities.

Ray decided to take on the enormous project[56] because "if you work with John Huston *and you succeed,* you'll never be without work again in Hollywood." He was right. After *Moby Dick,* Bradbury's reputation was established. By thirty-six, he'd won job security in a town of highly talented, very competitive people. Young Ray was a long term planner.

Yeats remarked on how difficult it was to fully immerse himself in the rituals and symbolism of the Golden Dawn Society (which influenced his early poetry, *Celtic Twilight* and *Wandering Aengus,*[57]) because his father's skeptical voice lingered in the back of his mind. His father's views also interfered with his attempts at what is now called Active Imagination.

While dialoguing on paper with the spirit guide, "Leo Africanus,"[58] he became distracted by concern as to whether or not his spirit guide was an actual historical figure. Yeats stopped his imaginative process to research Leo's life "as a poet from Fez," then gave up on him.

Many Capricorns who, like Yeats, have studied astrological symbolism, mythology and spiritual techniques, remark that these pursuits enhanced their imagination, intuition and creativity. For Yeats, they were also an important part of the journey to Wholeness.

When Yeats was thirty-seven, Maud, his muse, converted to Catholicism and married the war hero, John Mac Bride. As a Catholic, she'd never be free to divorce. Yeats was devastated.[59] He wrote a poem to send her away—stating that she could only "burn

---

56 He later based his story, *Green Shadows and White Whales,* on the experience.

57 Solar and lunar imagery. Ellmann, cited above, 106; Yeats *Journal,* with astrology notes.

58 Yeats wrote his questions on one side of his notebook and Leo's "answers" on the opposite page.

59 Ellmann 182-3. In 1907 he wrote, "I fear that I have lost—my center as it were—has shifted from its natural interests, and that it will take me a long time finding myself again." And the lines, (Maud had taken,) "All till my youth was gone/ Without a pitying look,/How shall I praise that one?" 166.

down his Troy" *once*—and began to see other women, actress Florence Farr and Olivia Shakespear, ("Diane Vernon.")

His "spiritual marriage" to Maud Gonne and his long marriage to Georgia Hyde-Lees were important to Yeats' creative development. He seemed closest to women who shared his esotericl interests, Maud, Florence Farr, and his wife, Georgia.[60]

At forty-three, Yeats met Ezra Pound, his brash, young American secretary who introduced him to Noh plays, convinced him to "modernize" his style, come out of the *Celtic Twilight* "into the Twentieth Century;" write tersely, drop those abstractions and go for the emotions!

James Joyce's long relationship with Nora Barnacle, the prototype for Molly Bloom, grounded him and also stimulated his imagination. An alcoholic who wandered across Europe with his wife and two children, Joyce saw Nora as his "Ireland" and his anchor.

Margaret Mead was forty-seven when Gregory Bateson left her. But Ruth Benedict's death the same year seemed to affect her more.

It's interesting that Fonda, Buchwald, and Mead all had Jupiter-in-Fall on, or close to, the Ascendant. While it's true that their hard work resulted in success, *they also had their share of Jupiter's good luck.* Buchwald ended World War II in Paris as a stringer for the *Herald Tribune.* Fonda won roles worthy of Oscars. Mead always found ritual events in 'her' villages to write about, while others fieldworkers might be six months in a village not far from Margaret's and find nothing worth documenting.

The Mask After Midlife
Beyond Insecurity and Vain Regrets - Forgiving Others, Forgiving Self

John Greenleaf Whittier, a Capricorn Rising poet, wrote, "For all sad words of tongue and pen/the saddest are/ It might have been."

At fifty, in "Man and His Echo," Yeats described something many of us have experienced. He woke in the middle of the night with regretful thoughts and had difficulty getting back to sleep.

The poet wrote:

> All that I have said and done

---

60 She agreed to call herself "George" before the wedding because he and Ezra Pound decided it was easier to rhyme than Georgia.

Now that I am old and ill,

Turns into a question till

I lie awake night after night

And never get the answers right.

Did those words of mine send out

Certain men the English shot?

Though we haven't written plays encouraging young men to risk their lives for Irish independence, by fifty most of us have had similar experiences. We've had our share of vain regrets. The road to hell is also said to be paved with *those,* along with good intentions! In the middle of the night, we, too, may come to terms with the human condition. And, like Yeats, we don't always "get the answers right."[61]

During a TV interview with Barbara Walters when she was fifty-one, Jane Fonda apologized to Vietnam veterans and their families for her "careless and thoughtless remarks" made during the anti-war protests of 1972. She came to realize that her anger over the war and her empathy for the suffering people in Hanoi didn't excuse her hurtful words.

On a personal level, the Chiron Return (around the age of fifty) connects sensitive people with their inner "wounded healer." This seems particularly true in the healing professions. Many Capricorn Rising people, in attending to others' needs, have put their own needs on hold.

When Tom Hayden ended their sixteen-year marriage, Jane Fonda felt wounded and vulnerable. She missed the "usness" and the holiday traditions.[62] She surrounded herself with women friends, went into therapy and read *Leaving My Father's House,* by Jungian analyst Marion Woodman.

Slowly, Jane "grew a membrane over the wound." She learned that Woodman was right; vulnerability *did* open to humility. Three years later she married Ted Turner. (Fire Sun

---

61 In his astrology journal, Part II of *Memoirs,* (London, Macmillan,) 1977. Yeats also regretted not taking the stage in defense of his friend, playwright J.M. Synge as his father did, "ignoring the craven men hiding in the gallery, Diary entry 50, about progressions to his Natal Mars.

62 She'd really enjoyed dressing up as the Easter Bunny every year with the family around her.

Signs move on faster than the other Elements.) Fonda resolved to work on her fear of intimacy. Unfortunately, she chose a man with the same problem.[63]

Sometimes, in their fifties, Capricorn Rising suffers from an illness like Yeats, ("now that I am old and ill') and become more aware of their waning vitality. But productive, purposeful Capricorn still sees so much to be done. What is this fatigue, this lack of vitality? When will my energy return? In "Lines Written in Dejection," Yeats expressed it well,

> The holy centaurs of the hills are vanished;
>
> I have nothing but the embittered sun;
>
> Banished heroic mother moon and vanished,
>
>
> And now that I have come to fifty years
>
> I must endure the timid sun.

And he continued working in spite of the "dejection," throwing himself into the play, "At the Hawk's Well."[64]

Astrologers will appreciate the symbolism. Chiron is, of course, a "heroic," youthful, energetic centaur. But Yeats and his friends were getting older. "Heroic Mother Moon" is banished. Maud Gonne, who'd rallied large crowds in her youth, was forbidden by the British government to return to Ireland. And when she came back in disguise, she looked older. A Sagittarius Sun Sign, Maud was represented by both the Centaur and "The Arrow," the title of Yeats' poem which ends, "This beauty's kinder, yet for a reason/ I could weep/ That *the old is out of season*"

The timid sun in "Lines Written in Dejection" is the Ego, the Sun Sign. At fifty, our "half century birthday," many of us exhale deeply, as if subconsciously releasing the Ego's unfinished desires and, often, its responsibility for grown children.

A few Capricorn Rising clients, nearly all of them women, have embarked on an

---

63 Fonda had lost her mother to suicide; Ted's father was also a suicide. She and Turner both feared abandonment.

64 For Yeats, (Sun-in-Gemini,) the hawk was a symbol of "the mind's eye" and the analytical thinking process. In his astrology journal (*Memoirs* Part II,) he lamented constantly stopping to analyze instead of following his instincts and impulses. He "should have" defended Lady Gregory's son Robert; he wished he'd been more spontaneous on many occasions. Ellmann, pp.215-16.

advanced degree at fifty or have adopted a grandchild. A few male clients have decided, like Yeats, that they want heirs, married younger women and started new families in their fifties. But that's unusual. Most are ready to leave parenting and career responsibilities behind.

At the end of his fiftieth year, Yeats had a mystical experience. His wife said it "remained with him all his life." He wrote this verse about it:

> My fiftieth year had come and gone,
>
> I sat, a solitary man,
>
> In a crowded London shop,
>
> An open book and empty cup
>
> On the marble table-top.
>
> While on the shop and street I gazed
>
> My body of a sudden blazed;
>
> And twenty minutes more or less
>
> *It seemed, so great my happiness,*
>
> *That I was blessed and could bless.*[65]

At fifty-two, the poet married for the first and only time. During his honeymoon with Georgia Hyde-Lees, (then studying Rudolph Steiner's esoteric teachings,) he was finally able to suspend his skepticism about the supernatural.

One night, his bride tried automatic writing.[66] Decades later, she told Yeats' biographer, Richard Ellmann, that her new husband was sad and moody over his rejection by Iseult Gonne.[67] To distract him, Georgia picked up a pencil and wrote a few cryptic phrases. Then, suddenly, the pencil began to move on its own, producing ideas, symbols, and

---

65 The long poem was originally called "Wisdom," but Yeats changed the title to "Vacillations," the verse is from Part IV. In his astrology Journal (*Memoirs*, Part II) he attributes his skepticism to his "Moon in Saturn's Sign," (Aquarius,) as well as to his father's influence.

66 Ellmann, cited above, xvi-xvii. The first version (1926) was very close to the automatic writing. He realized he needed more time to digest the information. The posthumous second version has the preface.

67 Maud Gonne's daughter. See below.

sketches. Yeats was excited! He remained enthusiastic about the automatic writing and the spirits who guided Georgia for years. He never needed to attend another séance.

An "oath bound man,"[68] Yeats was compelled to silence about occult techniques. But shortly before his death, he credited Georgia and her spirit collaborators with much of the material in a new preface to *A Vision*.

He wrote to the printer that he'd wrestled with the symbolism "like Homer's Odysseus had wrestled with Proteus, the Old Man of the Sea," and that he, too, needed to "get home to Ithica." By his seventies, *A Vision's* revolving gyres, the opposites, had come to symbolize Man and God; Life and Death. The unity or integration in the Thirteenth Phase of the Moon, indicated that the poet had "come home" to himself. He said that if he were young again, he'd write more about *Unity*.

Happy to leave administrative work at the Abbey Theater to the younger generation, Yeats also resigned from the Senate in his early sixties "because of ill health." Content with his work, his wife and two young children, the poet was surprised to learn that according to the critics, he was "doing his best work" in his old age! Like Yeats, many people with Capricorn Rising are happiest in the prime of life, after the Second Saturn Return.

In her fifties, Mead wrote that she'd "reached the age of committees;" she served on governmental, academic, and international councils. She taught seminars preparing anthropologists for field work. She'd written thirty-nine books and contributed to another eighteen. Too old for field work, she'd become a household word at home. She enjoyed mentoring graduate students.

Her practical articles and advice columns in *Redbook* magazine were widely read. During her travels, she stopped to see her daughter's family in Iran. Mead's visit to the Pacific was celebrated by village elders, who remembered her from long ago and had composed a song in her honor.

Like Yeats, Capricorn Rising may experience the "timid sun" at fifty. However, like Margaret Mead, after the menopause, many women, feel renewed "zest and enthusiasm" at sixty. This will depend, of course, on whether Natal Jupiter is in an angular house (1, 4, 7, 10) or makes aspects to Natal planets. If so, the Natal House and aspects are energized at sixty.

Mead and Fonda both experienced the Jupiter Return on their Ascendant; and they both seem to have felt the zest. Excited about new ideas, Mead took out her notebook

---

68 Yeats' used the phrase several times in "The Black Tower," written at the end of his life. He also used the past tense, as if he was no longer "oath bound," possibly because he'd left the Golden Dawn.

at dinner parties and jotted them down for lectures and articles. Fonda focused on her Foundation and on spirituality.

Jupiter symbolizes contentment and generosity of spirit. Fonda forgave her mother for abandoning her and, afterwards, had an easier time forgiving herself. A chapter of her memoir, *My Life So Far* is called, "Sixty."[69]

During the Second Saturn Return, she watched her forty-nine films and old home movies from her childhood. Observing "the continuity" of her life helped Jane "prepare for Act III," which began at sixty.

The Jupiter Return often coincides with renewed interest in spirituality and/or a desire to expand in new directions. Fonda felt "led," or guided by a Higher Power, during her divorces with Hayden and Turner. An openness to grace is an asset in healing old wounds.

Sometimes, however, Capricorn's spouse is ill-equipped for change or disinterested in it. When Jane asked for "a voice" in her marriage, her request frightened Ted Turner. An atheist, he was already disturbed by her new interest in Christianity.[70]

Art Buchwald also had Jupiter in the First House. At sixty, he too experienced the Jupiter Return in his Identity House. However, he was hospitalized for severe depression at sixty-three. And in his eighties, he still found it difficult to forgive others for his childhood suffering.[71]

Though all the examples faced challenges during the First Half of Life, Fonda and Mead began a new, relaxed, expansive and fulfilling cycle at sixty.[72] Bradbury was in great demand, writing for radio, TV, the movies and as the Future Pavilion designer for the World's Fair. Yeats "did his best work" and was happy in his marriage. While Buchwald remained as prolific and productive as ever, he wasn't as contented as the others at sixty.

---

69 She also regretted not having been a better mother and not having found the time for spiritual interests. She wrote that "out of regret comes restitution;" her foundation focuses on preventing pregnancy and improving the quality of life of adolescent girls.
70 He began looking for her replacement. When she was sixty-two, the couple divorced.
71 The humorist concluded his book *Too Soon to Say Goodbye*, "but if nothing else, I know I made an awful lot of people happy, " (cited above, 146.) Like so many other peoples,' this memoir, written at the end of his life, discussed his regrets.
72 On her "Jupiter Return year" birthday, Fonda's third husband, Ted Turner surprised her with "the gift that keeps on giving," for her 60th birthday, a $10,000,000 family foundation. Through the grant, she and each of her children have been able to promote the cause of their choice.

The Aquarian Progressed Mask - Uniqueness and Risk

Aquarius is Fixed Air and usually presents a more sociable *persona* than Natal Capricorn. Detachment, objectivity, originality (unique talents) and openness to risk are developed during this thirty-year-cycle.

By midlife, Capricorn Rising clients often tell me their workday feels like Hercules' task of mucking out the Augean stables. Divorce attorneys, doctors, nurses, social workers, teachers and administrators have all said they're tired of cleaning up others' messes.

By Midlife, Capricorn Rising professionals are tired of "romantics who, after four divorces, still refuse pre-nuptial agreements;" or "morbidly obese patients who, year-after-year, refuse to change their diet," or "clients who prefer pills to doing their inner work," or "parents who won't turn off video games and supervise children's homework."

Productive and prolific like the examples in this chapter, they'd like to free themselves from their routines. However, they're also concerned about their pensions! If, during the Aquarius mask-building phase, Capricorn became comfortable with risk and excited about learning new things, and if those risks worked out well for Capricorn, he's more likely to welcome an adventure after fifty.

As soon as they progress into Aquarius,[73] Capricorns begin to transcend their "Saturn" fears, embarrassment and other insecurities. They begin developing the confidence needed for their adult contributions to society (House Eleven.)

This was an interesting progression for Yeats and Mead, as both had the Natal Sun/Uranus conjunction. They resonated to the ruler of the new cycle, Uranus. Both also had Aquarian planets intercepted in the First House; they "found themselves" (assimilated these planets) through the creative imagination, in childhood, they wrote poetry and plays.[74]

The Aquarius Mask leaves its imprint on Capricorn's youth and young adulthood. An Air Sign, Aquarius favors writing and learning. The Mask may bring out the creative flair of a First or Second House planet in Aquarius.[75] If the progressed Mask aspects Natal

---

73 The age of ingress depends upon the *degree* on the Natal Ascendant, Yeats was one year old; Bradbury eight, Fonda fifteen and Curie eighteen.

74 Mead wrote a play at De Pauw which the school performed. The sororities "noticed her" afterwards but she'd lost interest in them. Yeats and a school friend wrote a play together in Ireland.

75 Though Bradbury had no Natal planets in Aquarius, he began writing stories on butcher paper at eleven. His teachers encouraged him. At thirteen, the progressed Aquarian Ascendant aspected two Virgo planets, (Venus and Saturn) by inconjunct.

Uranus (ruler of Aquarius) while moving through the First House, Capricorn Rising may discover a unique talent.

A Fixed Sign, Aquarius accentuates will power. Because Yeats was born with *the last degree* of Capricorn Rising, Aquarius became his new progressed Mask when he was a year old. A few years later, little Willie's father found him "stubborn and resistant" about learning to read; the boy preferred listening to ghost stories in the kitchen with the help!

Aquarius represents the Eleventh House Archetype of friendship and group interactions. It's the archetype of *belonging.* Several Capricorn Rising women have told me *long after midlife* about college experiences similar to Margaret Mead's, experiences that still rankled. They'd all wanted very much to belong to a sorority, so they "bid" several "Greek" organizations, only to be rejected by them all.

However, in the process, they discovered that they didn't fit the conventional mold! There was something "different' about them that sorority leaders feared or disliked. They were "too intellectual," "too foreign-looking," or, like Mead, didn't purchase their clothing at the right stores.[76]

First House planets are connected to one's sense of Self. Several women clients with strong Uranus aspects but different Rising Signs, for instance, have had similar experiences to Mead's. But when asked about sororities, they'll usually laugh about being rejected. It wasn't a particularly painful memory. One woman said, "I learned I was a *trend-setter,* not a follower!"

Like Mead, she, too, had transferred to a university where she "fit in" and was happy. But for Capricorn Rising, an Ascendant that values tradition, rules, and conventionality, to be seen as "different" comes as a shock! But it also clarifies *who they are,* in contrast to those who reject them!

It's helpful to look at the house where Natal Uranus, the planet ruling this developmental phase, is located. That House symbolizes the way in which their "uniqueness" will later become an asset. Mead's Sun/Uranus conjunction was in her Eleventh House. (Aquarius in the Natural Zodiac.) Her *potential,* her international (Sun/Uranus in Sagittarius) role as a cultural interpreter was not seen in the Midwest. Nor would it have been appreciated by girls who wanted to associate with those who looked and thought as they did; who spoke with a similar Midwestern accent.

Bradbury's Aquarian mask formed a trine with his Sun-in-Leo; Fonda's and Mead's

---

76 Mead, with Venus-in-Aquarius in the First, had designed her own dresses. The other girls all dressed in the latest trend, and bought their clothing in the same stores. Margaret helped her younger sisters avoid her mistake.

sextiled their Sagittarian Suns. Buchwald's Aquarian mask sextiled his Tenth House Libra Sun. This cycle brings out the more Yang Air and Fire Natal planets.

Young Marie Sklowdowska,[77] however, had a square between the progressed Mask and her Natal Scorpio Sun. When she progressed into Aquarius, she was working as a governess in Poland. She fell in love with the son and heir of the noble house, but her story had a sad ending. He was unable to tell his parents he wanted to marry a servant. Maria told him that she was glad she "hadn't married a coward!" She moved to Paris and immersed herself in science. With Uranus on her Seventh House cusp, she said later in life, that "in a sense I was married to Science."

When, on Mead's thirtieth birthday, she felt the "worse depression I've ever experienced," her progressed Ascendant was in twenty-eight degrees Capricorn. For her, the end of the long progressed cycle coincided with the Saturn Return. She was in a remote village; her husband having "gone off with the men."

This combination of a Saturn Return with the progressed Ascendant changing Signs sometimes feels like the darkest hours of the night, the hours that preceed the dawn of a new cycle.

The Pisces Progressed Mask - Imagination, Intuition, Vision

By the end of the Aquarian cycle, most Capricorns have assimilated some Airy objectivity. Curie's move to Paris after her failed romance is one example. Mead, with Venus and Moon-in-Aquarius, detached and moved on in her personal and professional life. My California clients tend to follow this pattern, many have moved cross-country, or, like Curie, from abroad.

Pisces is Mutable Water. William Butler Yeats was a late bloomer, like many Gemini Sun Sign people. He entered the thirty-year Pisces cycle much more objective about his writing than his personal life. The Yeats family lived in London and sometimes spent summers in Ireland. Though artists and other talented people came to visit his father, young Willie wrote his Irish friends about his "terrible loneliness" in England.

Then, one day when he was twenty-four, (a Jupiter Return year) the "stunningly beautiful" Maud Gonne paid the family a visit.[78] With the aid of his Piscean poet- *persona*,

---

77 Curie's maiden name.

78 January 20, 1889. Yeats' sister Elizabeth described Maud in her diary as "keeping the hansom cab waiting during the visit" and "wearing slippers instead of shoes." She said that all the young men in Dublin were smitten with Maud. And *Willle* had asked her to dinner!

Yeats, the young man who ordinarily hesitated, analyzed, and was of two minds about nearly everything, took a risk and invited her to dinner the next evening. Miss Gonne accepted; they immediately became friends. She was to remain his muse and his obsession for fifteen years [79]

When they met, Yeats' progressed Ascendant was conjunct his First House Chiron (the Wounded Healer.) Over the next ten years, the Pisces Ascendant slowly formed a Mutable T-square to the Natal Sun/Uranus conjunction in his Fifth House (romance) and Jupiter (in Rulership) in his Eleventh. Finally, the Pisces Mask formed an inconjunct to his North Node/Saturn conjunction in the Eighth (others peoples' secrets, values, needs and resources.)

As the Ascendant brought out *his own Natal planets*, Yeats saw Maud as exciting and stimulating, (Uranus) kind and spiritual, (Jupiter,) as someone who "understood him (Sun/ego) better than anyone else." And yet, she was *unattainable*. She lived in Paris, where he sometimes visited her; she was in and out of his life (Uranus) in London and Ireland.

He later wondered, was she loving or was she cold? (Saturn.) Did he see the real woman or the beautiful Mask, the *persona* of the inspiring speaker at nationalist ralleys. In his poem, "The Mask;" the lover poses the questions and the Mask responds.

While the previous Uranus-ruled cycle, brought clarity to Capricorn, the Neptune-ruled Pisces cycle is more likely to be confusing. For Yeats, the symbols and rites of the Golden Dawn, spirit guides met in séances (Leo Africanus and others) and poetry were useful ways of delving into the Unconscious and sorting things out. In Yeats' mind, his muse was a virgin sacrificing herself for her cause, Irish independence. On some level he must have suspected Maud of having a secret life in Paris, though she didn't tell him about it for many years. (By then, he'd progressed into Aries Rising.)

Whether Capricorn Rising's work involves the arts, sciences, professions, administration or property development (Saturn is fortunate with land and property) the Pisces cycle expands and enhances their vision. Jupiter, the largest planet in the Solar System, ruled Pisces for centuries, before Neptune was discovered and has its effect. It symbolizes big dreams.

Marie Curie's Natal Pisces Moon in her Second House was probably conjunct her husband Pierre's Ascendant, though his birth data seems not to be as accurate as hers. Years older than she, Pierre saw the potential of her student research. As physicists, they

---

79 Though he twice asked her to marry him, unfortunately for Yeats, Maud, the daughter of a former military officer, (by then a diplomatic attaché,) preferred men of action to poets and mystics.

shared the same vision— that gamma rays would benefit humanity— and dedicated their lives to it. They were right, radium had definite practical uses.

Curie is the least materialistic of the Capricorn Rising examples.[80] She and Pierre(Pisces Rising) refused to patent their discoveries, stating that "the knowledge belongs to science, not to us." Pierre died three years after they won the Nobel Prize[81] in physics, leaving Marie a widow with two children at thirty-nine. Though women were not admitted to the Academy of Sciences, she was given Pierre's classes at the University of Paris.

Like Mead in anthropology and Curie in physics and chemistry, the imaginative Pisces cycle also results in success in the arts and entertainment. Pisces forms a symbolic sextile (opportunity aspect) to Capricorn Rising. Neptune, ruler of Pisces, is a visionary ruling planet.

Three years into the Pisces progression, Ray Bradbury's Ascendant conjuncted Uranus, his only First House planet. (It was almost in his Second.) His science fiction book, *The Martian Chronicles* appeared that year. Ray became famous in the genre at thirty.

"Dandelion Wine" followed, with its subtle message about prohibition. *Fahrenheit 452*, on censorship, appeared next. Two decades later, in the 1970's, Bradbury wrote the screenplay for *Moby Dick*, which became a successful movie. Christopher Isherwood's reviews of his stories helped establish Bradbury's reputation as a Hollywood screenwriter.

Jane Fonda graduated from movies like Barbarella to more challenging roles. She received an Oscar for *Klute*.

The Aries Progression - New Beginnings

Aries is Cardinal Fire, Mars-ruled, and squares Natal Capricorn. Capricorn Rising enters the Aries' progression after Midlife, when careers are well established. Ray Bradbury, for instance, had written for radio and the movies earlier. Then, during the Aries progression, he began adapting his stories for television. He wrote for "The Bradbury Show" and revised "I Sing the Body Electric" for "The Twilight Zone."

Similarly, many clients and friends have reinvented themselves; reworked old articles and other material, learned to blog and published online newsletters about their current

---

80 See the list of quotes at the beginning of Capricorn Rising. Albert Einstein said that fame hadn't changed her at all. Her Pisces Moon had an impact.

81 They won it for their radium discovery in 1903, sharing the prize with Lucien Berquerel, who also studied gamma rays.

interests and causes. The internet is fast becoming their new medium the way television became Bradbury's.

Mars symbolizes energy. Margaret Mead experienced renewed vitality (zest) at sixty during the Mars-ruled (Aries) progression. Often progressions coincide with and enhance planetary cycles like the Jupiter Return.

Mars is also the planet of discovery. Marie Curie received a second Nobel Prize in 1911, this time in chemistry, for isolating the new element, Polonium.[82] She soon put the prize money to use, purchasing war bonds and financing x-ray machines. A hundred mobile ambulances were fitted with the technology and dispatched from Paris to the front.

Curie talked doctors into taking x-rays and taught them how to use the machines. At first, they resisted; they saw no need to "waste time" with new technology while wounded soldiers awaited surgery. But Marie patiently demonstrated the equipment and proved that x-rays could quickly locate the exact place for an incision. And smaller, more precise cuts reduced the risk of infection. The doctors were finally convinced.

Marie even drove an ambulance herself. One day, it went into a ditch. She climbed out, covered with bruises. The next morning, Marie sent for an ambulance in better repair and set forth again! For Curie, wartime sacrifice was not financial or physical, but "my lost hours in the lab."

These Capricorn Rising examples were (and are) characterized by their vision and strong convictions. Each responded to "their" war (the Mars/Aries theme) in their own way, and each influenced the culture through their work.

Bradbury, who'd decided in youth not to fight but to "live for his country," helped develop a new mythology for the Space Age. Fonda, like her second husband Tom Hayden, held strong anti-war convictions, though she later apologized for the words she chose to express them.

Yeats became known as Ireland's national poet, "the poet of the Revolution." Future generations of school children would recite his poems with pride, particularly, "Easter 1916" which ended, "a terrible beauty is born."[83]

He mentioned his strong (Seventh House) Mars several times in *Memoirs*. Yeats was well aware of the extremes to which the "god of war" can go.[84] His poem, "Remorse for Intemperate Speech" (1931) ends with, "Out of Ireland have we come/Great hatred, little room/Maimed us at the start/ I carried from my mother's womb/A fanatic's heart."

---

82 Curie disproves the rule that scientists and mathematicians lose their creativity by thirty.
83 His friend and critic, Maud Gonne, liked the ending, but not the beginning. The stone, in her view, was not a good image for a patriotic poem.
84 He believed his Mars was seen as "irritable and arrogant" and resulted in trouble with others.

Mead also had an angular Mars, but hers was Exalted and conjunct the Ascendant degree. She seems to have fought her generation's war (World War II) as a Pacific regional analyst for the US Government, though the information is still classified. While living in Washington D.C, she and other social scientists involved in the war effort organized a commune in rural New York for their children,[85] whom they visited whenever possible. Applying her fieldwork knowledge at home, Mead demonstrated that a village can, when necessary, raise a child.

For Capricorn Rising, both inner and outer battles seem to characterize the Mars-ruled Aries progression. Fonda won a second Oscar, this time for *Coming Home*, a movie about the Vietnam War. But she still struggled with insecurity and fear of abandonment; she had to "work up the courage" to tell her husbands what she wanted and needed *for herself*. She also appeared with her father in *On Golden Pond*, a film on love and loyalty, about "a withholding father and his angry daughter."[86]

At thirty-seven, Yeats learned of Maud's secret life. He'd barely recovered from the fact that his "virginal ideal," whom he'd believed celibate and sublimating her energy into Irish nationalism, had in fact been the longtime mistress of French politician Lucien Millevoye. She shared this with Yeats "as she sat sobbing by the fire." After having two children with her lover, (Iseult and a son who died,) Maud was dumped in favor of a new mistress. Yeats was first stunned, then sad for her, and, finally, outraged.

However, the worst blow came a few years later, when he received the telegram announcing her marriage to John Mac Bride, who Yeats considered "a lout" and "a clown." The poet went from shock to fury, lashing out at Maud in his journal and poems. He wrote to others that she had led him on, that she "consumed my youth." Surprised at this reaction, Maud told others she'd "done nothing of the kind!"

As Yeats' progressed Ascendant went void-of-course between Aries and Taurus Rising (e.g. it made no aspects from either Sign) he wrote Lady Gregory that he was "losing his center;" that he could "feel it shifting."

During the Aries progression, Capricorns with Air and Fire planets often see a new marriage as an adventure. Like Jane Fonda when she married Ted Turner three years

---

85 Sometimes one parent worked in Washington while the other lived in New York with their children. However, neither of Catherine Bateson's parents could live with the group full time. Margaret visited as many weekends as she could.

86 Jane quoted a line in the film, "we all do the best we can." Jane got Henry Fonda his part in the movie. Katharine Hepburn observed Jane practicing a dive over and over for a scene, and congratulated her on overcoming her fears. She also told Jane that "Hank Fonda" was like Spencer Tracey. Both men "made harsh remarks but didn't mean to hurt anyone."

after her divorce from Hayden, many seem eager to take a chance on Life. The Aries cycle builds confidence.

However, with a preponderance of Earth and Water Natal planets, Capricorn Rising is more conservative. Less adventurous, they take longer to move on. On the whole, however, during the Aries progression, Capricorn exhibits a positive attitude towards learning new skills.

Taurus Rising
Establishing a firm foundation for "Act III, the Last Act"

Taurus, like Capricorn, is an Earth Sign. The progressed Mask forms a comfortable trine to the Rising Sign. It's a Fixed Sign; Capricorn Rising prefers to be settled now. The Irish bard with the Gemini Sun, for instance, was ready to *put down roots*. Jane Fonda speaks of missing her children while constantly on the move between Atlanta and Turner's various ranches.

Taurus enhances Capricorn's practicality. Yeats had progressed into Taurus when he met Ezra Pound. Confident in himself as a poet, Yeats allowed young Pound to underline every abstract word in his poems, then removed them. He said he'd "become a romantic *realist.*" The same year that he met Pound (1908,) his father moved permanently to New York City. As correspondents, the relationship became much easier relationship for them both. Distance offers perspective, and also freedom.

This progression brings out the talents of any Natal Taurus planets in the Fifth (Creativity; children) or Sixth (Health) Houses. Ruled by Aphrodite, Taurus seeks peace, love, warmth and companionship. After Yeats progressed into Taurus, he and Maud became reconciled as friends;[87] he proposed to Iseult and married Georgia ("George") Hyde-Lees. The late bloomer, having matured, decided that he wanted heirs.

During the early years of his marriage, Yeats restored an old tower named Thoor Ballylea.[88] In his poem of the same name, he claimed to have bought it for "my wife

---

87 1909.

88 In the mundane sense, buying a tower might symbolize the desire to "lord it over others;" to "look down upon one's land like a feudal lord." But in Yeats' case, the tower and the land around it were sold separately; he didn't own the surrounding pastures. Ellmann sees Yeats' poem, "The Winding Stairs" in *The Tower* collection as "an emblem of spiritual ascent," (cited above 143) and is probably more accurate.

George," but his joy in a home that was also a piece of Irish history comes through the poem strongly.

Yeats in his early fifties, is a man of substance, a property owner in his natal place. Owning the tower meant that he was no longer a guest of friends, relatives, or his patroness, Lady Gregory, when he arrived from London. He now "belonged" in Ireland.

In the Taurus cycle, Capricorn appreciates nature. Located in the quiet countryside, the tower was far from Dublin political and theatrical intrigues, and Yeats could write in peace. Though the couple attended plays at the Abbey theater in Dublin and spent part of every year in London,[89] most of his writing and Georgia's automatic writing was done in the tower.[90]

Financial planning is featured in the Taurus progression. The least materialistic example in this chapter, Marie Curie, regretted not doing more for her country, Poland. Prescient, she "knew" that many useful radium-based discoveries lay ahead. She wanted to endow a lab in Crakow, but as she'd never patented her discoveries, she had no money to fund it.

In spite of her dislike of travel and speaking abroad, she went to the US to raise money during the Harding and Hoover administrations. She happily returned, once with $50,000 and once with a gram of radium, worth a fortune at the time, for the lab in Poland.

Taurus is also about comfort. During the first few years of Taurus, Capricorn Rising usually says, "I no longer want to live like a graduate student." They acquire bigger homes and more comfortable cars. However, after a few years have passed, some of them resemble the Unicorn staring into the "Abyss of Materialism." (See "The Esoteric Ruler.") They complain about "high property taxes and insurance costs." Their yard becomes "too big to maintain." Everything seems too expensive. The astrologer hears, "things have gotten out-of-control! I want my life back!"

Children and grandchildren are usually seen as a great blessing during Taurus. As Capricorn Rising reaches what Jane Fonda called, "Act III, the Last Act," and the pace of their busy professional lives slows, many Capricorn Rising women wonder why they were always too busy to "really appreciate" their children.

During Taurus, several enjoyed making photograph albums for their descendants, or taking trips to research genealogy. Most of the women really enjoy spending time with grandchildren. Jane Fonda said her heart opened completely to her grandson, Matthew, in

---

89 As a Senator, he eventually spent more time in Dublin.

90 At the end of his life, in "The Black Tower," Yeats wrote that the old king (Ego) no longer needed to defend his tower, it was time to send the soldiers away. Eventually, a new king would come to occupy it.

a way it had never opened before. Curie loved working in the lab with her daughter Irene and her son-in-law. Mead made an elaborate family tree for her grandchildren.

While some Capricorn Rising men enjoy spending time with grandchildren, others continue to put work (or golf) first. Some enjoy their involvement with a civic, religious or other voluntary organization, the Rotary, or Doctors without Borders. Accustomed to receiving praise and feeling fulfilled *outside the home,*[91] they continue in the same pattern.

Spirituality may become important to Capricorn Rising in this progression. For some, like Yeats, it's always been important while others, like Fonda, develop an interest around sixty, during the Jupiter Return.[92] And a few, like Art Buchwald, never seem to move past their cynical defenses.

The Gemini Progression - The Inconjunct

Gemini is Mutable Air and Mercury-ruled. Mentoring was a joy for Yeats (through his letters and prefaces,[93]) Mead (through her seminars,) and Curie (training her daughter and others in the lab; teaching at the Sorbonne.)

Yeats, Buchwald, Mead, and Bradbury all lived long enough to begin this progression. All of them were still working![94]

Mead, ignoring pancreatic cancer, continued to travel, speak, and write articles to the end. Her health worried others (her daughter, students, and sponsoring organizations,) more than it concerned Margaret herself.

"Inconjunct insights" open Capricorn's thinking to new people and ideas. Yeats helped Swami Purohit with several English translations, the life of the Swami's guru, the *Bhagavat Gita,* the *Upanisads* and the *Yoga Sutras.*

During this "Peter Pan" Gemini progression, Yeats also underwent "rejuvenation surgery," then seemed to return to puberty. Many younger women were drawn to the sexy, famous poet in his old age! Yeats was still writing and revising the week before his death.

---

91 House Ten is opposite House Four.
92 Though several years before that, she'd asked Ambassador Andrew Young what "being saved" meant. He told her the word "saved" meant "Whole" in Greek.
93 Like the one he wrote about writing for Lady Dorothy Wellesley.
94 Fonda, of course, is still alive. She'll be a progressed Taurus for many years to come. She's currently working with her foundation and performing in an "indie" film, in the role of a hippie grandmother estranged from the rest of the family.

Mead traveled to the Pacific islands and visited a young American anthropologist at work. Ever practical, she told villagers, "since disposable grass skirts have been replaced with cotton cloth, soap is essential!"

When interviewed on his eightieth birthday, Bradbury said he'd planned his work for the next twenty years." Forty short stories were underway, some of which were revisions of earlier attempts.

The inconjunct aspect is associated with surprises. Buchwald dictated his last book from hospice, surprised to have lived past everyone's expectations, including his own. He ended *Too Soon to Say Goodbye* with his friends' eulogies so that he could read and enjoy them before his death.

These Capricorn Rising examples were happily productive to their last breath. My older Capricorn Rising clients and friends seem to be following this pattern.

Capricorn Rising Bibliography

Avery, Jeanne, *The Rising Sign*, "Capricorn," (New York: Doubleday,) 1982.

Bailey, Alice A, *Esoteric Astrology*, "Capricorn," (New York: Lucis Press,) 1972.

Banner, Lois W., *Intertwined Lives: Margaret Mead, Ruth Benedict and their Circle*, (New York: Alfred A. Knopf,) 2003.

Bateson, Catherine, *With a Daughter's Eye, A Memoir of Margaret Mead and Gregory Bateson*, (New York: Harper Perennial,) 1984.

Buchwald, Art, *Too Soon to Say Goodbye*, (New York: Random House,) 2006.

Curie, Eve, *A Biography of Madame Curie*, trans, Vincent Sheean, (New York: Doubleday Doran,)1938, and (Cambridge: Da Capo Press,) 2001.

Ellmann, Richard, *Four Dubliners: Wilde, Yeats, Joyce and Beckett*, (Washington DC: Library of Congress,) 1987.

—— *Identity of Yeats*, (New York: Oxford University Press,) 1964

—— *Ulysses on the Liffey*, (New York: University Press,) 1972.

—— *Yeats: The Man and the Masks*, (New York: Norton,) 1979.

Fonda, Jane, *My Life So Far*, (New York: Random House,) 2006.

Foster, RE, *W.B. Yeats: A Life, I, The Apprentice Mage, 1865- 1914*, (Oxford: University Press,) 1998. (The "official" biography commissioned by the family.)

—— *W.B. Yeats: A Life, II, The Arch-Poet, 1915-1939*, (Oxford: University Press,) 2005.

Gorski, William T, *Yeats and Alchemy*, (Albany: SUNY Studies in the Western Esoteric Tradition,) 1996.

Hathaway, Nancy, *The Unicorn*, (New York: Viking Studio Books,) 1980.

Heindel, Max and August Foss, *The Message of the Stars*, (Oceanside: Rosicrucian Press,) 1980.

Henn, Thomas R, *The Lonely Tower: The Poetry of W.B. Yeats*, (New York: Methuen,) 1979.

Howard, Jane, *Margaret Mead: A Life*, (New York: Random House-Balantine,) 1984.

Kafka, Franz, "A Fable," in *The Transformation and Other Short Stories*, (New York: Penguin,) 1992.

Kinsley, James, ed, *The Poems and Fables of John Dryden*, (London: Oxford University Press,) 1963.

Maddox, Brenda, *Nora: The Real Life of Molly Bloom,* (Boston, Houghton Mifflin,) 1988.

McEvers, Joan, *12 Times 12: 144 Sun/Ascendant Combinations,* (San Diego: ACS,) 1983.

Mead, Margaret, *Blackberry Winter: My Earlier Years,* (New York: William Morrow and Co,) 1972.

—— *Letters from the Field 1925-1975,* (NY: Harper Perennial,) 2001.

—— *To Cherish the Life of the World: Selected Letters of Margaret Mead,* Margaret Caffrey, ed, (New York: Basic Books,) 2006.

Moore, Virginia, *The Unicorn: W.B. Yeats' Search for Reality,* (New York: Macmillan,) 1954.

Pflaum, Rosalynd, *Grand Obsession: Madame Curie and Her World,* (New York: Doubleday,) 1989.

Raine, Kathleen, *Yeats the Initiate,* (London: Allan and Unwin,) 1986.

—— W.B. Yeats, *The Learning of the Imagination,* (Dallas: Institute of Leaning and Culture,) 2001.

Tolstoy, Leo, *The Death of Ivan Ilyich,* Lynn Solotaroff, trans, (New York: Bantam,) 1981.

Weller, Sam, *The Bradbury Chronicles: The Life of Ray Bradbury, Predicting the Past, Remembering the Future,* (New York: HarperCollins,) 2003.

Yeats, W.B., *The Collected Poems,* Richard J Finneran, ed, "Among School Children," "The Man and the Echo," "Lines Written in Dejection," "The Black Tower," (New York: Scribner, 1989). (SH)

—— *The Collected Works of W.B. Yeats: Prefaces and Introductions,* William H O'Donnell, ed, (New York: Macmillan,) 1989.

—— *Memoirs, with material not included in earlier editions,* Dennis Donoghue, ed, (London: Macmillan) 1977. Part II, astrology journal.

—— *The Gonne-Yeats Letters,* (New York: Syracuse University Press,) 1992. (The spiritual marriage; their synchronous dreams.)

—— *W.B. Yeats and Lady Augusta Gregory,* ed, Kathleen Worth, "Where There is Nothing, There is God" and "The Unicorn from the Stars," plays (Washington DC: Catholic University of America Press,) 1987.

—— *A Vision,* (London: Macmillan,) 1926; 1956 eds.

Yogananda, Parmahansa, (Mukunda Lal Ghosh,) *Autobiography of a Yogi,* (Los Angeles: Self Realization Fellowship Press,) 1971.

CHAPTER FIVE

Aquarius Rising - Author, Visionary, Volunteer

Andre Maurois, "Growing old is no more than a bad habit which a busy person has no time to form."

—— "Old age is not white hair and wrinkles; the true evil is not the weakening of the body, but the indifference of the soul."

—— "The first recipe for happiness is: Avoid too lengthy meditation on the past."

Alice Munro, "The complexity of things - the things within things - just seems to be endless. I mean nothing is easy, nothing is simple."

—— "I can't play bridge. I don't play tennis. All those things that people learn, and I admire, there hasn't seemed time for. But there is time for looking out the window."

—— "That's something I think is growing on me as I get older: happy endings."

—— "I have recently re-read much of Chckhov and it's a humbling experience. Like Shakespeare, his writing sheds the most perfect light. There's no striving in it, no personality. Well, of course, wouldn't I love to do that!"

Evelyn Shrifte, "When I met Joyce Carol Oates, I thought she was a genius," Vanguard editor.

Robert Louis Stevenson, "To know what you prefer instead of humbly saying 'Amen' to what the world tells you you ought to prefer, is to have kept your soul alive."

—— "To be what we are and what we are capable of becoming is the only end of life."

—— "Marriage is one long conversation checkered by disputes."

—— "A friend is a gift you give yourself."

—— "Keep your fears to yourself, but share your inspiration with others."

Sylvia Plath, "Is there no way out of the mind?"

—— "I took a deep breath and listened to the old bray of my heart. I am. I am. I am."

—— "Let me live, love and say it well in good sentences."

F. Scott Fitzgerald, "The test of a first-rate intelligence is the ability to hold two opposed ideas in one's mind at the same time and still retain the ability to function."

—— "I like people and I like them to like me, but I wear my heart where God put it, on the inside."

—— "Genius is the ability to put into effect what is on your mind."

—— "At eighteen our convictions are hills from which we look; at forty-five they are caves in which we hide."

—— "You don't write because you want to say something, you write because you have something to say."

—— "My idea is always to reach my generation. The wise writer writes for the youth of his generation, the critics of the next, and the schoolmasters of ever afterward."

Will Durant, "Every science begins as philosophy and ends as art."

—— "It may be true that you can't fool all the people all the time, but you can fool enough of them to rule a large country."

—— "Science gives us knowledge, but only philosophy can give us wisdom."

Joyce Carol Oates, "The ideal art, the noblest of art: working with the complexities of life, refusing to simplify, to "overcome doubt." *(Journal*, 1972-1983)

—— "If you're a writer, you locate yourself behind a wall of silence and no matter what you are doing, driving a car or walking or doing housework you can still be writing, because you have that space."

—— "When you're 50 you start thinking about things you haven't thought about before. I used to think getting old was about vanity—but actually it's about losing people you love."

—— "Keeping busy" is the remedy for all the ills in America. It's also the means by which the creative impulse is destroyed."

Truman Capote, "Fame is only good for one thing - they will cash your check in a small town."

—— "Most contemporary novelists, especially the American and the French, are too subjective, mesmerized by private demons; they're enraptured by their navels and confined by a view that ends with their own toes."

Carl G. Jung, "Follow that will and that way which experience confirms to be your own."

—— "Man's task is to become conscious of the contents that press upward from the Unconscious."

—— "Everything that irritates us about others can lead us to an understanding of ourselves."

—— "I have treated many hundreds of patients. Among those in the second half of life - that is to say, over 35 - there has not been one whose problem in the last resort was not that of finding a religious outlook on life."

—— "The word "belief" is a difficult thing for me. I don't believe. I must have a reason for a certain hypothesis. If I know a thing, then I know it - I don't need to believe it."

—— "Where love rules, there is no will to power; and where power predominates, there love is lacking. The one is the shadow of the other."

Bill Moyers, "When I learn something new - and it happens every day - I feel a little more at home in this universe, a little more comfortable …"

—— "What's right and good doesn't come naturally. You have to stand up and fight for it - as if the cause depends on you, because it does."

—— "Freedom begins the moment you realize someone else has been writing your story and it's time you took the pen from his hand and started writing it yourself."

—— "I think at the heart of so much restlessness of the day is a spiritual vacuum. There's a yearning for meaningful lives, a yearning for values we can commonly embrace. I hear an almost inaudible but pervasive discontent with the price we pay for our current ma-terialism. And I hear a fluttering of hope that there might be more to life than bread and circuses."

C.W. Leadbeater, "He has the most remarkable aura of anyone I've ever seen, without a particle of selfishness in it." Clairvoyant, about Jiddu Krishnamurti as a boy.

Barack H. Obama, "Yes, we can!"

—— "Change will not come if we wait for some other person, or if we wait for some other time. We are the ones we've been waiting for. We are the change that we seek."

The Aquarian Mask

I'm the brilliant Mask of Aquarius. Unless Mercury is badly aspected to Saturn, my quick and clever mind will come up with the right response (or retort) faster than anyone else's.

In my youth, teachers were impressed with my intelligence. They were certain I'd read and reflected on the assignment, when, in fact, I'd often skimmed it on the way to class. Some even considered me a genius, a prodigy. I may have finished elementary school ahead of my class, skipping one or more grades.

While I happily delve into topics that interest me, if a subject bores me, I'm content to watch the Earth Signs do Life's "extra credit work."

It's true that I share a ruling planet with Capricorn, (see Chapter Ten, Saturn) but unless I have a high percentage of planets in Earth, "striving" does not appeal. Alice Munro (quoted above) is right about that.

I'm no plodding mountain goat! If I'm interested in a task, I'll succeed through stubborn perseverance.

Unless I have several planets in Pisces, I'm seldom nostalgic or sentimental about the past, nor do I dwell upon past suffering. I enjoy today and anticipate tomorrow's exciting prospects.

Biographer Andre Maurois, who wrote about literary figures, and historian Will Durant both studied the past, but neither man was bogged down in his personal narrative, nor did he obsess on past childhood grievances. Carl Jung wanted to study Egyptian history as a young man. They used Saturn well; I try to do the same.

I'm grateful for the help of friends and consider myself a good friend to others, but when I've outgrown a friendship I'll detach and move on.

If I'm a writer, I'm often known for my original style. Ideally, my work appears effortlessly executed like Capote's *In Cold Blood,* or the best of F. Scott Fitzgerald. I aim high.

I'm calm, cool and collected under stress, like Condaleeza Rice and "no drama Obama."

I have a breezy, whimsical sense of humor like Truman Capote's. He joked that "Venice is like eating an entire box of chocolate liqueurs in one go." And, "you should never invite an Englishman to visit. He'll move into your closet rather than pay for a hotel."

I'm an impermeable shield; insults bounce right off me. Though I may have some sensitive Water or Nervous-Nellie Mutable planets, I conceal them well. Those planets can nap later, or like Fitzgerald, drown their sorrows in wine, releasing anxiety and inhibition.

Like Fitzgerald, for whom youth was life's best, most exciting phase, I live in the moment and anticipate tomorrow's prospects. With Fire planets, especially Aries, I try to keep fit and youthful looking as I grow older.

Though I'm an optimist, I expect periods of feast and famine. Happy years full of simple pleasures are better appreciated in contrast with sad ones. If I had children in my youth, I was probably not Supermom or Superdad. After midlife, however, spending time with my grandchildren leaves me refreshed and rejuvenated. They and many other interests keep me young.

Like Bill Moyers, (see above) as I grow older, I delight in learning or discovering new things.

Like Carl G. Jung's, my scientific mind may open to metaphysics and spirituality as the years go by. Jung reached a point where he no longer cared what other medical doctors thought of his interest in alchemy and astrology. Regardless of my profession, I may reach that point by my late forties.

Like all of the examples quoted above, I'll shape my own life; as Moyers said, "no one else can write that story for me."

My symbol is The Cup. It may be a wine bottle or the bottomless Grail Cup, poured out for Humanity, (especially those most in need,) through voluntary work, like Barack Obama's community organizing.

The Cup—or Cause—is unique for every Aquarian. Carl G. Jung stood for Individuation, the Creative Imagination, and making the Unconscious conscious. Bill Moyer's contributes to the culture through public television (PBS;) John Dean, President Nixon's former counsel, author and TV "pundit," attempts to protect democracy from ever-expanding Presidential power.

The Cup is also Rumi's symbol of ecstasy, for those who seek unity with the Divine in poetry or spiritual techniques.

Astrologers see me as "detached to the point of indifference;" as "aloof in the extreme," or "proud and arrogant." When accused of socially "cutting others dead;" breezing past or ignoring people to whom I've been introduced many times. I shrug my shoulders. Those Water Signs take everything personally!

In truth, though I have an optimistic vision for *Humanity's* future, I do find certain *individuals* boring. Making small talk with them is tedious. I'd rather go find my friends.

And most of all I value my freedom, so, please don't try to fence me in!

How To Recognize Aquarius Rising

Aquarius walks with a proud, stately bearing. Their large, domed heads provide space for their well-developed brains. Aquarius Rising has large eyes, (unless a planet close to the Ascendant tells us otherwise,[1]) that gaze at you fearlessly, and large "drooping lashes."[2] I don't know that all my clients' eyes are fearless, but they are clear, and intelligence shines through them.

Aquarians have wide foreheads and thin, usually smiling, lips. Their jaws jut forward slightly, expressing a strong, determined will. At social gatherings, Aquarian voices can usually be heard over the crowd. When a conversation interests them, they'll assert their opinions.

The body type is usually square, though heredity and ethnicity have an influence. The

1 Saturn close to the Ascendant may indicate smaller features.
2 Max and Augusta Heindel, *Message of the Stars,* (Oceanside: Rosicrucian Press), 1980, 108-9.

classical Aquarius Rising body is flat, rather than rounded, both front and back. Most Aquarians are of medium height, around 5'5", though some are shorter or taller.

Though I've encountered a few Aquarius Rising loners (in computer engineering and laboratory research,) this is usually an extraverted Mask. Gregarious in youth, Aquarius has a wide circle of friends and acquaintances. But by midlife, they seem more concerned with quality of friendships than quantity of acquaintances. In extreme old age, however, they're delighted to receive more birthday cards than anyone else in the nursing home.

Aquarius Rising people who watch their diets carefully, use alcohol in moderation and exercise regularly have long, productive lives. With few exceptions, my Aquarian friends and clients have assimilated these practices into their routine. Free spirits who live life on their own terms, most have very strong bodies. Their calves and ankles, the areas associated with the Sign, are very strong in holding yoga poses.

Many Aquarians spend too much time indoors with their books and computers, though, and would benefit from more walks in the fresh air.

Aquarius is considered the most eccentric Rising Sign. Several vegetarians have told me that relatives find their diets eccentric or "weird." Others, however, were raised by New Age parents, vegetarians themselves, and have always considered their unusual diet "mainstream."

There are some manic Aquarians, like the extreme example, daredevil Richard "Evel" Kneivel, who attempted motorcycle leaps over Snake River Canyon, Idaho and a tank of sharks. In spite of numerous accidents, resulting in broken bones, he lived to be sixty-nine![3] This manic, restless energy is symbolized by Uranus' House position or its aspects to the Ascendant.

Manic Aquarians are addicted to the "rush" and become bored if they're too long without it. Prodigy chess champions, for example, have difficulty retiring. Ideally, they say, they'd "like to go out at their peak," but because they miss the excitement, it's difficult to stop competing.

If the Sun is in the Eighth House (the "Scorpio House" in the Natural Zodiac), Aquarius Rising may suffer from depression, which often results from jealousy, another Eighth House/Scorpio tendency.

Two famous Aquarius Rising writers with Sun-in-the-Eighth are Sylvia Plath (*The*

---

3 Kneivel had Jupiter in his First House; Uranus in the Fourth square Moon in the Seventh, Sun-in-Libra and a close Mars/Neptune conjunction in Virgo. He suffered from Hepatitis C.

Bell Jar) and F. Scott Fitzgerald, (*The Great Gatsby; Tender is the Night.*) Plath committed suicide after her husband's affair and their breakup.[4]

Scott Fitzgerald's "zany," manic wife Zelda seems to have helped him through his depression. Her dramatic Leo Sun/Ascendant fell in Scott's Seventh House and seemed to lighten his darker moods. Zelda encouraged their American friends to visit them in Paris, entertaining everyone with amusing anecdotes. Meanwhile, she attempted to find her own creative path in ballet and short-story writing without threatening her husband's ego. Scott and Zelda were both alcoholics.

Today, some therapists consider exercise the best antidote for depression. Walking will not only raise the heartbeat and improve the circulation (the Leo-Aquarian polarity is associated with the heart and circulatory system) but is also said to raise endorphin and serotonin levels in the brain, leaving people with a more positive outlook on Life, themselves, and their work. About a year ago, a literary agent was asked why there seem to be fewer alcoholic authors now than in Fitzgerald's time. The answer was, "today, everyone goes to the gym."[5]

Many Aquarians suffer from insomnia; they have trouble slowing down their overactive brains at bedtime. They wonder, as Sylvia Plath did, (see the quote, above) "is there no way out of the mind?"

Yoga breathing techniques (pranayama) and certain hatha yoga sequences designed for insomnia are highly recommended. If Uranus, Mars, or Mercury is in Mutablility, or all three are in a Mutable T-Square, a longer yoga practice may be needed at night.

Known for their originality, many Aquarians are trend-setters, and are often considered ahead of their times. As teenagers, "Uranians" are the first in their group to appear in sequined T-shirts and torn jeans, or with tattoos and body piercings in unusual places. By the time their peers are following the new trend, Aquarius is Rising bored with it and on to something new.

After midlife, Aquarius Rising may change their colors from primary to pastels, or from dark colors to light. Or, women may change from slacks to skirts. The Mask may be entering a new cycle. It's interesting to check the aspects from progressed Mask to natal planets to see which planets are highlighted.

---

4 She was married to poet Ted Hughes. Plath had a close Mercury/Uranus inconjunct, This aspect is associated with being "high strung." Joyce Carol Oates, who also had Aquarius Rising , thought isolation was part of Plath's problem, she was "cut off" from the community. Oates herself had the campus community and her writer-friend, Gail Godwin.
5 The interview was in the *New Yorker* magazine in 2008 or 2009, unfortunately, I lost the reference.

The Moon and Venus, for instance, are associated with creating a more feminine image. Progressed Mask to Natal Saturn may coincide with a more businesslike look. Perhaps Aquarius Rising will change careers in a year or two and the Unconscious is sending advance signals.

The Mundane Rulers - Saturn and Uranus

The study of the human mind is an occupation that suits Aquarius Rising well. The two scientifically-oriented ruler of Aquarius, Uranus and Saturn were assets in Carl G. Jung's profession, psychiatry. Uranus in Houses 1, 4, 7, 10 indicates a unique, innovative approach. Uranus is associated with the spirit of adventure, risk-taking, scientific objectivity, exploration[6] and new discoveries.

Though Jung began his studies with pathology at the Burghholzli Mental Hospital, by his mid thirties his interests were no longer limited to the brain and the other organs. However, even after he became famous as the founder of Analytical Psychology, he encouraged students, especially the men,[7] to become medical doctors. Both traditionalist Saturn and pioneering Uranus influenced his thinking all his life.

Jung had Saturn in his First House opposite Uranus conjunct the cusp of his Seventh (from the Sixth House side). F. Scott Fitzgerald had both planets conjunct the cusp of his Tenth House.[8] But in his case, perfectionist Saturn (endurance; longevity) strove for literary immorality and Uranus symbolized his original style. The two rulers have roles to play, but we must also listen to what the other planets have to say.

As Saturn has already been discussed in the last chapter, Capricorn, where it's the sole ruler, readers are encouraged to review the "Mundane Ruler" and "Esoteric Ruler" sections, on discipline, focus, and the work ethic in Chapter 10.

Jung wrote about the impulse to individuate and the importance of the second half of life. In his view, midlife began at thirty-five (see the quote, above)[9] which was true when

---

6 Astronomers Edmond Halley, for whom the comet is named, and Tycho Brahe had Aquarius Rising. In classical times, the muse Urania ruled astronomy, Uranus is now considered the ruler.

7 Biographer Deidre Bair was surprised to learn that he encouraged the men to study medicine, but encouraged brilliant women like Marie-Louise von Franz to study other subjects. Von Franz studied classics and helped Jung translate alchemical texts. The field of medicine was open to women in Switzerland at the time. Elizabeth Kubler (see Pisces Rising,) received her credential there.

8 From the Ninth House cusp.

9 His break with Freud at age thirty-six was a major midlife change.

life expectancy was seventy. Now, however, people live longer and retirement age is edging upward, Social Security benefits will soon *begin* at seventy. Midlife seems to begin later as well, closer to the mid-forties, just after Uranus-opposite Uranus.

It's helpful to note which of the two ruling planets is stronger in the horoscope. Check the house position of the traditional ruler, Saturn, then, find Uranus. Is one of them in a stronger House (1, 4, 7, 10)?[10]

For example, Jung had Saturn in his First House and Uranus in his Sixth, (conjunct the cusp of his Seventh), the Mask's two rulers were opposed. *Both* were strongly placed by house position. His father (Saturn in the Identity House) was not a very strong personality. He was a minister who'd lost his faith but remained in the church.

As young man, Jung found a stronger role model and mentor in an older, pioneering psychiatrist, Sigmund Freud, and acquired a new "Saturn figure" with whom to identify. But when Freud proved intolerant of Jung's unusual interests in psychic phenomena, poltergeists, parapsychology and his personal experiences that transcended time and space,[11] the relationship no longer worked for Jung. With Uranus, ruler of his Ascendant conjunct his Sun, with Saturn opposite Uranus and symbolically, opposite his Sun (by Sign, not degree), Jung needed distance from Freud. He wrote about his need to separate from his new "father" in order to individuate.

This issue is important not only for the Saturn Ruled Signs, Capricorn and Aquarius, but for others, who, like Jung, have a First House Saturn. On or shortly after the Saturn Return, many clients have distanced themselves from their father, grandfather, or a male mentor by moving to California. With distance, they found it easier to work out their own Identity (House One) and "be themselves."

For Jung, remaining in the Freudian family would have meant giving up the research into astrology that led to *Aion* and the "wedding experiment." His path led him through

10 While many people with Aquarius Rising will have a First House Saturn, Uranus, the other ruler, takes 84 years to go through the twelve Signs, so fewer people will be born with a First House Uranus. Aquarius Rising people born in the late 1990s-2002 will have Uranus in the First, the Second or the Twelfth Houses. They may expect the outer world to conform to their values and opinions. With Uranus near the Ascendant, they'll insist upon having the freedom go to their own way.

11 Freud insisted on the "dogma" that psychological aberrations have their roots in sexuality. Jung, who believed that *dogma* had destroyed his father's faith, didn't want to create any new ones. In the second half of life, Jung believed, people were looking for meaning or spirituality; it was the absence of these that lay behind their suffering. He and Freud had other differences, too. Unlike Jung, Freud saw nothing at all creative about the Unconscious.

Gnosticism and alchemy; it intersected with the road Freud dreaded most, "the occult."[12] As a Leo Sun Sign, it was important to him to follow his own path.

On transiting Saturn conjunct his Natal Uranus, then opposing Natal Saturn, Jung broke with Freud. He called it breaking with The Father, which is still an apt description today. It happens in the lives of lab assistants who work with famous scientists and in the lives of disciples who work with famous Gurus. Letting go seems harder to do with Saturn in the First House; the identification with Father seems deeper.

"Breaking with the Father," finding one's own way, in accord with one's own talents, is definitely an archetypal process!

Having found the Saturn's and Uranus' Houses in the horoscope, we next check for aspects from each of the rulers to the Sun and Moon (the luminaries). Does either ruler aspect the Sun (ego) or Moon (feelings, emotion, creativity?) Which planet forms the most aspects? Which forms the closest aspects?

Jung's Uranus was in *exact square* to his Exalted Moon in Taurus, situated in the psychic Fourth House. His strong intuitive gifts came into play in his medical practice, his dreams, his visions and his research.[13]

After transcending Saturn's limitations and declaring his independence form the Freudians, Jung's intuitive, lunar side opened. Jung's Moon-square-Uranus was free to explore, to go where no psychiatrist had gone before[14] and make his own discoveries.[15]

Aquarius Rising women have told me that they appreciated reading about the Water Carrier's Cup, the Holy Grail, in *Archetypes of the Zodiac*. Two astrology students, one in financial services and another in lab research, confided that both mundane rulers seem arid, dry and *masculine*.

The Cup, on the other hand, is a feminine, womb-like symbol. The research scientist

---

12 Though he became interested in astrology in 1911, he was in his seventies when the wedding experiment was conducted (1950-52) and *Aion* was written..

13 He also had inconjuncts from Venus and Mercury *in Cancer* to his Ascendant degree. A good, intuitive listener, Jung was slow to pin diagnostic labels on his patients.

14 The relationship between Saturn and the Moon is discussed in Chapter 10, Capricorn. In astrology, the Moon and Saturn are interesting counterparts, the Moon has a twenty-eight *day* transit cycle and Saturn has a twenty-eight *year* cycle. In the Natural Zodiac, Saturn rules the Tenth House (Career) which is opposite the Fourth House (Home/ Personal Life). We all struggle for balance between planning and creativity, practicality and imagination.

15 Because the progressed Moon and transiting Saturn both have twenty-eight year orbits, progressed Moon-square-Natal-Moon occurs within a year or so of Saturn-square-natal-Saturn. There's a natural focus on the Creative Imagination at the end of every seven-year Saturn cycle, the square, opposition, and conjunction (Return) years.

said that while she understood the importance of altruism, (the Water Carrier who pours from the bottomless "Cup" to those in need,) she also "saw" the Grail Cup as a symbol of the Self, a source of *personal* inspiration on her journey to Wholeness.

After reading *Archetypes,* she bought a chalice at a metaphysical bookstore and placed it on her alter as a reminder her receptive, feminine side. "The source from which scientific discoveries emerge is surely *a lunar source,* the Creative Imagination," she said. I found the insight valuable.

After this conversation, I looked for biographies of women with Aquarius Rising, wondering how they moved beyond the masculine planets, Saturn and Uranus, beyond scientific methodology and clinical impartiality, to feeling and intuition.[16]

Two women authors have Aquarius Rising, Alice Munro, Canadian winner of the Man Booker International Award[17], whose short stories are featured in the *Atlantic* and the *New Yorker,* and whose novel, *The Lives of Girls and Women* became a Hollywood movie, and Joyce Carol Oates, well-known American author and creative writing teacher.

Oates has written myriad novels, short stories, essays and critical reviews. She once remarked that she hates the word *prolific,* which most of my Capricorn Rising clients consider a compliment. She'd probably find the Saturn term *productive* just as bad! "Insightful, innovative, and original," the Uranus' adjectives, would probably appeal more to her.

One of the few professors to teach at a major American university without a doctorate,[18] Oates is valued by academia as a prestigious novelist[19] and an excellent creative writing teacher.

Saturn is in her First House (conjunct the Second House cusp) and makes a symbolic square to her Moon. (It's too loose to be called an aspect.) Though she admits to being obsessive about her work, (see below, The Mode: Fixity) she also sees it as play. Oates

---

16 If Aquarians neglect their feminine side, they may become so totally absorbed in their work that Life seems arid, narrow and lonely. Successful Aquarians sometimes have an arrogant attitude like Fitzgerald's. He became angry when airport bookstores didn't stock his novels; he once yelled at an employee, *"don't you know who I am? I'm Scott Fitzgerald! I wrote the Great Gatsby!"* Behind the attitude, though, was fear of being forgotten. His literacy legacy was important to him.

17 In 2009, for her body of work. A master craftsman, she manages to say as much in a short story as many authors do in a novel. She's unsentimental and often uses the omniscient narrator perspective.

18 Princeton University.

19 Winner of the National Book Award, Oates was twice nominated for the Pulitzer prize and is rumored to be on the short list for the Nobel in literature.

has Jupiter-in-Pisces (Rulership) in her First House, and like many others with Sun-in-Gemini, she loves both her careers.

Uranus is in her Second House, conjunct the cusp of her Third, (Mind; Communication.) Interviewer Alfred Kazin said that though she answered every question, she responded in such an aloof, detached way that he "wondered if she were really there." When asked about this later, Oates said that in the 1950's and 1960's, after she'd already been published in national magazines, she was reviewed under the headline, "Local Housewife Writes Play." *Housewife indeed!*

The Aquarian Mask is a very effective shield; it can throw an interviewer off his game. It's good at deflecting personal questions. When asked if she and her husband had children, she responded, "No. I suppose I lack the maternal gene." Yet, as a teacher, she helps many budding novelists. Her Moon is in the Twelfth House, opposite Venus and Pluto in Cancer in the Sixth (Service.)[20] In Alice Munro's horoscope, neither Saturn nor Uranus is in a particularly strong House, but Natal Saturn (opposite Sun/Pluto) makes more aspects than Uranus. Uranus-in-Pisces is intercepted in Munro's Second House. (Finances) The couple experienced financial upheaval during her first marriage, but life became easier in her forties. Her second husband[21] was better off financially, and her career gained momentum.

She also has Moon Exalted in Taurus in the Fourth, square her Ascendant Degree and three Cancer planets, (including the Sun and Exalted Jupiter,) in her Sixth. In a 1974 interview with the *London Free Press,* Munro said, "I'm so glad I had my children when I did. I'm terribly glad that I had them. Yet I have to realize that I probably wouldn't have had them if I'd had the choice."[22]

---

20 She wrote in her journal, "the maternal instinct seems lacking in me." Quoted in *Invisible Writer: A Biography of Joyce Carol Oates*, by Greg Johnson, (NY: Dutton,) 1998, p. 160. Moon-in-Detriment in Capricorn or Aquarius is discussed in Chapter 10. For the 1972 Kazim interview, see Johnson, p 178. Munro, too, was asked personal questions like "how do your children deal with the embarrassment of not having a normal mother?" Alice responded, "if they still have any embarrassment, they gallantly cover it up. Since adolescence, my daughters have become friends," Sheila A. Munro, *Lives of Mothers and Daughters: Growing up with Alice Munro,* (NY: Union Square Press,) 2001, 206; 239.

21 She marred a man she'd known in college, but had not dated at the time, geographer Gerald Fremlin.

22 *Ibid*, Sheila A. Munro, the interview is quoted on page 39. The memoir is about Alice Munro and her oldest daughter Sheila's attempts at finding her niche as a writer. Neptune and Venus are both inconjunct Alice Munro's Ascendant degree, forming a Yod to it. Munro has both a T-square and a Grand Trine.

Alice dropped out of college at twenty to marry, then set up her typewriter next to the washing machine. While her children napped, she hid from her neighbors and wrote in the laundry room. After her divorce, (see the Mask after Midlife) she traveled from campus to campus, as writer-in-residence. At sixty-nine, she's developing new stories and adapting her earlier work for movies and CBC documentaries.[23]

I've observed a similar pattern to Munro's and Oates' with Aquarius Rising women, particularly with those with the Moon in *Houses 4, 8 and 12.* I wonder if other astrologers have noticed it as well.

The imaginative or psychic houses seem to absorb the Moon's energies in creative projects; parenting comes second, if at all. Yet, Aquarius Rising Mothers seem, like Munro, very happy to have their children as friends once they've become young adults. Through enjoyable conversations, Aquarius Rising learns from the perspective of Gen X or Gen Y. Curious about the future, they like to keep up with the trends.

The Esoteric Ruler - Jupiter

Aquarius the Water Carrier is said to be an altruist, a true humanitarian. Some say he symbolizes Mankind at his most generous. In art, Aquarius is usually represented by an angel or by a young man holding aloft his bottomless water pot.[24] When I first came across the Water Carrier symbol, I thought of Rudhyard Kipling's poem about the water carrier in the British army, the one that ends, "you're a better man than I am, Gunga Din."

"Aquarius must be like Gunga Din! Amidst flying bullets, without a thought for himself or his safely, Gunga Din dashed across the battlefield to ladle out water for the thirsty troops. Aquarius must be the Zodiac's most unselfish Sign," I thought.

Later, I learned about the different behavior patterns of the mundane and esoteric (spiritual) rulers. At the mundane level, a well-aspected natal Jupiter seems to inflate the Ego's prowess and expand its ambitions. Evel Knieval's First House Jupiter enhanced his adventurous, risk-taking nature and his desire for fame.

Transiting Jupiter also provides opportunities like travel and study, which *expand our awareness.* This is especially true of the Return Years (ages 12, 24, 36, 48, 60, 72, etc). While Knieval thought up greater personal challenges (involving shark tanks and jumping over

---

23 John Updike compared her to Chekhov, and other reviewers compare her to Faulkner. To me, she seems more like Flannery O'Connor.

24 See the reference to different types of Cups in "The Mask" section at the beginning of this chapter. The Grail Quest is discussed in the Aquarian chapter of *Archetypes of the Zodiac.*

canyons and rivers), other Aquarius Rising people learned foreign languages, studied, traveled or lived abroad,(Jung, Capote, Fitzgerald,) or acquired graduate degrees at home.

A Jupiter Return sometimes coincides with a Saturn cycle. When this happens, Jupiter tends to ease Saturn's tensions and/or loneliness. Jung's break with Freud occurred after Saturn-square-Saturn at thirty-five. Then, on the Jupiter Return, at thirty-six he went to Africa. The voyage expanded his perspective on human nature.

At the end of his life, Jung's editor at Bollingen Publicatons asked him to make a list of the important events for his autobiography. He replied that the inner life was more important to him than the outer, so there were few such events, *but he'd like to write about his trip to Africa.*[25]

Our openness to cultures that view life differently from ours seems enhanced in Jupiter Return cycles. Because we're ready to expand our horizons, our journeys, like Jung's Africa trip, are often memorable.

The Second Saturn Return (58-60) also overlaps with the Jupiter Return at sixty. Clients who told me how exhausted they were at the end of the Second Saturn Return have also mentioned feeling energized by a "Jupiter Return trip." However, most of these clients chose a country they'd always wanted to visit, and most of them stayed a month or longer.

Though travel in itself is a mundane Jupiter experience and only rarely results in spiritual ecstasy or healing as it did for Simone Weil in Assisi, (see Chapter 9) when outside their familiar comfort zone many people seem to release tensions; learn, adapt and grow.

Esoteric Aquarians practice unselfish, impartial love. The difference in levels can be subtle; it involves the individual's intentions and motivation.

At the mundane level, Aquarius Rising will show up to serve on a committee if it's convenient for him. If he does, it's likely that his friends are on it, too. He'd prefer to be chairman and ensure that his ideas are used. But if he or a close friend *isn't* elected chairman, and if the particular committee *isn't* that important to his resume, he'll probably drop out. He's likely to decide the committee wasn't a good opportunity after all.

If he does stay, he's unlikely to put his energy into *fighting for the cause*—he's not an

---

25 In the end, Bollingen didn't bring out *Memories, Dreams, Reflections,* though they had published Jung's *Collected Works. MDR* was a different kind of book, about his inner life. It was unusually revealing for someone with Aquarius Rising. Even today, it's still his most popular book.

Aries or a Sagittarian—but he'll write brilliant letters and give inspiring, even rousing speeches. He makes useful contributions.[26]

President Barack H. Obama, a former community organizer, has Aquarius Rising. Without detracting from the value of his service as a young man in the inner city, one might note that it didn't proceed entirely from unselfish love. It provided an entry into Chicago politics; he moved onward and upward.

The "Angel," or esoteric Aquarian, on the other hand, will drop whatever she's doing at a moment's notice and rush to the airport, fly cross-country to help a friend who just lost her husband or her child, in Iraq.

She'll contact everyone in her friend's address book; run errands, tidy up, cook, pick people up at the airport, take them to the memorial service and drive them back afterwards. She'll do whatever menial chores are required. She'll stay as long as needed. Sometimes she's exhausted afterwards. No gold stars appear on this Water Carrier's resume. But then, angels don't expect them.

During the Second World War, (which gave Jung nightmares long before it began,) so many German-Jewish psychologists arrived in Zurich that Swiss analysts at his Institute began to complain to Jung. Why was he referring patients to German Jewish refugees instead of *them,* Swiss psychologists who could use the business?

When, at the end of his life, Jung chose his German secretary, Aniela Jaffe to transcribe and edit his autobiography, *Memories Dreams Reflections,* others were unhappy with his decision. They argued, "the war is over! It's time to give a Swiss the task and the royalties?" "Why not a member of your own family! Why *her*? Nobody even likes her!" But Jung knew she would do it well *and* she really needed the money.[27]

Though esoteric Aquarians may be detached, they're not indifferent to others' suffering. Jupiter is compassionate, merciful and generous. Sometimes though, even for the angels, one "Jupiter obstacle" remains, pride.

---

26 Jeanne Avery was the first to make this point in print, in *The Rising Sign: Your Astrological Mask,* (NY: Doubleday,) 1982, "Aquarius." It's especially interesting now, with an Aquarius Rising U.S. President whose critics would like him to respond with more *fire.* "No Drama Obama," however, sees himself as a "problem solver" whose time is better spent resolving problems than venting about them.

27 Bair, cited above, 604. Aniela Jaffe was lonely and practically penniless in her old age. Jung, not only brought many refugees to Zurich during the war, he even accepted financial responsibility for patients who, like Aniela, couldn't pay him. He remained supportive to them in peacetime. Authors Jolande Jacobi and Aniela Jaffe are the most famous, but he helped many others, people he barely knew. He wrote to England on behalf of Heinrich Zimmer, and to the US, asking friends to help Jews settle abroad.

Walidad the Simple Hearted

There was once an old grass cutter who lived alone at the edge of a jungle in India. He had a sense of wonder and a great appreciation for beauty. Walidad was also "a man who knew who he was."

Prudent and resourceful, he had collected his meager savings over the years, dropping the coins into a pot.

One day, he noticed that the pot was full. He didn't need coins anymore now that he was a hermit. But, what to do with them? One day, he had an idea. He walked to the nearest town with his coins, had them melted and fashioned into a golden bracelet. He would give it to the young Princess of the East, for he admired her youth and her great beauty.

When the bracelet was ready, he sent it anonymously. Now that he had disposed of his worldly possessions, he would enjoy his solitude, and she would enjoy the bracelet. He thought the problem was resolved.

But he was wrong. When the messenger arrived at the Eastern palace, the King and Queen stared at the anonymous gift and were filled with grave concern. The bracelet was quite valuable. What mysterious stranger had designs on their daughter?

After discussing the problem, they decided she could keep it, for they had no desire to offend an important potentate. No doubt it was sent by a handsome prince who lived in a faraway kingdom. Eventually, they would meet him. But first they must send a tasteful, equally expensive gift.

And so, several months later the poor grass cutter looked out of his hut in amazement. There was his messenger coming across the grassland laden with heavy bolts of silk. Now, what was he to do with those?

He asked the messenger for the name of the most handsome, virtuous man he'd ever heard of, someone who could put the silk to good use.

"Well, there's the prince of the West," said the messenger.

"All right, take him the cloth, but don't tell him it came from me," sighed the grass cutter, feeling more irritated than peaceful.

The Prince of the West was pleasantly surprised, though somewhat confused by the anonymous gift. He accepted it and sent off a dozen thoroughbred horses with the messenger.

"Oh, no!" said the old grass cutter when he saw the horses. He gave the messenger two and sent the rest to the Princess of the East.

"Ten beautiful Arabian horses just arrived from my mysterious young suitor," said the princess happily to her father.

"Well, we certainly can't refuse those horses," said the King, "the Prince would be so insulted you'd never get to meet him. But this gift exchange is becoming very costly!" He sent the mysterious Prince ten mules laden with silver.

"What now? Mules bearing silver chests!" sighed the old man. He gave six to the messenger and sent the other six to the Prince of the West.

A wealthy man who would not be outdone, the Prince of the West sent twenty elephants and twenty camels bearing precious jewels. After receiving two camels and two elephants, the messenger left for the East with the rest.

The King of the East was astonished to see a long caravan coming, elephants, camels and jewels that glowed in the sunlight! "This can only mean one thing," he thought, "that Prince intends to marry my daughter!" He demanded that the messenger take the royal family to the suitor at once.

The frightened messenger could not tell the King the truth, lest he be killed for disrespecting the King and Queen and deceiving the Princess. In fear and trepidation, he led the royal family through the jungle towards the grasslands and the hermit's hut.

When they were half a day's ride from their destination, the travelers set up their tents for the night. But as soon as the others were asleep, the messenger leapt on his horse and galloped off to warn the old man.

"The king will surely kill us in the morning for this deception," he shouted. He rode back to camp in dismay.

The old man was ashamed to meet the Princess. He looked down at his rags in sorrow. Pride led him to the edge of a cliff. He paced back and forth, but was afraid to throw himself into the chasm. Finally, he collapsed in sleep.

Suddenly, a bright light shone upon him and two angels woke him. "Why do you despair?" said the first. One touched his rags, while the other waved towards his hut. He saw it transformed into a palace, and looked down at his own rich robes. He wandered through the palace in confusion, till two servants appeared to place him on a bed of soft cushions.

At dawn, a trumpet sounded in the distance. His servants quickly dressed him before the royal party arrived. The messenger, who rode in front to guide them, stared in bewilderment at the old man and the palace. The servants, meanwhile, were setting out a rich feast.

"If you want to marry my daughter, you have my permission," said the King, after eating his fill.

"Oh, no, I'm much too old for her," said Walidad, the man who knew who he was. "She must meet and marry the Prince of the West; I know for a fact that he's a *very* generous man.

And so the two met, fell in love and married in the old man's palace. Finally, the wedding party left with salutes; fanfare of flags and sounding trumpets. Walidad waved a frond of sweet smelling grass in farewell. He was not at all sad to see them go.

Having transcended pride and fear of humiliation; his spiritual journey was nearing its end.

The Element - Air

Air is about intelligence, communication skills, group interaction, networking, friendship, and "relating" in general. The Air Houses are the Relationship Houses in the Natural Zodiac, 3, 7 and 11.

Aquarius is the last and most complex of the Air Signs. Of the twelve Rising Signs, Aquarians are the most likely to compartmentalize personal and professional life; new friends and old friends, new loves and old loves, and to treat their children, adopted children and stepchildren equally. (The Eleventh House is the House of Children the World Gives Us.)

No matter how many projects Aquarius takes on, the Uranus-Aquarian seems to live "in the moment" while keeping up on everything, current events, hobbies, and the lives of old friends in faraway time zones.

The Saturn-Aquarian is a more patient listener than the other Air Signs. When both Saturn and Uranus are strong by house and aspects, Aquarius offers insights and/or elicits valuable insights from their students, clients and patients.

We often recommend Aquarius Rising professionals because they receive rave reviews like, "another great discussion! I feel so smart when I leave Professor Jones' class," or "I hear myself saying such amazing things in Dr. Smith's office, what a brilliant therapist! It's like looking at myself from across the room for an hour." Or, "I went to see Miss Doe feeling resistance; I didn't feel ready for the promotion, but I left convinced I could do it." (Or, the reverse, "I went in feeling ready and she convinced me I wasn't.")

Co-workers or clients usually enjoy Aquarius' whimsical sense of humor, especially when the Mask is enhanced by planets in Air. But Aquarian perspective, detachment and impartiality are often more appreciated at work than at home.

Children of Aquarius Rising parents have told me in frustration that Mom "always seemed just as interested, or more interested, in what the neighbor kid said as she was in *my* stories about *my* day."[28] The neighbor's child may have been a better story-teller! Like F. Scott Fitzgerald when his American guests turned up in Paris, or Truman Capote at a dinner party,[29] Aquarians enjoy a good story, especially one they might use later. Others' stories are new material for writers.

The Saturn Rulership notwithstanding, Aquarians seldom take themselves, their work or their lives *quite* as seriously as Capricorns. Air cannot exist in a vacuum; the Element is about Ideas and Ideals, which are to be circulated, discussed, and set into motion.

Every Air Ascendant has a Fire Sign, on the Seventh House Cusp, which means that Air Signs need other people to make things happen. There seems to be a connection between their health and their ability to circulate their ideas. Aquarians seem more content when they have an audience, in teaching, writing, publishing, volunteering, or just getting together to brainstorm about their new project with friends.

Aquarius, the Eleventh Sign, is analogous to the Eleventh House in the Natural Zodiac. Friendship is the most important Eleventh House theme. Ever curious, Aquarius keeps the dialogue open, communicating long distance, if sometimes infrequently, by email.

Conferences and other group gatherings are also Eleventh House activities. Aquarians are energized by new, useful information and concepts. At astrology conferences, they'll sit up all night talking. While others may purchase CDs and listen to certain talks several times, Aquarius has usually absorbed the information by the time the conference ends.

The Mode - Fixity

All the Fixed Masks have *presence,* but each has a different kind of magnetism. Unless Mercury is badly aspected, the Aquarius *persona* exudes intelligence and mental prowess. The Aquarian Mask isn't clever or glib like Gemini's, Aquarius actually seems brilliant.

Immanuel Kant, Karl Marx, Carl G. Jung, President Barack Obama and former Secretary

---

28 Sheila Munro said this about her mother, Alice Munro (see below.)
29 Capote supposedly lost several women friends who recognized themselves in his stories; Jacqueline Kennedy Onassis' sister, Lee Radziwill for instance. But he didn't mind being a character in others' stories. He enjoyed telling people that he was a "thinly veiled" character in Harper Lee's, *To Kill a Mockingbird.*

of State Condeleeza Rice wore (or wear) the aloof, cool, calm, and collected Aquarian Mask. A journalist who covers political campaigns observed a major difference in style between Bill Clinton (Libra Rising) and Barack Obama; while candidate Clinton would rush across the street to shake *your* hand, candidate Obama will smile, wave, and wait for you to cross to *him.*

High intelligence can be sexy. Both genders love to spar with Aquarius Rising! But intelligence can also come across as smug or elitist. Like the other Fixed Signs, Aquarians hold firmly to their opinions. Though not easily swayed by political partisans or evangelicals, like their Fixed polar opposite (Leo), most Aquarians are proud and vulnerable to flattery.

Like the other Fixed Signs, (Taurus, Leo, and Scorpio) Aquarius is known for perseverance and stubbornness. By the time they reach their forties, though, most Aquarians have become adept at identifying no win situations, letting go more quickly and moving on. (See below, The Mask after Midlife, F. Scott Fitzgerald.)

Aquarius is probably the most persuasive of all the Fixed Signs. Elizabeth Kubler-Ross (Pisces Rising) said that in her student years she often saw Doctor Jung walking along the streets of Zurich, smoking his pipe. Others would greet him and have brief conversations, but she'd cross quickly to the other side of the street. Determined to become a country doctor, she was superstitious about introducing herself to the great man. She knew several students who did so, and they all ended up as psychiatrists!

Not all who wear the Mask are brilliant. Sometimes, a high school dropout with Aquarius Rising and an excellent vocabulary may manage to convince an employer that he or she graduated from a prestigious university. Aquarius does so well at the interview that he's hired at once to teach, do PR work, or recruit others. He may even be chosen as the new head of sales. The interviewer may be so impressed that he doesn't bother checking with the Ivy League school on the resume.

But someday, when Aquarius is having lunch with co-workers, a stranger will appear at their table and say, "I heard you were at Harvard while I was there. A group of us are getting together next Thursday night. Why don't you join us? I'm embarrassed to say I don't remember you, but *I'm sure the others will!*" Eventually, there'll be a day of reckoning!

Some astrologers consider Aquarius Rising tolerant. I find that unless the Sun or Moon is in a Mutable Sign, "Saturn Aquarians" are often rigid in their views. Mutable planets have a live and let live approach to life.

The esoteric ruler (Jupiter) is also important. Travel expands Aquarius' horizons; they'll return from visiting countries with different forms of government, religions, cultures and economic systems still preferring their national approach, but realizing that people abroad are just as patriotic as they are and just as determined that theirs is the right way.

Fixity is often obsessive, especially when Aquarius Rising is enhanced by a Fixed Sun or Moon.

Zelda Fitzgerald resorted to acting out when she wanted her Aquarius Rising husband's attention; she complained to friends that he neglected her because of his work-obsession. His Fixed Taurus Moon (Exalted) on the Nadir was in square to his Ascendant. He adored Zelda; he "never met another woman as fascinating," but writing came first.

Emma Jung, the second richest woman in Switzerland and the mother of Jung's five children, shared her husband's attention and affection with analyst Toni Wolff.

Jung's horoscope was "triple" Fixed. With a Third House (Mind) Taurus Moon and a Leo Sun/Uranus conjunction on his Seventh House Cusp, Jung was attracted to brilliant women, and they, in turn, were fascinated with him. His Sun/Uranus seemed to provide the very insights they were seeking.

The Mask in Youth

Will young Aquarius Rising follow Saturn and Uranus into science? When both planets are in prominent houses, and form many aspects to other planets, it's quite possible.

A strongly placed Saturn might symbolize business or the professions. With Aquarius, anything's possible!

There are of course many other influences involved. The Sun Sign sets the agenda, and the Mask adapts. Parental influence, especially the father's, is important. If dad is a stockbroker, banker, doctor or attorney, the Aquarius Rising son may plan to follow him, eventually, into the family firm. He may wear the professional uniform, the dark suit and power tie, until his mid thirties or early forties.

A strongly-placed Moon (by House or aspect) may indicate literary or artistic talent. Truman Capote had Uranus in the First House (Pisces) and Moon/Saturn conjunct (Scorpio) in the Tenth.[30] His was an unusual *persona;* he was famous for his velvet jackets, his cravats, and his high-pitched voice.

For Capote, Uranus made more aspects than Saturn; restlessness and rebelliousness

---

30 Uranus-in-Pisces was in opposition to Mercury-in-Virgo and in square to Jupiter-in-Sagittarius, forming a "high strung," restless Mutable T-square. It helped that Jupiter and Mercury were both in Rulership. The missing point of the T-square was Gemini in the House of Creativity.

prevailed over discipline. Drugs and alcohol (Mars-in-the-First opposite Neptune-in-the-Seventh) distracted him from his work. Though his IQ was "genius-level," he didn't do well in school.

Determined to avoid college, which he considered "bad for writers," Capote went to work at seventeen, sorting articles and clipping cartoons for the *New Yorker.* He continued his association with the magazine for decades, long after *In Cold Blood* had become a best-seller and *Breakfast at Tiffany's* a movie. He enjoyed traveling abroad with the cast of "Porgy and Bess" and sending articles home to the magazine.

Novelist and short story writer Alice Munro has an Exalted Taurus Moon in her Fourth trine Mars and Saturn. A regional author, she writes of life in southwestern Ontario. She has the Sun, Pluto and Jupiter (Exalted) in Cancer and has three children, all girls. Several of her short stories feature the mother-daughter relationship theme.

As mentioned above, (Mundane Rulers) Alice has Uranus in her Second House. Earning one's living as a writer was "very unusual" in her region. When she was a child, "the only publisher we knew of produced textbooks. The only author we'd ever met was the baker's 'eccentric' (gay) son." Alice's choice was either to be "respectable" (Saturn) and marry before she became an old maid at twenty-five or to be viewed as eccentric. (Uranus.) Though highly intelligent, (she'd skipped a grade in school,) she dropped out of college to marry[31] when her two-year scholarship expired.

According to her daughter Sheila, Alice cultivated the respectable persona of wife and mother, but thought of writing as her real work.[32]

During her Saturn Return, (age thirty) the Munro in-laws visited from Eastern Canada and stayed a long time. In her new role as hostess, Alice had no time to write, and after they left, she found she couldn't write at all. She had panic attacks and developed an ulcer. At that time, the Saturn Return occurred in her Twelfth House opposed Sun/Pluto in the Sixth. Four years went by before she was able to write again.[33] Then, at thirty-five, she was surprised to find herself pregnant with a third child, her daughter Andrea.

---

31 She and her husband, James Munro, met as students. A manager for Eatons, the stationary chain, he was assigned to the Vancouver store and they moved West. He eventually opened Munro's Bookstore on Victoria Island.

32 Catherine Sheldrick Ross' biography of Munro is entitled, *A Double Life.* The title alludes to Munro's remark that she lived an "ordinary life" as wife and mother, and lived a separate life through her work, Sheila Munro, cited above, 100.

33 *Mothers and Daughters,* cited above. Sheila Munro said her mother had a public personality for the neighbors, and a second personality while doing her "real work." It sounds similar to Yeats' poem about himself as the "smiling public man." (See Capricorn Rising.) And also to Jung's "Personality Number One" and "Personality Number Two, in *Memories, Dreams, Reflections.*

Joyce Carol Oates, whose novels span many different genres, also has more aspects to Saturn than Uranus, though both ruling planets aspect Neptune, the storytelling planet, in the Seventh House. Her Moon is in the psychic Twelfth.

Daughters usually have more freedom of choice than sons. With a Leo or Libra Sun, Aquarius Rising girls may choose art, design, or music. If they're born at the end of Aquarius, the Mask will progress into Pisces early, contacting natal Water planets. They may choose a non-traditional (Uranian) direction, like the arts or computer design, instead of teaching, nursing, or social work, the conventional (Saturn) professions for women.

The color and style of her apparel provide a clue to the path she chooses, and the ruling planet she favors at the time. Does she wear the bright colors, long hair, long skirts and shawls or capes of an artist? In college, does she dress and style her hair like her peers, or does she dress with Uranus-flair?

The father's daughter tend towards a sophisticated Armani look. She wears dark business suits with colorful scarves or blouses. However, if her Armani suit conceals several tattoos, she's likely to break out in a Uranian, unconventional way (as if changing her planetary ruler) in her forties.

For "father's daughters" and "father's sons," the Uranus-opposite-Uranus cycle (between 39 and 42) often coincides with a shift towards originality, unconventionality, and sometimes brings out the eccentricity that astrologers associate with this Rising Sign.

If Uranus' placement is much stronger than Saturn's in the horoscope, Aquarius may not feel a need to change his Mask at thirty or forty; Truman Capote didn't. The Aquarian free spirit may already be liberated and unconventional enough!

The Saturn-square-Saturn transit, which occurs in the mid-thirties, often coincides with breaking off from authority figures. This has been true of many Saturn-ruled astrology clients.

Jung broke with Freud at thirty-six. At thirty-four, Jiddhu Krishnamurti, protégé of C.W. Leadbeater and surrogate son of Annie Besant (see Aries Rising) announced that he was dissolving the Order of the Star and leaving Theosophy.

The Order had prepared him to become the "vehicle" through which the Great Teacher would one day come. Besant was present at the 1929[34] gathering of 3,000 Theosophists when he made the announcement. Later, he returned all the Order's property to the Theosophical Society, including a castle in the Netherlands. He intended to continue his work "of setting people free to find the Truth," but he "would be no guru and would accept no followers."

---

34 C.W. Leadbeater was then living in Sydney Australia, working on behalf of Theosophy.

The "Sage of Ojai," (California) had both Saturn and Uranus in his Ninth House, (Philosophy and Religion) but too far apart for a conjunction.

Krishnamurthi included this anecdote in his resignation speech:

> You may remember the story of how the devil and a friend of his were walking down the street, when they saw ahead of them a man stoop down and pick up something from the ground, look at it, and put it away in his pocket. The friend said to the devil.
>
> 'What did that man pick up?'
>
> 'He picked up a piece of the truth,' said the devil.
>
> 'That's a very bad business for you, then,' said his friend.
>
> 'Oh, not at all,' 'the devil replied,
>
> *"I'm going to help him organize it."*
>
> I maintain that truth is a pathless land, and you cannot approach it by any path whatsoever, by any religion, by any sect. That is my point of view, and I adhere to that absolutely and unconditionally.

Many Aquarius Rising people have voiced similar opinions in their late thirties and early forties.

Saturn is associated with society's "shoulds," "oughts," and "musts." And, as Robert Louis Stevenson said, (see list of quotes, above) in order to keep your soul alive, it's important to know what *you* prefer rather than continue on humbly saying "amen" to everyone else's preferences.

When we reach an age that's a multiple of seven, (14, 21, 28, 35, 42, etc,) we often feel restricted by others' expectations, or by conditions beyond our control. With her Gemini Sun Sign, Joyce Carol Oates has *two* professional images to maintain. In her youth, she was also a perfectionist.

During her Saturn Return, Joyce and her husband, Professor Raymond Smith, lived near the University of Detroit campus. In 1967, riots and looting occurred nearby. Until the house sold a year later, they both commuted from Detroit to Windsor University, across the lake, in Ontario, Canada.

Joyce juggled two successful careers, one as "Mrs. Smith," the professor, and the other as Joyce Carol Oates, award-winning novelist. However, public lectures resulted in panic attacks and stomach pain.

Her husband had arranged a sabbatical in London, and, fortunately, she was able take a leave of absence and accompany him.[35] Joyce didn't like to fly, so they sailed. At thirty-three, she feared having a nervous breakdown. She described her feelings in the novel, *Plot*. She didn't want to return to Windsor where she was stalked by fans. A student once took a cab fifty miles to her house.

Oates has Natal Saturn in her First House (conjunct the cusp of her Second), sextile Mercury, and closely inconjunct Neptune. During the Saturn Return year, transiting Saturn activated these natal aspects. Over the next two years, it formed squares to Chiron (she mourned the loss of her grandmother, to whom she was very close) and to her three Cancer planets.

As her literary reputation grew, she felt adrift, or at sea (Neptune) and "rootless" (Cancer planets.) For Joyce, the stress resulted in "an almost total lack of appetite;" she became anorexic and suffered from insomnia.

She felt that her life was out-of-control, which is frightening for a First House Saturn person, especially when Saturn-in-the-First also rules the Ascendant. A client once described it as, "the feeling that the Mask is going to crack along the tension lines."

On the ship to England, Oates wrote author Gail Godwin that she felt "spiritually exhausted," and "hoped to escape with the blob of protoplasm that's left." In their London apartment, she sat by the French windows and stared out at Hyde Park.

Then, one day, Oates had what she called "a spontaneous mystical experience that lay beyond the scope of language," lasted for five to eight minutes and made her "aware of the relative unimportance of (her) ego." At first it was frightening, but she surrendered to the "selfless experience."

She felt as if her atoms were splitting apart and she was dissolving. She suddenly realized that she didn't exist in the way she'd always thought; in fact, "she" didn't exist at all. Her ego surrendered to a larger, transcendent reality.

When she returned to normal awareness after the "psychic upheaval," her "conscious attitude" was transformed. Oates' perspective had shifted from narrow "skepticism and existentialism." She was filled with "abundant energy" to begin new manuscripts, and for years afterward had numinous dreams. Her insomnia was gone, and she began to gain weight.

For a short time, a Portuguese figure named Fernandes "seemed to possess" her. He

---

35 First Raymond commuted to teach at the Windsor, while Joyce combined teaching at the University of Detroit and Wayne State with writing novels, poems, and short stories. Then, around the time Raymond became English Department Chairman, Joyce was also hired at Windsor. By then, she was as prolific as the Capricorn Rising authors (see Chapter 10.)

wanted her to tell others his stories for him. She "transcribed" and published several as "his translator."[36]

She told Gail Godwin that she used to think it was "myself versus the world, but I now I know it was myself versus different parts of myself."

After her mystical experience Oates "felt very guilty" about the dark, tragic ending of her novel, *Wonderland*. Because she "had made a grave error," she wrote her editor, asking permission to rewrite it and offering to pay for the printer's plates herself. The editor agreed.

She now felt the need to take a moral position in her novels. It was no longer enough simply to show the reader society's dark side in a detached, "existentialist" way.

After reading about others' similar experiences, Oates wrote, "we're all fireflies in the Void." She wrote that we need to let go of our childish prejudices and past suffering. We need to live in the moment.[37]

The Mask After Midlife
"La Volonte a quoi faire?"
Georges Bernanos

"You say that you want to be free. *But free to do what?*" the astrologer asks the forty-year-old client. In the early stages of his Uranus-opposite-Uranus cycle, the client is usually unable to answer. He just feels a strong urge to make a change. One man said he felt as if all the oxygen was being sucked out of the room, and he'd die if he remained any longer in the same circumstances.

This cycle is best understood and appreciated by hindsight, after the dust settles. I don't know if there is a seven year itch, but there's definitely an *early forties itch!* Between ages thirty-nine and forty two, regardless of Rising Sign, we're all "free spirits," whether or not we choose to act on the impulse to change our lives.

Aquarius Rising will often break free and develop their unique gifts at this time. Even if

---

36 Johnson, cited above, 206-08. If her mind were allowed to daydream she'd be in Portugal, a place she had never visited, "with a refined, perhaps snobbish bachelor in his fifties." The "Fernandes' collection" received bad reviews.

37 Johnson, cited above, pp 206-219. Jung was one of the authors she read. Zen seems to have helped in understanding her vision. Several of my clients with Aquarius Rising are practitioners of Buddhist meditation techniques, such as mindfulness and, especially in the Pisces progression, loving kindness and compassion.

they've pushed very hard against the "Saturn limits" between thirty-five and thirty-seven, their personal, professional, creative or spiritual lives may take a new direction around forty.

The House where Natal Uranus is located and the House opposite it, where Uranus is transiting, together signify the "breakthrough environment." The Aquarian Mask will change as the new *persona* reflects the lifestyle shift. Aquarius' spouse and co-workers may experience this as (Aquarius') "delayed adolescent rebellion."

This is true not only true of Natal Uranus in Houses 1, 4, 7, or 10, but of Houses Two and Eight as well. Sometimes an Eighth House inheritance or the sale of joint property following a (Seventh House) divorce enables Aquarius Rising to move on.

With Natal Uranus in Houses Six or Twelve, Mutable Houses in the Natural Zodiac, the cycle may involve creativity, spirituality, or both. Sometimes there's a change in religious affiliation or a separation from the meditation group, and sometimes the change is more subtle. They may move from one art form to another, or leave a service-oriented profession (House Six) for psychic work or artistic projects (House Twelve.) One client, an editor with Uranus in the Sixth, said that she, "left a hectic job to write *my own* books," enjoying the solitude (Twelfth House) of her mountain cabin.

Transiting Uranus opposing a Natal Sun/Uranus conjunction may signify a breakthrough in self-awareness or lead to a new discovery. For Carl Jung, both occurred. As psychoanalyst with Natal Sun/Uranus in his Sixth House (Health and Service), Jung saw patients, wrote, and lectured. He also had family responsibilities. By his late thirties, he was a very busy man.

When he was forty, after a frightening vision of a deluge, Jung made time for his inner journey of self-discovery. He bought a "costly notebook" for the project, which he called *The Red Book;* closed the door to his home office and told his family not to disturb him. He'd been having "an incessant stream of fantasies" and he was ready to "pursue the inner images."

Jung wrote in his notebook that by forty, he'd attained reputation, financial security, everything he'd ever wanted, and his desire for more such "trappings" ebbed away. *But he had lost touch with his soul.*[38]

On Uranus opposite his Natal Sun/Uranus, Jung began to dialogue with his inner

---

38 "My soul, where are you? Do you hear me? I speak—I call you, are you there? I have returned. I am here again....I am with you." The images, or figures, that appeared next seemed to have a life of their own, apart from his. *The Red Book,* Sonu Shamdasani, ed, (NY: Norton & Norton,) 2009, *Liber Novis,* 231-32. The dialogue with Philemon is in *Liber Secundus,* 312 -314. See also the epilogue.

images, the parts of his psyche represented by Philemon and Baucis, Elijah and Salome, Simon Magus, Helen, a black Snake (his anima) and an Egyptian figure, Ka. He filled the notebook with his questions and their answers.[39]

Philemon taught him that magic couldn't be understood by the rational mind nor could it be taught, but a seeker could discover it himself. And that magic could be very useful in helping others.

Jung, whose Sun was in Leo, described the "humbling process" of opening himself to these inner figures as "climbing down a series of ladders to myself." In the beginning, he saw himself wearing a heavy suit of mail. His anima (the black Snake) asked him why he needed such powerful defenses!

He also sketched in his notebook. He drew his tower at Bollingen, which he said symbolized the continuity of his past, present, and the person he was to become. Jung's Bollingen tower, Yeats' Thoor Ballylee, and the philosopher-poet's tower in Nietzsche's *Prologue to Zarathustra,* were havens of solitude away from the busy pace of urban life.[40]

Jung continued his "descent into Hell" through a desert where he met and questioned an early Christian hermit. As he neared the end of his journey, the images began to change. Salome, who was blind in the beginning, could see when he met her again. When Jung realized that *he* had healed Salome, who was a part of himself, he knew that he was closer to Wholeness.[41]

When Jung first took the time to get in touch with his soul, he thought of his journey as personal. Later, though, he found that he'd also made an important psychological discovery. Previously, psychiatrists had thought of the personality as unified, except for psychotic patients. Jung had proven that Wholeness does not come easily, that the human personality is complex.

Jung's descent into the world of images is now known as Active Imagination. Today, Jungians enter into similar dialogues with their dream- images.

---

39 Ka was "rooted or grounded" while Philemon represented "meaning." By studying alchemy, he learned to integrate them. Jung once told analyst Barbara Hannah that he never let a figure leave until it had explained why it had come. Barbara Hannah, *Jung: His Life and Work,* (NY: Perigree,) 1981, 115.

40 See Capricorn Rising, "Yeats," and Scorpio Rising, "Nietzsche." Most of "George" Yeats' automatic writing was done in their tower. Jung worked with *The Red Book* for sixteen years. Then he received *Secret of the Golden Flower,* which, "explained the alchemical symbolism." After that, his research took a new direction. He and Marie-Louise von Franz (Scorpio Rising) explored alchemy.

41 In his autobiography, *Memories, Dreams, Reflections,* (NY: Vantage Books,) 1973, 176-188, Jung explained that Salome's ability to see meant that *he* was now able to see; he "got the message."

Some of us, like Jung, have a prominent Uranus, and, like Jung, we began a project that was "just for ourselves" in our early forties. Later, we were surprised to find that others, intrigued with our results, attempted the same process or activity. Uranus is the planet of the unexpected; Uranians are explorers and trend-setters.

Jung wrote that his sixteen years spent with the *Red Book* were the most important of his life; everything that came later was derived from those years. Afterwards, it was merely a matter of classification.

As transiting Uranus continued on through his First and Second Houses, Jung assimilated the discoveries made on his inner journey. His Mask reflected his changing interests. In his youthful photo, (1900,) he wore a business suit and an earnest expression suitable for a young doctor. This Mask contrasts with the midlife photos of Jung in Deidre Bair's biography.

In the later photos, "Herr Professor Jung" is dressed in tweed jackets or in shirtsleeves, holding his pipe. He was unconcerned that, as Toni Wolff warned, other doctors would see him "as a quack or a charlatan" for taking up "alchemy, folklore, mythology and discussing his patients' art."[42]

Similarly, clients with *both* Saturn and Uranus strong by house placement will often move from the former ruler to the latter by their latte forties. They re-invent themselves; their Masks adapt to suit their new identities. If a relative says, "you're becoming eccentric," they may respond with, "no, I'm authentically myself." Conventional opinion ceases to matter. By fifty, they can answer Bernanos' question. They know *what it is* that they needed to be free to do.

In the more extraverted Houses, the Uranus cycle favors risk-taking in the *outer* world. Some people become entrepreneurs. While new ventures undertaken in their early forties don't always succeed, most Aquarians are happy that they "bet on themselves," cut loose and tried new things, like self-employment or a different career.

F. Scott Fitzgerald left Paris in his forties and moved to Hollywood, hoping to launch a new career as a screenplay writer. Zelda was miserable there, surrounded in her forties by young, talented actresses. She returned to Montgomery, Alabama.

Fitzgerald complained that he wasted nearly seven years of his life attempting to save

---

42 She and others noted that he no longer discussed patient case histories at his seminars. And their friendship ended abruptly. Bair, cited above, 395;399. He replied that the alchemical process was a metaphor for Individuation. On her gravestone, he wrote the Chinese character for spinster or nun, an odd way or perceiving a former mistress. Emma, on the other hand, he called his "queen." (Leo was on his Seventh House Cusp. It's reminiscent of Scott Fitzgerald and his wife, the Queen of Jazz.)

"Tender is The Night." In the end, he failed to persuade the Hollywood studio to use the dialogue in his novel. They insisted that it wasn't credible coming from the box office stars chosen for the main roles. Later, he wished he'd started *The Last Tycoon* earlier instead of going to Hollywood.[43]

But his time there wasn't entirely wasted. Fitzgerald learned that he was a novelist, not a playwright. And more important, the stubborn author learned that in a no win situation, it's better to give up and move on sooner, rather than later.

When Saturn-Aquarians who are credentialed in business or the professions change careers on Uranus-opposite-Uranus, they seem to do so with minimum upheaval. Teachers, for instance, become real estate or insurance agents. However, if the change doesn't work, Saturn-Aquarians seem more upset than Uranians. Sun-in-Earth people who have a strongly-placed Saturn, for instance, really hate losing money, especially if the new career doesn't provide a salary or pension benefits. Some return to teaching.

The Uranians are likely to say, by hindsight, "well, I wasn't getting any younger. I thought, "if not now, when *will* I try this? And I'm glad I did."[44]

In the 1980's, many Baby Boomers who went through the Uranus cycle were involved in Multi-Level Marketing (MLM.) One client with Natal Uranus in her Second told me that after the third MLM product, her friends stopped returning her calls! A Uranus cycle may coincide with involvement in a cultural or economic trend like MLM.

Sometimes a trend or an original (Uranus) project lasts six-and-a-half to seven years, coinciding with Uranus' transit through one of the twelve Signs. I've noticed this pattern in the lives of clients who are writers and artists.[45] For instance, F. Scott Fitzgerald's books usually took six to seven years from start to finish. And six years elapsed between Truman

---

43 One screenwriting collaborator remarked that though everyone thought the man a genius, working with him was like interacting with all the Karamatzov brothers at once. Others found his style too literary for films. Arthur Krystal, "Slow Fade, F. Scott Fitzgerald in Hollywood," *The New Yorker,* November 16. 2009, pp. 36-41.

44 Robert Louis Stevenson relocated to Samoa on Uranus-opposite-Uranus, in hopes his health would improve. It was a major change for the Scottish barrister-turned-novelist. The Samoans called him "Storyteller." He lived to forty-four. His last, unfinished manuscript, *Weir of Hermiston,* is considered his best work. *Treasure Island* and *The Strange Case of Dr. Jekyll and Mr. Hyde* are his most popular books.

45 It takes the same length of time for the progressed Moon to move through a quadrant of the horoscope (three houses) marking the beginning and end of a particular cycle of creativity. While Saturn Returns occur once every 28-30 years, Uranus returns to its Natal position only once, around the age of 84. (Uranus takes seven years per Sign, times twelve Signs, equals 84 years.)

Capote's trip to Kansas to research the murder case and the publication of his novel about it.[46]

Jung's autobiography, *Memories, Dreams, Reflections* also took six years from the first three chapters, which Jung wrote himself, through Aniela Jaffe's interviews, transcription, editing, and translation.

After *MDR* appeared posthumously, Jung's astrologer-daughter, Gret Baumann-Jung wrote an interesting article about the transits of Saturn and Uranus to his birth chart at the time the autobiography was published. She demonstrated how, even after death, transits to the Natal chart continue to describe a person's influence and changing public image.[47]

MDR remains Jung's most popular book. Because he was open about his personal experiences and feelings, his public image changed. His earlier books were read mainly by other psychologists. But in *MDR*, he revealed his inner life in "a moving and lyrical style."[48] Readers of his autobiography appreciated Jung for more than his brilliant, objective, clinical insights. After sharing his personal journey, Jung was no longer viewed simply as a cool, distant, detached scientist.[49]

On Uranus-trine-Uranus around age fifty-six, insights and changes from the early forties are absorbed. The frenetic restlessness, urgency and/or boredom diminish. On the Second Saturn Return at fifty-eight like many of us, he experienced the loss of old friends. During Great Depression, others were unable to continue funding the Vision Seminar workshops,[50] but he wasn't troubled about finances; intuitively he knew the money would come.

By the end of his life, he seemed comfortable with subjectivity. *MDR* was written *as*

---

46 *In Cold Blood.*

47 Monika Wikman, "On the Life and Work of Gret Baumann-Jung," *Spring Journal*, 1999, Issue #66: "Divinations," pp.146 -161. When *MDR* appeared, transiting Jupiter was trine Jung's Natal Uranus and transiting Saturn made its Third Return, reinforcing his Natal Saturn-Jupiter trine. Gret also wrote that *during his most creative years,* his two Ascendant rulers were often transiting Jung' Natal Saturn, Uranus, or Jupiter (And the progressed Moon, ruling Jung's "new" Cancer Mask, was conjunct progressed Uranus, for changes in image. The Moon also symbolizes the General Public. *MDR* reached a wider audience.)

48 Bair,cited above, 639-40.

49 One woman said that his books were "like food." She added that though she didn't completely understand them, they nourished her.

50 According to Bair,(cited above, 400) so many deaths in his circle of friends made him aware of growing older. Most of us experience this, as well. Edith Rockefeller Macormack and others had financial setbacks during the Depression.

Jung's progressed Mask was changing to Cancer, the Zodiac's most personal Sign. Readers felt as if he were sitting with his pipe in their living room recounting his story, with its challenges, dreams, images, and sense of resolution. They felt that his story was, in many ways, their story, too.

Midlife changes involve the awareness that our physical energy is waning. During pregnancy and the birth of her third child (a surprise at thirty-five), Alice Munro found she lacked the energy of her twenties, when her first two girls were born.

Tension built gradually. When she came home at night from working in her husband's bookstore to find her teenage daughter, Sheila, vacuuming and cleaning, Alice wept. She remembered herself as a young girl cooking and cleaning for her own mother, who was terminally ill by the time Munro was a college student.

The same year that she received an award at a dinner attended by President Trudeau, she also asked for a divorce. At forty two, she'd invited to spend a year as writer-in-residence at Nelson College. An interviewer marveled that she took only two trunks from the house after twenty years of marriage. After Nelson, she accepted several other one-year appointments.

F. Scott Fitzgerald, after decades of pills and alcohol, died of heart failure. He had just finished his first draft of *The Last Tycoon.*

In his forties, Jiddu Krishnamurti lectured on how the images in our minds—political, spiritual, social, or mythological—interfere with seeing the truth about ourselves. From his Eastern perspective, he also wrote that experiencing union with all Life is more important than individuality.[51]

After Joyce Carol Oates' spontaneous mystical experience in her mid-thirties, her nervous tension and restlessness seemed to abate.[52] She remained happily married to Raymond Smith, retired professor and literary journal editor, for forty five years.

Aquarius Rising usually finds such experiences far more meaningful than religious

---

51 References to his life and thought are taken from Mary Lutyens, *Krishnamurti: The Years of Awakening,* (London: J. Murray) 1975. A longtime friend, she became his official biographer.
52 Oates began a journal in 1973, after her "experiment in consciousness" and continued it until 1983 (NY: Harper Perennial) 2008. Her health (heart condition), friendships with other authors, loving marriage, and the evolution of her writing are discussed.

dogma or blind faith. As Jung remarked,[53] the real problem for his middle-aged patients was "that of finding a religious outlook on life." The Uranus cycle in the early forties is often characterized by acting out or groping for a new outer world identity. But for many, it's also characterized by an awareness of an *inner* emptiness and a desire to fill it. By the Uranus/Uranus trine at fifty-six many Aquarians seem to have found their way to psyche's imaginative core; then, energized, they returned to the outer world.

Pisces Rising - Art, Music, Imagination, Meditation

Pisces is Mutable Water. It's an imaginative cycle in which artistic, musical, or poetic talents often appear. But most Aquarians find it's not as compatible with mathematics. This may be a playful cycle in which many Aquarius discover a talent that brings them joy, peace, solace or contentment for the rest of their lives. Unfortunately, some listen to an adult who tells them not to waste time in an imaginative activity because they won't be able to earn a living with it.

Neptune rules the Pisces cycle. Musicians and composers Leonard Bernstein, G.F. Handel and Stephen Sondheim (West Side Story)[54] all had Aquarius Rising and a prominent Neptune.

Music is a source of joy for Condaleeza Rice. As a child, she wanted to become a concert pianist. At fifteen, she won an opportunity to play with the Denver symphony orchestra. Though she gave up that dream in favor of political science, decades later her desire to play at Buckingham Palace was fulfilled. While Rice was Secretary of State, she played for the Queen.[55]

Joyce Carol Oates, too, loves to play the piano. Some of her poems have been set to music and are available on the internet.

---

53 See "Jung," in the list of quotes for Aquarius, above. See *Stages of Life: Structure and Dynamics of the Psyche, CW* II, part VI. Such experiences as Jung described in *MDR* and Oates and Krishnamurti described in their journals have lasting benefits. The experience of immortality; of life beyond the Ego, removes the fear of death. Yeats (Capricorn Rising) had a similar experience at fifty. Simone Weil (Sagittarius Rising) described her experience at Assisi, and its affects on her life and her health.

54 Handel had Neptune in early Pisces in his First House, Bernstein had Neptune in Cancer in the Fourth, Sondheim's Neptune was in the Seventh, his Mars and Mercury in Pisces in the First and Second Houses.

55 The audio is available on YouTube.

F. Scott Fitzgerald wrote a musical instead of attending his classes at Princeton.[56]

Aquarian children usually have above-average vocabularies for their age. Teachers enjoy their lively curiosity and thought-provoking questions. Parents remark on how alert Aquarius Rising is to his surroundings, even to reminding mom or dad that "tonight is the night to put out the trash."

The Mask's transition from Air to Water, therefore, often comes as a shock. Parents may notice that instead of being reminded by Aquarius Rising to take the trash out, *he* needs to remind Aquarius to take his homework with him in the morning. Or, the parents may receive a note from Aquarius Rising's teacher about his daydreaming, gazing out the window instead of paying attention. They may complain that his homework is carelessly done. He may lose track of time and arrive late, or lose interest in his classes.

Jung, whose Pisces Mask moved through his intercept, (see Introduction, FAQs,) described a sense of being in a cloud, then coming out from under it. Others have had similar feelings.

The Pisces Mask is moodier, and may take longer to emerge from its moods. (With Water planets for the Mask to trine, moodiness is accentuated.) Some love to draw, but are frustrated in art class when asked to copy a picture. Jung, for instance, was good at sketching, but unable to copy a goat's head or a Greek statue with empty slits for eyes. The imagination may resist, especially if the artistic subject seems false.

The creative imagination is often messy. Younger children like to finger paint. Watercolor, too, can be intriguing. Magical surprises happen; the colors run, creating new patterns and shapes. The results are unpredictable; the technique resists planning. It's fun and playful. Jung felt that stones were alive, and liked to arrange or paint them. He returned to stones later in life, when he needed to find joy and playfulness.

Reading or listening to poetry sometimes inspires young Aquarius to write his own. Joyce Carol Oates has a Seventh House Neptune. Alice Munro has hers there, too. A talent for descriptive imagery may reveal itself early in life when the Mask opposes or inconjuncts Neptune. Oates' favorite childhood story was *Alice Through the Looking Glass*. She returned to the theme as an adult. At the time of her spontaneous vision, she'd recently finished writing the novel, *Wonderland*.

Carl Jung, whose Natal Sun/Neptune trine is exact, (both planets in three degrees,) got in touch with his Neptune and his Leo identity early in life.

Between ages ten and eleven the Pisces Mask sextiled Neptune and inconjuncted Jung's

---

56 When placed on academic probation the following year, Fitzgerald left the University for the military.

Sun. These two major aspects set the tone for his Pisces Progression. When another boy knocked him down at school, he stayed down longer than necessary. When the adults were worried; he discovered he had power! Giving in to fainting spells kept him out of boring classes. He "went with" the feeling of faintness and allowed himself to collapse. Then one day, he overheard his father tell a friend how concerned he was about his boy.

His parents knew it wasn't epilepsy, they'd had the child examined. But his father lacked sufficient funds to provide for a child who, when grown to manhood, would be unable to support himself. Ashamed, young Carl began to use his strong Leo will to control the fainting urges.

At thirteen, he experienced himself as two personalities. He observed them both with detachment. He once became enraged when a friend's father shouted at him for not following instructions and standing up in a small boat.

It seemed to him that the rage belonged to a different personality, an old, prosperous, authoritative man who owned a splendid carriage. He'd seen this "eighteenth century man" in his daydreams, and identified with him.

But the rage also belonged to his Leo nature, His firey, powerful, authoritative Sun Sign rebelled at the idea of an adult berating *him*. It was insufferable! What an audacious adult!

But he also identified with the second personality, the thirteen-year-old boy with holes in his shoes. Powerless, that personality struggled with algebra trying, Pisces-like, to get through the class on his "visual memory" of the blackboard diagrams.

Jiddu Krishnamurti wrote in his autobiography (at eighteen)[57] that his father beat him for not doing well in school. He said Jiddu *could* do well, but instead walked around with a vacuous expression and refused to learn. Jiddu had long conversations with his mother, who had died when he was ten, and also with his deceased sister.

Jiddu easily fell in and out of meditative trances. He also suffered bouts of malaria. He believed he would have died had not C.W. Leadbeater, a clairvoyant, "discovered" him and Annie Besant hired a tutor. Jiddu was a natural at yoga and meditation. Leadbeater developed a rigorous academic and athletic routine for him and his brother, preparing them for higher education in London. Jiddu found he had a talent for languages. He learned English in sixteen months and later, quickly learned Italian and French.

On August 17, 1922, after the progressed Mask had sextiled Sun-in-Taurus, and a year later, conjuncted his Pisces North Node, Jiddu experienced pain at the nape of his neck, swelling, delirium, loss of appetite, and finally, mystical union.

---

57 Eighteen was the age of his first Nodal Return, which occurred in his First House.

The pain lasted two days, ending in "God-intoxication and a deep peace." "I have drunk at pure, clear waters; I have seen the light. Nothing will ever be the same. I experienced the compassion that heals sorrow, the fountain of joy and beauty," he wrote. Every night in early September he was in pain, then entered the trance state. Besant and Leadbeater called it The Process. They interpreted it as a sign of the descent of their anticipated World Teacher.

Later, as an old man, Krishanmurti told his biographer he was delighted to discover that the experience was a total surprise to Besant and Leadbeater. He finally had something *they hadn't planned,* something that was his alone! Until then, he said, "the boy" (meaning himself,) "did anything he was told to do." His confidence improved; he saw himself as an individual, outside the expectations of his elders in Theosophy.[58]

Three years later, his brother, confidante and companion through his years of travel in Europe, Australia and America, died. Depressed, Jiddu craved solitude. By thirty, he'd lost his faith in Theosophy, but not in his personal connection to the divine.

Aries Rising - Independence, Authenticity, Courage

Aries is Cardinal Fire; Mars rules this cycle. There's a downside to the highly imaginative and introspective Pisces progression: decisions involving others seem difficult to carry out. The Pisces progression often brings out feelings of embarrassment, shame, guilt, or financial fear, especially in years when the progressed Mask contacts Natal Earth and Water planets. Aquarius may remain too long in an unhappy situation.

The Aries cycle, however, is in symbolic sextile to Natal Aquarius Rising, enhancing the Airy restlessness and spirit of adventure. Professional risks are taken. Aquarius grows in courage and confidence as the Mask brings out Natal Air and Fire planets.

At thirty four, Krishnamurti's progressed Ascendant was in the last degree of Pisces, about to change Signs. As often happens, the year the progressed Mask changed was significant. For Jiddu, the Mask's first aspect was an inconjunct to his Tenth House Saturn. He was about to take a stand, set limits for himself and others, and accept personal responsibility.

---

58 He was twenty-seven at the time of the vision. But he had, in fact rebelled before. He'd refused to go to the university in London, after Annie Besant had arranged his education. He and his brother preferred to travel and hike. Prior to 1922, the Pisces Mask formed a trine with Saturn and Uranus in the Tenth, and a second trine to Mars and Jupiter in the Fifth, creating a Grand Water Trine across his horoscope.

In the spirit of the new Fire progression, Jiddu gave a speech (see above, The Mask in Youth) to a large gathering of Theosophists, dissolving the Order of the Star and announcing the return of all its properties.

His break with Theosophy was a leap in the dark, especially in 1929, the year the Great Depression began. With the backing of a few supportive friends, he began to write and lecture. Although he wasn't the Avatar of the Age Besant had envisioned, the Sage of Ojai" eventually reached a worldwide audience.

The Aries Mask slowly made a Grand Trine to Jung's Natal Leo and Sagittarian planets; it also formed sextiles to his Ascendant degree and his First House Saturn. At the end of the Aries cycle, Jung broke with Freud. He began studying astrology and years later he prepare his famous "wedding experiment" with the aid of his astrologer-daughter, Greta.

When Uranus-opposite-Uranus, with its urge towards freedom occurs during the Aries progression, independence and authenticity are its themes.

Though Alice Munro took a separate apartment, she felt guilty about leaving her youngest daughter, Andrea. She returned to the house every night for dinner. Her husband and older daughters knew the marriage was over, but kept up the pretence longer for Andrea's sake.

Then at forty-two, on the onset of Uranus-opposite-Uranus, as the Aries Mask formed an inconjunct with Natal Mars, Alice accepted a writer-in-residence appointment, asked for a divorce and left the city. She set aside the conventional Mask of "ordinary housewife and mother."

In his early forties, on the onset of Uranus-opposite-Uranus, Firtzgerald's Aries Mask moved into opposition with his Natal Mercury-Venus conjunction in Libra. He left Paris for Hollywood, hoping to establish a new career as a screenwriter. Zelda was unhappy and moved to Alabama.[59]

Taurus Rising - Stability and Routine

Taurus is Fixed Earth and is ruled by Venus. Taurus is a square to Aquarius, so there are some challenges. An introspective cycle, Taurus brings out the Earth and Water planets. On the whole, it seems an easier cycle for the Saturn-Aquarians who are more comfortable

---

59 She was institutionalized shortly afterwards. Fitzgerald stayed in a nearby hotel and wrote the story, "Crack-up," about her nervous breakdown. Her friends were angry that her suffering became his subject matter.

with stability. Many find the restless Aries cycle and Uranus-opposite-Uranus stressful. The Aries Mask and the Uranus cycle seem to energize Uranian-Aquarians, however.

Not everyone with Aquarius Rising goes through Uranus-opposite-Uranus during the Aries cycle. For Jung, Krishnamurti and Joyce Carol Oates it coincided with Taurus-Mask building. Introspective cycles work well for writers and those who teach groups of like-minded people. During Taurus, Jung, Joyce, and Krishnamurti were all privileged to teach those who valued their insights, as well as have solitude for writing.

Venus-ruled progressions may coincide with an interest in art. Jung sketched in his notebooks; participants' art was displayed at some of his workshops and seminars. The Taurus cycle may bring out the Natal planets' talent for imagery, lyrical poetry and design, especially if Aquarius Rising has Sun or Moon in Taurus or Libra and/or a prominent Neptune.

Venus is also associated with calming activities. Jung had enjoyed arranging stones as a boy. As he grew older, he enjoyed designing, building, and adding decorative inscriptions to his stone tower at Bollingen.

When, at the age of forty, Joyce Carol Oates had accepted a one-year appointment at Princeton University, she was beginning Uranus-opposite-Uranus. At first glance, the astrologer might think, "oh no! Even though it's a prestigious university, and it'll be a stimulating year, why risk her career by moving during a cycle of upheaval? Remember Fitzgerald and Hollywood!"

But the move worked out well for Oates and her husband. During the Taurus progression, she settled into her new routine quickly. Venus, ruler of the cycle, symbolizes socializing well, and ease in adjusting.[60] She was soon comfortable with the faculty and students. Oates would stay at Princeton long beyond the one-year contract, in fact she's still there.

She described the nervous excitement of Uranus-opposite-Uranus. Before leaving Windsor, she wrote in her journal, "I feel a thrill of panic at the prospect of what may await;" she had "all I can do to contend with the images that rush forth in the fullness and complexity of my ordinary days."[61] She added that she also looked forward to solitude; she "felt like Emily Dickenson." The deluge of images during the introspective Taurus cycle is similar to Jung's experience at the same age, forty.

On Uranus-opposite-Uranus she broke with her publisher, Vanguard, even though she liked her editor, Evelyn Shrifte, and had been with them since her first novel. She felt taken for granted, and Dutton was willing to pay almost twice as much for her new novels.

---

60 Though there were challenges. The house was filthy, and her first semester very demanding.
61 Johnson, *Invisible Writer*, cited above, 276. She was also apprehensive that her new novel, *Son of the Morning*, might receive poor reviews at the same time she arrived at Princeton.

Taurus seeks a comfortable living. As the progressed Ascendant moves through the Second House, practical decisions are made. Oates' agent, in her late seventies, was also replaced. Joyce wrote in her journal, "1978 was a watershed year."

Jung's decision at forty, to shut himself in his home office and go with the flow of the images, was also a good one. He assumed the Taurus Mask in 1913, by 1916 it had conjuncted Neptune in his Third House (The Mind) and squared Sun-in-Leo in the Sixth (Health; Service.)

His inner Magician and Wise Old Man, Philemon, taught him that magic was often useful in healing. His inner Christian Anchorite taught him humility and told him that there was more to understanding the *Bible* than the minister's son had previously thought. His Anima, a black Snake, laughed at his defenses (suit of mail.) Exasperated, she tried to bite him, but Jung's armor was in her way.

In an introspective cycle like Taurus, going with the images is often the most practical approach, particularly for those who practice the art of healing (psychology) the art of writing, and the visual or performance arts.

Jung was right, the experiences of our forties, which seem "like a lava flow," are sorted out later, in our fifties.

By Uranus-trine-Uranus around age fifty-six, we've assimilated the insights and discoveries, they've become part of us and/or our work.

At fifty-six, the last year of Jung's progression through Taurus, Friedrich Wilhelm gave him *The Secret of the Golden Flower,* a key to understanding and organizing his images. Alchemy became his new direction and Jung no longer needed *The Red Book.*

The Taurus progressed cycle usually feels stabilizing. When it's over, some Aquarians find that their Uranus discovery, or method, is also useful to others. Jung later shared his insights on Active Imagination in England, America, Germany, and Ascona, Switzerland.

Gemini Rising - The Air Trine

Gemini is Mutable Air, ruled by quixotic Mercury. The progressed Mask forms a symbolic trine to Aquarius Rising. In this progression, many Aquarians take an objective look back at their life experience. Jung, in his seventies, said that he'd been "a dilettante," collecting information from various sources, and putting it together.[62]

---

62 An interesting choice of words, because Gemini is the dilettante's Mask.

In 1930, the year he read *Secret of the Golden Flower,* Jung's Mask was changing from Taurus to Gemini. By fifty-five, around the time of Uranus-trine-Uranus, he'd "classified" his discoveries.[63]

By the second Saturn Return at fifty-eight, he simplified his schedule. Unless new patients were in urgent need, Jung no longer accepted them.[64] As a young medical doctor, his theories had been based on patient cases, but from his fifties on, new theories came to him while "walking across (the bridge of) alchemy to the collective unconscious."

Several famous people came to see him. Hermann Hesse (Sagittarius Rising) came for analysis. Jung met James Joyce (Capricorn Rising) whose daughter Lucia's condition was degenerating into schizophrenia, and F. Scott Fitzgerald, whose wife, Zelda, was temporarily incarcerated in the Burgholzli Mental Health Institute. He and H.G Wells discussed flying saucers, space, and "the mythology of the future."

Jung gave the famous Eranos seminars in Ascona (1933-53), traveled and lectured at Harvard, Tavistock, England, and the Berlin psychological club. But by his mid sixties, after his voyage to India, where he became severely ill, he began thinking of himself as an old man.[65]

Too old for active duty in World War II, his services were required by his neutral country as a medical practitioner and as a psychologist. He was assigned to Zurich and the outlying rural areas.

On Uranus-square-Uranus, the unexpected often happens. On Saturn-square-Saturn his old cycle (travel; lecturing abroad) ended. Travel outside Switzerland was no longer possible. A more restricted Saturn-cycle began.[66]

During the early to mid 1940's meat was rationed, but dairy, vegetables and pipe tobacco were plentiful. Jung received a tip that he was on the Nazi's Black List to be tortured and killed after their (planned) invasion of Switzerland. The patriarch, however, refused to leave his children and grandchildren or abandon his wartime duties.

---

63 Through alchemy, he also came to understand his earlier "stream of dreams" differently. He decided that he didn't need to "kill Siegfried" in his dream. Although he'd outgrown the youthful hero stage of life, part of him was "still Siegfried," but he was other dream figures as well. (Bair, 196.)

64 D.H. Lawrence's Santa Fe friend Mabel Luhan, among others wanted very much to see him, but Jung responded that she was not sick, therefore she didn't need his help.

65 He refused inoculations prior to the trip. He contracted amoebic dysentery, which weakened him and seems to have contributed to his heart condition. In January 1944, Jung fell and broke his leg. At 69, he was diagnosed with a myocardial infarction.

66 He did, however, leave two years later for a more anonymous rural area.

Isolated from news or visitors from abroad, he began writing what many consider to be among his best books, *Aion* and *Mysterium Coniunctionis*. He and his wife celebrated their Golden Anniversary. When Emma died shortly after his eightieth birthday, he carved a stone for the woman who was "the foundation" of his life and took it to Bollingen Tower.

After Emma's death, Jung withdrew. He "chiseled in stone" so long that some of his friends began to worry about him.[67] By his eighty-fifth birthday, however, he was writing again. In spite of poor health, he finished an excellent essay for *Man and His Symbols*.[68] Jung and his only son, Franz, were reconciled.

When Joyce Carol Oates' husband, Raymond Smith, died suddenly in 2008, she was busy writing and teaching as usual. After his death, she experienced herself as "a teacher hired to impersonate a writer." In her loneliness, she wrote, "a writer's life is no life at all."[69]

She was shocked when two students stayed after class to tell her how sorry they were about her loss. Joyce hadn't thought they knew that their teacher, "Mrs. Smith," had lost her husband. Her two identities had collided; she "felt shaky" after the students left.

She finished her husband's last task, returning submissions to the *Ontario Review*[70] with notices that the journal was discontinued. She wrote, "I am sorry to inform you of the unexpected death of Raymond Smith."

But she realized the word "unexpected" was wrong! "It was melodramatic. It was too subjective. *It sounded self-pitying*. And they had no need to know." She removed it. But later, she was "embarrassed to say," she reinserted it.

Her personality, "my self," she wrote, "was never a factor in my teaching, or my career." She said that students and friends "literally kept me going" after Ray's death. In her *Atlantic Monthly* article, "I'm Sorry to Inform You," she wrote about her devotion to her writing students, who "had become my lifeline in my grief."

She mentioned that part of her job had always been "to impersonate Joyce Carol Oates, who doesn't exist except on the spines of books."

In 2009, she announced her engagement to Professor Charlie Gross, a psychologist on

---

67 Aniela Jaffe's "cryptic remark" is quoted in Bair, cited above, 476.

68 He chose to write it in English, which he then found "much easier than German."

69 Joyce Carol Oates, "I am sorry to inform you," *Atlantic Monthly Fiction Edition*, 2010, 39-74. She was seventy when Raymond died.

70 This section is based on Oates' article in the *Atlantic Monthly Fiction Edition*, 2010, "I Am Sorry To Inform You," 76-83. Oates said that while other faculty members seemed happy when students read their books, she wasn't. She thought of Mrs. Smith and JCO as separate identities.

the Princeton faculty. With Leo on the Seventh House Cusp, Aquarius Rising can fall in love quickly.

Oates still has many years left of the Gemini progressed Mask, which brings out her Aquarian Air. But she'll eventually reach a comfort zone, as Jung did, about sharing personal, subjective feelings.

On the trine from Gemini, there may be recognition. If the rumors prove true, Joyce Carol Oates may receive the Nobel Prize in literature. The Jupiter Return Years, sixty and seventy-two, seem to coincide with a deepening interest in spirituality. Young people often see wisdom in Aquarius Rising, and look to them for advice.

In old age, the Aquarian who had lost his faith in Theosophy became known as "the Sage of Ojai. The Aquarian that Toni Wolff had feared would be seen as a charlatan became known as the "Sage of Kusnacht."

Cancer Rising - The Inconjunct

Cancer, Cardinal Water and Moon-ruled, is the most personal Sign. It's about home and hearth, family and feelings. Aquarians who live into this progression are challenged to become more subjective, less impersonal, and more open about their feelings.

As his progressed Ascendant entered Cancer, Jung began the interviews with Aniela Jaffe for his autobiography, revealing his inner life. Alice Munro amazed her daughter Sheila by arriving, offering to babysit her young grandsons, leaving Sheila time to write. In her seventies, Alice still writes and revises stories for films and CBC.

Joyce Carol Oates has several Natal planets in Cancer which the progressed Ascendant will eventually conjunct, one-by-one. The Mask's initial contact will be to Chiron,[71] in the first degree of Cancer. Chiron will set the tone for the Cancer cycle.

George E. Vaillant, M.D, author of *Aging Well,* wrote that in late old age, many of the happiest interview subjects were also the most productive. This seems true for both Saturn-ruled Signs, Capricorn and Aquarius.

Andre Maurois (Aquarius Rising) said, "old age is not white hair and wrinkles; the true evil is not the weakening of the body, but the indifference of the soul."

Two types of people often seem younger than their chronological age, the curious, who are interested in life and other people, and the creative who are in touch with *psyche.*

---

71 The asteroid that symbolizes the Wounded Healer.

Aquarius Rising Bibliography

Bair, Deirdre, *Jung: A Biography,* (New York: Little Brown,) 2003.

Baumann-Jung, Gret, "Some Reflections on the Horoscope of C.G. Jung," (Psychological Club, Zurich,) 1974, trans, Daryl Sharp. A reprint of this paper was kindly provided by Monika Wikman. (Baumann-Jung used a different formula and thus has a different year for the beginning of Jung's Gemini progression from mine. I used Tropical Placidus for his Natal chart and the Solar Fire formula for Secondary Progressions.)

Barks, Cathy W, and Jackson L Bryer, eds, *Dear Scott, Dearest Zelda: The Love Letters of F. Scott and Zelda Fitzgerald,* (London: Bloomsbury Publishing, PLC,) 2003.

Berman, Ronald, *The Great Gatsby and Fitzgerald's World of Ideas,* (Tuscaloosa: University of Alabama Press,) 1997.

Bruccoli, Matthew J., and Judith S. Baughman, *Conversations with Scott Fitzgerald,* (Jackson: University of Mississippi Press,) 2004.

Chinen, Allan B, *In the Ever-After: Fairy Tales and the Second Half of Life,* "The Simple Grasscutter," (Wilmette: Chiron,) 1989. (A modern version of the Indian story, "Walidad the Simple-Hearted.")

Cox, Ailsa, *Alice Munro,* (Tavistock: Northcote House in Association with the British Council,) 2004.

Fitzgerald, F. Scott, *F. Scott Fitzgerald on Writing,* Larry W. Philips, ed, (New York, Scribner,) 1985

—— *Tender is the Night,* (New York; Scribner,) 1995.

Hannah, Barbara, *Jung's Life and Work,* (New York: Perigree,) 1981.

Jaffe, Aniela, ed, *Memories, Dreams, Reflections* by C.G. Jung, (New York: Vintage-Random House,) 1973.

Johnson, Greg, ed, *Conversations with* Joyce Carol Oates, *1970-2006,* (Toronto: Ontario Review Press,) 2006.

—— *Invisible Writer, A Biography of Joyce Carol Oates,* (New York: Dutton,) 1998.

Jung, C.G, *Aion,* CW, IX , Part 2, (New Jersey: Princeton University Press,) Bollingen Series, 1975.

—— *Mysterium Coniunctionis,* CW, XX, (New Jersey: Princeton University Press,) 1976.

—— *The Red Book,* (New York: W.W. Norton,) 2009.

—— *Structure and Dynamics of the Psyche*, "The Stages of Life," CW VIII, Part 6, 1981.

Krystal, Arthur, "Slow Fade, F. Scott Fitzgerald in Hollywood," *The New Yorker*, November 16, 2009.

Lutyens, Mary, *Krishnamurti: The Years of Awakening*, (London: J. Murray,) 1975.

—— *Krishnamurti: The Years of Fulfilment*, (London: J. Murray,) 1983.

—— *The Life and Death of Krishnamurti*, (London: J. Murray,) 1990.

Maurois, Andre, *An Art of Living*, reprinted by (n.p. HydroScience Inc,) 2007. Includes, "The Art of Growing Older."

McGuire, William, ed, trans. R.F.C. Hull, *Freud-Jung Letters: The Correspondence Between Sigmund Freud and C.G. Jung*, Bollingen Series 94, (Princeton: University Press,) 1974.

Munro, Alice, *Friend of My Youth*, (New York: Knopf,) 1990.

—— *The Love of a Good Woman*, (New York: Knopf,) 1998.

—— *Runaway*, (New York: Knopf,) 1994.

—— *Something I've Been Meaning to Tell You*, (Toronto: Mc Graw-Hill,) 1974.

Munro, Sheila, *Lives of Mothers and Daughters*, (New York: Sterling,) 2008.

Oates, Joyce Carol, *Expensive People*, (New York: Vanguard,) 1958.

—— "I Am Sorry to Inform You," *Atlantic Monthly Fiction Edition*, 2010.

—— *The Journal of Joyce Carol Oates, 1973-1982*, (New York: Harper Perennial,) 2008.

—— *Them*, (New York: Modern Library,) 2000.

——*What I Lived For*, (New York: Dutton,) 1994.

Philips, Gene D, *Fiction, Film and F. Scott Fitzgerald*, (Chicago: Loyola Press,) 1986.

Vaillant, George E, MD, *Aging Well*, (New York: Little, Brown and Company,) 2003.

CHAPTER SIX

Pisces Rising
Creativity, Spirituality, Inner Peace

Gertrude Stein, "A rose is a rose is a rose."

Thomas Merton, "A life is either all spiritual or not spiritual at all. No man can serve two masters. Your life is shaped by the end you live for. You are made in the image of what you desire."

Deepak Chopra, "The physical world, including our bodies, is a response of the observer. We create our bodies as we create the experience of our world."

—— "Nothing is more important than reconnecting with your bliss. Nothing is as rich. Nothing is more real."

—— "If you and I are having a single thought of violence or hatred against anyone in the world at this moment, we are contributing to the wounding of the world."

—— "In the midst of movement and chaos, keep stillness inside of you."

—— "The less you open your heart to others, the more your heart suffers."

Allen Ginsberg, "Follow your inner moonlight; don't hide the madness."

Algernon Charles Swinburne,

"And the best and the worst of this is

That neither is most to blame,

If you have forgotten my kisses

And I have forgotten your name."

Elisabeth Kubler-Ross, "Learn to get in touch with the silence within yourself, and know that everything in life has purpose. There are no mistakes, no coincidences, all events are blessings given to us to learn from."

—— "Love is the only thing that will never die."

Hazrat Inayat Khan, "Everything in life is speaking in spite of its apparent silence."

—— "Our success or failure depends upon the harmony or disharmony of our individual will with the divine will."

Thomas Merton, "We are not at peace with others because we are not at peace with ourselves, and we are not at peace with ourselves because we are not at peace with God."

George Sand, "Guard well within yourself that treasure, kindness. Know how to give without hesitation, how to lose without regret, how to acquire without meanness."

—— "It is a mistake to regard age as a downhill grade toward dissolution. The reverse is true. As one grows older, one climbs with surprising strides."

—— "Life in common among people who love each other is the ideal of happiness."

Charles-Augustin Sainte Beuve, "Tell me who admires and loves you, and I will tell you who you are."

Clara Barton, "You must never so much as think whether you like it or not, whether it is bearable or not; you must never think of anything except the need, and how to meet it."

Elisabeth Kubler-Ross, "For those who seek to understand it, death is a highly creative force. The highest spiritual values of life can originate from the thought and study of death."

—— "It is not the end of the physical body that should worry us. Our concern must be to live while we're alive - to release our inner selves from the spiritual death that comes with living behind a facade designed to conform to external definitions of who and what we are."

H. Inayat Khan, "I have seen all souls as my soul, and realized my soul as the soul of all."

—— "Muslim or Hindu are only outward distinctions, the Truth is one, God is one, life is one. To me there is no such thing as two. Two is only one plus one."

Ringo Starr, "That's all drugs and alcohol do, they cut off your emotions in the end."

—— "I just feel good. I feel like I have a purpose."

Roger Zelazny, "I try to sit down at the typewriter four times a day, even if it's only five minutes, and write three sentences."

Allen Ginsberg, "I want people to bow as they see me and say he is gifted with poetry, he has seen the presence of the creator."

—— "I think it was when I ran into Kerouac and Burroughs-when I was 17- that I realized I was talking through an empty skull... I wasn't thinking my own thoughts or saying my own thoughts."

Sam Shepard, "I feel like I've never had a home, you know? I feel related to the country, to this country, and yet I don't know exactly where I fit in... There's always this kind of nostalgia for a place, a place where you can reckon with yourself."

—— "I'm a writer. The more I act, the more resistance I have to it. If you accept work in a movie, you accept to be entrapped for a certain part of time, but you know you're getting out. I'm also earning enough to keep my horses, buying some time to write."

Judith Krantz, "Surely the whole point of writing your own life story is to be as honest as you possibly can, revealing everything about yourself that is most private and probably most interesting for that very reason."

Thomas Merton, "Perhaps I am stronger than I think"

——"By reading the scriptures I am so renewed that all nature seems renewed around me and with me. The sky seems to be a pure, a cooler blue, the trees a deeper green. The whole world is charged with the glory of God and I feel fire and music under my feet."

"Lead me from the Unreal to the Real

From Darkness to Light;

From Ignorance to Wisdom,

From Death to Immortality."

Brihadaranyaka Upanishad

The Dual Mask of Pisces

I'm the Mask of Pisces Rising, the most permeable, suggestible, sensitive and subjective Mask.

At my best, I project what Elisabeth Kubler-Ross called "personal, unconditional love," without a martyr, victim or messiah complex. At my worst, I'm addicted to drugs, alcohol, cigarettes, and/or romantic relationships which turn out badly

Sometimes I'm a shallow-water fish. In this phase, I love fashion and glamor; I spend more time on my appearance than any other Mask except Libra. My "come-hither" look and sweet, seductive smile are famous with the opposite sex. Decades later, Judith Krantz's husband Steve still remembers that flirtatious glance at their first meeting!

Mars-ruled Aries is on the cusp of my House of Finances. If Mars is afflicted, I'm an impulsive spender, unless I have several planets in Earth or am weighed down by old, fusty Saturn.

With Jupiter prominent, I have expensive taste which I like to indulge. I'll gladly take a blissful daydream or fantasy over boring reality.

Unless Mars is prominent and I enjoy exercise, by midlife I tend to be overweight. With a strongly-placed Neptune, I love my wine or cocktail. It helps me escape the mundane world, though I do feel bloated afterwards.

Unless I have several planets in Air, I disagree with Carl Jung about the need to make the Unconscious conscious; *I* think awareness is overrated. To me, an overly-examined life is like a novel full of dull characters.

I prefer to put my dream images on canvas, into poetry, song, decorating or jewelry design. Words like clinical, analytical, impartial, and objective do *not* appeal. My world is personal and subjective; feeling, emotion, imagination and intuition matter most.

In decision-making, intuition is quicker than weighing all those "pros and cons."I prefer to go with the flow. I'm curious to see my story unfold without undue interference from Mercury, editor and critic.

Sometimes, though, I'm a deep water fish, like Deepak Chopra, Thomas Merton, Elisabeth Kubler-Ross and Hazrat Inayat Khan (see above quotes.) Sometimes, I'm mystical, otherworldly. With planets in the psychic houses (4, 8 and 12), especially Jupiter, Neptune or the Moon, I may become a healer, a monk or a nun.

I laugh at the expressions on my friends' faces after I've exchanged my deep water persona for the shallow, glamorous one, or vice versa. They may not recognize me at first! The last time they saw me I was my old, glamorous self. Now I'm at the movie theater, in a long brown skirt and T-shirt, passing out the Dalai Lama's flyers on Tibetan rights.

Or, last time, I was dressed as a Mormon missionary. But today I encounter them as I emerge from a luxurious beauty treatment at the spa.

Unless I have Sun-in-Leo, Scorpio, Cardinality or several Tenth House planets (Career), fame and power are not important. Like Roger Zelazny who taught fencing while writing science fiction novels, or actor Sam Shepard whose day job supports himself, his horses, and his plays, I care more about the quality of life than money or prestige.

The most Yin of all the Masks, I'm quite sensitive to the world around me. Negativity and toxic fumes seem to go right to my core. As a young person, others could tell that my feelings were easily hurt. But I soon learned to stare into space and daydream about something pleasant. Teachers who accused me of inattention were usually rude or unkind.

Though I love yoga and meditation retreats, I often wonder why I don't find time for these practices at home. The same is true of writing workshops. All my life, I've been told how imaginative and talented I am, yet I find myself too busy to write at home. Family needs and social life are my first priorities.

If my horoscope were high in Fixity, or Saturn in a stronger House, astrologers say, perseverance and discipline would come more easily to me.

Astrologers have accused me of poor judgment, usually about my romantic choices. They see me as an Absolutist, like Sagittarius Rising. I do tend to see issues as either black or white, without any subtle shades of gray.

Well, Gertrude Stein was right, "a rose is a rose is a rose." How can it be otherwise?

And I like the Biblical quote that Thomas Merton chose, "you cannot serve two masters," a reference to God and materialism.

To me, inner certainty comes from my intuition and belief system. If I ollowed them in every decision, all day long, I couldn't go wrong. But it's impossible to do! We all make mistakes; that's how we learn.

Like Alice in Wonderland, "I sometimes give myself very good advice," advice that feels right, but discover I cannot follow it!

How To Recognize Pisces Rising

Other astrologers seem to notice Pisces' eyes first. Pisces Rising usually gazes out at the world from underneath thick, curly eyelashes. Their eyes are large and liquid. Self-protective and easily hurt, Pisces, when feeling vulnerable, responds with a blank stare. But as soon as they feel comfortable with someone, their eyes become very expressive. If Pluto aspects the Ascendant or Sun-in-Scorpio trines it, they can even be hypnotic. Like Judith Krantz, (above) most Pisceans quickly master the art of flirting.

Across a crowded room, a Pisces' woman's eyes communicate "you'll have a lot of fun with me!" Or, (if there's a strong Pluto) "I'm your destiny; you'll absolutely love taking care of me!" Pisces Rising men often have a puppy-dog-appeal. Their eyes signal, "I can't survive without you. I'd love it if you cooked for me; entertained my friends, dropped off my clothes at the cleaners, redecorated my apartment and/or spruced up my wardrobe. And I'd be forever grateful if you'd set out my vitamins every morning."

Unless there are Sixth House (Health) planets or planets in Virgo, health concerns are usually delegated to the partner. (Virgo is on the cusp of the marriage house. If the spouse has Virgo planets, he or she seldom minds assuming the responsibility, at least when the relationship is new.)

When I think of this Ascendant, though, the first feature that comes to mind is not the eyes but the smile. Pisces has a genuine, warm, welcoming smile. Perhaps their greatest asset, that gentle smile draws people and success like a magnet, particularly in areas like the media, sales, fund-raising, or publicity. The smile is subtle, but powerful.

With their shape shifting talent (see Mundane Ruler) acting also comes naturally. One talented Pisces woman told me she was happiest when on stage, that it was "wonderful to become someone else for a few hours."

Pisceans have beautiful skin unless addicted to cigarettes, alcohol, or drugs. Poor diet also affects the complexion. By their mid-thirties, the screenwriter-valet, who parks cars for the big names in the film or music industry, and the aspiring actress or supermodel may console themselves with too many French fries or gooey desserts, to the detriment of their health and their dreams. The liver and/or the pancreas usually suffer the ill effects.

Astrologer and healer Max Heindel[1] seemingly met many shallow water fish (see above, The Dual Mask) with medical problems. His description of the Ascendant Sign is not flattering, "Pisces Rising is short, flabby and fleshy. Even when not grossly overweight, they seem to have several chins. They have small hands and feet; they waddle when they walk.

They don't recuperate quickly. They're lazy. They lack common sense and good judgment. People seem to dislike them without knowing why. Unless the Sun is in a tall Sign like Aquarius or Capricorn, they're short in stature. Their noses are long and flat. If they try to become mediums, they can be taken over by low-grade spirits."

Heindel is not as good at describing the *other* Pisces fish who swims in deeper waters.

He's accurate about height, though. My clients also range from short to average height. And those who have the Sun in the two Signs he mentioned, *or* in Sagittarius, are taller. Former talk show host Phil Donahue has Sun-in-Sagittarius.

Author Gertrude Stein was tiny, shorter than most of my Pisces Rising clients. Stein is known for *Alice B Toklas*, the book about her lover, Alice's restaurant and their circle of ex-patriot friends in Paris and for the famous line, "a rose is a rose is a rose."

Gertrude's Moon was in the Seventh House. The closest aspect to her Ascendant was a Jupiter inconjunct. It's interesting that her partner owned a restaurant in which the couple helped their fellow ex-patriates feel at home in Paris. The nurturing Moon/Cancer archetype includes food. Jupiter symbolizes foreigners; foreign places.

Stein spent several years in medical school, like Kubler-Ross, Deepak Chopra and many other Pisces Rising people with Cancer or Virgo planets.[2]

Novelist Judith Krantz was the shortest girl in her freshman class at Wellesley College. Sixteen that year, her class photo is very attractive. She listed as her goals, "to date as many

---

1 Max Heindel and Augusta Foss Heindel, *Message of the Stars*, (Oceanside: Rosicrucian Press), 1973, 109-111.

2 Dr. Kubler-Ross had Cncer Moon-in-the-Fourth (Rulership.) She also had Neptune exalted in Leo in her Sixth, opposite Jupiter-in-Aquarius, (esoteric Rulership) in her Twelfth. Dr. Chopra has Moon-in-Virgo in his Seventh. Neptune-in-Libra is also in the Seventh.

men as I can, read all the books in the library, and graduate." She added that grades didn't matter.[3]

Though usually slender in youth, Pisces tends to gain weight around the abdomen at midlife. By fifty, many Pisceans appear bloated, especially if Moon is prominent by House position (1, 4, 7, 10) or aspects the Ascendant degree. The Moon, ruler of the tides, is associated with fluid retention.

A square or opposition from the mundane ruler (Neptune) to the Moon may indicate a different "fluid problem," excessive alcohol consumption. These two planets jointly are said to rule the endocrine and immune systems, so attention to diet is important. One or two glasses of wine per day is the recommended limit.

But alcohol isn't always the drink of choice. Some Pisceans keep the coffee pot on all day long and have a cup with every client. Others are seldom seen without a can of caffeinated soda. Going to the Virgo polarity usually results in Virgo consequences like insomnia and digestive disorders. It's better to speed up the metabolism with a walk or, after fifty, choose a nap instead of caffeine.

Some have fallen arches or flat feet. Yoga poses that involve lifting the arches; spreading the toes, pressing into the sides of the feet and the back heels are beneficial for Pisces.

Students often ask, "how do we distinguish the shallow water fish from the deeper fish? Both fish are friendly, hypersensitive, usually have talent in music or the arts, and are skilled communicators. Both are impulsive spenders. Both seem intuitive." All this is true. And yet there are important differences, which become clearer when we know them better.

Pisces Rising is like a porous membrane that quickly assumes, then reflects back, the qualities that his or her new acquaintance seeks in a friend or lover. Unless the rest of the horoscope has manipulative or narcissistic tendencies—like five or six First House planets—this chameleon-like behavior is an unconscious process for Pisces.

In other words, it's easier for us *to project the attributes we're seeking* upon Pisces Rising than on the other Ascendants. Pisces seems to accept our projections and reflect them right back to us. It takes awhile to get to know who Pisces Rising is, to see beyond the Mask.

The astrology student mentioned the example of impulsive spending, Mars ruling Aries on the Second House. The shallow water fish are somewhat narcissistic. They impulsively spend *on themselves.* The deeper fish is instinctively generous. He or she will impulsively

3 With Jupiter inconjunct Neptune and Mercury inconjunct the Moon, Judith enjoyed reading and social life. Many Pisces Rising students begin college as literature or fine arts majors. However, in the Twenty First Century, they later change their major to "something more practical."

spend on others, the spouse or lover; the children, the sick neighbor or elderly grandmother who'd love that expensive nightgown and robe.

Most of us would look at the price tag, put the expensive item back and go to the sale rack. Or, we'd wait until the person's birthday to buy it. Of course, if there are several planets in Earth, or Saturn is in the Second House (Finances) this impulse is easier to control.

Spending is a concrete example, but it works for the other traits in the student's question, too. Deeper fish mature as they grow older. In youth, they were hypersensitive about others' reactions *to them*. They were more narcissistic. As adults, they transfer the worry to their children, "am I embarrassing my child?" Or, "is that teacher too critical of my child? Their feelings are hurt *for someone else*. "My husband's boss doesn't appreciate by him!" The sensitivity is still there, but Pisces is growing up. Fears that were vague in youth become more specific, less personal. More mature Pisceans are more likely to feel guilty themselves than "guilt-trip" others.

It's true that both fish seem intuitive, But the shallow fish is certain all his dreams are predictive; that dream events will literally happen to himself or others. It's very difficult to convince them that their dreams aren't literal.

Like the medium with poor judgment that Max Heindel mentioned, the shallow fish may open himself to dangerous people or experiences because he believes in his psychic powers. He believes he's in control, therefore he can deal with whatever transpires. Since he prefers his daydreams to reality, a logical (Mercury) approach won't persuade him.

With a hypnotic aspect (Pluto to the Moon or the Rising Sign,) he may be able to persuade others to follow him. If they do, it'll be like the blind leading the blind.

A deep water fish has a natural affinity for allegory and symbolism, but doesn't use mystical symbols to recruit or manipulate others. He sees dream events symbolically. He doesn't attempt to "guilt trip" others into facilitating or compensating for his addictions.

Heindel had a point; there *are* lazy fish who manipulate others. Pisces Rising drug addicts sometimes attempt to convince their child to drop out of school and support them. "Your mother is sick and you need to take care of her." Their behavior is not only self-destructive, it harms others, too.

Deep water Pisces intuitives have different problems. Heindel mentioned that Pisces is often slow in recuperating after an illness. I associate this with their difficulty in setting boundaries. Absorbing others' projections and overcompensating for others can be unhealthy, as can overextending their schedules.

Inhaling the spouse's secondhand cigarette smoke and bad moods is also an unhealthy practice. With Jupiter in a prominent house or closely aspects the Ascendant, Pisces Rising is probably attempting too much.

Pisces, the Twelfth Sign, is analogous to the Twelfth House (Solitude). Pisceans who find time for solitude are more in touch with the Soul and the Creative Imagination, more peaceful and content.

Pisces has many talents; the deeper fish is generous with his. Unless Saturn is in a strong house or aspects the Ascendant degree, it can be very hard for them to say "no." It often feels wrong to them after years of saying "yes."

Friends will ask them to read auras at birthday parties, channel messages from deceased relatives, interpret dreams and "listen to my day; listen to my problem." Friends may be incensed when Pisces has a schedule conflict and is unable to play the organ at their child's wedding. Everyone seems to forget that Pisces Rising has a life of his own.

I sometimes mention during client sessions that Jiddu Krishnamurti, who had Aquarius Rising, wore the Pisces progressed Mask for several decades. Yet during the Pisces cycle he refused to be imposed upon by being treated like a spiritual teacher or Messiah. He set boundaries, and he lived a long time.

Pisces at its best is "gentle, loving, kind and idealistic," as Joan McEvers said in *12 Times 12: 144 Sun/Ascendant Combinations*.[4]

Many Pisceans have beautiful symbolic dreams, daydreams and illusions. Jung once said that a patient, a cobbler's schizophrenic wife, had lovely delusions. Pisces' romantic illusions, too, are lovely. When they explain that it would be "too depressing to go through life *without* my rose colored glasses," we see their point, though it looks to others as if they're repeating the same scenarios again and again with a series of new loves.

A woman with Pisces Rising and four Pisces planets in her First House came to see me at age twenty-eight on her Saturn Return. She had no planets in Earth or the "Earth Houses" (2, 6, and 10) but, after a long struggle with alcoholism, she sought grounding.

The day that we discussed the meaning of the Saturn Return year, I wasn't expecting a miracle. I knew hers was a difficult journey. However, two years later she left her life as an exotic dancer and the environment of drugs and alcohol. She converted to Catholicism and, shortly thereafter, she became a nun. She found peace in the rituals of her new religion.

The change of *persona* from exotic dancer to nun was dramatic. As Pisces Rising moves from shallow to deep water, the Mask changes, too.

---

4 (San Diego: ACS Publications,) 1983, 254.

The Mundane Rulers - Jupiter and Neptune

Until Neptune's discovery in 1846, Jupiter was considered Pisces' ruling planet. From classical times through the mid Nineteenth Century, astrologers looked to Natal and transiting Jupiter for an understanding of the Sign. The largest planet in the Solar System definitely left its imprint on the Pisces Archetype!

Though Neptune is now viewed as Pisces' ruler, many jovial traits remain, such as optimism, generosity and cheerfulness ("after this bad stretch; the divorce, unemployment, losing my house, my child's illness and all, things will look up. You'll see. Everything happens for a reason!")

And, Jupiter can go beyond inclusiveness, or expansiveness, to grandiosity: "I won't become just *any* old saint! I'm going to be a *saint of the altars!* Statues will be made of me and young girls will join convents because of me," said a Pisces Rising client. (A recent convert to Catholicism, she'd been reading the saints' biographies.)

"I'm not going to be just *any* model, I'm going to be a *super*model, on the cover of *Vogue Magazine*, and then I'll be a fashion designer with my own product line," said Pisces Rising, on her sixteenth birthday.

"I always leave a copy of my latest screenplay—I've written over twenty—on the car seats where I work as a valet. Famous directors and producers frequent the restaurant, so any day now, I'll be discovered. You'll hear my name at the Academy Awards."

Jupiter not only inspires big dreams. Prescience and faith are among its attributes. Jupiter rules the House of Religion. (House Nine.) Evangelical minister Jim Bakker, for instance, has an impulse to share the Gospel.

We associate Jupiter with *largesse* and *noblesse oblige* (it was also the planet of royalty), with the impulse to help make the world a better place. From the Twentieth Century to the present, the modern media has enabled Pisces Rising to reach a wider audience, as Robert Redford and Phil Donahue did at the height of their fame. All of them had Jupiter in a prominent house (1.4.7.10,) in its own House (the Ninth or Twelfth) or conjunct the Sun.[5]

Whatever their politics, Left or Right, Bakker, Redford and Donahue have a sense of purpose and strong convictions. Yet to those whose worldviews differ from theirs, they may seem like "extremists."

Jupiter is also associated with two other important attributes, luck and wisdom.

---

5 Deepak Chopra has a wide Sun/Jupiter conjunction in his Eighth House. He brings Eastern wisdom on health and happiness to the West through his inspiring self-help books.

Where Saturn's Rulership is about a person's place in history and his legacy, (Jung, Fitzgerald, Joyce and Yeats were all concerned about theirs) Jupiter's seems more about his role as a cultural influence.

Neptune's attributes differ from Jupiter's, though the storytelling planet has an equally powerful influence on the culture.

When visual and imaginative Neptune aspects the Sun, Moon or Ascendant in the horoscope of writers and artists, it indicates the ability to create a world of one's own.[6] Roger Zelazny achieved this in his science fiction novel, *Lord of Light.* He had a Grand Trine in Earth, including the Sun, Jupiter and Neptune in Houses 3, 7, and 11, excellent positions for a writer.

Neptune, however, is not as uplifting as Jupiter. Director and producer Brian De Palma's films *(The Untouchables, Carrie, Dressed to Kill, Mission Impossible)* borrow from Alfred Hitchcock themes. With Sun, Neptune, and Mercury conjunct in Virgo, De Palma's films present the world as a threatening place. The trines to Sun/Neptune from Saturn/Jupiter in Taurus add realism.

Many Pisceans are interested in dreams, mythology, folklore and/or art. Pre-Raphaelite artist Algernon Swinburne, who influenced a generation, including William Butler Yeats' father, John B. Yeats, chose his themes from mythology.[7] He had Neptune sextile Venus, a fine aspect for an artist. But his Neptune was also opposite Mars/Jupiter. A masochist, he supposedly enjoyed being flogged.

A cognate of *nebulous*, Neptune has a unique allure; the opposite sex is drawn to mysterious Pisces. The lover, spouse or partner also hopes to allay Pisces' fears and dispel their confusion. Because Pisces Rising craves emotional security, they're happy to let their new love take charge.

Later however, Pisces may come to resent the spouse, (or series of them,) for being controlling. "Why am I never in the driver's seat in this relationship?" Pisces wonders. But Pisces abdicated the driver's role early, letting the partner compensate in the Virgo areas, like paying the bills, doing computer downloads or hiring and firing gardeners. It may be that over the years, Pisces never suggested taking his or her turn at these tasks.

It's as if Pisces is challenged to go wide (Jupiter) *and* deep (Neptune) at the same time. Extraverted Jupiter seeks as many diverse experiences as possible, while introverted Neptune needs time to reflect on each experience. In general, Neptune works well with

---

6 See *BTM, Part I,* Marcel Proust had Neptune conjunct his Ascendant. Through his book, *In Search of Times Past,* readers gain access to a vanishing world.

7 As a boy, Ireland's future poet laureate, W.B. Yeats, saw the paintings and listened to his father discussing symbolism with others in Swinburne's circle.

Earth and Water planets, while playful Jupiter appreciates adventurous Fire and humorous Air.[8]

Neptune aspects may also indicate musical talents. Conductor Zubin Mehta has Neptune is in his Seventh House; Ringo Starr, the former Beatles' drummer, has Neptune conjunct his Seventh House cusp.[9] Actress and singer Whitney Houston has Neptune trine her Ascendant.[10]

Poet Allen Ginsberg had Jupiter in the Twelfth (Aquarius, esoteric Rulership) opposite Neptune (Leo, Exalted) in his Sixth.[11] Twelfth House mysticism comes through his poetry. He wanted readers to know that he'd been in "the presence of the Creator" and that his poems were inspired. (See above list of quotations.)

Pulitzer prizewinning playwright ("The Buried Child") Sam Shepard has Neptune in his Seventh and Jupiter inconjunct his Ascendant degree. He's written over forty plays and acted in several movies, including "The Right Stuff." He was nominated for an Oscar. Shepard has Neptune-trine-Uranus.

Judith Kranz has Jupiter conjunct her Ascendant (Rulership). She was fortunate in her social circle. At Wellesley College she once received a "B" grade on a story and vowed never to write another one. She did, however, succeed with articles submitted to *Good Housekeeping* and other magazines.

At twenty-five, Judith Tarcher met her husband, director Steve Krantz[12] at Barbara Walters' Fourth of July party. It was love at first sight; they were soon married.

"Felix the Cat" and his other animated films had made Steve a millionaire. At twenty-seven, after the birth of their first child,[13] she worked part time from home as a freelance writer.[14] For fifteen years, recognizing Judith's gift for storytelling, Steve patiently encouraged her to write a novel

Her first one, *Scruples,* went to her husband's publisher. It was an instant success; she'd discovered a new career at fifty!

---

8 In the individual horoscope, though, the two ruling planets could be in any of the four Elements. In De Palma's, Jupiter-in-Taurus (Earth) enhanced the three Earth planets in his Seventh House.

9 From the Sixth House side. It trines Uranus and squares Venus.

10 She has Jupiter/Moon conjunct in Aries in the First House.

11 The Pulitzer Prize and National Book Award winning author also has Mars and Uranus conjunct his Ascendant, which came through in his poem "HOWL!" which is in the anthology entitled, *HOWL!*

12 Walters is the television journalist from 20/20 and "The View."

13 Her first son was born when she was 27.

14 She contributed to many of the popular magazines. Her most famous article was for *Cosmopolitan,* "The Myth of the Multiple Orgasm."

Though the Talking Cure (psychoanalysis) may not appeal to Pisceans, they often find the Writing Cure effective. Judith let go of her Wellesley concerns about not being "literary" and developed her talent by writing entertaining novels. Krantz no longer cares if reviewers find her novels "trashy." She discovered that many women readers, like herself, "find shoe-shopping sexy."

While Jupiter is associated with Ninth House religion and scriptural study in preparation for a life of service in the larger community, Neptune is associated with the Twelfth House, mysticism and solitude.[15]

Thomas Merton, a Trappist monk with Pisces Rising, had five planets in Aquarius, including Mercury/Jupiter in the Twelfth inconjunct Neptune. Merton was the son of two artists who lived in Greenwich Village, New York. His mother was French, his father a New Zealander. When Thomas was six, his mother died. He spent two years with French grandparents in the countryside. His father died while Thomas was in boarding school.

Merton thought of himself an atheist. At Cambridge he drank, smoked, went to jazz clubs and slept with several women in an attempt to "fill the emptiness" he felt since his father's death. After his exams, he decided to attend Columbia University, New York. However, before leaving Europe he visited Rome, where he had a mystical experience in a Catholic church. He then began reading William Blake's poetry and biographies of saints.

The next time his Cambridge friends visited New York, they were shocked to hear of Merton's conversion to Catholicism. A year later, after visiting Gethsemani Abbey, Kentucky, he decided to enter the Trappist Order.

Merton's autobiography, his most famous book, *The Seven Storey Mountain*, drew widespread attention.[16] Soldiers returning from World War II, students, even teenagers, flocked to the monastery after reading it. Tents were assembled on Abbey grounds for all the guests and applicants.

A pacifist, Merton corresponded with Daniel P. Berrigan (Scorpio Rising) during the Vietnam War. At the end of his life, he lived alone in a cabin at the Abbey, enjoying his solitude.

He died in Bangkok during a visit to various spiritual leaders in Asia.

---

15 A European Trappist once told me, "you don't need a degree to become a monastic. I'm the only one here who attended a university. The other monks think my writing is an excuse to get out of helping with farm work." The schedule revolved around prayer and work. Short intervals of sleep were interspersed with chanting in the chapel. They took a vow of silence. This monastery is an example of a Twelfth House environment.

16 Fifty years later, it was on a list of the 100 most important books of the Twentieth Century.

In mythology, Neptune is associated with sacrifice. In Homer's *Odyssey*, before setting sail, the Trojans neglected to toss a sacrifice into the ocean for Poseidon. As a result, they were lost at sea for fifteen years, attempting to find their way home

In astrology, too, Neptune is associated with sacrifice. In its Natal House, one desire is often sacrificed in order to fulfill another. For example, some women with Neptune in the Fifth House have sacrificed creative potential in the first half of life; they "hadn't the time or energy" after caring for their children. Others have given up quality time with children, or having children altogether, to pursue another form of Fifth House creativity.

Carl Jung said that Prometheus paid a price for stealing the fire of creativity from the gods, and that creative people, too, pay theirs.

Vain regrets are sometimes voiced in nursing homes, "if only I had done things differently."

But fortunately, there's time in the second half of life for creative projects, if those have been neglected, or for playing with grandchildren or with step-grandchildren, if Pisces Rising missed the parenting experience.

Sometimes we, too, have regrets about unfulfilled desires in the Neptune-ruled House, the one with Pisces on the cusp. For Pisces Rising, that's also the *persona*.

Unless there are several First House planets, Pisces Rising is inclined to sacrifice their own desires to help others achieve theirs.[17] Many Pisceans are at peace with this sacrifice; it feels right to them. Some, however, are resentful. When Pisces cannot make the sacrifice whole-heartedly, without reservations, it's better to say, "no." When a situation doesn't feel right, it probably isn't.

Dionysus' Dual Identify

During the last three decades I've been privileged to work with idealistic former monks and nuns who have Pisces Rising. They come from Eastern, Western and New Age communities. And of course, I've met many glamorous, fashionable, "worldly fish" as well.

The great majority of my Pisces Rising clients are heterosexual; several are gay or lesbian.

---

17 Aries First House planets are seldom self-sacrificing, nor is Mars in the First. Ginsberg, a founder of The Beats, had Mars/Uranus conjunct on his Ascendant and followed a unique path, as did Kubler-Ross, with the same two planets in the middle of her First House.

A small number are bisexual. When mentioning the fact, they often remark, "everyone is really bisexual, though most people pretend not to notice."

Some have undergone therapy to rid themselves of "gender confusion" and have emerged from the process more confused than ever.

This story about Dionysus the Shapeshifter is for them.

Dionysius was a deity whose followers, mostly women, belonged to a mystery cult. They "went mad with ecstasy." Every year around the time of the grape harvest, in a region not far from Athens, there was an elaborate ritual. Dionysus came to the festival in a procession, riding in his traveling cart. He usually assumed the form of a bull.

When the festival was over, the Great God willingly sacrificed himself. He was torn apart by his worshippers, like the broken, trampled grapes. In the ritual, Dionysus died, was reborn, and sailed away until the next harvest.

In the beginning of this story,[18] Dionysus was very lonely. He missed his Mother, Semele, who had died and gone to the Underworld (Hades). Determined to descend, find her, and carry her out, he dived into Lake Lerna and sank to the bottom.

He was gone a long time looking for Semele.

His worshippers, waiting along the lake, began to worry. Then, suddenly, they gasped; he was emerging alone. He'd been unsuccessful.

"But wait! Is it really Dionysus?" asked a follower.

"No, it's a woman!" said another, sadly. She feared the Great God was a captive in Hades.

"*No! It's Dionysus, dressed as a woman!*" shouted a third.

The worshippers were confused. Dionysus stood on dry land, looking down at her apparel. She was surprised, but not at all embarrassed by the missing phallus.

However, she immediately began constructing an altar of fig-tree wood, on which she placed a phallus she'd fashioned herself.

Though he was unable to rescue Semele, every year thereafter Dionysus descended into Hades and visited his mother. This myth demonstrates both the sacrificial spirit of Pisces and Pisces' efforts at integrating Masculine and Feminine.

---

18 Carl Kerenyi, *Dionysus: Archetypal Image of Indestructible Life,* Bollingen LXV (2) NJ: Princeton University Press, 1976, 175-81. Aeschylus wrote a play based on the tragedy , "Semele, or the Water Carriers." More stories about Dionysus can be found in *Archetypes of the Zodiac,* "Pisces."

The Esoteric Ruler - Pluto

Neptune the Earthshaker, whose Trident alternately roils and calms the seas, who speaks through the symbolism of nightly dreams, escapist daydreams, creative imagery and mystical experience, is a subtle, ethereal force *compared to Pluto.*

Neptune is actually quite Yin, though we may not think so after a dream in which our house floods and all our possessions are swept out the door! In hurricane country, Neptune's dream-visits are often memorable.

Through dreams, art, music solitude and meditation, Neptune beckons us inward, urging us to honor our intuition and be true to our feelings.[19]

Neptune represents surrender, sacrifice, and faith in a Higher Power beyond the ego, a power whose grace, sufficient to our needs, is always there to guide us. Neptune's visions often result in humility and acceptance; the ego usually experiences itself as a small, almost negligible part of the Whole.[20]

These are Neptune's better attributes. But there's also a downside to Neptune; escapism, laziness, apathy, lack of vitality, (a weak immune system) and displaced mysticism, (the tendency to seek an altered state of consciousness by means of alcohol or drugs.) Sometimes, there's an urge to save others rather than do one's own inner work, (a Messiah Complex.)

Dionysus had a strong desire to rescue his mother. It proved an impossible task, but he got in touch with his feminine side in the process.

Pluto, the esoteric ruler, is quite different. Pluto is relentless. Squares, oppositions or inconjuncts to Pluto may indicate a compulsive, obsessive or addictive personality. Pluto aspecting the Ascendant degree makes a powerful impression on others.[21]

---

19 What Yeats called our "heart's core."

20 One example of such a vision is author Joyce Carol Oates' experience, her personality change, and the changes she made in her novel afterwards, "to take a moral stance." See Chapter 11, "Aquarius Rising." Another is Elisabeth Kubler-Ross' Cosmic Consciousness experience, recounted in *The Wheel of Life: A Memoir of Living and Dying,* (NY: Touchstone,) 1997, 217-223. Though she had a series of out-of-body experiences, this was the most meaningful. It happened soon after her divorce, validated her work, and enabled her to persevere with the international seminars. The name of her foundation, Shanti Nilaya, "going home in peace," came to her during the experience.

21 Many Leo Rising Baby Boomers have it conjunct their Ascendant. Magnetic personalities, they're persuasive salesmen, whatever their profession. With a Pluto trine to Pisces Rising, the eyes seem hypnotic.

Pisces easily becomes attached to the source of their financial or emotional support, even when that person is verbally, emotionally or physically abusive.

As strange as it sounds, some Pisceans victims become attached to their emotional pain. Exasperated friends and relatives have told them, "call me after you've left him (or her). I no longer want to hear about your relationship." After the last listener opts out, some seek professional help.

Many Piscean have remarkable faith in God and in Life ("things will turn around, my story will have a happy ending if I'm patient a little longer"), yet lack faith *in themselves.*

Years go by before their esoteric ruler transits Venus, Mars, the Moon or the South Node. The transit may last a year or two. Then, as Pluto wanes, the other person may break off with Pisces Rising.[22]

Occasionally, Pisces will "bottom out" on the addictive relationship themselves, usually because they fear for their children.

When the progressed Mask forms aspects from Aries, self-confidence improves. Pisces has an easier time believing that they can build an independent life for themselves.

Spiritually, long Pluto transits[23] seem similar to what St. John of the Cross and (Pisces Rising) St. Theresa of Avila called, "the dark night of the soul." There are no visions, no Divine messages, no beautiful symbolic dreams, no images to inspire art or poetry, no short story ideas, no signs or omens. Neptune's astral realm is strangely silent.

"Pluto dreams" are more like the two that Jung mentioned in *Memories, Dreams, Reflections*. In one, a turd fell from underneath God's heavenly throne onto the Basle cathedral and in the other (after asking for a Sign) he dreamt of a pile of manure. Such dreams catch our attention! Like Jung, we tend to remember the humble dreams.

The last Sign of the Zodiac, Pisces has the spiritual task of releasing attachments to people, places, objects, and images, everything that symbolizes personal security in the material world. The esoteric ruler is there to help.

The deep water fish is a veteran of many inner battles. While other Ascendants may have difficulty letting go of power and prestige, no Ascendant is better equipped than Pisces to re-invent itself for the second half of life. Though there were times when the shopping mall was their playground, on the whole, mystical fish don't take the material world very seriously. They adapt quickly to prosperity or recession.

---

22 On Pluto conjunct Venus, they tend to find a new love, leave town, or die. In one case, the man went to jail for tax evasion.

23 Pluto was once stationery on a client's South Node' it barely moved for three years. The transit coincided with a regressive state of min. He tried to turn back the clock and start over with his old love from college. Married with several children, she didn't welcome his midnight calls.

Neptune is kind; Pluto transforms. Esoteric Pisceans often contribute to improving others' quality of life. Two Pisces Rising doctors have gone beyond the medical model to the art of healing. The first is Elisabeth Kubler-Ross, a Swiss psychiatrist whose childhood aspiration was "to become a country doctor." Decades later, in the second half of life, she achieved her childhood goal in a unique way. While living and working in the United States, she taught seminars on living and dying, and promoted Hospice. Like a rural doctor in Switzerland, she sat for "thousands of hours" by the bedsides of dying patients.

The second is Deepak Chopra, who specialized in endochinology. The son of a New Delhi cardiologist, Chopra wanted to be an actor or a journalist in his youth. He came to the U.S. for his internship and residency, then went into private practice.

After writing for the New England Journal of Medicine and serving as Chief of Staff at two American hospitals, he left his lucrative career to write self-help books.[24] *Business Week* listed him among the top one hundred motivational speakers. He, too, achieved his childhood dreams in a unique way. Motivational speakers and actors have similar talents.

With Pisces resilience, he took a detour at midlife. Chopra's career risk turned out quite well for him. Countless Westerners also benefited from Ayur Vedic medicine and Eastern wisdom presented in a modern, readable style.

As mundane ruler of Scorpio, Pluto symbolizes determination, will power, and willfulness. As esoteric ruler of Pisces, a strongly-aspected Pluto has the same traits. Pluto enables the Yin Rising Sign to take a stand independent of family or peers, even if scorned by them.

Kubler-Ross' husband Emmanuel, also a doctor at the University of Chicago Hospital, was embarrassed by her "superstitious" behavior; the children also seemed uncomfortable with it. (She consulted an invisible spirit guide named Salem, photographed flower fairies, and even conversed with her former patients, recently deceased.)

Manny asked for a divorce, pointing out that he and the children seldom saw her. Booked as an international speaker, she was constantly on the road. Elisabeth observed that Manny was entrenched in an affluent suburb, intent upon acquiring more possessions. They'd grown apart. Elisabeth decided that their father could offer the children a more stable life. Heartbroken, she packed, then kissed them goodbye while they slept.

---

24 He also "gets the message out" on television. A friend of Michael Jackson's, Chopra was interviewed after the pop star's death. He reasserted his opinion on the dangers of pharmaceuticals. "One reason I left (Western) medicine is that pills don't *cure* insomnia, poor digestion, or many other problems.

When she left Illinois for California at fifty, she'd never written a check herself. Her husband bought her a house which he put in his own name as an investment.

Deepak Chopra's wife supported him in his midlife career change. But his will to follow his own path was tested by his teacher, Maharishi Mahesh Yogi, who'd trained him in meditation techniques, and suggested Dr. Chopra study Ayur Veda. Later, affronted by Chopra's growing reputation, the Maharishi seemed to feel that the doctor was encroaching on his territory. Dr. Chopra, however, had no desire to be a guru. After breaking with the Maharishi's organization, he explored his own interest, the "mind-body complex."

When Kubler-Ross and Chopra came to America as outsiders, they both noticed what was missing from the US medical model. With their unique backgrounds and knowledge, they each developed an alternative method.

Kubler-Ross, who came from a country where doctors had a "bedside manner" and took a personal interest in their patients, focused on the needs of the dying, while Chopra focused on preventive medicine, (patients taking responsibility for their own health through diet and exercise), Ayur Vedic medicine, and the link between the mind and the body's well being. Both Kubler-Ross and Deepak Chopra believed that real solutions came from intuition. Both also believed that doctors needed to listen to patients, and that patients needed to listen to their bodies.

As esoteric ruler of Pisces, Pluto is considered an evolutionary force for societal change. For esoteric Pisceans, Pluto's role is not limited to will power and/or developing a unique personality. Pluto still symbolizes a sense of purpose, determination and will power or willfulness. But it also represents something more, an impulse to change the culture. Kubler Ross and Dr. Chopra are remarkable examples of Pluto as esoteric ruler of Pisces.

In the previous chapter, esoteric Aquarius was the embodiment of impersonal, unconditional Divine Love. But Kubler-Ross spoke instead of *personal,* unconditional, unselfish love." She said in several of her lectures that it is the only thing worthwhile in life, the only thing we take with us when we die. She expressed this love by sitting for thousands of hours at the bedsides of dying people.

Both Chopra and Kubler-Ross acted on their intuition when making life-changing decisions. And, finally, they have kindness in common. Though they come from different cultural backgrounds, Chopra and Kubler-Ross are in agreement on the importance of thinking only positive thoughts about others.

Elisabeth believed it was impossible to help someone we feel hatred, anger or hostility towards. She gave an example from one of her seminars.[25] There were about eighty health

---

25 In the collection of lectures, *The Tunnel and the Light*, cited above, "the Schnook," 117-123.

care givers present, nurses, social workers, theology students, priests, ministers and rabbis who worked with the dying.

The first hour of the class consisted mostly of questions and answers. Elisabeth introduced a dying patient, who briefly described what he or she needed from the hospital staff, and who then took questions from the group. The second hour, after the patient left, they discussed what could be done differently to help the person.

But that day the usual format didn't work; the patient unexpectedly died ten minutes before the class met. There was no time to obtain doctors' permissions to interview another patient; Elisabeth was on her own. She went to the stage, explained the situation and then suggested they use the time to discuss whatever they considered to be the cancer ward's greatest problem.

Surprisingly, the answer was unanimous. The Department Head was the greatest problem! Nobody liked him. There were degrees of dislike, but everyone considered "the arrogant big shot" their worst problem.

While others were speaking, Elisabeth flashed back to her own confrontation with the Chief. He didn't like talking to patients, so he'd sent several charts to her, the doctor in charge of psychosomatic cases. He'd expected her to "improve their attitudes."

She studied the x-rays, found tumors in all of them, and informed the Chief they were not psychosomatic cases. They were all really dying, so psychiatry wouldn't help them. *He* could listen to their needs. A minister or social worker could do more for them than she. In the end, the Chief wasn't happy with her and she didn't like *him*, either.

The class deliberated, then decided that the Chief couldn't be helped by somebody who disliked him. The negativity would interfere. He needed to feel compassion or kindness.

Eventually she asked the group, "is there *no one* here who likes him at all? Even a little bit?"

A shy nurse raised her hand. Staring at the floor, she said that she was the only one there at night when he made his rounds. She didn't like him, but she felt very sorry for him. Before entering each patient's room, he'd put on his professional, clinical mask. When he came out, his jaw dropped. Then he'd replace the mask and continue down the hall, emerging a little more ashen from each room. By the time he finished, he looked dreadful.

Though it wouldn't be appropriate for her, a mere nurse, to reach out and touch the arm of the "big shot," she'd been tempted to do it many nights. And also, to mutter something like, "it's okay, you're doing the best you can."

The group discussed the situation and unanimously agreed the nurse was the only one who could help him, and indirectly, help change things for them all. She felt compassion; she shared his anguish.

The nurse, terrified, insisted she couldn't do it. Elisabeth assured her it was possible, but not from the thinking quadrant of the brain. (Mercury). She'd have to be in the spiritual, intuitive quadrant (Moon/Neptune.) Some night, she would "know." And she could just "say whatever comes out."

Elisabeth forgot all about the class. Then, several days later, a young woman, practically hysterical, burst into her office. It was the nurse. "I did it! I did it!" She shouted, dancing around the office. Kubler-Ross finally recognized her from the previous week.

"Three nights went by before I could approach him," she began. "My mind said not to do that, but I remembered my commitment, and that I'd promised not to think first. The third night, I quickly walked over and reached out—but I don't think I touched him—and I said, "God, it must be difficult."

He grabbed her, started to sob, pulled her into his office and cried in her arms. He told her about being in medical school learning his specialty, which he thought would really help people, while his friends were dating, getting married and earning a living. He'd postponed living and now, he felt impotent. His patients were all dying; there was nothing he could do. He'd been taught that his role was to prolong life, but that was impossible.

The nurse let go of the "shoulds" and "oughts" of the hospital bureaucracy and listened to the doctor "human being to human being." A year later, he called Kubler-Ross for help. Because of his position as Chief he refused to go to her office, so Elisabeth arranged telephone consultations.[26]

Pluto transits also have an archetypal meaning beyond the individual horoscope, a meaning for the larger society.[27] Like bureaucracies, business models become rigid over time and crack along their fault lines. During a Pluto-in-Capricorn recession, for example, the United States is dealing with banking regulations, infrastructure repair, alternative fuels; a growing elderly population, the pressures of demographics and unemployment

---

26 Kubler Ross, *The Tunnel and the Light,* cited above, "the Schnook," 117-122.
27 Pluto will be in early Capricorn through spring, 2014. Capricorn rules the banking system, bank managers, the stock market, property, and the capitalist economic model. In 2014, at ten degrees Capricorn, Pluto will oppose the United States' Sun-in-Cancer. Slow moving and thorough, Pluto cannot be out waited in hopes that everything will eventually return to normal. Pluto was in Cancer, conjunct the U.S. Sun, in the late 1920's. By the end of the Great Depression, Franklin Delano Roosevelt and the Congress had established Social Security, Unemployment Insurance, and the Federal Reserve bank.

(so many people prefer to live on the coasts and in the Sun Belt), health care costs and the deficit. Changes will come as the Pluto opposition wanes.

During another cycle of turmoil, World War II, Carl Jung said that love must triumph over power. In the language of astrology, Venus and Jupiter must not yield to Pluto.

In the Twenty-First Century, Age of Pisces values like kindness and compassion will be challenged. Two thousand years ago when the Piscean Age began, Jesus of Nazareth taught a gospel of unselfish love. "You shall love the Lord your God with all your heart, and with all your soul, and with all your strength, and with all your mind; and your neighbor as yourself."[28] At the end of the Age, will we still follow this teaching?

Or, in a time of recession and budget deficits, will we treat the elderly and the poor as unproductive, unsuccessful citizens who burden the rest of us with their "self-created problems?" Will we reduce or deny their funding? Cancer is a thrifty Sun Sign but fortunately, Cancer is also nurturing.

The Element - Water

Water is about feelings, intuition, psychic ability, and shared memories. Like Cancers, Pisceans are sympathetic and empathetic. Unless there are many hard aspects, they're kind, sentimental and nostalgic. Pisces is the Sign most likely to cry during sad movies. Like the other Water Signs, they prefer to make major decisions from intuition rather than logic. Friends with Water Signs rising, especially Pisces, have written beautiful poetry.

Of all the Rising Signs, Pisces does the best with natural remedies. Many have adverse reactions to antibiotics. Neither Kubler-Ross nor Deepak Chopra liked pharmaceuticals; my Pisces Rising friends and clients feel the same way. Many of them tell me they'll only take half an aspirin, as "those things can't possibly be good for a person." Yet, like Kubler-Ross, they'll smoke, drink "bottomless cups of coffee" and eat lots of chocolate. Or, like Allen Ginsberg, they like laughing gas, marijuana, and experimented with LSD in the "sixties."

If he has Virgo planets, Pisces may read *Consumer Reports* and consult a mechanic

---

28 See Matthew Chapter 25:35-45. "When I was hungry you gave me to eat; when I was thirsty, you gave me to drink. When I was naked, you clothed me. When I was a stranger, you welcomed me. When I was in prison, you visited me. Whatever you did for the least of my brethren, this you did unto Me." See also, the Sermon on the Mount, Matthew 5 and Luke 6, 20-49 And Luke 10: 27, "Love the Lord your God with your whole heart, soul mind and your neighbor as yourself." *New American Standard Bible*, @1995.

friend before purchasing a new car. But in the end, he'll disregard the facts and follow his intuition. He'll sit awhile in a care he likes to see if it "feels right." If it does, he'll buy it.

This annoys the mechanic friend who spent time with Pisces, and the relative who gave him *Consumer Reports* for his birthday. Both expected Pisces to make a more "logical" choice, but that's a small matter. He's happy with his purchase. He's also grateful to the relative and the mechanic for helping him eliminate the wrong cars. It is, after all, *his* car and *his* choice.

Hypersensitive in youth and self-protective as adults, Pisceans tends to share their deepest feelings with only a few close friends. As a result, they feel lost for awhile when a friend moves away; their world has shrunk. The Water Element is about merging or dissolving. Sufi mystic Hazrat Inayat Khan spoke of it mystically, "I have seen all souls as my soul, and realized my soul as the soul of all." Merging with the Divine is wonderful.

But sometimes Pisces Rising merges with a spouse or partner to the point where Pisces can no longer distinguish the "I" from the "We."

In that case, losing the person is harder for Pisces than any other Rising Sign, even Cancer and Scorpio. Max Heindel's point (above, How to Recognize Pisces Rising) about Pisces taking longer to recover than other Signs is true emotionally as well as physically.

Kubler-Ross was right when she said, "give others as much love as you can because nothing is more important." Still, if the beloved dies and Pisces lives on, Pisces needs to know who he or she is as an individual, in order to survive.

Sometimes Pisces Rising develops an ability to "see" or visualize an obstruction in someone else's body, then "go there mentally" and dissolve it.[29] Massage therapists with Water Signs Rising, particularly Pisceans, often hold their hands over the person's body, close their eyes and hone in on the exact spot that's causing distress. Then they'll spend an hour on it.

Over the years, several Pisces Rising people have told me, "we're all cells in the same cosmic organism, Humanity. Whatever hurts one of us hurts everybody else." Negative thoughts, whether spoken or left unsaid, damage the ecosystem. But positive, compassionate thoughts will help repair the hole in the ozone layer."

Deepak Chopra said, "if you and I are having a single thought of violence or hatred against anyone in the world at this moment, we are contributing to the wounding of the world."

---

29 Elisabeth Kubler-Ross seems to have been healed in her sleep. She dreamed that a group of men worked on her body as if they were repairing a car. When she awoke, a slipped disc no longer bothered her. She could pick heavy objects up from the floor again. A bowel obstruction was also gone and her digestion much more efficient.

To Pisces, this in not an abstract theory, but the way the world works. It's practical knowledge, applicable to daily life.

And since *they* easily intuited this, surely the rest of us are aware of it, too! "Why do people persist in doing mean things to each other?" Pisces wonders.

Pisces Rising horoscopes that are low in Fire and/or have Mars located in a weaker house usually find it difficult to assert or defend themselves. Nicole Brown Simpson, for instance, had nearly all her planets in the more passive Elements, Earth and Water. The exceptions were her Seventh House Moon-in-Libra (Air),[30] Uranus, an outer planet in Leo, and the South Node in Aries, which stood alone in her First House.

A beautiful young woman with Venus ruling both her Sun (Taurus) and Moon, Nicole married football hero O.J. Simpson at eighteen, the year the North and South Nodes returned to their places in her Natal First and Seventh Houses.

She was pregnant with their daughter. Two years later, she had another child, a son. Nicole was a battered wife. In spite of several calls to the police for domestic violence, she stayed with him for fifteen years.

With Mars-in-Cancer (Fall) trine Jupiter in the Eighth House (Others' Finances), she did well enough in the divorce settlement to purchase two cars and a town house in an expensive area.[31] With Neptune in the psychic Eighth she no doubt had beautiful daydreams and lofty goals. With Saturn in Capricorn in her Tenth House in sextile to her Ascendant, it probably seemed as if she'd fulfill them through marriage. But after the Saturn Return, the marriage ended.

O.J. Simpson had many affairs. With Pluto-in-Virgo conjunct her Seventh House Cusp,[32] Nicole probably didn't receive as much attention as she felt she needed and deserved. And she was probably perceived as needy, demanding and manipulative.[33]

Dr. Elizabeth Kubler-Ross and poet Allen Ginsberg had Mars and Uranus in the First House. Neither had difficulty in being assertive or making risky midlife decisions.

Dr. Chopra has Mars-in-Scorpio (Rulership) trine his Ascendant. With Mars conjunct Mercury in his Eighth House (a psychic House), his intuitive decisions generally work out well.[34]

Mars, Uranus, the Sun, Jupiter and the North Node were all lined up in Aquarius in

---

30 The Libra Moon in the Seventh House tries hard to please relationship partners.

31 She had Sun-in-Taurus in her Second, opposite Jupiter. O.J. also has Sun-in-Taurus.

32 From the Sixth House side.

33 In horoscopes where Air and Fire are low, a strongly-placed Pluto usually comes through as manipulative.

34 Chopra also has the Sun-in-the-Eighth. His is in Libra (Air).

Thomas Merton's chart, opposite his Leo Moon. With Pluto on the Nadir opposite Venus at the Midheaven, his childhood was difficult. He acted out during his student years, then settled into the Houses where most of his planets were located, Houses Eleven and Twelve, the Friendship (Trappist community) and Solitude Houses. He wrote, meditated, and corresponded with several famous or influential people (Leo Moon).

The Mode - Mutability

Pisces is the last of the Mutable Signs. Astrologers usually associate this easygoing, flexible mode with tolerance of others' beliefs. In youth, however, the two Jupiter-ruled Mutables, Sagittarius and Pisces, are often absolutists on the subject of religion and adamant about their political beliefs. While Sagittarian fire is argumentative, Pisceans may worry that their "deluded" friend or family member won't get into heaven or that dad's vote is taking the country in the wrong direction.

With Saturn or Pluto in the First House or aspecting the Ascendant, or with a high percentage of Fixed planets, Pisces Rising finds it easier to set boundaries. With a Cardinal Sun Sign like Cancer (Kubler-Ross), Libra (Deepak Chopra) or Capricorn (Clara Barton, Judith Kranz), Pisceans have an easier time knowing their own minds and finding their own way in life.

Otherwise, Pisces Rising is even more suggestible than the other Mutable Signs. From childhood through old age, environment has a strong influence on this Ascendant. The esoteric ruler, Pluto, in a Fixed Sign will strengthen will power.

In new environments, Mutables often change their views. Family members are often surprised when their most religious child comes home from college influenced by a teacher or a new love with very different beliefs or opinions. After relocating, most Mutables adapt more quickly and easily to life in their new region than Fixed or Cardinal Signs. Some even change their political or religious affiliation.

Mutables are often gifted communicators. The Mutable Mask is very receptive to new information, especially when presented by a strong personality, someone they admire. However, Pisces may attempt too much. With planets in Virgo, Gemini or Sagittarius, information overload puts the nervous system under stress. Meditation, yoga, and massage are helpful.

As a young woman, Elisabeth Kubler-Ross knew she was highly suggestible. When she encountered Carl Jung (Aquarius Rising) on his walks, she felt "an eerie familiarity as if they would hit it off magically together." Yet she walked across the street rather than introduce herself to him.

A medical student in Zurich at the time, she knew several others who, after speaking once or twice with Herr Doktor Jung decided to specialize in psychiatry. Avoidance seemed the safest strategy to protect her dream of becoming a country doctor.

Later, as a psychiatrist in the United States,[35] she was sorry to have missed her opportunity to meet Jung. By then, she was applying his ideas in her quadrants of the brain[36] approach to children dying of cancer. At the time, however, following her intuition was the right choice.

As the years go by, most Pisceans are happier with the intuitive decisions than the decisions influenced by others. When faithful to their intuition, there are fewer vain regrets.

Like the other Mutables, Pisces is curious about so many areas of life that finishing a long project can be challenging. The more new people Pisces meets, the more opportunities appear and the more distracted he becomes.

While it's true that Mutables are restless, it's also true that Pisceans may feel more joy in helping a close friend or relative with his project than in finishing theirs. Pisces giving up his own project may seem sacrificial to others, but not to him. As Jupiter's children, Pisceans instinctively follow their bliss.

When his projects matter, a flexible deadline helps with focus.

First House Aries planets, brought out by the progressed Mask, lend the persona vitality, authority and pioneering spirit. Nurse Clara Barton had Saturn and Jupiter conjunct in Aries in the First House, trine Mercury in Sagittarius.[37] Allen Ginsberg and Elizabeth Kubler-Ross, with Uranus in the First House, were original thinkers.

Mutables are usually open to new opportunities, even when they involve a major change like relocation. As they grow older, their openness and adaptability helps them adjust to life changes.

Of all the Mutable Signs, Pisces, the most Yin, seems the most receptive to Grace.

---

35 She said that in Zurich, psychiatry was at the bottom of her list of possible specialties, but later as a married woman trying to become pregnant, psychiatry offered an easier schedule at the hospital than her other options.

36 Physical, intellectual, emotional, spiritual/intuitive. Children who are dying of cancer have a "wide open spiritual quadrant" which becomes stronger as the physical quadrant declines. *The Tunnel of the Light,* cited above, 41-49.

37 She had Neptune at the Midheaven and Pluto conjunct the Ascendant.

The Mask in Youth

Early childhood environment is especially important for Pisceans. Whether good or bad, the home environment affects them deeply. Long after their siblings have forgotten childhood incidents, Pisces Rising remembers.

As children, Pisceans are more likely than other Signs to visualize themselves happily engaged in performing certain tasks. If Jupiter and/or Neptune is strongly-placed in the horoscope, they're also likely to accomplish these or similar tasks as adults.

Sometimes, like Allen Ginsberg's and Deepak Chopra's, their parents will offer them encouragement and/or financial assistance. Allen's father, Louis Ginsberg, was also a poet.[38] Surrounded by poetry books as a boy, he easily memorized many long poems. Deepak Chopra's father was a medical doctor, a Chief of Staff in New Delhi.

Thomas Merton's parents were Greenwich Village artists. His grandfather left a trust fund for Tom and his brother's education.

Judith Krantz, who has Jupiter on her Ascendant, attended Wellesley. She and her supportive husband, Steve had a long and happy marriage.[39]

Hazrat Inayat Khan grew up in a home where poets, musicians and philosophers gathered. He learned to play the Vina and decided to seek his own experience of God after hearing about others'.

It isn't always a smooth path from the visualization or the daydream to its actualization. Like Elisabeth Kubler, Pisces usually faces many challenges along the way.

The youngest of triplets, Elisabeth weighed only two pounds at birth. One day, she overheard an adult refer to her as "that two pound nothing," and became determined to prove herself *at least* equal to everyone else.

With Mars and Uranus in her First House and Sun/Pluto/Node trine her Ascendant, she defended her sister Eva, whom their pastor had punished for "not memorizing her Psalm."

---

38 As well as a high school teacher. See, *Family Business: Selected Letters Between a Father and Son, Louis and Allen Ginsberg,* Michael Schumaker, ed, (NY: Bloomsbury,) 2001. Because of his mother's mental problems, Ginsberg's was a more troubled childhood than most of the other examples.

39 Steve Krantz died of pneumonia in 2007.

Later, Elisabeth refused to be confirmed in the church where Eva was mistreated.[40] Expecting a journalist to appear on Confirmation Day and photograph the triplets, her father was embarrassed.

When his friend Reverend Zimmerman came to speak to her, Elisabeth, then sixteen, told him that God was too big to be confined to any one church or be defined by Man. She also disliked the fear, guilt, and shame religion instilled. Avoiding Elisabeth's arguments, the Reverend told her to make the highest possible choices every day, that was all God expected. She was appeased. Then, to her father's relief, the triplets were confirmed and photographed together.

Her sisters were docile in following their father's plans. One went to finishing school and the other to the gymnasium. But when Elisabeth was she was to become her father's bookkeeper, she refused. Her "creative mind and restless nature would die sitting behind a desk." Her father replied that she'd have to go away and work as a maid. She was shocked, but quickly agreed to go. Her goals were to save money; find work at a lab, and eventually attend medical school.

Elisabeth lasted a year as a maid in the home of a very snobbish woman, then worked in a cosmetics lab. Her boss was a manic depressive whose moods ranged from enthusiastic to skeptical and depressed. By the time he went bankrupt, she'd accumulated her math and science credits at the university.

Back home again, her father gave her three weeks to find a job. If she didn't succeed, she was to to begin immediately as his bookkeeper. Whenever she felt self-pity, she visualized herself in his office. At the end of the third week, Elisabeth received an apprenticeship in dermatology. Excited, about the job, she didn't tell her father about working in a windowless room of the hospital basement, or taking blood samples from prostitutes with late-stage venereal diseases.

By 1944, Swiss hospitals were filled with traumatized refugees. They came in waves, "hundreds at a time," many from as far away as France. With little time to sleep or eat, she fell behind in her lab work. She and her "accomplice," Mr. Baldwin ordered hundreds of extra meals from the hospital and distributed them to refugee children.

When summoned by the new boss, Elisabeth expected to be fired for stealing food and/ or neglecting her work. Surprisingly, Dr. Weitz, who'd watched her from afar, agreed that

---

40 The pastor had accused the girl standing next to Eva of coaching her during a Psalm recitation, when in fact Eva was "letter -perfect." (The other girl had covered her mouth to cough.) The minister knocked the girls' heads together so loudly that "the crack of bone-on-bone made the whole class shudder." Elisabeth threw the Psalm book at his face and "hit him in the kisser." *The Wheel of Life,* cited above, 42.

the refugees needed food. He could see that this work "made her very happy and was her destiny." Dr. Weitz, who'd seen great suffering in Poland, invited Elisabeth to accompany him to the camps when the war and her apprenticeship ended. Inspired, she agreed.

But then "the other shoe dropped." She and the accomplice, "two lowly lab techs," were told that if they couldn't repay the full amount of the meals or the equivalent in ration cards, they'd be terminated. Devastated, she encountered Dr. Weitz and explained her predicament. Disgusted at the bureaucracy, he told her not to worry. He'd get the ration cards from Zurich's Jewish community, and he did. Elisabeth also followed through on her promise, the trip to Poland.

After facing difficult challenges, Elisabeth realized her dream of becoming a doctor. Like many Pisceans, she was assigned some of the worst cases, (VD patients,) which other apprentices had refused. She believed her commitment to medicine had been tested; that had she "been in it for the money," she'd have quit.

During the war and later, in Poland, she learned that not everyone shared her idealism. This can be a painful lesson for Pisces Rising, especially when the Earth Element is low or lacking. Pisces clients are very sad when they come up against the problem of budget limitations while working at places like hospitals and animal shelters.

One Pisces Rising woman called in during a Jerry Lewis Telethon and signed up twelve of her friends, committing them to send money for disabled children. Her friends were shocked when the letter of gratitude and the bill arrived later from the foundation.

When they called her about it, she said, "I know you have a generous heart. Had you been listening to the telethon that night, I knew you'd have signed up to help Jerry's Kids. So, I simply did it for you!" But they weren't as generous as she'd imagined!

In spite of their Neptunian gifts of intuition and visualization, Pisceans don't achieve every dream. Elisabeth Kubler wanted to go to India, for instance, but the project was cancelled. However, they're usually quick to spot the silver lining behind their disappointment. Elisabeth said that had she gone to India, it's doubtful she'd have married Manny Ross.

My Pisces Rising clients rarely have more than three children and seldom more than two. Several have spent many years in convents or monasteries. Others, writers or artists, have opted for quiet lives and solitude time to practice their craft.

Pisces Rising authors who had no children include Clara Barton, Thomas Merton, Allen Ginsberg and Gertrude Stein. Deepak Chopra, Judith Krantz, Elisabeth Kubler-Ross and Nicole Simpson each had two children. Science fiction and fantasy author Roger Zelazny had three, as does actor and playwright Alan Shepard.

Sufi mystical poet and musician Hazrat Inayat Khan wandered through India in his youth, then toured Europe and American reciting poetry and playing music. Eventually, he married and had four children.[41]

The Mask After Midlife

Pisceans tend to be late bloomers. For many, the first half of life is about finding themselves and learning their craft. Before she married, Judith Tarcher had worked in the Paris fashion industry, where she met many celebrities. At home, she wrote for *Good Housekeeping*.

When she was fifty,[42] her first novel, *Scruples* appeared and became instant best-seller. She had a new career! Krantz has been a prolific author in the romance genre ever since.

Elisabeth Kubler-Ross published her "ground-breaking" book, *On Death and Dying,* at forty-three. Like Krantz, Elisabeth's life also changed dramatically at fifty, the year that the asteroid Chiron returned to its natal place.

Everyone has a Chiron Return, but the Wounded Healer cycle seems particularly significant in the lives of medical practitioners. Chiron's return impacted her Second House, (Finances, Values/Sense of Purpose).

In her youth, Elisabeth, with Sun/Pluto/Node in Cancer trine her Ascendant and Cancer Moon wanted to become a pediatrician. She also had a strong desire for children of her own. After a series of miscarriages, she gave up pediatrics for psychiatry, with its less demanding schedule, and Kenneth and Barbara finally arrived. Just as she'd hoped and predicted, she had two children, a boy and a girl.

By fifty, however she'd begun to sacrifice time with her family to travel and lecture on the needs of dying patients, particularly children with cancer. Featured in *Life Magazine*,

---

41 His son Pir Vilayat Khan, co-founder of Omega in Rhinebeck, NY, and his daughter Noor are the most famous. The former followed him as head of the Sufi Order International. The latter, Noor, a British spy during World War II, was captured and put to death at Dachau. His grandson is the current head of the order.

42 Krantz and Kubler-Ross both have Chiron in the First House, but close to the cusp of the Second.

in great demand as a speaker after *On Death and Dying,*[43] the modern shaman was caught up in the momentum of her work.[44]

Though highly intuitive in working with patients, Elisabeth was quite surprised when her husband, Manny, told her that he wanted a divorce.[45] She thought he was joking! She seemed unaware that he felt neglected, though she did note his inability to relate to her sense of purpose or her new California friends, like the medium who channeled Salem, her spirit guide.

This is a common pattern for Pisces Rising. Years pass while they're caught up in intuitive, spiritual or creative work. They seem (or prefer) not to notice the dwindling enrollment at their parochial school; they're unaware that with many leaving the convent or monastery, Pisces' position as cook is in jeopardy. Or, they're unconcerned that their New Age Healing Center is losing patrons, and Pisces will need to develop a new massage clientele. Mundane changes may catch them off guard. Or, like Elisabeth and Manny Ross, Pisceans may be growing in a different direction from family members.

Unless there's a problem with drug or alcohol addiction, Pisces Rising is resilient and rebounds quickly. The Jupiter-Neptune Rulership symbolizes faith that God, or Life, will open new doors when old doors close. In Kubler-Ross' case, Manny paid for the land for her Shanti Nilaya healing center and her new house in Escondido, California.

In their fifties and early sixties, Pisceans may take awhile settling into their new life or lifestyle. Kubler-Ross, for instance, discovered that the critics were right, her psychic friend Jay Barham was a charlatan, (although Salem, her guide, "was real.")

Soon after she refused to write the preface for Barham's book, Elisabeth's house burned to the ground. The fire department suspected arson.

Unfazed, she relocated to Headwater, Virginia and purchased a farm. She intended to establish a community and a hospital for orphans whose parents had died of AIDS. During the 1980's, however, there was widespread fear of an AIDs epidemic. The local zoning commission denied her the permits. Once again, Elisabeth's house mysteriously burned to the ground.

---

43 *On Death and Dying* includes the famous five stages of grief: denial, anger, bargaining, depression and acceptance.

44 In the years that followed *On Death and Dying,* Kubler-Ross estimated that over 100,000 people attended her lectures. Though she didn't found hospice herself, she promoted it, and she became known as the founder of Thanatology.

45 She said it was Father's Day and the family had just finished dinner. They were in the restaurant parking lot when he delivered the ultimatum. He then got in his car and drove away, leaving her and the children to go home alone.

True to her sense of mission, she continued to travel and lecture on the needs of the dying; "doctors must be honest about the time remaining to patients so that they could 'sort out unfinished business,' particularly in their relationships, and move on to the Afterlife. Patients need hands-on care, unconditional love, personal attention, and thousands of hours of listening."

She suffered two strokes in the 1990's. At the end of her life, she settled in Arizona. When Manny's investments failed, she sent him money. "Why were you surprised (to receive the funds)?" she asked. She added, "*I didn't divorce you, you divorced me.*" Pisces Rising is often kind and supportive to the former spouse long after the divorce.

Deepak Chopra, too, went through several changes of affiliation in the second half of life. After leaving Western medicine, he was first associated with the Transcendental Meditation organization. He tried affiliating with Sharp Hospital in San Diego and other institutions. Though it was a "stressful," period,[46] his house didn't burn down! And he eventually established his own foundation and Ayur Vedic medical center.

Like Kubler-Ross, Chopra was also berated by critics, especially his medical peers. Cardinal Sun Signs, both focused on their own unique approach. Kubler-Ross believed that *the healer's* physical, mental, emotional and spiritual quadrants of the brain must all be involved in helping the patient transition to the Afterlife. Chopra, however, focuses on self-help; *the patient* must engage his own body-mind continuum to prevent disease or recover from it. Both Pisces Rising healers exemplify Pisces' personal, unselfish, unconditional love. Both took personal risks to help fill society's needs.

Inayat Khan and Kubler-Ross[47] both inspired a son who continued their work. Chopra's son, too, is currently involved in films and graphic novels (formerly called comic books) about Hindu myths and Indian philosophy.

Progressed Ascendant in Aries

Aries is Cardinal Fire, and Mars-ruled. This is an energetic cycle. As the progressed Mask moves through Aries, it puts Pisces Rising in touch with Natal Fire planets by forming conjunctions or trines to them, and with Natal Cardinal planets by forming squares or oppositions.

---

46 He used the word stressful about his break with the Maharishi's group.

47 A photographer by profession, Kenneth Ross serves as President of the Elisabeth Kubler-Ross Foundation and does speaking engagements on her philosophy of dying, "death is like graduation."

During the Mars-ruled cycle, placid Pisces Rising is less patient, more easily ruffled, even irritable if the new Mask conjuncts Natal Aries planets. But there advantages. The new Aries persona is not as *overtly* embarrassed, uncertain, guilty, fearful, or worrisome. Though Pisces still takes criticism to heart, the Aries Mask conceals hurt feelings.

Natal Mars-in-the-First in Aries (Rulership), is quite courageous, acting and reacting impulsively. The year that the progressed Ascendant conjuncts Natal Mars is often memorable. Gentle Pisces Rising may shock authority figures with sudden, out-of-control rage. For example, as the Aries progressed Ascendant conjuncted her First House Mars, sixteen-year-old Elisabeth Kubler threw the Psalm book at her pastor, hitting him in the face.

For the Pisces teenager, an angry outburst like Elisabeth's[48] is as more likely to result from outrage that *someone else* was mistreated as from concern that Pisces *himself* was being treated unfairly.

Clara Barton, who was called the "Angel of the Battlefield" during the American Civil War, progressed into Aries at the age of four. At six, her progressed Mask made its first aspect to a Natal planet, a square to Neptune, mundane ruler of Pisces, in two degrees Capricorn. As often happens with a strongly-placed planet like Clara's Tenth House Neptune, this first contact from the new Mask set the tone for a lifetime of compassionate service.

The youngest of five children, Clara was home schooled. Her older siblings each enthusiastically taught her their "best" subject. With Sun-in-Capricorn conjunct Uranus, she learned quickly. She later wrote a book about her childhood,[49] mentioning her family's encouragement when, at sixteen, she began teaching.

In her late teens, the Aries Mask formed a trine to Mercury-in-Sagittarius in her Ninth House. An inspiring teacher, she established a free public school in Bordentown, NJ. Over the next three years, the Aries Mask squared the Moon, (also in Capricorn in her Tenth,) then went on to conjunct Jupiter and Saturn in her First House. Her Capricorn organizing skills were engaged. The "natural" teacher (Sagittarius) was also a natural authority figure

---

48 A photographer by profession, Kenneth Ross serves as President of Elizabeth Kubler-Ross Foundation and does speaking engagements on her philosophy of dying, "death is like graduation."

49 *The Story of My Childhood*, (NY: Baker and Taylor,) 1907. Her father fought in the American Revolution and served in the state legislature. With Saturn in her First House square her Capricorn Moon, Clara followed his example of public service. She said, "you must never so much as think whether you like it or not, whether it is bearable or not; you must never think of anything except the need, and how to meet it." (See above, list of Pisces Rising quotes.)

(Capricorn.) At this time, Clara experienced the joy of her Natal Fire Mercury-Jupiter trine.

By her early twenties, the confident Aries Mask had already helped in overcoming shyness and integrating the energy of four outer planets, two of which, Jupiter and Neptune, ruled her Ascendant. A third, her First House Saturn-in-Aries, ruled her Sun and Moon, the planets that represent personal goals and inner satisfaction, respectively. Clara's sense of purpose and dutiful nature were awakened.

The fourth outer planet, Uranus-in-Capricorn represented her quick, insightful, yet practical approach to problem-solving. Later, it would also describe her "day job." Clara was the first women to work in the U.S. patent office where new discoveries (Uranus) are investigated and recorded. Like many with Pisces Rising, she probably found the office routine calming. And her Sixth House Mars-in-Virgo (trine Moon in the Tenth) was good with details. Eventually, she lectured for the Suffragettes, who were fighting for women's right to vote.

Any outer planet that's strongly-placed by House (1, 4, 7, 10) or aspects the Sun, Moon or Ascendant connects a person to the issues of his generation and the themes of his era.

Pluto is the most powerful and relentless of the outer planets. (We feel Uranus' restlessness in our early forties, for instance, but our Unconscious, our inner Hades, is always with us. And while asserting our will power sometimes works during a Uranus cycle, Pluto represents forces beyond our control. See Scorpio Rising, *Sturm und Drang*.) With Pluto transits, our only choice is how to react to change.

With her esoteric ruler, Pluto, conjunct her Pisces Ascendant, Clara was involved with serious "life and death" issues beyond the concerns of the classroom or the patent office. Whenever she saw a need, she responded.

Aries learns through experience. Though nursing schools are named for her today, they didn't exist in Clara's time. She developed her skills as she went along. In her forties, during the Civil War, she helped supply and care for wounded troops on both sides.

At first she worked alone, without supervision. Over time, she won the support of generals and the help of other nurses.

After the war, President Lincoln commissioned Clara to identify missing troops. Hers was the sad task of visiting unmarked graves in Georgia.[50] In search of missing soldiers, she also corresponded with veterans and reported back to their families[51]

Later, Clara was put in charge of disaster relief. She arranged for water, blankets and

---

50 She identified 22,000 soldiers, one-tenth of the missing troops.
51 She eventually became head of the new Missing Persons Department.

other supplies to be sent to flood victims on Galveston, Texas and to yellow fever sufferers in Florida.

When she suffered a breakdown in 1869, her doctor recommended she take time off and travel. Clara reached Paris at the end of the Franco-Prussian War, in time to observe the Red Cross in action in the newly-liberated city.

She returned from Paris with rheumatic fever. At home, she established an American chapter of the International Red Cross, serving as its president for twenty-three years. By the Spanish-American War, largely because of Barton's efforts, the US had began to take the Red Cross' international mission seriously.[52]

She lobbied Presidents James Garfield and Chester Arthur on behalf of ratifying the Geneva Conventions.

With Venus-in-Aquarius in her Twelfth, volunteer work brought inner satisfaction. But with the North Node there as well, Clara also met many challenges working alone.

While most Pisces Rising people seem to settle into a comfortable work and/or family life routine during the Taurus Progression, Barton, with fifty percent of her planets in Cardinality, remained single. On Neptune-trine-Neptune at age fifty-six, she began a new career as Superintendent of a woman's prison. She retired at seventy-eight and lived to eighty-six.

Judith Krantz also has Pisces Rising, Capricorn Sun,[53] and Jupiter/Saturn in the First House (without Pluto on the Ascendant or Neptune at the Midheaven). But Judith's Jupiter/Saturn conjunction is on the Ascendant, while Clara's was in the middle of her First House. Barton's horoscope was fifty percent Cardinal; Krantz' is fifty percent Mutable.[54]

For Judith Krantz the Aries progression was adventurous. It involved learning, social life and Paris (Ninth House planets.) While Clara Barton's family had considered her a shy child (Pluto conjunct Pisces Rising,) Judith was quite sociable; in college, she planned to date as many men as possible.

But Judith had a serious (Saturn) side too; she also planned to read as many books as possible. While she was at Wellesley, her Aries progressed Mask turned a Natal Fire Trine (Moon/Neptune in Leo to Mars/Saturn in Sagittarius) into a Grand Trine. After graduation, she worked for a Paris fashion magazine. At the end of the Aries cycle, she returned to the US and contributed articles to *Good Housekeeping*.

---

52 Contributing to the Armenians in Turkey and elsewhere.

53 Sun/Mercury in the Eleventh House.

54 Both also had a Mutable Rising Sign and Midheaven (Tenth house Cusp) which is normal for Pisces Rising unless there's an intercept.

The Aries progression helps in developing self-confidence. Though Judith didn't attempt novels until later, by the end of the cycle she'd seen her name in print.

Poets Allen Ginsberg, Thomas Merton and Hazrat Inayat Khan all had one or more Twelfth House planets, enhancing Pisces' mysticism. Ginsberg and Merton had Air Sun Signs, Gemini and Aquarius respectively, while Hazrat Inayat Khan had Sun-in-Cancer. Aries Rising brought out the restless nature of the Air Element.

With Jupiter in the Fourth House (early home life), Inayat Khan had the happiest childhood.[55] Both Merton's parents died during his student years, he lived in France with his grandparents and then attended boarding school.

Ginsberg's mother was in and out of mental institutions. She had shock treatments and, eventually, a lobotomy.[56] With Jupiter in the Twelfth (its Sign of esoteric Rulership) Merton and Ginsberg eventually found solace in solitude, books and like-minded friends, but on the sextiles from Aries to their Natal Suns, they both "acted out" during their college years.

Aries is a restless cycle. Before meeting his own teacher (Murshid,) Hazrat Inayat Khan, poet, musician and mystic, wandered around India and studied with several different Sufi Orders.

Like many others with the Moon-in-Pisces, he dreamed of his teacher years before they met. When they did meet, he "felt" that someone important was about to enter the room, then, suddenly, there was his teacher, the man from his dreams.

The Murshid predicted that Inayet Khan would travel to the West and teach. Two years after his teacher died, when Khan was twenty-eight, he left for Europe. During the last five years of the Aries cycle, Inayat briefly established a school in France, then moved to America. He met his wife as the Ascendant progressed into Taurus.

Deepak Chopra, has been quoted by physicians, playwrights, world leaders and New Age healers. He had no First House planets for the Aries Rising Mask to conjunct, but it formed a trine to Venus-in-Sagittarius in his Ninth. He remarked that he "always knew" he'd study abroad. His intuition was right.

By the time Dr. Chopra was twenty-seven, his progressed Aries Ascendant opposed his Natal Libra Sun. He'd begun to have his doubts about Western medicine. However, by then he was licensed in internal medical and endocrinology, had taught at Tufts and was Chief of Staff at New England Memorial Hospital, Boston.

---

55 With Jupiter in the Fourth, Khan was also an internationalist, a citizen of the world. Merton had Pluto and Saturn close to his Fourth House Cusp.
56 He wrote about her in his poem, "Kaddish for Naomi Ginsberg."

Progressed Ascendant in Taurus

Taurus is Fixed Earth and Venus-ruled. Taurus makes a symbolic sextile to Pisces Rising. In the Taurus cycle, Pisces Rising is usually content settling into a routine. Venus represents romance and personal happiness. Outer achievements must be balanced with inner fulfillment.

Hazrat Inayat Khan married, settled in Santa Fe, New Mexico, and had four children during the Taurus cycle.[57] Judith Krantz married and had two sons. Allen Ginsberg met Peter Orlovsky. They had a forty-year relationship.

In Taurus, family concerns are important to most of my clients, even the more mystically inclined.[58] Most Pisceans prefer to focus on the "quality of life," living their dream, rather than taking on new responsibilities or working longer hours.

If the Uranus-opposite-Uranus cycle transit (ages 39-41) occurs during Taurus Rising, there will be some upheaval in this otherwise tranquil progression.

Around the time Deepak Chopra progressed into Taurus, his son Gotham was born. Dr. Chopra settled into career and family life, but his inner discontent with Western medicine was growing. It bothered him that while prescription drugs reduced symptoms, they failed to cure disease. And he believed that more needed to be done in preventive medicine.

He remembered that when Western medicine had failed his grandfather, Ayur Vedic helped. Perhaps he should find time to study Ayur Veda. But on the other hand, should the father of two young children give up a lucrative career? It would be a substantial risk. His Libra Sun weighed the possibilities and consequences.

Then, in 1981, when the progressed Ascendant formed an inconjunct to Neptune in his Seventh House, Chopra began studying Transcendental Meditation. Four years later, as the progressed Ascendant formed a sextile to Natal Pisces Rising, he met Maharishi Mahesh Yogi. The guru "strongly suggested" that Chopra study Ayur Veda. Others had suggested it before, but during the *Taurus* cycle, on this sextile, it seemed *more practical*.

With Mars/Mercury trine his Natal Ascendant, Chopra quickly mastered Vedic medicine. Initially, he affiliated with the Maharishi's organization. But on Uranus-opposite-Uranus the relationship became "too stressful;" Dr. Chopra broke away.

Attempts at affiliation in our early forties, so often made with high hopes or great effort,

---

57 Unfortunately, he died of influenza on a trip to India in 1927, on Progressed Ascendant sextile Natal Pisces Rising. He was forty-five.

58 Though there are exceptions, like Clara Barton, with her Tenth House Capricorn planets, and Kubler-Ross, with her Sun/Pluto/Node conjunction.

seem not to last. For Dr. Chopra, with Natal Uranus on the Nadir and transiting Uranus crossing the South Node into his Tenth House, a long association was very unlikely.

But to his Libra Sun Sign, it probably seemed as if a joint venture with the Maharishi "ought to work," and to his Seventh House Virgo Moon, his only Earth, it probably seemed more logical to use an existing structure than start anew and organize his own.

In 1996, as the Taurus progression waned, Dr. Chopra founded The Center for Well Being. The new, Gemini Rising cycle would soon find him writing, lecturing, and appearing on TV to discuss philosophy and healing.

Elizabeth Kubler-Ross, with Sun and Moon in Cancer, wanted very much to settle into a family-oriented cycle after her marriage. It took a long time.

Elisabeth and her husband moved from Zurich to New York, where his relatives lived, then to Colorado, where Manny had an opportunity in neuropathology, and finally to Chicago, where he had an even better opportunity.

Halfway through the Taurus progression, she wrote her mother that she'd "finally become Americanized;" she now wore slacks instead of skirts and ate sugary breakfast cereal. Now if only she could have a child!

Elisabeth gave up pediatrics for psychiatry because the hours at the hospital were more manageable, less stressful. At last, after four miscarriages, she had her long-awaited boy and girl.

Progressed Ascendant in Gemini

Gemini is Mutable Air and Mercury-ruled. It's a symbolic square to Pisces Rising, which presents challenges. The restless Air Element usually accentuates Pisces' Natal restlessness, sense of wonder, and curiosity about life. But there's also a positive side to Gemini Air. Many Pisceans have said they've "gotten a second wind" in their fifties or sixties.

In this progressed cycle, Pisces Rising may embark upon a second career that involves communication skills; writing, lecturing, consulting, blogging or storytelling.[59] The Mutable Mask enhances Natal Mutable talents.

Allen Ginsberg, a Natal Gemini Sun Sign, met his Buddhist teacher, Chogyam Trungpa Rimpoche two years after progressing into Gemini. He studied meditation with the Rimpoche at Naropa College, Boulder, Colorado and developed a creative writing program for the school. Though he'd previously considered himself a "non-academic poet," during

---

59 Progressed aspects to Natal Mercury may describe new interests or endeavors.

the Gemini cycle he discovered that he enjoyed teaching. He divided his schedule between Naropa in summertime and the rest of the year at Brooklyn College, NY, where he taught until his death in 1997.[60]

Some, like Chopra, and Kubler-Ross, were involved in very different careers during the first half of life, but became prolific authors and/or prized lecture-circuit speakers during the Gemini cycle.[61] Or, Pisces Rising may shift from one type of Mercury activity to another, as Judith Krantz did when she gave up writing articles to focus on novels. Or Pisces may diversify, as Ginsberg did when he added teaching to his writing and poetry readings.

Often, within a year or two of progressing into this dual Sign, Pisces Rising reaches a crossroads. The year that Elisabeth Kubler-Ross entered Gemini, *On Death and Dying* was published. After it became a best-seller, her reputation grew to surpass her husband's. She traveled constantly, promoting Hospice and lecturing about the "last taboo subject," death.

An Air Sign, Gemini is curious about learning new things. On the whole, this curiosity is an advantage for Pisces; so many older people are afraid to leave their familiar routines.

Elisabeth's family, however, thought she carried curiosity and restlessness to extremes. When she discovered a psychic in Southern California who channeled spirit guides,[62] they didn't share her enthusiasm. During the "mercurial" progression, they were concerned about her reputation. Perhaps Elisabeth would no longer be taken seriously as a professional.

Around the time of her Jupiter Return at age forty-eight,[63] she visited the psychic more frequently. She preferred California, where many people thought as she did, "but Manny was entrenched in the Chicago suburbs and wanted to acquire more material things." They'd "grown apart."

When Elisabeth was fifty, Manny asked for a divorce.[64] When her daughter was only thirteen, she kissed her children goodbye and left for California and her mission, helping the dying release their attachments.

At fifty, Judith Krantz published her first novel, *Scruples*. Soon she was publishing one

---

60 The progressed Ascendant was in 28 Gemini when he died.
61 Ginsberg traveled as far as China and Russia, giving readings and accompanying himself on the harmonica. He won the National Book Award as the progressed Mask in Gemini entered his (Natal) Third House.
62 This seemed to be the last straw for Manny, even worse than Elisabeth's seeing flower fairies.
63 Her Jupiter was in Aquarius in the Twelfth House.
64 The Chiron return, and transiting Saturn square Chiron.

best-selling book after another. Several of her entertaining stories have been adapted as made for TV movies or mini-series, including *Secrets* and *Torch Song.*

Gemini is the Zodiac's most versatile Sign. In his youth, Thomas Merton had enjoyed writing poetry *(A Man in the Divided Sea).* At thirty-three, he'd written his spiritual autobiography, *The Seven Storey Mountain,* several books on silence, solitude and meditation *(Seeds of Contemplation, The Palace of Nowhere).*

But as the Gemini Mask began to trine his Stellium (five planets) in Aquarius, Merton's work began to reflect his era. His essays covered humanitarian themes like social and economic justice (the Social Gospel) and Ecumenism. On progressed Ascendant trine his Mars, he wrote essays on the Vietnam War. His world view expanded. On progressed Ascendant trine Natal Sun/Uranus, the Catholic monk became interested in Asian mysticism.

While representing the Trappist Order in Thailand, he wrote in his *Asian Journal*[65] (based on his travels and conversations with Eastern monastics) and began his last book, *The New Man.*[66]

Thomas Merton died in Bangkok while changing a light bulb, at the age of fifty-three. His *Collected Works,* including his correspondence, totaled 6,000 pages.[67]

Both Pisces and Gemini are associated with the nervous system. In the Gemini progression, few Pisceans seem able to pace themselves. Most pack their schedules as full as they did when younger, enjoying the opportunities and stimulation. However, overextending themselves in the Gemini cycle often catches up with Pisces later.

Progressed Ascendant in Cancer

Cancer is Cardinal Water and Moon-ruled. It forms a symbolic trine to Pisces Rising. Pisces is in his Element. The progression will bring out the Earth and Water planets with soft aspects. It forms hard aspects to Natal Cardinal planets, and to others' Cardinal planets as well.

Clara Barton, still president of the American Red Cross in her eighties, finally retired after a conflict with another authoritative woman. The progressed Ascendant was moving into opposition with her Moon, having already opposed three Tenth House planets in Capricorn. At eighty-seven, she must have been tired! Clara lived to be ninety-one.

---

65 Published posthumously as *The Asian Journal of Thomas Merton.*
66 The title is very descriptive of the Sun/Uranus in "futuristic" Aquarius.
67 It was published by HarperCollins. His letters are of particular interest to historians.

In horoscopes with many planets in Air and Fire, the calmer Cancer cycle may seem boring at first. The same is true of horoscopes with Mars in the First House. Kubler-Ross, for instance, with Mars in Aries, liked to be active. She had difficulty slowing down as she aged. The same was true of political activist Allen Ginsberg, with Mars/Uranus conjunct his Ascendant. Both the Thanatologist and the poet went at life full-speed ahead.

That may work for the first five decades. After sixty, however, a different approach and different skills are required; patience, sublimation of desire, acceptance of our changing bodies. We learn to pace ourselves, simplify and adapt. Some people have more energy in the mornings and others at night; we all learn to work with our biorhythms.

Many Pisces Rising clients have told me how much they enjoy playing with their grandchildren, painting (especially in watercolor), yoga class or yoga DVDs, and listening to quiet, calming music. Most Pisceans have a talent for play and relaxation.

"The new cycle is great! I take a lot of naps. I'm glad that others no longer expect me to be as productive," one client observed, four years into the Cancer Rising cycle.

"Is there anything you *don't* like about it?" I asked. "Yes. Loud noises really bother me now. I don't like taking my grandchildren to the movies anymore. The sound track is too loud. And, if someone is watching a TV show with police sirens blaring, I leave the room."

Physical and/or emotional sensitivity seems enhanced. Taste in food may change. If Pisces spends too much time alone, old habits such as abuse of alcohol or painkillers, or overindulgence in comfort foods may return. As a result, Pisces may feel bloated and out-of-sorts. Cancer, the Sign of the Crab, sometimes has crabby moods, which discourage visitors from coming as often. Family members enjoy reminiscing about the *happy* memories, but during the Cancer Cycle, Pisces sometimes needs to discuss the sad ones.

The year her progressed Ascendant transitioned from Gemini to Cancer, Kubler-Ross had two strokes, which she diagnosed herself. Her son insisted she go to the hospital; she eventually gave in and went. She described herself as a terrible patient. A few days later, she "released (herself) to her own care," much to the doctors' chagrin, and went home.

Elisabeth, like most water Signs, felt comfortable in her own house performing her own "calming rituals." The hospital had, of course, denied access to her *ritual substances,* coffee, cigarettes and chocolate.

The second stroke left her paralyzed. Two years later, as the Progressed Ascendant conjuncted her Cancer Moon, Elisabeth moved to Arizona near her son Kenneth and his family. She "complained to God that it was taking so long to meet death face-to-face."

When she died at seventy-three Kenneth said, "mother reached acceptance (the last stage of the dying process) several years ago."

For Pisces Rising, family is one of the greatest joys in old age, balanced with solitude time for reflection. Music is often mentioned as an important part of life.[68] Pisces, for instance, usually enjoys the choir more than the Sunday sermon. The introspective among them look back on their life story and reflect on the creative moments, the birth of a child, the birth of a book, or of a poem written to commemorate a happy occasion.

When I ask imaginative Neptune-ruled Pisceans how they define creativity, their definitions are similar to George E. Vaillant's in *Aging Well*, "creativity is putting into the world something that was not there before."[69] Pisceans seem to excel at creativity, each one fashioning his life in his own way.

When I ask Pisces Rising, "what does spirituality mean?" there are many answers; "a personal experience of God;" "thinking the best of others; a positive attitude attracts positive results," "my prayer that my grandchildren will be happy after I'm gone. I've done all I can for them."

"Meditation and the support of my Sangha," (Buddhist community), "I'm at peace knowing that my generation has done its part. The world is a better place than it was during my childhood. There's a lot more opportunity for young women and minorities."

Pisces Rising Bibliography

Barton, Clara, *The Story of My Childhood*, (New York, Baker and Taylor,) 1907.

Burt, Kathleen, *Beyond the Mask, Part I*, (Carmel: Genoa House,) 2009.

Chopra, Deepak, MD, *Healing the Heart: A Spiritual Approach to Coronary Artery Disease*, (New York: Harmony,) 1998.

—— *The Path to Love: Spiritual Strategies for Healing*, (New York: Three Rivers Press,) 1998

—— *Perfect Healt: The Complete Mind-Body Guide*, (New York: Harmony,) 2001.

—— *Perfect Digestion: The Key to Balanced Living*, Perfect Health Library Series, (New York: Three Rivers,) 1997.

---

68 According to her website, late in life Judith Krantz became interested in "boards, music and death;" "Her Compassion and Choices," is an organization dedicated to providing options for the dying. She also serves on the Board of the Music Center of Los Angeles County.

69 Vaillant, *Aging Well*, (NY: Little, Brown and Co,) 2003, 245.

—— *Why is God Laughing?* Deepak Chopra and Mike Myers, (New York: Three Rivers,) 2009.

Chopin, Fredrick, *Chopin and George Sand, Letters and Music,* CD, Berlin Chamber Orchestra, 1999.

Eisler, Benita, *Naked in the Marketplace: The Lives of George Sand,* (London: Unwin-Counterpoint,) 2007.

Ginsberg, Allen *HOWL! And Other Poems, by Allen Ginsberg and Gary Miles,* (New York: Harper Perennial,) 1995.

—— *Family Business: Selected Letters Between a Father and Son, Louis and Allen Ginsberg,* Michael Schumaker, ed, (New York: Bloomsbury,) 2001.

Heindel, Max and Augusta Foss Heindel, *Message of the Stars,* (Oceanside: Rosicrucian Press,) 1980.

Kerenyi, Carl, *Dionysos, Archetypal Image of an Indestructible Life,* trans, Ralph Manheim, (New Jersey: Princeton University Press,) Bollingen Series LXV, 2, 1970.

Khan, Hazrat Inayat, *The Essential Writings of Sufism,* (Boston: Shambhala,) 1999.

—— *Music,* (York Beach, Weiser,) 1977.

Krantz, Judith, *Princess Daisy,* (New York: Bantam,) 1984.

—— *Scruples,* (New York: Bantam,) 1989.

—— *Scruples Two,* (New York: Bantam,) 1993.

—— *Till We Meet Again,* (New York: Bantam,) 1989.

Kubler-Ross, Elisabeth, *On Death and Dying*: *What the Dying Have to Teach Doctors, Nurses, and Their Own Families,* (New York: Macmillan,) 1976.

—— *The Tunnel and the Light: Essential Insights on Living and Dying,* Goran Grop, ed, (New York: Marlowe & Co,) 1992.

—— *The Wheel of Life: A Memoir of Living and Dying,* (New York: Simon and Schuster-Touchstone,) 1998.

McEvers, Joan, *12 Times 12: 144 Sun/Ascendant Combinations,* (San Diego: ACS,) 1983.

Maurois, Andre, *Leila: The Story of George Sand,* (New York: Harper,) 1954.

Merton, Thomas, *The Asian Journal of Thomas Merton,* (New York: New Directions,) 1975.

—— *The Seven Storey Mountain,* (New York: Harcourt,) 978. (Autobiography.)

—— *The Vision of Thomas Merton,* Patrick F. O'Connell, ed, South Bend, (Notre Dame: Ave Maria Press,) 2003. (From his journals and letters.)

—— *New Seeds of Contemplation*, (New York: New Directions,) 1964.

—— *The Way of Chuang Tsu*, (Toronto: Penguin,) 1969.

—— *New American Standard Bible*, (Anaheim, Foundation Publications,) 1997.

Pryor, Elizabeth Brown, *Clara Barton, Professional Angel*, Studies in Health, Illness and Caregiving, (Philadelphia: University of Pennsylvania Press,) 1988.

Sainte-Beuve, Charles A, *Volupte: The Sensual Man*, Marilyn, Gaddis-Rose, trans, (Albany: SUNY,) 1995. The literary critic's autobiographical novel about his affair with Victor Hugo's wife.)

Sand, George, *The Story of My Life*, (Albany: SUNY,) 1991.

—— *Indiana*, Sylvia Raphael, trans, intro by Naomi Schor, (New York: Oxford University Press USA,) 2001.

Shepard, Sam and Richard Gilman, *Seven Plays (Buried Child, Curse of the Starving Class, The Tooth of Crime, La Turista, Tongues, Savage Love, True West)* (New York: Dial Press,) 1984.

Stein, Gertrude, *The Autobiography of Alice B. Toklas*, (New York: Vintage,) 1990. (About Stein's lifelong companion.)

—— *Picasso*, (Mineola: Dover Publications,) 1994.

Swinburne, Algernon Charles, *Poems and Ballads & Atalanta in Calydon*, (New York: Penguin classics,) 2001.

Zelazny, Roger, *Lords of Light*, (New York: HarperCollins-Eos,) 2004.

—— *The Great Book of Amber: Chronicles of Amber*, (New York: HarperCollins-Eos,) 1999

—— *Today We Choose Faces*, (Boston: Gregg Press,) 1978.

Vaillant, George E. MD, *Aging Well: Surprising Guideposts to a Happier Life*, (New York: Little, Brown & Co,) 2002.

ACKNOWLEDGEMENTS

Beyond the Mask is now in print because of the help of many friends. I particularly want to thank Jungian analyst Monika Wikman and Ray Hillis of the Santa Fe Alchemical Society; my friend and former secretary Dagny San Miguel, my poet friend Joyce Brady in San Francisco, astrologer Catalina O'Brien of Nevada City, my literary friend Jeannette Scollard in Carlsbad, and multi-talented Vicki Gloor of Del Mar, for their support, advice, and encouragement.

I'd also like to thank my Jungian mentor for fairy tales and storytelling, Robert Johnson. His contribution to the Patterns in Health program in Del Mar and his weekends at Pacifica Institute led to my inclusion of elder stories and other tales.

My gratitude goes to the late Lois Rodden and the staff at Astro-Databank.com for the celebrity horoscopes. I hope many readers will avail themselves of this useful information, now available on the internet through Astrodienst: www.astro.com

The help of Kay Carlson and Susannah Garrett who transcribed my lectures is very much appreciated. This was a daunting task for two women without a background in either astrology or Jungian terminology.

A special thank you to Patty Cabanas of Stoney Creek Editorial. Without her keen eyes and refined copyediting skills, this combined volume of *Beyond the Mask* would never have made it to print. www.stoneycreekeditorial.com

And most of all, I'd like to thank my husband Michael Burt for his patience.

Recommended Reading

Re-Imagining Mary: A Journey Through Art to the Feminine Self
by Mariann Burke, 1st Ed., Trade Paperback, 180 pp., Index, Biblio., 2009
— ISBN 978-0-9810344-1-6

Threshold Experiences: The Archetype of Beginnings
by Michael Conforti, 1st Ed., Trade Paperback, 168 pp., Index, Biblio., 2008
— ISBN 978-0-944187-99-9

Marked By Fire: Stories of the Jungian Way
edited by Patricia Damery & Naomi Ruth Lowinsky,
1st Ed., Trade Paperback, 180 pp., Index, Biblio., 2012 — ISBN 978-1-926715-68-1

Farming Soul: A Tale of Initiation
by Patricia Damery, 1st Ed., Trade Paperback, 166 pp., Index, Biblio., 2010
— ISBN 978-1-926715-01-8

Transforming Body and Soul: Therapeutic Wisdom in the Gospel Healing Stories
by Steven Galipeau, Rev. Ed., Trade Paperback, 180 pp., Index, Biblio., 2011
— ISBN 978-1-926715-62-9

Lifting the Veil: Revealing the Other Side
by Fred Gustafson & Jane Kamerling, 1st Ed, Paperback, 170 pp., Biblio., 2012
— ISBN 978-1-926715-75-9

Resurrecting the Unicorn: Masculinity in the 21st Century
by Bud Harris, Rev. Ed., Trade Paperback, 300 pp., Index, Biblio., 2009
— ISBN 978-0-9810344-0-9

The Father Quest: Rediscovering an Elemental Force
by Bud Harris, Reprint, Trade Paperback, 180 pp., Index, Biblio., 2009
— ISBN 978-0-9810344-9-2

Like Gold Through Fire: The Transforming Power of Suffering
by Massimilla & Bud Harris, Reprint, Trade Paperback, 150 pp., Index, Biblio., 2009
— ISBN 978-0-9810344-5-4

Divine Madness: Archetypes of Romantic Love
by John R. Haule, Rev. Ed., Trade Paperback, 282 pp., Index, Biblio., 2010
— ISBN 978-1-926715-04-9

Tantra & Erotic Trance: Volume I Outer Work & Volume II Inner Work
by John R. Haule, 1st Ed, Trade Paperback, Vol. I 210 pp., Vol. II 214 pp., Index, Biblio., 2012
— ISBN 978-0-9776076-8-6 & ISBN 978-0-9776076-9-3

Eros and the Shattering Gaze: Transcending Narcissism
by Ken Kimmel, 1st Ed., Trade Paperback, 310 pp., Index, Biblio., 2011
— ISBN 978-1-926715-49-0

The Sister From Below: When the Muse Gets Her Way
by Naomi Ruth Lowinsky, 1st Ed., Trade Paperback, 248 pp., Index, Biblio., 2009
— ISBN 978-0-9810344-2-3

The Motherline: Every Woman's Journey to find her Female Roots
by Naomi Ruth Lowinsky, Reprint, Trade Paperback, 252 pp., Index, Biblio., 2009
— ISBN 978-0-9810344-6-1

Jung and Ecopsychology: The Dairy Farmer's Guide to the Universe (DFGU) Volume 1
by Dennis Merritt 1st Ed., Trade Paperback, 250 pp., Index, Biblio., 2011
— ISBN 978-1-926715-42-1

The Cry of Merlin: Jung, the Prototypical Ecopsychologist: DFGU Volume 2
by Dennis Merritt 1st Ed., Trade Paperback, 250 pp., Index, Biblio., 2012
— ISBN 978-1-926715-43-8

Hermes, Ecopsychology, and Complexity Theory: DFGU Volume 3
by Dennis Merritt 1st Ed., Trade Paperback, 220 pp., Index, Biblio., 2012
— ISBN 978-1-926715-44-5

Land, Weather, Seasons, Insects: An Archetypal View: DFGU Volume 4
by Dennis Merritt 1st Ed., Trade Paperback, 220 pp., Index, Biblio., 2012
— ISBN 978-1-926715-45-2

Becoming: An Introduction to Jung's Concept of Individuation
by Deldon Anne McNeely, 1st Ed., Trade Paperback, 230 pp., Index, Biblio., 2010
— ISBN 978-1-926715-12-4

Animus Aeternus: Exploring the Inner Masculine
by Deldon Anne McNeely, Reprint, Trade Paperback, 196 pp., Index, Biblio., 2011
— ISBN 978-1-926715-37-7

Mercury Rising: Women, Evil, and the Trickster Gods
by Deldon Anne McNeely, Revised, Trade Paperback, 200 pp., Index, Biblio., 2011
— ISBN 978-1-926715-54-4

Four Eternal Women: Toni Wolff Revisited—A Study In Opposites
by Mary Dian Molton & Lucy Anne Sikes, 1st Ed, 320 pp., Index, Biblio., 2011
— ISBN 978-1-926715-31-5

Gathering the Light: A Jungian View of Meditation
by V. Walter Odajnyk, Revised. Ed., Trade Paperback, 264 pp., Index, Biblio., 2011
— ISBN 978-1-926715-55-1

The Promiscuity Papers
by Matjaz Regovec 1st Ed., Trade Paperback, 86 pp., Index, Biblio., 2011
— ISBN 978-1-926715-38-4

Enemy, Cripple, Beggar: Shadows in the Hero's Path
by Erel Shalit, 1st Ed., Trade Paperback, 248 pp., Index, Biblio., 2008
— ISBN 978-0-9776076-7-9

The Cycle of Life: Themes and Tales of the Journey
by Erel Shalit, 1st Ed., Trade Paperback, 210 pp., Index, Biblio., 2011
— ISBN 978-1-926715-50-6

The Hero and His Shadow: Psychopolitical Aspects of Myth and Reality in Israel
by Erel Shalit, Revised Ed., Trade Paperback, 208 pp., Index, Biblio., 2012
— ISBN 978-1-926715-69-8

The Guilt Cure
by Nancy Carter Pennington & Lawrence H. Staples
1st Ed., Trade Paperback, 200 pp., Index, Biblio., 2011 — ISBN 978-1-926715-53-7

Guilt with a Twist: The Promethean Way
by Lawrence Staples,1st Ed., Trade Paperback, 256 pp., Index, Biblio., 2008
— ISBN 978-0-9776076-4-8

The Creative Soul: Art and the Quest for Wholeness
by Lawrence Staples, 1st Ed., Trade Paperback, 100 pp., Index, Biblio., 2009
— ISBN 978-0-9810344-4-7

Deep Blues: Human Soundscapes for the Archetypal Journey
by Mark Winborn, 1st Ed., Trade Paperback, 130 pp., Index, Biblio., 2011
— ISBN 978-1-926715-52-0

Fisher King Press publishes an eclectic mix of worthy books including Jungian Psychological Perspectives, Cutting-Edge Fiction, Poetry, and a growing list of Alternative titles.

Phone Orders Welcomed — Credit Cards Accepted
In Canada & the U.S. call 1-800-228-9316
International call +1-831-238-7799
www.fisherkingpress.com

9087141R00220

Printed in Great Britain
by Amazon.co.uk, Ltd.,
Marston Gate.